IMMIGRANTS
TO FREEDOM

Regional History Series
The American Jewish History Center
of The Jewish Theological Seminary of America

EDITORS

Salo Wittmayer Baron
Moshe Davis
Allan Nevins

Volume One. Louis J. Swichkow and Lloyd P. Gartner. The Jews of Milwaukee. Published by The Jewish Publication Society of America, 1963.

Volume Two. Max Vorspan and Lloyd P. Gartner. The Jews of Los Angeles. Published by Huntington Library and The Jewish Publication Society of America, 1970.

The present title is Volume Three.

*"And seek ye the peace of the city . . . for
in the peace thereof shall ye have peace."*

ודרשו את שלום העיר
.כי בשלומה יהיה לכם שלום. . . .

(Jeremiah 29.7)

IMMIGRANTS TO FREEDOM

Jewish Communities in Rural New Jersey since 1882

JOSEPH BRANDES
in association with
Martin Douglas

University of Pennsylvania Press
Philadelphia

9/26/2000

To Sol Satinsky
(1900—1966)

Whose service to the
future derived from his
sense of obligation to the past.

acknowledgments

Without the cooperation and devoted assistance of many individuals and organizations this work could not have been completed. Special appreciation is due The American Jewish History Center: to Professors Allan Nevins and Moshe Davis, co-directors, as also to Professor Lloyd Gartner, for their scholarly guidance; to Dr. Gladys Rosen, Executive Associate, whose tireless efforts and gracious manner provided effective coordination.

In Vineland, the encouragement of the late Dr. Arthur Goldhaft, continued by Dr. Tevis Goldhaft and other members of Beth Israel Congregation, played a major role in initiating the local research; Judge I. Harry Levin aided with primary information, giving much of his time and counsel; Ben Z. Leuchter, editor of the *Vineland Times Journal,* generously made available all past issues; the families of Moses Bayuk, Jacob Crystal, and other pioneers supplied useful contemporary data. The technical assistance of David Feldman and Sam Tepper in the task of photostating numerous primary sources deserves acknowledgment as well.

Records of the Baron de Hirsch Fund, the Jewish Agricultural Society, and library collections of The Jewish Theological Seminary of America, the Vineland Historical and Antiquarian Society, YIVO Institute for Jewish Research, the New Jersey State Library, Dropsie University, and the Jewish Division of the New York Public Library, all provided the essential brick and mortar of research.

Appreciation is due to the distinguished scholars serving as editors of this regional history series, and to the editors of The University of Pennsylvania Press for their patience and unstinting cooperation.

The affectionate devotion of our respective families is an especial cause for gratitude: to Margot Brandes and the children, Cheryl, Lynn, Susan, and Aviva; to Shirley Douglas and the children, Alfred, Beth and Michael, the latter also for their helpfulness in assembling local newspaper records. In the study of history, one may hope, are formed some of the links which unite one generation to another.

preface

An intriguing yet unexplored chapter in the history of the Jews in America is the settlement of small Jewish agricultural enclaves in towns and villages of the American interior. It is a complex story involving such diverse elements as the ideological "back-to-land" movements which originated in Europe, organized efforts of the Baron de Hirsch Fund and the Alliance Israelite Universelle, as well as American Jewish communal groups which sought to direct and channel immigrant absorption. The roots of this history reach deep into the political and social forces that propelled mass emigration from Tsarist Russia to America in the last decades of the nineteenth century.

As the pogroms of the 1880's raged and savage impulses were given legal sanction by Alexander III, Sabato Morais' insight about Russian Jewry was the practical counsel of escape: "The only hope for the Jews in Russia is to become Jews out of Russia." *Tsar* both in the Hebrew language and in reality meant "oppressor."

But, *where* to go? *How* to go?

In the midst of the tyranny and suffering, an ideological debate took place as to where group emancipation might best be achieved, in Palestine or America. Epitomized in the words *Am Olam* meaning both "Eternal People" and "World People," one orientation emphasized the cooperative settlement of *Eretz Yisrael*, the Land of the Eternal People; the other pointed westward, to the free countries overseas.* A small minority pioneered in *Eretz Yisrael*. Most, however, moved to the West—in Europe itself, to England, South America, and mainly to the United States.

*The Hebrew press of the period is replete with discussion, letters, and feature reports on the mass emigration. For selected translations and annotated documentary sources in English from the Hebrew periodicals Ha-Melitz and Ha-Yom, see Joel S. Geffen's studies in American Jewish Historical Quarterly, LI (March 1962), 149-167; LIX (December 1969), 179-200.

In the two decades following 1880, the American Jewish community was confronted by the unprecedented responsibility of helping more than half a million immigrants to adjust to life in America. The newcomers far exceeded the resident Jewish population of 1880, comprising virtually twice the number who had come during the preceding two centuries. Devoted communal and spiritual leaders identified themselves with the new arrivals. In their brothers' suffering they witnessed a modern Exodus.

A leading advocate of Russian Jewish immigration to America was Rabbi Benjamin Szold of Baltimore. Speaking in the cadences of biblical thought, whose idiom and moral perceptions guided him, he said:

> From Russia comes the horrible news of millions of people suffering the pangs of hunger. You fancy that because we in America are free, we can repose in peace. I say that so long as a single Jew, in any corner of the earth, can with impunity be insulted on account of his faith, thus long not one Jew anywhere is free. The Russian people will not always continue to be a dumb beast of burden. The time will come when . . . it will demand that its human right be respected. Then it will remember that here are men and women holding out their hands to us for bread.

With this complex historical background in mind, one can begin to comprehend the purpose and development of the agricultural colonies in rural New Jersey. Indeed, *Immigrants to Freedom* is more than a story of acculturation to America; it is a social and human history of the years of open American immigration.

The distinctive quality of this particular agricultural Jewish immigration is its conceptual and organizational framework. These immigrants *chose* America. Their quest for physical emancipation from Russia included moral and Jewish imperatives: the urge for individual transformation as well as group transplantation. A contemporary source, *Migdal Zophim* (The Watch Tower) by Moses Klein, vividly illustrates this double imperative. As he described the newcomers' homesteads, the streets, the schools, and the synagogues in three Jewish colonies—Alliance, Carmel, and Rosenhayn, in that triangular district of southern New Jersey bounded by Vineland, Millville, and Bridgeton—Klein sought to validate the ideological position that agriculture offered the best solution to the Jewish problem.

Based on thorough documentation, including specialized primary sources as well as general Americana, this volume skillfully portrays the growth, aspirations, and failures in the rural communities. The first group of Russian Jewish arrivals in Alliance in 1882 numbered but four hundred, with thousands of others to come in successive immigrant waves beyond World War II. Their synagogues and other communal institutions still testify to the sources of cultural energy they brought to the New World. Today, the center of community life has shifted to Vineland proper with its substantial Jewish population.

Situated between New York and Philadelphia, these agricultural colonies sought to realize their declared destiny without becoming submerged by either metropolis. Somehow, it was Philadelphia that became the "godfather" rather than New York. This was evident not only because of the Philadelphia Jewish community's earnest philanthropic aid but also because of its spiritual and social ties to the colonies. For example, Rabbi Bernard L. Levinthal continued, after Sabato Morais, as a frequent visitor and speaker in the colonies near Vineland. The educational impulse, too, was motivated by Philadelphia; and young people of the colonies met their betrothed and had their weddings in the City of Brotherly Love.

It cannot be said that these rural colonies made major contributions to American agriculture—except by their very stubborn resistance to urban life and employment. As Professor Brandes comments, "there were few Luther Burbanks among them." But it is possible to notice the significance of their particular enterprise in forming agricultural organizations (marketing cooperatives, joint ventures for purchasing feed, and poultry and egg producers' associations) as well as in their educational and scientific achievements. In the latter category, the Baron de Hirsch Agricultural School in Woodbine (1894–1917) was a pathbreaker.

The pioneering generation quickly became rooted in the new American surroundings. Then Jewish destiny called upon them, as it had upon earlier Jewish settlers, to assume responsibility for Jews in other parts of the world. During the early decades of the twentieth century, aid and succor had to be given to countless newcomers; and in the third and fourth decades the children of the refugees from Russian pogroms embraced the brands plucked from the Holocaust of the Nazi era. In our own time, a shoot from the stock of *Am Olam,* "World People," made its way to the "Eternal People," settling in the Land of Israel in the cooperative village of Orot in the Shefelah, the coastal plain of Israel.

Precisely because of the overarching importance of Jewish agricultural settlement in the United States as part of immigration history, the co-directors of the Seminary's American Jewish History Center included the story of the rural communities of South New Jersey in its Regional History Series, together with the histories of the urban communities of Milwaukee, Los Angeles, Cleveland, and Miami. From the Center's inception, Professor Louis Finkelstein, Seminary Chancellor, Professor Allan Nevins, Professor Salo W. Baron, and I sought to find the historical balance between local community rootedness, national awareness, and world Jewish perspective. And it was in this spirit that Sol Satinsky assumed the Chairmanship of the Center's Board of Directors, inspiring the founding members of the Board, who readily sponsored its program in active cooperation with the Jewish Publication Society. In that same spirit we acknowledge our profound gratitude to Daniel G. Ross, Joel S. Geffen, Reuben Kaufman, Richard K. Manoff, Irving Neuman, Gladys Rosen, Herbert Salzman, and Dore Schary.

Immigrants to Freedom is dedicated to the memory of Sol Satinsky, an alumnus of the University of Pennsylvania, a scholarly collector of Lincolniana, who, above all, loved learning and men of learning. As Professor Simon Greenberg, Vice-Chancellor of the Seminary and his lifelong rabbi and friend, said:

> The personality of Sol Satinsky was molded by an extraordinary sensitivity to history. He felt that the past obligated him. This sensitivity to history was the source of his inspiring loyalty to America, to the Jewish people and his own immediate kin. It dominated his thought and largely determined his action.

History, it can be said, lives in the details which are universally valid. *Immigrants to Freedom* is not a volume of past circumstances; it details the continuing quest of the Jewish people to find a more perfect union with lands and peoples of expanding freedom.

MOSHE DAVIS

CONTENTS

IMMIGRANTS
TO FREEDOM

Introduction

Since its discovery, the New World has beckoned as a haven of refuge for the downtrodden of the Old. Millions, oppressed by religious, social, or political persecution, languishing for lack of economic opportunity, were drawn to America in search of freedom and a better life.

The specific factors causing the immigrants to leave home and their dreams of what awaited them in the land beyond the ocean, form a varied pattern within world history. Inevitably, any understanding of either their reasoning or their achievements defies generalization. They came as individuals or with families, often within groups whose common religious orientation offered strength in a strange environment. And, sometimes, as with the Puritans, these religious bonds were augmented by economic and political concerns.

Diversity characterizes the history of American immigration. National origins, races, religions, and social philosophies, are commingled within the great stream which has nourished this country. A majority of the new arrivals came from rural communities, and the prospect of becoming independent farmers remained a natural attraction until the end of the nineteenth century. Yet even before the age of urbanization, many, such as the Irish in the 1840's, also flocked to the cities. Later, while Scandinavian farmers still tamed the northern Great Plains, Eastern and Southern Europeans toiled in the new steel and textile mills or in urban construction crews.

From the first enduring settlement in New Amsterdam (1654), diversity marks the history of Jewish contributions to the immigration stream. Over the centuries, Jews entering the gates of freedom have included heirs of Spanish-Hebrew culture, scholars and tradesmen from the Low Countries and Germany, teachers and carpenters from East European villages, even ex-farmers from Russia's Kherson province.

One of the significant, though relatively unknown, chapters in the history of the great westward surge of people and ideas is the establishment of Jewish immigrant colonies in the rural setting of southern New Jersey. The first of these was Alliance, founded near Vineland in 1882, soon followed by others, some with biblical names like Carmel and Mizpah. Within a dozen years of its founding, the Woodbine colony in Cape May County was incorporated (1903) as a virtually all-Jewish borough.

These organized colonies in the countryside, seemingly autonomous if not separatist, represent a divergence from the mainstream of late nineteenth-century migration to America. Most notably, perhaps, the South Jersey settlers did not seek to work out their future on an individual basis in the cities of an increasingly urban and industrial America as did the vast majority of their impecunious East European fellow immigrants who settled in the cities, partly, at least, for lack of funds. Land, in an economic sense, has never been free. The Homestead Act of 1862 notwithstanding, money has always been an essential, often prohibitive prerequisite for settling on the soil: money for inland transportation, for tools and equipment, for subsistence before the first good harvest, all this in addition to the price of a family homestead was required. Besides capital, East European Jews frequently lacked experience in farming as well as, some thought, a natural bent for this ancient occupation. Moreover, there were other reasons to favor settling in the city: more and better-paying jobs, a chance at a variety of small businesses, a richer cultural and social life, and wider educational horizons, especially for the children. And the city environment provided immigrant groups an opportunity to further ethnic and religious concerns; the newcomer could find nearby the consolation of his mother tongue, his native church or synagogue, home cooking, or even the varied biases and prejudices from "the other side." Of course, there were also the harsh realities of overcrowding, abject poverty, unrelieved toil, and the pervasive slum, but this ghetto contained aspects of freedom: there was no Tsarist terror or forced conversion, no censorship, no invisible walls implacably blocking movement both outward to new communities and upward on the social scale.

Why, then, did thousands of Jewish immigrants deviate from the ingathered majority by settling in rural South Jersey? Was there anything unique in their relationship to other Americans, whether Christian or Jew? In what ways was their life different from that of their brethren in the burgeoning metropolis? For both were, in a real sense, pioneers, the one on an urban frontier, where the American city was undergoing radical change, the other on the frontier of an area still largely undeveloped, where one literally had to build from the ground up.

Among those seeking homes on the rural frontier were men and women inspired by popular leaders like Michael Bakal and Moshe Herder, who taught the dignity of manual labor. They were members of an ideological movement based on a return to the soil as a means of salvation for the oppressed Jews of Russia, and assuming, with Tolstoy, that "all the world honors and protects the bread producer," that farming embodied the most honest and useful kind of toil. They had as a precedent the selfless *narodniki* (populists), including Pavel Axelrod and Lev Deutsch, youthful intellectuals concerned with the welfare of Russia's vast peasant class. Some of these idealistic agrarians had even abandoned their university studies for hard labor in the fields alongside the peasants; unfortunately, however, the latter were often suspicious to the point of hostility. In free America, things would be different; the intelligentsia would transform themselves into true tillers of the soil. Or at least, so they hoped.

Some of the rural settlers envisioned in the well-balanced communities a way to overcome anti-Semitism, as well as achieve a more creative life. It was their goal to disprove the stereotype of the Jew as Shylock, petty trader and middle man. In these objectives, they acquired the support and benevolent guidance of established Jewish communities in Western Europe and the United States. Philanthropic organizations like the Alliance Israélite Universelle, the Hebrew Emigrant Aid Society, and the Baron de Hirsch Fund, provided funds to purchase land for colonization and leadership to organize the settlers and establish them in their new homes. The Western Jews hoped to develop within these agriculturally-based communities a beneficial social and economic climate for the strangers in the land, an alternative to the poverty-ridden immigrant slums of London's East End, New York's Lower East Side, or Boston's West End.

Colonization encompassed deeply felt humanitarian impulses for the rescue and resettlement of Europe's displaced and unwanted. Before the end of the nineteenth century, some of the benefactors were also concerned about their own image in the Western countries where opposition to "the new immigration" from the poorer regions in Southern and Eastern Europe was mounting. In the eyes of some assimilated Jews, their "oriental" coreligionists who swarmed into the cities as peddlers or tailors, speaking a strange tongue (Yiddish) and seeming uncouth in clothes and manners, were a source of embarrassment. To counteract this was the somewhat naïve hope, shared by many in both communities, of destroying the old canard that Jews could not be farmers, and thus restoring the good name of Israel. The existence of many thousands of Jewish farmers in Russia, in spite of harsh repressions, was a fact seemingly unrecognized.

For a variety of reasons, the idea of rural colonization swept the Jewish world of the late nineteenth and early twentieth centuries. Western agrarianism included a nostalgia for biblical Israel, though without the political connotations of the modern Zionist state. Intellectuals, dreamers, agrarian pioneers, community leaders, philanthropists, and just plain immigrants joined forces in an endeavor which brought East and West together for the collective good of a suffering people. At its most urgent level, rural settlement was a technique for saving lives, first from Russian pogroms and later from the Nazi holocaust. At another, though not unrelated level, it took the form of an apology to stem anti-Jewish or anti-immigration sentiment in Western Europe and the United States.

Support of colonies such as those in South Jersey could produce less denominational controversy than that of pioneering Palestine settlements of the same era. Farming per se was traditionally an honorable profession, endowed by physiocratic and Jeffersonian thought with all kinds of moral and practical virtues. Individual proprietorship, hard work, and thrift, along with other middle class American values, were safe and popular shibboleths. By contrast, the notions of religious-national revival, collective ownership, and utopianism seemed immoderate to such Jewish notables as Baron Maurice de Hirsch in Europe, or Jacob Schiff and Mayer Sulzberger in the United States. Leaders of Reform Judaism, including Rabbi Isaac Mayer Wise, could enthusiastically preach agrarianism in the New World as an extension rather than a negation of their precept that "America is our Zion and Washington our Jerusalem."

Programs of settlement and retraining were not only practical, but also on the noblest level of traditional Jewish charity: they would enable the poor to stand on their own feet. Philanthropists like Schiff and de Hirsch strove for viable communities where Jews could take care of their own, without becoming a burden to external relief agencies. Self-help was the doctrine preached by these leaders, a goal toward which they helped as many immigrants as possible in a harsh, competitive era, for even native farmers and laborers were subject to the painful economic adjustments from the 1880's onward.

Consequently, the South Jersey colonies developed as a privately subsidized social experiment, with neither the strongly socialist nor the nationalist connotations of the settlements in Palestine. Utopian dreams of immigrant theoreticians, however, remained, in the long run, unfulfilled. Among the colonists, of course, were those ideologically imbued—nationalists, agrarians, socialists, so-called radicals of all sorts—for they were representatives of that great self-assertive intellectual ferment which characterized the East European awakening. Nevertheless, agrarian or other ideologists were in the minority, perhaps even among the first groups of settlers. Most of them shared

7

with other immigrants an overriding concern for economic opportunity and the promises of a free society. In South Jersey, they
found an underpopulated region, hungry for settlers. Although its
resources were severely limited, there was space aplenty, a fact also
recognized by other Europeans. Thus, by 1882, the Vineland area's
ethnic mixture already included, among others, Italians specializing
in viticulture. The Russian Jewish settlements, however, constituted
a distinctively new kind of community based on group colonization
and almost self-contained institutions.

In large measure, the organizational sponsors of the Jewish
colonies retained control over their nature and development, not the
immigrant intellectuals or radicals. Those who wished to do things
differently lacked the power; a few were expelled as troublemakers.
Policy decisions usually came from above, a situation which sometimes created friction between immigrants and their benefactors:
although the settlers resorted to pleas, petitions, protests, and
walk-outs, effective democracy in basic matters did not function
consistently. At issue was not doctrinal ideology but rather such
practical matters as subsistence pay and farm and home mortgage
extensions. Attempts to attract private investment from the city
brought conflict between factory owners and proletarians and
between philanthropists and entrepreneurs over wages, hours, and
concessions to business. On one side, the philanthropists had too
large an investment at stake and too great a burden in caring for
additional waves of immigrants to allow either settlers or local factory operators too free a hand; on the other, the colonies as a whole
could not tear themselves loose from a state of dependence. Moreover, the cultural gap made mutual understanding difficult: what
represented efficient management to the American and Western
European benefactors seemed like a cold, almost alien bureaucracy
to their Eastern coreligionists. Even language was a barrier. In the
meantime, continued development required further subsidies, causing disillusionment on both sides; despite such problems, many individual families did succeed in farming, industry, and the professions.

Knowledgeable and influential, the Western leadership prevailed,
though its supposed victories were matched by confrontation, stale-

mate, and eventual decline. Unlike the Palestinian colonies, the major goals sought in New Jersey were social and economic integration rather than national or cultural revival. Americanizing the immigrant included lessons in private enterprise not socialism, in producing for a market economy, and in thrift and paying off mortgages. In the long run, however, this capitalist-style individualism and rural colonization proved inconsistent. Integration and economic success were closely related, and the weakening of ethnic or ideological identities, especially among the younger people, provided little basis for keeping the individual on the farm if he saw greater advantages in the city. After all, mobility for purposes of personal gain has always been respected in capitalism, and above all in laissez-faire America.

The Western Jewish leadership and the Eastern refugees who accepted their terms (usually there was not much choice), felt themselves no less justified than their Zionist or socialist or "Russified" contemporaries. All strove, in their own way, for the eventual emancipation of the Jewish people, and for dignity and meaning in a world where modern democracy and nationalism had failed to secure the social rights of minorities or, as in Russia, to stay the despotism of an ancient bigotry. At the most basic level, Western Jews felt compelled to respond repeatedly to the needs of their Eastern coreligionists for physical survival; here the sense of collective responsibility was clearest.

Concerning ideology, economics, cultural and religious development, however, the gulf between the two communities persisted. And the social confrontation was made more complex by the divisions among the immigrants, too, attempting to retain some of their own wealth of cultural patterns, yet forced also to seek new directions within the American setting, choosing among middle class or proletarian values, urban or country life, orthodoxy or secularism. The result, at times, was disagreement not only between colonists and benefactors, but also among the colonists themselves. All the while, of course, remained the problem of confronting the world outside. Internal development was often self-consciously molded according to the pattern and reactions of gentile society.

Thus the colonizing experiment represents both a kaleidoscope and a mirror of the major forces in modern Jewish life. Agrarianism, Americanization, Zionism, a testing of traditional values, all were to be found here in microcosm. If it was not motivated by a single unifying ideology in any schematic sense, if it sometimes seemed diffuse and amorphous in character, the same can also be said of Jewish life as a whole in Europe or in the United States or, to a lesser degree, in Palestine. Combining pragmatism with humanitarian idealism, individualism with group responsibility, the New Jersey colonies were in the mainstream of traditional Jewish ethics; self-help and mutual aid were not exclusive. Perhaps it was precisely because of these nondoctrinaire qualities that they were able to arouse such enthusiastic if often arm's-length support among Western communities.

There was intensive interest, as reflected in both the Jewish and the non-Jewish press, in the successes and failures of the rural colonies. Would these Russians, as they were often called, prove that Jews too could be farmers? And throughout was a kind of safety valve theory: if enough immigrants were settled on the land rather than crowded into slums, this would not only ease conditions in the city, but might also inhibit, or delay, the ever-growing threat of the closed door. All these were elements in the unique relationship between Eastern and Western communities.

Another significant aspect of the relationship is indicated even in the selection of the Vineland-Bridgeton-Millville triangle for the first settlement in 1882. The organizers deemed it close enough to Philadelphia and New York to provide adequate contacts or supervision, and markets for the settlers' products, yet far enough away to avoid the encroachments and temptations of the city. Tracts of land were purchased, homes and public facilities provided for, and, with clearing and cultivation, began the first year. An excellent training school for agriculture complete with demonstration farms and livestock was eventually established as part of the almost self-contained new town of Woodbine. Time and substantial investments of capital and labor gradually overcame the hardships of pioneering.

East Europeans in Alliance and Woodbine strove to give life to the idea of working God's land as free farmers, to draw dignity from their roots in the soil. Here they were not enchained by the feudalistic restrictions of the Old World, which over the centuries had forced Jews to scrounge for a living in the urban and rural slums of Europe as petty retailers, craftsmen and middlemen. In spite of adversity many persisted as tillers of the soil through long lifetimes; some were ingenious in drawing a livelihood from the land, whether in small fruits, viticulture, or poultry, and bequeathed good farms to their children.

The very first years, however, were marked by change and urgent adaptation to unstable business conditions, to the general decline of agriculture, urbanization, and the need to diversify. For example, an early adaptation was the growth of textile and clothing manufacture along with agricultural activities, thus supplementing the meager earnings of the average farmer and his family. Many abandoned farming altogether, in favor of the factory. The problems of optimum land use, as well as the application of human and capital resources, were to figure significantly in the viability of the colonies.

Throughout, active channels of communication between the colonists and their city brethren grew stronger with technological advances; such communication was undoubtedly a factor in the character of the Jersey colonies and their survival far beyond the lifespan of other such experiments in more isolated areas (as in Oregon, Louisiana, or Kansas). From the community in the cities came visiting rabbis, philanthropists, preachers, lecturers, Christian missionaries, Yiddish entertainers, small businessmen, radicals, labor union organizers, vacationers, do-gooders, and always new immigrants. To the city went news of the settlers' changing fortunes, the products of their farms and factories, and also discontented colonists who would wander thence in search of better opportunities. Especially in time of trouble, the two communities would solidify: in response to the Kishinev pogroms, for example, colonist farmers and tailors united with the better established city Jews to hold protest meetings and fund drives; and when colonists joined their city cousins in strikes against sweat shop bosses, they received a pat on the back from the Jewish *Forward* for their working class solidarity.

Except for a few, they were neither Socialists nor anarchists, but they turned out in force to hear Eugene V. Debs and Emma Goldman. Not many were active Zionists, but they paid heed to Zionist appeals and in one way or another shared the dream of the Promised Land. They were pioneers in industrial unions as well as farmers' associations; they formed workmen's circles and literary clubs as well as cooperative marketing organizations. There was hardly a Jewish cause or social movement not represented in the life of the colonies; there was even the Jewish Chautauqua Society.

For the historian and social scientist, important aspects of social change and acculturation in modern America are vividly illustrated by these communities. For, in addition to the first pioneers of the 1880's more came in the 1890's and the twentieth century, including sizable numbers during the Nazi era. Each wave of these immigrants into the area was somehow unlike its predecessors, not only in country of origin but also in its social, economic, and even political emphasis. Each found its own type of haven. And the children of the immigrants, in a rapidly changing society, continued the experiment by adopting new solutions, even if they conflicted with those prevailing before.

Whether or not they stayed on the farm—most of the children did not—the new arrivals experienced in the New Jersey colonies a unique training ground for freedom. In their own town of Woodbine, green farmers and rural factory workers practiced the arts of self-government without the encumbrance of big city political machines. They served as councilmen and mayors as well as on committees to clean up and beautify their community.

Life among fellow Jews who were also fellow immigrants involved fewer sacrifices of one's identity; there was less of an immediate language problem and fewer urgent challenges to background or beliefs than in the often high-pressure melting pot of the city. For the process of immigration involved an uprooting of previous patterns, an abrupt and often painful reversal of familiar group associations and values. It was a hard road from the old, deepseated organic identity of East European Jewry to the middle class secularism of Americanization. The transformation, and one may well debate its desirability or ultimate form, was probably easier

12

in the all-Jewish environment of the colonies. Moreover, here were the means for the "huddled masses" to evolve into a self-supporting, well-informed citizenry drawing sustenance from the most honest of all occupations.

But the heyday of American agrarianism was over, and the farmer's revolt in the twilight of the nineteenth century was symptomatic of this decline. In a sense, the spirit of Hamilton rather than Jefferson was dominant in the United States, as industrialization, technology, and big business flourished in a nationwide economy now reaching even overseas. Opportunity drew people away from the farm, and the lure of quick advancement was in the city.

In the long run, the experiment was not to prove impressive in terms of size or total impact. It absorbed only a minute fraction of the masses thronging to these shores. Its utopian aspects were eventually overshadowed by pragmatic adjustments. Here were no great ranches or "bonanza" farms. The meager yield of a sandy earth was, of necessity, soon supplemented by the sewing machine, especially in an era of falling farm prices. Numerous settlers eventually dispersed to the towns and cities nearby. Nonetheless, there remains this heritage of Jewish agrarian idealism, self-help, and philanthropy, individualism and group planning, all converging from the partnership of Western and Eastern communities. It forms a significant chapter in the development of America's pluralistic society and in the history of a people straining from oppression to freedom.

"Give me your tired, your poor..."

The people left of the sword found grace in the
wilderness . . . Again I will build thee and thou shalt
be built . . . the planters shall plant and shall eat.
Jeremiah 31:2, 4:5

1

European Backgrounds: Emancipation
Stifled by Pogroms

Modern Jewish history has been influenced crucially by those epic changes within Europe which transformed the Continent into belligerent camps brooking no tolerance for each other or for outsiders. The century between the end of the Napoleonic Wars and the outbreak of World War I was ostensibly a period of relative calm, as Britain attempted to maintain a balance of power in international relations. The absence of widespread warfare during these years could be contrasted with the bloody religious battles of the Reformation period, the dynastic wars of the eighteenth century, and finally, the violent continental upheavals caused by the French Revolution.

And yet the Continent was not really at peace in the nineteenth century. Revolutionary movements, such as those which exploded in 1848, continued to press despotic governments for greater political and economic freedom. The ideologies of capitalism, socialism, nationalism, and imperialism caused feverish reactions and counterreactions in the body politic of Europe. Industrialization brought with it rapid change, economic instability, and even a decline in the status of entire social groups, such as the landed gentry and the craftsmen.

Under these circumstances, the almost traditional Jew-hatred, practiced for centuries, found expression in new and more virulent forms of anti-Semitism. Thus, Adolf Stöcker's Christian Social Workers' Party, organized in 1878, preached a program of opposition to any culture that was not "Germanic and Christian"; the problems of the lower middle class were blamed on a "conspiracy" of the Jews. In 1882, the first International Anti-Jewish Congress met at Dresden under Stöcker's chairmanship.[1]

Years before, the ghetto walls had been battered down in the wake of the French Revolution. Its rationalist ideology, sweeping through Western Europe, led to the emancipation of Jewish citizens in the form of equal treatment before the law, freedom from special taxes, and equal rights of domicile and vocation. But removal of legal disabilities offered in reality little protection against the forces of reaction and bigotry. By the second half of the nineteenth century, these forces drew added strength from the new doctrines of racism, such as those preached by the Pan-German movement. In France also, Jew-hatred was seized upon as a useful propaganda tool by reactionary nationalists and royalists, and culminated in the infamous Dreyfus Affair.

The emancipation achieved early in the nineteenth century, however, failed altogether to reach the majority of European Jewry, those living within two great empires, the Russian and the Austrian. In the latter, the Hapsburgs did not extend basic citizenship rights to the Jews until 1867. Up to that date, the Jews of the vast Austrian Empire continued to suffer the humiliating disabilities of medievalism: no right to own or lease land; severe restrictions on place of residence, including virtual exclusion from major cities; and denial of access to both education and the respected trades and professions. Emancipation removed the legal basis for oppressive discrimination, but equality of opportunity was far from assured.[2]

Eastward, in the Empire of the Tsars, the situation was much worse. Most of the Jewish population, about five million before the end of the nineteenth century, was forcibly concentrated in an area

16

of western Russia known as the Pale of Settlement. Only a privileged few, who were considered most useful to the state, were permitted to move about within the Russian interior to practice their trade or profession. Inside the crowded Pale, hundreds of thousands of impoverished people struggled for economic survival mainly as small retailers, artisans, and peddlers.

Alexander III, ascending the throne in 1881, sought to combine the traditional autocratic policies of the Tsars with more severe measures of forced Russification. The regime sharpened its weapons of reactionary nationalism in the name of Slavophile ideals, and then used these as a basis for further centralization of power and a tool to oppress such non-Russian minorities as Poles, Finns, and Armenians, as well as Jews. A vast bureaucracy enforced the supremacy of three transcendent and intertwined universalities: Mother Russia, the Tsar, and the Orthodox Church.

Legal emancipation of the serfs, followed as it was by the new dislocations of market capitalism, failed to improve the economic condition of either the mass of Russian peasants or the growing Jewish minority. The forced pace of modernization included railroad building and government monopolies in such consumer industries as the manufacture and sale of whiskey. In the process, traditional jobs like wagon driver, innkeeper, artisan, miller, or agent for the nobility, that were open to lower and middle class Jews were eliminated, while religious prejudice made Jews virtually ineligible for other positions in the changing economic structure. Chronic depression for almost two decades after the early 1870's aggravated the overall situation.

The Jewish community, which was especially vulnerable, provided a convenient scapegoat for the nation's problems. On the one hand, the autocratic regime labeled them radicals and proletarian agitators; on the other, the bureaucracy fanned peasant prejudice by attacking the few wealthy Jews as usurers, and the whole Jewish population as "Christ killers." None other than Tsar Alexander himself saw fit to remind his subjects "that it was the Jews who crucified our Lord, and spilled his priceless blood."[3]

A series of government-inspired pogroms shook Jewish communities from Kiev to Warsaw in the spring and summer of 1881. "The entire behavior of the police," wrote the Austrian consul in Kiev, "leads one rightfully to the conclusion that the disturbances are abetted by the authorities."[4] In May of 1882, the Tsar issued a set of decrees intended to restrict the degraded Jewish population to the Pale's urban ghettos: moving into rural areas was virtually prohibited; village councils were empowered to expel "undesirables"; strict quotas limited their entry into schools and universities; similar quotas and other restrictions reduced their number in the professions and crafts. As a result, Jewish existence in Russia was subjected to a stranglehold economically, politically, socially, and psychologically.

Attempts at Defense and Self-Help: National Revival and "Return-to-the-Soil"

As hopes for emancipation in Eastern Europe waned, Jewish leaders and intellectuals strove desperately for solutions within a context of nationalism and social reform. Programs for national amelioration, as adapted to Jewish needs, often represented a defensive response to the twin dangers of anti-Semitism and assimilation. At the same time, influenced by centuries of a separate and flourishing ethnic life, especially in Eastern Europe, Jewish leaders emphasized the common heritage of religion, history, language, and the dream of redemption through Zion.

A decade before the nadir of Russian oppression, Perez Smolenskin thundered against the blandishments of assimilationism and demanded a positive loyalty to the Jewish People and their heritage. An influential author and journalist, he had a particular impact on the youth. His eloquent essay *Am Olam* ("Eternal People"), published in 1872, proved a most effective reply to those who placed their hopes in some sort of benevolent Russification.

Still more direct was the message contained in the prophetic *Auto-Emanzipation* ("Self-Emancipation") published early in 1882 by an Odessa physician, Dr. Leon Pinsker. Common bonds of religion and culture were not enough to assure a people's survival, Pinsker argued, and cited as evidence the Diaspora's tragic history. What the Jewish people needed to achieve acceptance and self-

18

respect was a *land* which they could call their own, preferably the land from which their forefathers had been exiled; only thus could they end their condition of servile impotence. The pamphlet, soon translated into Russian and Yiddish, reached a wide audience of the oppressed. Events in 1882 also seemed to bear out the truth of Nahum Sokolow's early Zionist essay, *Sina't Olam le-Am Olam* ("Eternal Hatred for the Eternal People"). For leaders of the Jewish rationalistic enlightenment, the example of other oppressed minorities striving for cultural and political identity gave added impetus to the hope of national revival, and, as a legitimate expression of a great contemporary movement, their aspirations might provide a positive image to replace that of the rootless Jew in a Christian world.

As a slogan, "Am Olam" was interpreted both as "Eternal People" and "People of the World." While Smolenskin and Pinsker, forerunners of political Zionism, stressed a return to Palestine, others pointed to different lands as perhaps more practicable and more hospitable. The People-of-the-World approach suggested that Jews might be better off in a world outside Russia, a world improved through democratic reform; countries like the United States and Argentina seemed to offer a better opportunity to rebuild one's life in dignity than could be hoped for in a barren Palestine under Turkish rule.

Throughout southern Russia and the western Pale, in cities and hamlets, student societies and common people became embroiled in the urgent debate over their own future. Some of the young intellectual *narodniki* ("populists") favored integration with the Russian peasantry, but found themselves rebuffed by the anti-Semitism preached even within liberal groups, as well as among the Slavophile writers. Other Jews, working through the Society to Propagate Manual and Agricultural Labor, hoped to make their people more "productive," more "useful," and thereby merit acceptance and win integration. Jacob Gordin established a sect based on the virtues of manual labor as well as biblical purism; he was to continue his career in America as a theorist and successful Yiddish playwright.

Emigration became a most urgent if painful necessity with the pogroms of 1881-1882. Some prepared to embrace both Zion and farming in a great national-cultural revival in Palestine. At the same time, more were aroused by the prospect of emigration to America and the hope of socio-economic improvement. Am Olam clubs were formed in Odessa, Kharkov, Kiev, Vilno, and other cities of Russia, to prepare for the New World migration. The members, young men and women of better than average education, were highly sensitive to the suffering of their people; like many other Jews, they had eagerly absorbed the ideas of emancipation and the secularist enlightenment, including the doctrines of utopian socialism. One such group had on its escutcheon the design of a plow with the Ten Commandments, above which were the words "Am Olam" and this motto: "Arise from the dust, throw off the contempt of the nations, for the time has come!" A member of another group wrote: "Our slogan is work on the land, our goal is the spiritual and physical revival of our people. In the free America, where various nationalities live side by side in peace, we Jews can also find a haven."[5] More an amorphous movement than a disciplined political party, they sought new solutions for an ancient oppression.

Their preference for a universal humanism, operating through enlightenment and political reform, usually minimized the concept of Jewish nationality. Some found it necessary to explain that American federalism could not encompass a "separate Jewish State bearing the name Israel," though group settlement might permit a new life on a communal basis. One of the Am Olam's founders, Michael Bakal, sacrificed a prospective career as rabbi to devote himself to the movement, giving concrete expression to its ideology of manual labor as an artisan in Odessa. He and Moshe Herder, a teacher-poet, were able to attract not only intellectuals like H. L. Sabsovich of Odessa University, but a broader following as well. Thus, it was hoped, the massive exodus would acquire some order and leadership. "Just ordinary craftsmen and tradesmen who managed to get by in Russia, sold all they had and joined the groups seeking to build a new Jewish life in America. They did this with religious zeal and self-sacrifice," recalled Abraham Cahan, an adherent of the Am Olam and later editor of the American Jewish *Forward*.[6]

Among these idealists were some who would move successfully

beyond the rigors of planning, travel, and adjustment to build agricultural colonies in New Jersey and other states. From the outset
they were confronted with crucial decisions that would affect both
their own future and any historical evaluation of their movement.
There remained, for example, the alternative of Zion. In the same
year as the Am Olam left for America (1882) several thousand
other Russian Jews, most of them also aspiring to an agricultural
life, settled in Palestine. They were motivated principally by *Hibat
Zion* ("love of Zion"), and among them was a group of about three
dozen zealous youths who, using as their watchword "BILU" (from
the Hebrew initials of "House of Jacob, Let Us Go") pledged to
work only as farmers or laborers. Could members of "the House of
Jacob" find roots in American soil as well? Confronted with the
choice, the Am Olam answered affirmatively. Their leaders included
men who would become pioneers in New Jersey, not only Herder
and Sabsovich, but also Sidney Bailey and others. Their philosophy
was based partly on idealization of agricultural society, of honest and
truly productive labor; to till the soil was somehow to participate in
the divine, to place one's hand in the process of creation. But in
large measure they were also concerned with their own response
to anti-Semitism.

Along with other young Jews, the Am Olam had formed self-
defense clubs to repel the physical threat of pogroms. More significantly, however, they attempted to cope with what they considered to be the roots of anti-Semitism in the battleground of ideas
and education. They were concerned with changing the stereotype
of their people as peddlers, merchants, unproductive middlemen, by
proving that they could return to agriculture, as in biblical times.
Yet, in their own soul-searching and fault-finding, some Jewish
intellectuals reflected too much the views of their oppressors, the
charges of exploitation which had become part of the arsenal of
anti-Semitism. It did not matter, seemingly, that the Jewish merchant or peddler struggled on the edge of poverty, or that a mere
pittance was often his reward for performing the vital economic
functions of the market, especially as a link between agriculture and
the slowly developing commerce and industry.

Nor was there adequate recognition of the great numbers of

Jewish artisans, craftsmen, factory workers and, in spite of Tsarist restrictions, farmers. Following the May Laws of 1882, which prohibited Jews from acquiring rural property, thousands of Jewish families continued to work on the land, especially in the many long-established agricultural colonies throughout the provinces of Kherson and Ekaterinoslav. From Bessarabia and other regions, relatively few Jewish farmers, mainly those forced out by pogroms, migrated to the United States. They seemed to have no connection with the Am Olam movement, whose concern was so largely with the emigration of the nonfarming majority. Yet, by 1900, the Jewish agricultural population within Russia grew to about one hundred thousand.[7]

It is possible to question the assumptions of the Am Olam without minimizing their achievements. Their neo-physiocratic notions of true economic value as derived from agriculture seem as out-of-date in the era of industrialization as does their romantic utopianism. Hardly any of them possessed practical experience in farming, yet they were willing to adopt it as both a way of life and a response to anti-Semitic charges. Since the formation of their movement in the early 1880's, the trend had been towards urbanization, technology, and specialization and away from agriculture and the rural community pattern. Their goals were not clearly defined, nor were they organized into well-disciplined and indoctrinated cadres. Nonetheless, this can scarcely detract from recognition of the group's courage in seeking through agrarianism a solution to Jewish problems. Their misreading of economic and social trends may have made life in the New World more difficult for them at first, but it also focused their attention on some basic dilemmas posed by the Old World ways of life.

In the Old World, those who favored concentration on the secular training of the Jewish masses as a means of improving their lot hailed the philanthropic proposals of Baron Maurice de Hirsch to construct a network of vocational and technical schools in Russia as well as in Austrian Galicia. But could occupational skills, and even scholarly eminence, overcome the effects of Tsarist bigotry? From the New World, Philadelphia journalist Moses Klein counseled that this was only wishful thinking: there was no assurance, he warned, that graduates of such schools would receive the right of residence in the interior of Russia or the opportunity of applying their acquired skills on an equal basis with other citizens. As if in summation of the Am Olam's major premise, Klein argued that "the sole benefit these 50,000 scholars [in the proposed schools] will derive from their education will reach them only after their emigration from Russia to other and more civilized countries, in which their intelligence and industry and their knowledge of art and science will probably be recognized, notwithstanding their Semitic origins."[8] He spoke both as journalist and civic leader as well as agent for the Jewish Emigration Society of Philadelphia, which lent its support to the colonies of South Jersey.

Not only the question of migration itself, but also its objectives were to reflect the conflicts of the time. Unlike the Zionist groups, the Am Olam had no clear desire to work toward a Jewish state; their mother tongue was Yiddish, but they did not feel compelled to perpetuate it. Some undoubtedly preferred the Russian language and culture. They were torn between a consciousness of being Jewish and a sense of unity with the whole world. Nor did the socialistic aspects of Zionism appeal to many: among those who settled in the Carmel colony of New Jersey were a few of strong socialist convictions, but in a country where private enterprise was the secular faith they made little headway. Clearest of all was the belief that a return to the soil was the path to recognition and self-respect. "We chose the 'land of the brave and the home of the free,'" said Sidney Bailey, one of the successful pioneer settlers, "and we came here, instead of going to Palestine, which was then under a Turkish regime. . . . Our goal was to own a home and land as a means of earning a livelihood . . . to get the blessings of a natural life from heaven and earth . . . to become true citizens of our adopted country."[9]

Many of the Am Olam, however, never succeeded in their dream of rural colonization, even on a temporary basis, for they simply lacked the resources to move away from the city in which they had disembarked. A member of one group eking out an existence in New York's sweat shops summarized their financial situation thus: "From the first month we have each contributed to our agricultural fund 15 cents out of every dollar; our common treasury now includes $34.40."[10] Much more would be required in funds and organization than the Am Olam's limited capabilities. Migrating Russian Jewry, stifled in its own homeland, required the material assistance of the less numerous but more prosperous communities of France, England, and America.

I Am My Brother's Keeper: The Role of Western Philanthropy in Resettlement Plans

The recurrent pogroms in Russia and the intensified oppression of the Jewish population shocked humanitarian sentiment throughout the world. Thousands of the terrorized and dispossessed managed to struggle across the Tsar's borders, bringing the full impact of their tragedy to the rest of the world. Even in far-off Vineland, New Jersey, the local press carried dispatches describing the expulsions from St. Petersburg and Kharkov, the forced baptisms, the pillaging of shops, destruction of homes, and the wanton attacks on innocent families.[11] For the vast majority of Jews remaining in Russia, it seemed, the May Laws and the pogroms virtually abolished freedom of movement outside their tenuous domiciles.

Along with news of the persecutions, came words of indignant response by civilized men. Early in 1882, the Vineland press carried accounts of protest petitions and a call for a mass meeting in London by such dignitaries as the Archbishop of Canterbury, the Bishops of London, Gloucester, Manchester and Oxford, Cardinal Manning, Matthew Arnold, Charles Darwin, the Earl of Shaftesbury, and others.[12] Less than a month later, on 21 February, it also reported passage of a resolution in the New Jersey Assembly "demanding protection for the oppressed Jews of Russia."[13] In New York, a great public meeting of protest was held in Chickering Hall, under the sponsorship of community leaders such as Judge Myer S. Isaacs.[14]

It would take more than expressions of protest and sympathy, however, to aid the "huddled masses" of refugees gathered in

24

Brody and other Austrian towns across the Russian border. In the West, the Jewish communities were endowed with both greater economic and political security including the freedom to organize effectively. An outstanding example was the Alliance Israélite Universelle, with headquarters in Paris and branches as far away as Philadelphia and San Francisco. In Philadelphia, its chief representatives were Moses Dropsie and the philanthropist Simon Muhr, who mobilized community support for the new immigrants and was to play a crucial role in assisting the New Jersey colonies.[15]

The Alliance, founded in Paris in 1860, was pledged to "defend the honor of the Jewish name whenever attacked . . . encourage, by every possible means, labor and the exercise of useful trades and professions . . . consolidate perfect freedom by intellectual and moral regeneration . . . [and] extend efficient aid to those who are suffering by reason of their being Jews."[16] Its operational scheme included election of a representative Central Committee and two-way communication with the membership in France and other countries. While predominantly Jewish in composition, it freely acknowledged the support of non-Jews in its humanitarian activities and attempts to arouse public opinion against persecution.

Relief for the victims of pogroms was organized primarily by the Alliance, whose representatives across the Russo-Austrian border and in Berlin were swamped by a tide of refugees requiring the basic necessities. Thousands fled across the border in 1881-82 because of the systematic Tsarist oppression which was intended, in part, to force their migration. Others, even in the relatively calm areas of Russia, caught the migration fever from favorable reports on American life which appeared at times in the Hebrew journals; some were misled by the false rumors of cash payments and free western land spread by competing steamship lines. The Alliance, too, was forced to deny exaggerated accounts of its ability to provide needy Russian Jews with generous resettlement aid.

At the same time, fearful that the mounting tide of refugees would overtax the resources and meager hospitality of Western Europe, the Alliance leadership thought instead of guiding them toward America, "that huge, free and opulent nation, where all

25

who want work can find it and establish themselves."[17] In any case, subsidized massive emigration was not part of the Alliance's planned response to Russian pogroms. Aside from tactical considerations, the burden would have been impossible. In 1881, in a circular distributed among threatened congregations, its Central Committee offered to defray traveling expenses to America only for "healthy, able-bodied, and industrious artisans," eighteen to thirty-five years of age.[18] Soon, from across the Atlantic there came critical voices, such as the *Hebrew Messenger* of 18 November 1881, complaining that too many refugees helped to America were of the peddling bent, unsuited for manual labor and especially for agriculture. Throughout the 1880's, the Board of Delegates of the Union of American Hebrew Congregations promised further assistance only to "these able-bodied men, capable of working."[19]

The philanthropists' emphasis reflected some of the attitudes of the Victorian age, yet it also betrayed a sensitivity to the incipient movement for immigration restrictions in the United States. It was still a few years before the Immigration Restriction League was organized officially, but opposition was mounting from various quarters. In New Jersey, the *New Brunswick Fredonian* in 1881 had raised its voice among others to maintain that "we must not be content to be a kind of dumping ground for all Europe."[20] The Vineland press echoed the complaint of the *New York Sun* that the newcomers "either cannot or will not work"; instead, continued the account, they would claim they were students and demand appropriate support, refusing jobs as farm or mill hands.[21] Such criticism made selectivity an early and persistent shibboleth.

Applying its own "careful and judicious" standards in 1882 the Alliance selected within a few months two thousand immigrants for America, many of them imbued with the ideals of Am Olam. The Central Committee's representative, Charles Netter, not only worked in the border towns where the refugees were temporarily located, but also provided transportation and the human amenities to alleviate the plight of the displaced. Nor was the migration ignored by fellow Jews in the villages and cities: at stopping points, local delegations presented flags and scrolls of the Torah along with moral

and material encouragement. It was in honor of the patron organization, however, that the first Jewish agricultural colony in New Jersey
would be named "Alliance."[22]

The cause of rescue and resettlement also owed much to the
philanthropic efforts of Baron de Hirsch, that great financier and
railroad builder of the late nineteenth century. His father, Joel
Jacob de Hirsch, had achieved success in the cattle business and in
banking, as well as attaining that rare distinction among European
Jews, the title of baron, granted to him by the King of Bavaria.
Maurice, the second Baron de Hirsch, was willing to risk the
family's wealth in projects which others considered too speculative,
such as the expansion of railroad lines eastward from Central
Europe to the Black Sea. Under his direction, numerous obstacles
were overcome to provide vital transportation for large areas of the
Austro-Hungarian Empire. Another consequence, as noted somewhat invidiously by the Vineland press, was that "the building of
these roads enriched de Hirsch beyond the dreams of avarice."[23]

As a result of his work and travels in Eastern Europe, Baron de
Hirsch became convinced of the need to aid his oppressed brethren
through expanding educational opportunities. It was to this end
that he had established vocational and business schools in Austrian
Galicia, later offering the vast sum of 10 million dollars to the
Tsarist government for its use in providing similar education for
Russian Jews. But the offer was rejected. And with the renewal
of pogroms in the 1880's, he too embraced the cause of emigration
as the only real means to secure freedom and economic opportunity.
Searching for a practical and humanitarian solution, Baron de Hirsch
eventually founded the Jewish Colonization Society, based on an
initial capital of 2 million pounds sterling, to aid in the establishment
of farm colonies in the New World, focusing on Argentina.[24]

With the advice of Oscar S. Straus, de Hirsch created (1889)
another interim fund of 2.4 million dollars, the income of which was
to be used specifically for agricultural resettlement in the United
States, under American direction. After long deliberations, the
Baron de Hirsch Fund was incorporated in the state of New York
(1891) by such notables as Judge Myer S. Isaacs (president), Jacob

H. Schiff (vice-president), Julius Goldman, and Straus, all of New York, and Mayer Sulzberger and William B. Hackenburg of Philadelphia. Thereby, the Baron not only provided emergency aid to the struggling colonies in the Vineland area, but also, and more significantly, he created the basis for long-range subsidies leading to the planned establishment of Woodbine and its agricultural school.[25]

Best known, however, for its immediate relief to the refugees landing in New York, was the Hebrew Emigrant Aid Society of the United States, founded in 1881 in the wake of the Russian pogroms. The Society provided temporary board and lodging, loans, job information, and even travel expenses to get away from the congestion of seaboard centers—west as far as Denver and south to Atlanta. Though short-lived, it was the earliest New World link in the chain of brotherly aid extending from the Alliance Israélite Universelle on the Continent and the Mansion House Committee of Jewish philanthropists in England. This working relationship was translated into concrete financial agreements, when, for example, the Alliance made a contribution of over $38,000 to the American organization's budget of $281,000 in its fiscal year ending 30 November 1882. It was in this same year that the Society reported initial expenses of $41,960.42 to establish the Alliance colony near Vineland.[26]

The impetus to settle Jewish immigrants on the land caught the imagination of other organizations also, though with less effect. For example, an ambitious plan to sell two hundred thousand Educational and Agricultural Fund certificates at $5 each was developed in 1882 by leaders of the Union of American Hebrew Congregations. Unfortunately, in spite of rallies in New York, Philadelphia, and New Orleans, mass subscriptions were not forthcoming. This effort too, however, was an indication of the ferment within the established Jewish community in response to the new immigration. The major motive undoubtedly was humanitarian. How much was it also a sense of insecurity in the face of impoverished coreligionists, who were foreigners nonetheless, flocking to the "tenement houses . . . to disease and a vicious life"? Underlying such proposals as the

Educational and Agricultural Fund there is indicated a sensitivity to non-Jewish opinion: let the immigrants become farmers "and make thereby the most effectual step to stamp out prejudice against the Jew."[27]

Tradition-oriented leaders of the American Jewish community recognized not only the moral obligation to help the newcomers adjust to the ways of their adopted country, but also saw in a more positive light their potential contributions to New World Judaism. Thus, rabbis Sabato Morais and H. Pereira Mendes urged their congregants to join with them in acts of personal aid and counsel to the immigrants, caring particularly to alleviate the deplorable conditions in the city slums. Even before he became a trustee of the Baron de Hirsch Fund and dedicated to the settlement of Jewish immigrants in a rural environment, Morais worked closely with the needy immigrants in both the urban and agrarian settings of his native Philadelphia and such nearby South Jersey colonies as Alliance and Carmel.[28]

The lay notables who formed the new Jewish Alliance of America (1891) also deplored the immigrants' "concentration in the seaboard cities." Communal leaders like the eminent physician Solomon Solis-Cohen and attorney Mayer Sulzberger reminded their American brethren that it "has always been the custom of Jews to allow no man to go unrelieved, and it is now especially a duty to apply this principle to these afflicted refugees." If they could be resettled in sparsely populated "interior districts," as the Alliance plan of action proposed, sufficient improvements would result in "their material conditions . . . their introduction into varied branches of industry [including agriculture] . . . their education in the rights and duties of American citizenship . . . [and, finally] their complete assimilation into our American commonalty would follow as of course."[29] Such, it was noted, was the history of the previous German-Jewish immigration which model it was hoped the newcomers would follow.

It became almost fashionable for the leaders of the American Jewish establishment—urban, affluent, successfully middle class—to vie with one another as spokesmen for the restoration of the image of an agricultural people. The immigrant "must not live in a new Ghetto," pleaded Judge Isaacs in New York, rather, "he must be prepared for American life and methods of work." True emancipation could only be achieved in this way, and by the return to the soil; "as in olden days, so in the near future, shall the critic whom a hostile power has retained to prophesy the incapacity of these Jews for citizenship be compelled to declare as he gazes on the happy settlements of the exiles, 'How lovely are thy tents, O Jacob, thy tabernacles, O Israel.' "[30] Thus did the president of the Barøn de Hirsch Fund envisage the rural colonies of New Jersey as living testimony against the modern Balaks and Balaams.

Judge Isaacs's early partner in Jewish agrarianism was a liberal immigrant from Eastern Europe named Michael Heilprin. Born in Russian Poland in 1823, he grew to an intellectual maturity that was at home with the culture of Western Europe as it was with Hebrew poetry. In 1842 his family fled from Tsarist persecution to Hungary; there Heilprin joined the independence movement led by Louis Kossuth, and after the revolution of 1848 was again forced to flee. Following an exile in Paris and his subsequent return to Hungary, Heilprin decided that freedom might be less elusive in the New World. His wide knowledge of languages and cultures, combined with a keen understanding of world politics, led him to a career as contributor to Appleton's *New American Cyclopaedia*, and later also on behalf of the anti-slavery movement for whom he composed an expert critique of attempts to use the Bible as rationalization for slave labor. In 1865, he joined the *Nation*, writing distinguished articles on world affairs for more than twenty years, and yet still finding time for his own scholarly two-volume *Historical Poetry of the Ancient Hebrews* (1879-80).[31]

Heilprin was ideally qualified in background, sympathy, and achievements, to provide a living bridge between the established American Jewish community of Sephardic or Germanic origin and the newcomers from Eastern Europe. Deeply stirred by the pogroms of 1881, he too saw a solution in "Jewish agricultural colonization."

The American public was, after all, sympathetic to the plight of the oppressed, even if there were some who felt "a vague dread of an overwhelming influx of foreign hordes ill-fitted for American conditions." Bias against the immigrants resulted from too "little faith" by those few who failed to "believe that among the wrecks of distant communities which a storm of persecution had driven to our shores, there was material for construction which might become an honor to this country, and to all Israel."[32] As early as March, 1882, Heilprin organized the Montefiore Agricultural Aid Society, named after the great Anglo-Jewish philanthropist. Its purpose was to assist those refugees showing an "ardent desire to devote themselves to agricultural pursuits."[33] Judge Isaacs became treasurer of the organization; Dr. Julius Goldman, of German background, was comptroller.

Heilprin, as secretary, labored arduously in the Society's dingy basement office on Philadelphia's State Street, not only on behalf of the agrarian principle, but also counseling the newcomers in their native language. His programs for assisting the agrarian colonies included a generosity that other leaders would find too easy to let pass: there should be no liens on property furnished to settlers, but rather a reliance on their personal honor, and settlers should certainly be allowed free movement to and from the colony. He also urged that organizational aid be supplied "without impairing the self-respect" of the people; for example, help in the form of agricultural equipment shared by all members of the colony, as well as community facilities such as a school, a library or a hospital would make the settlers feel less like mere recipients of charity. He continued to emphasize that "the Jewish agriculturist should be made to feel and consider himself a self-sustaining cultivator of the soil, an unsupported member of society."[34]

Nor did Heilprin fear to castigate the motives of some in positions of power who cared only for themselves: "the selfish or patriotic susceptibility of the already established Jews [who] revolt at the thought" of absorbing the new multitudes. America's resources, he assured the timid, were more than adequate, especially if the immigrants were channeled into rural areas. Agriculture might even be supplemented with local industry, if need be, to secure the prospect of self-sustaining colonies.[35]

In the cause of colonization to assure the immigrant's welfare, Heilprin was joined by many others, including the poet Emma Lazarus. Shortly before his death (1888) he presented his views to Straus, then American ambassador to Turkey, who had inquired regarding the prospects for potential Russian Jewish emigrants to the United States. Undoubtedly, Heilprin's program, including its organizational details, influenced the activities of the Baron de Hirsch Fund. Led by some of Heilprin's early associates, the Fund would mobilize much greater resources than available in the 1880's. That initial era of experimentation, "when dire necessity demanded the removal of many of the unfortunates from the over-crowded city districts," Heilprin predicted, would become a proving ground for the "colonizing attempts" in South Jersey and other areas of still-rural America. These pioneering efforts, pitted against the hard rock of inadequate resources and economic instability, none-theless would represent the urgent first steps in acculturation, and in shaping a significant partnership between the newcomers and their American benefactors.[36]

"At the Silesian Railroad Station"
Georg Brandes's Eyewitness Account of Jewish Refugees from Russia on their Way to American Farm Colonies (1882)

From 1877 through 1882, Georg Brandes lived in Berlin contin-uing to make creative contributions to literature and literary criti-cism. It was a temporary but productive absence from his native Denmark, where, in spite of his recognized achievements as scholar and university lecturer, he had felt the effects of anti-Jewish bias. In Berlin, Brandes found time to join with the Jewish Relief Committee, which received hundreds of refugees from Russia headed for America. The Committee, he wrote, was confronted with the arduous task of detaining those too weak for the burdens ahead of them, those lacking in manual skills, or those with small children. Many were in terror of being turned back, pleading that they would *"prefer to die of hunger. . . ." He took note especially of the idealists planning to establish their own communities in rural areas of the United States:**

Day by day, there arrived more groups of Russian Jews migrating at their own expense. . . . Among the first were sturdy young men, well-suited for pioneering (by now they are cultivating their own land in America, where they have built colonies and prospered). . . .

It is remarkable how such immigrant groups have planned their journey and indeed their future. Each has its own leader, usually a student; all group members take a vow to share all they own. And it must be understood that they pledged themselves to a full communal existence: to work on the land which they would receive in America through joint ownership of soil and tools; all income would belong to the group as a whole. They swore that no one would engage in commerce; only the managing committee would sell their produce, on a collective basis. In this, there is a mixture of Old-Russian and modern socialist ideas, with a wondrous infusion of national aspirations. When speaking to one of these impoverished but energetic students who lead this kind of group across the ocean, three different drives become apparent: More or less consciously, he feels that the collective type of land ownership in the Russian commune is in the natural order of things. He has been inspired by the relatively well developed socialist ideas so widespread in Russia with the translation of Lassalle's brochures. Ultimately, he is imbued with a profound determination and sense of duty to wipe away the old slur that Jews are capable only of trading and that they desire only to accumulate money.

Such student leaders and their compatriots are zealots and idealists. Suffering has neither failed to break down their courage, nor even diminished their optimism. They travel confidently to meet their New World. Will their socialism flourish there? Will they be able to maintain their cooperative spirit in a society where all is based on individualistic designs? Shall not their own individual talents, once allowed to develop, inevitably sunder the mutual bonds? It is but common sense to predict that, sooner or later, the groups will disband. But at least for the first-generation agrarian colonists the socialist orientation seems well suited.

* These observations, dated June 12, 13, 1882, appear in Chapter 62, "At the Silesian Railroad Station," of Brandes, *Berlin som Tysk Rigshovestadt* [*Berlin as the Capital of the German Empire*], pp. 485-492, translated into Yiddish by Uriel Weinreich: Appendix A of Elias Tcherikower, ed., *Geschichte fun der Yiddisher Arbeter Bavegung in die Fareinikte Shtatn* ("History of the Jewish Labor Movement in the United States") (New York, 1943), I, 391-396 (excerpts from pp. 392-393 trans. by author).

33

It is apparent that they have suffered and gone hungry. They are self-assured but not arrogant; they are craftsmen, not merchants; courteous, appreciative, but with none of the suspicion characteristic of the lower classes among other peoples. They are willing to speak informatively, but not necessarily to bemoan their fate. . . .

In the latter groups, there have also been substantial numbers of women. The horrors endured by these people have, from the outset, marked this migration as a mass exodus. Among these children of flight there were some who witnessed the massacre of their own parents, and they managed to describe it. There were survivors of the pogrom in Balta [March 1882], where the mobs broke into their homes with the acquiescence of the police, to plunder, wreck, and rape. . . . They scarcely managed to save themselves, with none of their possessions. A cigar-maker from Kiev, with whom I spoke today, told me succinctly and with no self-pity: "First they robbed us of all we owned, then they expelled us."

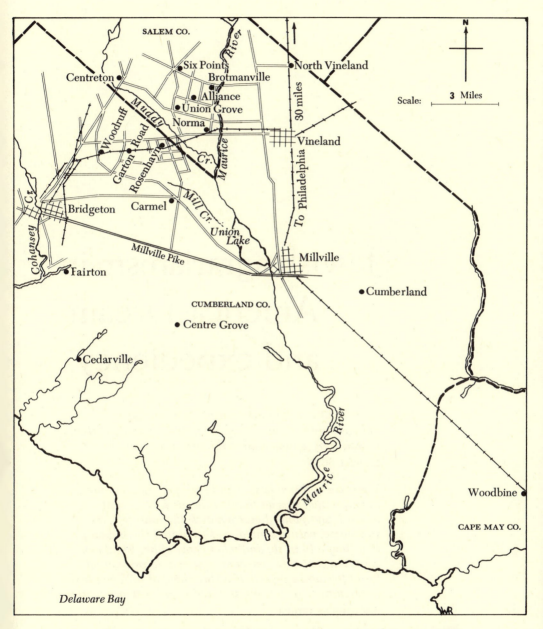

Locational map of Jewish Communities of South Jersey, 1919

Jewish agrarianism in America: Dream and expediency

And I will multiply the fruit of the tree, and the increase of the field, that ye may receive no more the reproach of famine among the nations.
Ezekiel 36:30

We were told two years ago to go to work and raise a big crop, that was all that was needed. We went to work and plowed and planted; the rains fell, the sun shone, nature smiled, and we raised the big crop that they told us to; and what came of it? Eight cent corn, ten cent oats, two cent beef and no price at all for butter and eggs—that's what came of it. Then the politicians said that we suffered from over-production.
Anonymous farmer[1]

2

The Agrarian Ethos:
Persistent Panacea

What made America unique in the eyes of Europeans were the very opportunities for which they sought vainly at home: freedom for the individual and an abundance of resources. On both sides of the Atlantic, truth was enhanced by exaggerated hope. The lure of land ownership in particular promised both economic and social advancement. Wave after wave of immigrants seemed to achieve the twin goals of material success and family security. Moreover, in the newly settled territories, at least, it seemed that Old World traits disappeared and institutional reform accelerated. Wealth in the form of land and natural resources was more evenly distributed; there were few vested interests; and mutual problems called forth cooperative efforts more democratic than the ways of Europe.

In the New World farmers could expect to support their families independently, to educate their children, to participate freely in the life of their new communities, and to see as well the value of their land increase as the country grew. Then, if they chose, they could move westward to some new frontier. The virtuous, healthy middle-class farmers seemed, to the mind of America and her admirers, the backbone of democracy. Throughout most of the nineteenth century, the comforting shibboleths of unlimited virgin land and opportunities for honest farmers persisted. Such prevailing beliefs were shared enthusiastically by American Jewish leaders proud of their patriotism and of their own achievements under conditions of equality. Yet, in the social philosophy of the farming frontier could be found much that demonstrated an ambivalence characteristic of America: materialism was mingled with idealism, pragmatic optimism with waste and opportunism, individualism with organized political pressure, and equalitarianism with a fear or hatred of the noncomformist. But most of all, before the turn of the century, the agrarian tradition had to bear the double blow of an apparent end to the frontier and a long-range economic decline of agriculture.

Hard years confronted the American farmer in the last quarter of the ninetenth century. From 1870 to 1897, prices fell in an ominous, inflexible pattern.[2] The more farmers produced, the more their relative share of the national income declined; they were caught in a vicious circle of debt, rising costs, a closing frontier, and a worldwide competitive market economy. The 1870's and late 1880's were especially painful years owing to both low prices and bad weather; regional farmers' alliances sought desperately for relief in cooperatives as well as in political action on both state and national levels. Yet, the symptomatic conditions like growing farm tenancy (highest in some of the most fertile areas) were not reversed.[3] On the western frontier, widespread destitution followed in the wake of drought, grasshopper plagues, and declining prices. The census of 1880 showed that 25.6 percent of the farms were operated by tenants, with each census for the next five decades to reveal a further increase in the percentage of tenant farmers.[4] As a foreshadowing of twentieth-century depressions, farm prices in 1896 reached the lowest level ever recorded.[5]

The long-run relative decline of agriculture in an increasingly urban and industrial America is indicated also by the following two estimates of population and income changes: From the start of the nineteenth century to the mid-twentieth, that segment of the population defined as rural dropped by 53 percent. Even more precipitously, agriculture's share in the national income plummeted from 40 percent to 6 percent.[6] Curiously enough, such unfavorable factors as increased farm tenancy continued during both prosperity and depression, attesting to the more burdensome costs of land, credit, machinery, and fertilizer; more farmers descended the ladder from ownership to tenancy than those who managed to climb it.[7]

In light of the difficulties confronting agriculture, the recurrent enthusiasm for rural colonization schemes among American Jewish leaders from the 1880's even into the 1930's may well be questioned. Though relevant economic data were limited or inadequately interpreted, some trends—as revealed in the census reports and other official publications, in agrarian discontent, in the flush of urban-industrial expansion—might have been more clearly understood. The myths of land ownership persisted. Most of all, however, it is apparent that *noneconomic* considerations provided the major impetus for settling the immigrants in rural communities.

First among these objectives was always the generous impulse to save refugees from oppression and to provide them with a wholesome social environment for becoming Américans. At the same time, the agrarian zeal within the established community persistently reflected a defensive and sometimes apologetic reaction to anti-Semitic charges, even if these were only implied. For example, the *Jewish Exponent* referred to a seemingly embarrassing article by George F. Kennan in a June 1889 issue of *Century* magazine, which contained allusions to the middle class Jewish *"mir*-eaters" who ostensibly exploited the peasants of Eastern Europe.[8] The *Exponent* pleaded that "Jews were *forced* by circumstances to become the most inhuman oppressors of the Galician peasants [sic]."[9]

The Union of American Hebrew Congregations had early joined in the struggle to dispel such unfavorable images of middle class exploitation. By 1885 its established Committee on Agricultural Pursuits urged the St. Louis Convention to encourage large numbers of "Israelites" to enter careers in farming. It asked for practical measures to make this possible, such as calling a national meeting for an independent American Hebrew Farmer's Association supported by all communities (this specific proposal was defeated by only a narrow margin).[10] In Philadelphia, the Hebrew Literary Society also addressed itself to this sensitive question: "Can the Jews become agriculturists?" asked one of its discussion papers. "If an affirmative answer be made, the objection that the Jews are not fitted to become an agricultural people vanishes. . . . In the ancient Biblical and early post-Biblical times the occupations of the Jewish nation were pastoral and agricultural. . . . It was more out of necessity than out of choice that Jews became . . . a commercial race."[11]

Existing agricultural colonies would prove the affirmative and more: "The sower of oats is as good as the sewer of coats," proclaimed Charles S. Bernheimer. Agricultural colonies would be true to the ancient agrarian ethos of the Jewish people, providing a sound environment for religion. "If our philanthropic Hebrews must be charitable," why not thereby create a class of "sturdy, self-supporting agriculturists?"[12] The theme was indeed warmly embraced by such philanthropic groups as the Jewish Emigration Society of Philadelphia, whose agent, Moses Klein, would delight in comparing the healthful Jewish farms of Carmel, New Jersey, with the "valley of death" in the ghettos of his own city or New York, where the battle for survival left no nourishment for the spirit and the future was no better than in Vilno or Bucharest. *"Farming alone,"* wrote Klein, "can solve the Jewish problem forced upon us for solution by eastern Europe and Asia."[13]

An editorial in Philadelphia's *Jewish Exponent* maintained that even if the immigrants did later choose to leave their farms because of changing conditions, "they will have gone through a humanizing school of healthy and honest toil which cannot but leave its unmistakable impression on their characters as well as those of their posterity. . . . The damning marks of the middleman or the three-balls man will no longer cling to their largely regenerated physiognomies or poison the very vitals of their capable natures."[14] This remarkable statement combining dubious notions of heredity and environment with a dose of prejudice can be traced to two forces: the fashionable Darwinism sweeping America by the 1880's, and the self-hatred phenomenon in the Jew (as well as other minorities).

"Can Jews be farmers?" was both battlecry and soul-searching question; it came from all parts of the country. Jacob Riis, eloquent critic of the dingy and unhygienic New York slums, also joined the call for rural colonies in an era of rapid urbanization and incipient reform. Writing for the *Review of Reviews,* he hailed South Jersey's Jewish farming communities in an article entitled "A Way Out of the Slums."[15] In the Middle West, Rabbi A. R. Levy of Chicago published a detailed survey in the *Reform Advocate* of numerous Jewish farm families throughout Michigan, Wisconsin, Minnesota and Iowa. These people, he affirmed, looked "in every way the true farmer," often indistinguishable from their Norwegian-born neighbors. Well-built, strong, and confident, they betrayed no signs of their "mercantile" origins, nor did they suffer the despair of Markham's "Man With the Hoe" (perhaps because the Baron de Hirsch Fund offered assistance with mortgage problems!).[16]

Throughout the 1880's and 1890's, much stress would be placed on the tenacity of successful Jewish farmers in New Jersey and other parts of the country who were supposedly driving themselves beyond their physical abilities in an occupation in which one was usually "born and raised." Some commentators observed that it was the well-educated among the immigrants who were often most eager to settle on farms because they were most sensitive to anti-Semitic charges in the Russian press, where the Jew was held in contempt "as an idler who knows only to buy and sell and cheat and to avoid manual labor." Those educated in the Jewish tradition could thus appreciate their agrarian heritage and avoid the peddling, tailoring, and cigar making of so many fellow immigrants. Other observers went even further to maintain that Jews *must* settle on farms in order to save the "race of Israel" from an envy aroused by their notorious success as "a nation of traders."[17]

Such Diaspora apologetics combined a tone of condescension with a defensive pseudo-Darwinism; it was as though peddling, tailoring, and cigar making were not also honest manual labor! They seemed generally ignorant of the fact that thousands of Jewish families in Russia supported themselves by farming. Paramount also was a concern for the continued well-being of the established Jewish community in the United States along with the fear, by some, of potential immigration restrictions. Even the American Zionists, who were more concerned with the success of agricultural colonies in a restored land of Israel, would be exhorted to help foster agriculture in America. Speaking on "The Jew and Agriculture" (that ever-popular topic), Rabbi Isaac Landman urged the Philadelphia Zionist Organization to increase the number of Jewish farmers in the United States from an actual five thousand to fifty thousand "and more" by 1908.[18] Consistent with his beliefs, Rabbi Landman himself played a leading role in establishing the Jewish colony of Clarion, Utah, where he claimed the "excellent soil" was superior to New Jersey's, producing four hundred bushels of potatoes per acre; there, the immigrant colonists would manage to overcome the challenges of "productivity, pauperization, isolation, and ignorance of agricultural methods." He neglected to add, however, that the arid land was dependent on precarious irrigation schemes: after a few years of unbearable hardships, the colonists of Clarion were forced to disperse, some to so distant a place as Los Angeles.[19]

Jewish social workers, participants in that new wave of community reform characteristic of the coming Progressive Era, also climbed onto the agrarian bandwagon. For example, they saw in the agricultural colonies an opportunity to rehabilitate juvenile delinquents. Thus, the Committee on Juvenile Aid of the Young Women's Union in Philadelphia sent Jewish youths who were on probation to board in South Jersey's rural communities, to live in "good homes in the country." In the words of one Jewish farmer, these boys "came from the city wild as animals," but the new environment, which included both secular and Jewish schooling as well as a better family relationship, "made good children of them."[20] Although environmental theories were criticized in the turn-of-century Philadelphia, they were also stoutly defended in an age of muckracking progressivism as one means of social uplift. To many social workers and other "humanitarian Americanizers, the immigrant seemed a blessing if redeemed and uplifted but a danger if left alone."[21]

As if to support the Yankee's apotheosis of an agricultural

population, contrasting with the occasionally stereotyped denigra-
tion of the Ghetto Jew,[22] the South Jersey colonies offered their
own evidence. "Let any unprejudiced observer come down to
Alliance and surroundings and see for himself how the Jewish
farmers have transformed a tract of rough brush land into a bloom-
ing garden covered with grapevines, fruit trees and vegetables . . .
[though] with inadequate means [and] a constitution enfeebled by
cruel persecution." So ran a somewhat plaintive letter to the
Exponent signed by "one of the Jewish farmers."[23] Other apologists
pointed to the isolation of the colonies as an advantage that encouraged individual self-reliance among a traditionally gregarious
people.[24] In this, there was a none too faint echo of that clannish-
ness which was supposedly a peculiar heritage from the ghetto past.

A unique literary measure of the persistent Jewish agrarianism,
even with the decline of American agriculture, would come in the
form of a full-length serialized popular novel, *Milly: A Jewess of
Today,* by Judith Solis Cohen. Published in 1909, its locale is the
South Jersey colonies as well as New York and the heroine's birth-
place, Philadelphia. First only a visitor from the city, Milly grows
to love Alliance and Woodbine, finding their older pioneers particularly impressive. For example, the Bershadsky family of the
novel appears to be a fictional version of the Lipmans and their
sons, of Alliance.[25] Miss Cohen's characters, while not immune to
soap opera effects, were intended to represent some typical figures
on the American Jewish scene: there is, for instance, the New York
banker's daughter who regrets her inability to communicate in
Yiddish with the hardy farmers, thus reflecting the gulf between
the acculturated and the immigrant generations. But the heroic
Milly, daughter of a poor grocer, has a strong sense of identification
with Judaism and an urge to help her brethren in some significant
way. She decides to organize a kindergarten and a recreational
program for children in the farm colonies and so finds fulfillment
in working with her own people.[26]

At the other extreme of the campaign for agrarianism were the
voices of the few professional farm managers and agronomists in
the American Jewish community. Among these were the agrarian

administrators H. L. Sabsovich and Bernard A. Palitz, both of whom were employed by the Baron de Hirsch Fund. Palitz leaned toward an emphasis on uplift and self-help. In an article on "Jewish Charity vs. Jewish Agriculture," he too joined the campaign to ameliorate the unfavorable public image of the lower middle class Jew: "The energies of the immigrant must be directed," he maintained, "not to the petty trades, not to the push-carts, or the pack on the shoulders, not to the tailor shop, but to the free, health-giving, ennobling, invigorating and plenteous farm life." Through agriculture, the Jewish immigrant could share in that communion with nature which formed the heritage of Americans and of free men everywhere. Here was true fulfillment (and, incidentally, hardly any cases of tuberculosis or other diseases to burden organized charity).[27]

Uniquely different considerations molded the views of Sabsovich, the leader who would earn the title, "Builder of Woodbine, New Jersey."[28] He did not merely advise or subsidize the Russian Jews; he was one of them. As a law student in Odessa during the terrible pogroms of 1881 he was a co-founder of the Jewish self-defense league, and later jailed by the Tsarist police for fighting the *pogromschiki* in the ghetto streets. After his release, he helped organize an Am Olam group, but a police crackdown on meetings along with tighter passport restrictions made this work impossible. Acting on his Am Olam principles, Sabsovich gave up the study of law only a year before graduation and enrolled in an agricultural college in Zurich, Switzerland. He was convinced that professional experience in agriculture was required for anyone hoping to lead the Jewish people back to the soil. After a three-year course amidst considerable hardships, he returned to Russia and there succeeded in obtaining a position as manager of a two-thousand-acre estate belonging to the liberal-minded director of a teachers' seminary.[29]

His task in this isolated region east of Rostov was to increase productivity among the farm tenants, who were native Don Cossacks and immigrant Letts. He succeeded in teaching these peasants improved methods of tilling, breeding, and sanitation; and while living among them, he won their respect for his knowledge and personal devotion. But the Orthodox priest in a nearby village who knew Jews only as "Christ-killers" and usurers finally made Sabsovich's position untenable, even though he had been accepted for years as "Gregory Konstantinovich" (the initials in his name stood for Hirsch Loeb). All the while, he retained his Am Olam convictions, having been foremost among the advocates of emigration to the United States rather than Ottoman Palestine or Argentina; and in 1887, armed with both a degree in agriculture and professional experience, he left for America.[30]

Sabsovich's journey and life's work would provide a slender human bridge between the Old World agrarianism and the New. In Russia there was a long-established chain of Jewish farm colonies founded partly under the resettlement programs of Tsars Paul and Alexander I. Yet many were intentionally located in inaccessible and primitive areas and subject to the stifling control of government overseers.[31] Looking towards the New World, Sabsovich soon learned that Jews recalled the romantic schemes of Major Mordecai Manuel Noah, who sought to establish in 1825 a colony on Grand Island, opposite Buffalo, New York—"Ararat: A City of Refuge for the Jews." This hapless venture was followed in 1837 by an agricultural settlement called *Shalom* ("Peace") near Wawarsing, in Ulster County, New York; but here, Jewish farmers struggled for a decade only to fail.[32]

Along with such American Jewish agrarians as Moses Klein, Sabsovich maintained that one of the major causes for these early failures was simply the lack of people, a practical limitation overcome by the new waves of immigrants from Eastern Europe. Thus, by the 1880's, the agrarian idealism of the Am Olam, the mass emigration from Russia, and the equally urgent need to provide for the multitude of new arrivals, all combined to give impetus to the colonizing drive and to Sabsovich's hopes. After a brief try at peddling (like so many other immigrants) and then tutoring, he landed a job as assistant director of the Agricultural Experiment Station in Fort Collins, Colorado. For the next three years the Sabsovich family, unlike most of their fellow immigrants, lived comfortably in this Western hamlet. In May 1890 a telegram

arrived from the Baron de Hirsch Fund in New York: they needed
a superintendent-manager for their proposed Jewish agricultural
colony (Woodbine). This was the opportunity for which Sabsovich
had waited; for its sake, he gave up a promising career in scientific
research and teaching, and declined a position as professor of
agricultural chemistry at Wyoming College. For the next fifteen
years he directed the growth of Woodbine, and then for the next
decade, as general agent of the Fund, he strove mightily in the
cause of Jewish agrarianism.[33]

Sabsovich's voice among the pro-farming chorus was clearly professional, tough as well as idealistic, thoroughly lacking the apologetic or eleemosynary tone of many zealots. The ideological cry
to take up farming "on account of the nobility of the farmer's life
and its importance to the nation and race will remain unanswered,"
he cautioned, unless proper guidance and training were offered.
Toward this end, Sabsovich would organize the Baron de Hirsch
Agricultural School in Woodbine (1894). He warned that the
weakening position of agriculture made training even more essential
for any city dweller in search of "a respectable, independent living."
Jews could succeed in agriculture, but only if they were ade-
quately prepared.[34] The experience of the abortive or founder-
ing settlements in the 1880's served as a point in evidence for
Sabsovich's caveat against untrained pioneers and inadequate
organizational support.

Ephemeral Utopias: Proliferation and Controversy

Unfortunately, practical advice was seldom heeded in the pell-
mell drive actually to settle immigrants in their own rural communities. The effort was dispersed throughout the United States, in
addition to other parts of the world (especially Argentina), as
well-intentioned individuals, self-appointed leaders, and organizations dissipated their strength in a variety of ambitious schemes. The
East, moreover, was at first ignored in favor of more colorful frontiers. As early as 1881, Judge Myer S. Isaacs announced some vague
plans by the Alliance Israélite Universelle to secure homesteads in
the southern and western states for Russian refugees.[35]

46

Undoubtedly, such trial balloons were welcomed by the established communities in America's eastern cities as well as by the Jewish Board of Guardians in England, who worried even then over "a very large accession to the mass of foreign poor in London."[36] In the New World likewise, Philadelphia's beleaguered Russian Relief Committee hopefully wondered whether a generous offer of land by the State of Louisiana could be accepted on behalf of "the Russians [who] are habituated to a cold climate." The New Orleans *Democrat* seemed to approve of Jewish colonization nearby, comparing it favorably with the great Irish influx of a generation before. When a colony was actually formed on Sicily Island about 160 miles northeast of New Orleans, praise came also from the immigration committee of that southern metropolis, as well as a regional journal, *The Jewish South*. But praise alone could not save the colony from typical disasters of the region; torrential rainstorms, malaria, yellow fever, floods, heat, and isolation soon brought an end to this colony as well as to its abortive successor in Arkansas.[37]

Other small groups of the Am Olam, idealistic but inexperienced, eventually founded colonies in Kansas, the Dakota territory, Iowa, Michigan, Colorado, even California, Texas, Washington, and Oregon. Each effort was accompanied by great hopes, intensive publicity in the Jewish press—usually calling for financial support—and endless debate on whether the Russians would actually take to farming. The Cincinnati *Enquirer*, marveling at the ambitious colonization plans of the early 1880's, urged Christians to lend their support as partial repayment for the Hebrews' contributions to civilization which they numbered as "law and religion . . . the system of exchange and banking . . . harmonizing the nations into a brotherly love." Isaac M. Wise, the renowned Reform rabbi of Cincinnati, worked with the Hebrew Union Agricultural Society on behalf of Beersheba Colony near Cimarron, Kansas. In his influential journal, *The American Israelite*, he pleaded, "Let us make as many Jewish free farmers as can be made."[38]

American Jewish leaders sometimes joined in the pioneering

directly. For example, Simon Muhr of Philadelphia personally explored the possibilities of colonization in Florida.[39] Martin Butzel, a prominent Detroit merchant, spent much of his time with the Michigan colonists at Palestine (near Bad Axe) assisting in their recurrent problems. Michael Heilprin afforded guidance and aid to the Oregon colonists as well as to those in South Jersey. Rabbi Wise's son Leo endured the hardships of homesteading in the Kansas colony, along with Charles K. Davis of Cincinnati. And M. H. Marks, a leader of that city's Jewish community, visited Beersheba, returning with word of "an assured success." By 2 July 1897, the first group of California-bound migrants left Philadelphia under the leadership of Ephraim Deinard. And shortly after returning from a meeting with Tolstoy and a tour of Russian agriculture, Rabbi Joseph Krauskopf, spiritual leader of Keneset Israel in Philadelphia, founded the National Farm School in nearby Doylestown; he too exhorted the Jews of his city to embrace the agricultural life, and eventually joined with Rabbi Isaac Landman to establish the colony in Utah, where the state government obligingly promised an irrigation plant as well as other facilities for the Philadelphians.[40]

Adding to the confusion of numerous and uncoordinated settlement schemes, were unconfirmed or premature reports appearing periodically in both the Jewish and wider press of philanthropic largesse on behalf of many colonies. For example, the *Vineland Evening Journal* featured a photograph of Jacob H. Schiff over the caption "To Back Jew Colony" and a related article quoting two would-be founders of a Jewish farm community in New Mexico. Likewise, the *New York World* reported a story, picked up by the *Jewish Exponent* and later denied, of a munificent grant by Julius Rosenwald of Chicago for the benefit of "Hebrew Farmers" in Wyoming.[41] In spite of the publicity, occasionally invidious, the funds available for agrarian settlements were far from adequate, and individual philanthropic contributions tended to be too erratic for consistent planning.

At the other end of the spectrum, the Socialist Yiddish *Forward* of New York took a jaundiced view of all the colonizing furor, labeling it a capitalist conspiracy to disperse the proletarian masses

Immigrant boys on their way to farms, a group sent out by Mrs. John Jacob Astor. (The Jacob A. Riis Collection, Museum of the City of New York)

Outside the American Consulate in Warsaw, 1919. (Courtesy of YIVO Institute for Jewish Research)

Faces of immigrants, about 1910. (Courtesy of YIVO Institute for Jewish Research)

Immigrants on their way to America aboard the S.S. Westerland.
(Museum of the City of New York)

Talmud class in the early 1890's. (Photograph by Jacob A. Riis The Jacob A. Riis Collection, Museum of the City of New York)

Immigrants on the farm, about 1905. (The Jacob A. Riis Collection, Museum of the City of New York)

A family in Carmel, New Jersey, 1889. (Courtesy of YIVO Institute for Jewish Research)

The dormitory and the classroom building of the Baron de Hirsch Agricultural School in Woodbine, about 1899.

to far-off places like North Carolina and Canada.[42] Closer to home, it criticized the Baron de Hirsch Fund for collaborating with the sweatshop bosses to oppress the laboring class of those New Jersey colonies that combined small industry with agriculture. Proletarians in New York must not be deluded into joining such colonies, warned the *Forward*. Its sharply critical tone was also aimed at Woodbine, whose superintendent was described sarcastically as "Herr Professor Sabsovich . . . lord of the manor . . . governor-general of the agriculture school . . . [and] a rabid anti-Socialist [*Sozialistenfreser!*]."[43]

The *Forward*'s idea of sound agrarianism was based on farmer-labor cooperatives, and included joint proletarian ownership of land and factories. Its writers remembered with nostalgia the Brook Farm experiments and looked forward to purely socialist rural communities. Private enterprise colonization, whether in far-off Argentina or Palestine, in the American West or nearby New Jersey, appeared suspect to Jewish Socialists.[44] If anything, however, utopian socialism and positivism caused a disastrous ideological split in at least one of the colonies, Oregon's New Odessa, where many other factors (such as fertile soil) were unusually favorable.[45] Of all the colonies established throughout the United States, only those in New Jersey would prove to be long-lived. The baleful facts stand out in the quarter-century report (1900-1924) of the Jewish Agricultural Society: "The New Jersey colonies are the only survivors."[46]

A vast catalogue of difficulties was used to explain the demise of the colonies in the South and West: poor soil, the climate, malaria or some other disease, prairie fires, lack of water or wood or equipment, floods, crop failures, inadequate markets, high interest rates, burdensome mortgages. Most important perhaps, inexperience, absence of trained leadership, the attractions of the city, and inadequate motivation especially for the Americanized younger generation, represented common denominators of weakness. The New Jersey colonies were not immune to such troubles either, even though they survived.

The agrarian ideal, Jefferson's conception of the good society as a society of farmers, had already begun to fade before the great onslaught of industrialism. In an age of rapid economic change, of corporate giants expanding overseas, of cities building skyward, and the coming era of aviation, Jefferson's favorite, "the heaven, even the heavens, are the Lord's, but the earth hath He given to the children of men" (Ps. 115:16), would seem ever less persuasive.[47]

Vineland, New Jersey: Frontier Economics in the New Jerusalem

As the conditions were unprecedented, so were the solutions. There were no manuals in the 1880's to prescribe the restoration of a Jewish farm society upon the soil of the New World. Yet, the pressures of massive immigration allowed for little delay, and the task of making farmers out of greenhorns was complicated by the fact that the philanthropists who decided where to settle were not themselves to be the settlers. This was not the first time in American history, however, that some contributed the capital or experience for others to use with little more than willing hands. In the spring of 1882, a South Jersey location was chosen for its proximity to the seaboard, its sparse population, and the relatively low land costs—selling points well publicized in New York by the eager land developers.

Thus, as on other frontiers, the union of land, labor, and capital marked the beginning of an economic and social development destined to take some unique turns. In this case, the human resources were represented by the helping hands of established American Jewry combined with one small segment of a vast new wave of immigrants which would eventually prove far more numerous than the existing Jewish community.

Three towns marked the roughly triangular area in which the first New Jersey colonies were established: Vineland, Bridgeton, and Millville, all in Cumberland County. From the center of the triangle, it was just over 30 miles north to Philadelphia, 115 miles to New York. About 40 miles to the east was Atlantic City; on the southeast lay Cape May County in the wake of the ocean winds; and the Maurice River wound through the light, sandy soil southward into Delaware Bay. The three nearby towns became important economic and cultural influences, for they were transportation hubs, sources of supply, and simply convenient landmarks in the vast New World.

The site of the first colony, Alliance, three miles outside of Vineland, was on twelve hundred acres thickly overgrown with scrub oak and pine woods.[48] The area was just across the Salem County line, in amorphous Pittsgrove Township. It was an hour's ride to Philadelphia then on the West Jersey Railroad. Vineland itself was a relatively new town, having been founded on 8 August 1861. It was an eastern illustration of the kind of speculative land venture which characterized much of urban pioneering on the frontier from colonial times through the nineteenth century. Its founder, Charles K. Landis, was a Philadelphia banker and lawyer who dreamed of a model city in the wilderness. He purchased thirty-two thousand acres in the then sprawling Millville Township; on them lived only fifty souls, most "charcoal burners" dependent on the forest for their subsistence. Landis planned here an urban center with main streets a hundred feet wide, with light industry, and a variety of cultural facilities to serve the surrounding farm areas. The thin, sandy earth of the pine barrens and flatlands, however, was not suited for the lucrative grain production one found in Illinois or the Russian Ukraine; only vineyards, fruit orchards, and truck farming were feasible. To discourage speculation, and to capitalize on the widespread appeal of land ownership, Landis sold lots of five, ten, and fifteen acres. By 1869 the population of his original domain, now split into Vineland and Landis Township, amounted to an impressive 6,500.[49]

Since Vineland itself was a pioneering experiment, it was a natural attraction for further colonization. *The Vineland Weekly*, back in 1865, maintained that "a population of 24,000 is needed"; though the large figure "would look to be incredible," it admitted, "good agriculturists and fruit growers" could be attracted to expand the local economy.[50] Nor were the prospects of colonization by foreigners ignored. Favorable notice was given to a settlement of Hungarians engaged in viticulture outside Egg Harbor City in neighboring Atlantic County. These new settlers, according to enthusiastic reports in the *Newark Courier* and the *State Gazette,* considered the area excellent for small fruits. "Thus do we gradually find the despised and neglected soil of South Jersey becoming appropriated to the cultivation of all kinds of choice agricultural products, and in a few years more its now wild forests will give place to the hand of improvement, and rich vineyards will be found at all available points."[51] By 1880, Italian farmers in Vineland were cultivating grapes. There were even small numbers of Germans, French, and Scandinavians,[52] though the Russian Jews of Alliance would achieve the first successful settlement on a group basis.

The Vineland area remained a miniature frontier always in search of more population. By-passed in the westward surge, which by the late 1870's reached out into the Great Plains and the Mountain States' mining golcondas, it sought to "talk up" its virtues to newcomers, both native and foreign. Its newspaper columns urged inhabitants to extol such local advantages as good roads, proximity to Philadelphia's fruit markets, the "comparatively mild" winters and summers ("a mean temperature of 55 degrees, which is considered the most agreeable and healthful"), pure water, low taxes, and generally "cheap living." Rail transportation to Philadelphia cost only $1.50 for a round-trip and the New Jersey Southern Railroad stopped on its way from Sandy Hook and Long Branch to Delaware Bay.

Industrial activities reported in the 1880's included manufacture of clothing, shoes, caps, carriages, and pearl buttons; but most praise was lavished on the agricultural opportunities, especially fruit-growing.[53] One traveler described Vineland's pears, peaches, apples, plums, apricots, and grapes as "infinitely superior" to California's. "For climate, health, and money-making," he concluded, "Vineland has the advantage." Even in far-off California, Los Angeles County land developers boosted their "Vineland of the Azusa" during the boom of the 1880's, a "new town to be modeled largely after the world-famous Vineland of New Jersey!" which was replete with "elegant tracts," fruit orchards, and a ban on saloons.[54]

Growth rates were not consistent, however. Between 1865

and 1886 the population of the original Vineland tract, covering land in Cumberland, Salem, Atlantic and Gloucester Counties, increased from six thousand to only eight thousand. Setbacks were experienced in the 1870's and early 1880's as a result of the adverse economic conditions affecting all southern New Jersey.[55] Partly because of this there were intensified efforts to encourage further land sales, especially for colonization by immigrants.

One leading citizen of Vineland, Augustus Seeman, rose to the challenge: he played a significant role in bringing Russian Jews to the area by contributing some timely local initiative to the efforts of philanthropists in New York. Seeman had been appointed commissioner of immigration for the State of New Jersey, a post which allowed him to aid real estate interests in his home territory. He also owned at that time a major share in Newton and Seeman, a Vineland realty firm. Operating from an office in Castle Garden, New York, the very gateway to the new promised land, Seeman could easily advertise the attractions of South Jersey. It was through his efforts that the Hebrew Emigrant Aid Society and Leach Brothers of Vineland negotiated an agreement for the land on which Alliance was established, a tract described as a mile north of the intersection of Landis Avenue and the New Jersey Southern Railroad.

Sold at $15 an acre, the land was only partially cleared of its heavy growth of timber. The state geological survey still referred to this region as the Oak Belt, "one of the wildest, most desolate" areas, according to Harshberger's contemporary *Geography*.[56] Initial expenditures by the Hebrew Emigrant Aid Society, between May and November 1882 included the following:

Land and Improvements		$12,129.92
Maintenance and "Final Relief"		19,049.02
New Housing		9,897.77
Transportation		883.71
	TOTAL	$41,960.42

Payments to Leach Brothers comprised not only the cost of land and improvements, but also construction of housing by George

Leach, who drew supplies from the family's local lumber business.[57]

Native residents recalled that the Vineand area had attracted attention before as a means of absorbing recent newcomers, though not without failure or recurring criticism. In 1878 a group of forty Italian immigrants entering Castle Garden claimed that they had been offered a work contract by a Vineland business agent. Citing *The New York Times* as the source for this story, the *Vineland Daily Journal* reported that these immigrants had to remain in New York, victims of an apparent hoax.[58] Local citizens were at times critical of both the foreigners in their midst and the firms which cooperated with them; they were wary of the different religion, language and cultural background. For many years, even Charles K. Landis felt compelled to defend the land deal made by the Leach Brothers. He was "asked many questions concerning the condition of the Jewish settlements" and embarrassed by "erroneous reports, circulated by people who were ignorant and prejudiced." Affirming confidence in the colonists' ability to make "the wilderness blossom as the rose," Landis reminded his fellow citizens to regard them in the spirit of 1776 as expressed by Richard Henry Lee:

> The eyes of Europe are fixed upon us; she demands a living example of freedom that may contrast, by the felicity of the citizens, with the ever-increasing tyranny which desolates her polluted shore. She invites us to prepare an asylum where the unhappy may find solace and the persecuted repose. She entreats us to cultivate a propitious soil, where that generous plant which first sprung up and grew in England but is now withered by the poisonous blasts of tyranny, may revive and flourish, sheltering . . . all the unfortunate of the human race.[59]

These eloquent words about a young democracy, repeated by a far-sighted real estate developer, were still fresh and relevant to the dreams of an Am Olam escaping European persecution. They still represented a challenge to both immigrant and American. How would the challenge be met in an America "without a frontier," when the democratizing influence of the West appeared to be on the decline? In a typically American blend of pragmatism and idealism, Landis championed the Jewish colonies as a stimulus to the local economy, for "they do much of their trading in Vineland."[60]

Alliance: *"Pioneer of All Jewish Colonies in America"*[61]

Four hundred immigrants, including 160 children, were brought by train to Alliance in May and June of 1882. In their words, they were "dumped off" at the nearest Jersey Central flag station, known as Bradway (later Norma), and taken to the "barracks" or "Castle Garden," named in mock honor of New York's famed depot. These temporary quarters consisted of several large frame buildings on the brow of a hill overlooking the western bank of the Maurice River. Although the basic construction had been performed in advance by Leach Brothers, immigrant carpenters themselves completed the interiors. Supplies, including food for the common kitchens, were provided by the Hebrew Emigrant Aid Society.[62]

An early start was made on clearing additional land and constructing small frame houses for the individual families, again with the aid of Leach Brothers. Before completion of this work, however, communal living was the rule. The largest of the buildings, about twenty by one hundred feet, housed twenty-six families in small rooms opening on either side of an unfloored passageway like cabins on a steamer. The rooms were just large enough for a bed and a small table and chairs; all were topped with high storage shelves. An observer from Philadelphia, noting on nearly every table bouquets of freshly gathered swamp flowers, especially magnolias, as well as individual family ornaments, remarked sympathetically how these Russians Jews attempted to improve the appearance of their humble abodes.[63]

Although New Jersey's ubiquitous Commissioner of Immigration Seeman accompanied each group of new arrivals, he was unable to spare them their early hardships. For example, only one of the three large houses contained an operating stove; much of the bedding, furniture, and farm equipment was delayed in transit. Assisting Seeman was another well-intentioned American, A. C. Sternberger, a native of Hartford who was appointed superintendent by the Hebrew Emigrant Aid Society. Sternberger's reports to HEAS President Henry S. Henry indicated an informed understanding of the colonists' problems. Citing evidence of their progress in clearing the land, Sternberger refuted vehemently the charges made by the *Philadelphia Inquirer* (1 July 1882) only a few weeks after their arrival. This otherwise liberal newspaper editorially scorned the refugees as "lazy, insolent, and degraded." Denying any basis for such generalized accusations, both Seeman and Sternberger praised the industry, intelligence, and good behavior of the colonists. "Their conduct," Sternberger reported, "has been in every respect exemplary, with very rare exceptions" caused by overcrowding and lack of basic necessities.[64]

Soon, other Philadelphians, including leaders of the Jewish community and journalist-civic worker Moses Klein, came to find out for themselves. One of the first notable visitors was Rabbi Sabato Morais, called in after a young child's death early in July of 1882. He responded promptly to Sternberger's appeal for a clergyman to conduct the funeral service and to consecrate a new cemetery, but his visit also reflected sympathy for the travails of the newcomers. The distinguished American rabbi of an eighteenth-century Sephardic synagogue (Mikveh Israel) was moved by this experience of meeting his coreligionists from far-off Russia. He prayed with them, visited their "hovels" in the evening, pressed the hand of each warmly, and although he spoke no Yiddish or Russian, their mutual knowledge of Hebrew served as a vehicle for fraternal communication. Upon returning to Philadelphia, Morais pledged to labor further with all his resources in the cause of these and other thousands of refugees and called for the Jews of his own city and New York to do likewise. Together, they could "redeem the fair name of Israel from aspersions, and elevate those whom brutality has cast down."[65]

Indeed, the appeal for support was timely. The cost of maintaining each immigrant family on the land before the first harvest had been estimated at about $500.[66] This included farm equipment approximating $100 per family (the first group alone numbered forty-three families). For the strenuous labor of clearing the area

56

for the crop of white and sweet potatoes and the garden vegetables, each family was allotted from $9 to $12 monthly. Their field work was supervised expertly but vigorously by a budget-conscious "native" foreman, a German-Jewish farmer named Frederick Schmidt.[67]

The scrub oak and swamp were pushed back, in spite of heat and mosquitoes. Family farms of 12 to 15 acres were assigned by lottery, and individual houses built, each with two rooms (one upstairs, one downstairs) and a cellar. Seemingly generous ten-year contracts for both homes and land were extended by the Hebrew Emigrant Aid Society (succeeded in 1883 by the Alliance Land Trust), providing for the eventual repayment of the original value of the land at 3 percent interest. But most could not maintain the payments and the debt would later become a serious point at issue between the immigrants and the business-oriented philanthropists.[68] The latter regarded the terms as unusually liberal, each contract amounting to $350 ($150 for the house and well, the remainder for land at $15 an acre) and payments on the *full* amount of principal and interest in equal annual installments not being required until the fifth year. And the HEAS and Alliance Land Trust affirmed one aspect of communal responsibility by requiring the colony to bear the debts of any who were ill or otherwise unable to manage.[69]

To immigrants confronted with the very limited opportunities in rural New Jersey for earning extra cash, this debt was staggering and it appeared even more burdensome when seen in the light of the economic flexibility and greater earning power of their individualistic big-city cousins. The situation was further complicated by the great pressure of additional waves of immigrants, some of whom were temporarily housed in the Alliance colony with no intention of settling them on the land. By early 1883, the population had grown to 650, most of whom still lived in the makeshift "Castle Garden" buildings.[70] HEAS itself suffered, moreover, from a lack of funds and was able to pay fully for only 33 farm lots plus the 150 acres of common property set aside for school, synagogue, industry, and other communal needs. The rest of the land was still owned by Leach Brothers. On the horns of this dilemma were two

57

possible solutions: Superintendent Sternberger could "weed out" those with no aptitude for farming, and plans could be made for an "industrial colony" to supplement local employment opportunities. Alliance Israélite Universelle came to the rescue through the intercession of Judge Isaacs, with a contribution of $3,000 for factory construction. By early 1883, 67 families were settled on individual farms, though they still required a monthly allowance of about $10 and were obligated financially to either HEAS or Leach Brothers.[71]

Life in Alliance remained exposed to the hardships of pioneering. Nearby swamps still brought swarms of mosquitoes and insects; potable water was not easy to obtain and when wells were dug some were rat-infested. Even as late as 1919, plumbing was not available in any Vineland colony. Heat was supplied by inefficient wood-burning stoves which also caused frequent fires. Because of the cost, lack of adequate roads, and lack of horses and wagons, the town doctor was too far away to be consulted for anything but the worst emergency. Dr. Arthur Goldhaft, son of a pioneering family, recalled how mothers would heal open wounds by making a poultice of sour black bread. Only the huge tree stumps seemed undisturbed (until, by 1916, the Dupont Company finally blasted the remaining trunks on Jacob Crystal's farm to demonstrate the power of its new explosives).[72]

During the first year especially, when there were as yet neither crops to tend nor sewing machines to work, the colonists resorted to picking strawberries and cranberries for local growers. Men, often with wives and children, walked miles in search of farms requiring pickers. It was hard work at low wages (only a few pennies per bucketful of berries), and a far cry from the ideal of an independent yeomanry. The Vineland press periodically reported that the new "installments of persecuted Russians" in Alliance were supplying much of the cheap farm labor. For example, "Dr. Brown sent a bus load of 30 Jewish cranberry pickers to his bog." On 4 October 1882 the paper noted, with an invidious pun, that "the Jews are rather flush with cranberry money this week." By 1886, it could still report that large groups, as many as "150 Jews residing at Alliance" were returning to their homes across the Maurice River from a stint in the cranberry bogs of Vineland. The settlers also cut corn for farmers near Palatine, Deerfield, and Elmer, all more than 8 miles from home; a few found jobs in the Vineland brick factory.[73]

Early visitors to the colony observed its daily life with interest. In the center of the compound, high above the buildings, flew the American flag. Men and women both worked at removing trees and clearing fields. Mothers were busy with their household chores and children. Indeed, women were present in large numbers, as adult males comprised less than one-third of the population in August 1882. Though the central kitchen featured a sixty-gallon cauldron for soup, there was no communal dining room, each family having meals in its own small abode. Necessary supplies could be charged at Mr. Simon's Commissary, with the obligation of repayment borne by HEAS. A temporary school, set up in the first weeks, emphasized English-language instruction as preparation for enrollment in the public schools of Vineland.[74]

"New Jerusalem," as the colony was called by its neighbors, earned some praise from these first curious visitors. For example, some commented with pleasure on the general cleanliness and advanced sanitation; two large bathhouses were "frequented by most of the colonists daily." They were described as a hard-working lot; a few even obtained jobs as mechanics with local firms. At the same time, it was feared that their strict observance of the Sabbath on Saturday would prove a stumbling block to outside employment. Sabbath day started with a morning service at eight in the meeting room, and no work was done on that day. Native Vinelanders were impressed that kosher beef was imported from Philadelphia, "dressed and marked in the peculiar Jewish style," but that bread, milk, other groceries, and hardware were purchased locally for the most part—a welcome addition of about seven hundred dollars weekly to Vineland storekeepers.[75]

The rhythms of life quickly assumed their natural tempo. The very first night the Am Olam families spent in the "Castle Garden" of Alliance, a child was born to Naphtula and Deborah Yoseph. The boy, Moe Yoseph, took to the new soil, and would spend his life-

59

time on the land assigned to his father; in the late 1950's, he was still tending the family farm, "a tall, stooped man something like a New England farmer in appearance."[76] The midwife for the delivery of Moe and other children of the colonists was herself a resolute pioneer, Bashe Goldhaft, who lost her own three babies through a combination of early hardships, including strenuous work in the fields, inadequate nutrition, and the prevalent "milk-sickness."[77] The first marriage ceremony was observed too within a few weeks of the founding, apparently in spite of opposition from the colony's administrators, who objected that while the groom was a resident of Alliance, the immigrant bride was a full-time domestic for the Seeman family in Vineland. They were married, nonetheless, "by a Canter [sic] from their own midst and a fiddler to furnish music." Even more festive was the second wedding, featuring the superintendent's coachman as the happy groom, and attended by the colonists as well as fifty "outsiders," with Van Flood's orchestra, Vineland's favorite, supplying melodies for all who came to "New Jerusalem."[78]

The Smaller Colonies

ROSENHAYN

In the same year that Alliance was founded, the Hebrew Emigrant Aid Society also established an "overflow" colony starting with six families in Rosenhayn. Although this agricultural hamlet midway between Vineland and Bridgeton had been surveyed and partially developed by real estate men, it was making little progress. The immigrants set to work at once clearing the land and building homes—"very industriously," according to local observers—but their efforts were short-lived. Lack of funds, poor soil, and a "kind of epidemic resembling lung fever" forced them to abandon their project. A few years later, the same fate was suffered by a nearby settlement nicknamed "The Seventeen" for the seventeen Jewish families who attempted farming here unaided by a sponsor.[79]

Encouraged by a seeming improvement in local economic conditions, a number of families came back to farms in Rosenhayn beginning in 1887. Within two years, its Jewish population was close to 300. Most depended on Vineland and Bridgeton or the new village shirt factory for employment, and of their 2,000 acres only about 260 were under cultivation. This was not, moreover, an exclusively Jewish community, nor was there a paternalistic combination of encouragement and pressure from some benevolent planning organization. By the turn of the century, the Jews numbered 539 of a total 920 in Rosenhayn; many of the non-Jews were recent Italian immigrants.

In spite of economic difficulties and recurring labor strikes, Jewish community life evolved around a new synagogue, religious school, library, meeting hall, an evening school for adults, and a public school for the children. The latter were "being assimilated to the native language, customs and attitude of mind" in a manner that was, to the editors of the *Mercury,* "simply astonishing." It claimed, in an enthusiastic pseudo-science, that "even characteristics of feature and other ethnological peculiarities seem rapidly to be melting away under the influence of the New Jersey air and soil, and ten-year-old boys and girls . . . no longer betray their foreign birth by the slightest trace of accent."[80] Such was the verdict from the adherents of the melting pot.

At least equally encouraging was a report to the first annual convention (1909) of the Federation of Jewish Farmers of America stating that the hundred Rosenhayn members were "all doing well." That year was a good season, especially for lima beans, sweet potatoes, and strawberries. A few of the young men who left the colony for greener pastures (usually in the city) returned again to try their luck at farming.[81] But as agriculture's share in the national income continued to decline, neither the melting pot nor good harvests could keep free people on their farms.

CARMEL

Three miles south of Rosenhayn, at a place called Beaver Dam, was another venture uniting land developers, idealists, philanthropists, and immigrants. The enterprising W. H. Miller had settled on his property some German immigrant families from

Philadelphia. When they abandoned their pioneer holdings and returned to the easier life of the city, Miller's colonization plan was rescued by Michael Heilprin, who saw an opportunity there for his persecuted Jewish brethren. Out of Beaver Dam, he helped create Carmel, named for the mountain in Israel on whose vineyard slopes trod the prophets Elijah and Elisha.[82]

Heilprin realized his dream of an all-Jewish colony with the aid of philanthropists Schiff, Goldman, Jesse Seligman, and Julius Hallgerten. In 1882, the same year that marked the birth of both Alliance and Rosenhayn, the first immigrant families came to Carmel. To replace those who found the stony soil unrewarding, others came in later years, including a few who had practiced farming in Russia.

With the death of Heilprin in 1888, the colonists felt orphaned, deprived of their moving spirit.[83] Lack of funds became a serious problem, partly because the New York organizations now concentrated on making Alliance a viable settlement. Finally, an appeal made through Rabbi Morais brought five thousand dollars from Baron de Hirsch. Leading citizens of Philadelphia, notably Simon Muhr and Mayer Sulzberger, took charge of the colony's financial affairs, and the Jewish Emigration Society of that city commissioned Moses Klein to explore further the needs of all the agricultural communities. Thus, Carmel was saved.

By 1889, its population under three hundred, it too was a village with its own synagogue, school, library, post office, and many high hopes: Perhaps its location on a proposed railroad line between Bridgeton and Millville would bring even greater prosperity.[84] How many other speculative and idealistic ventures in pioneering America were founded on similar hopes! The railroad never came to Carmel, although more Jewish families thought the area promising enough to invest in it their own labor and capital, thus causing a minor land boom. Here as in Rosenhayn (which did boast a railroad station) some dreamed of finding their fortune in real estate. One bemused Jewish farmer in Alliance thus described the phenomenon for the Hebrew journal *Hamelitz* of St. Petersburg, Russia: Rosenhayn's "inhabitants believe that a big city will be built there, for the Americans have prophesied that Rosenhayn is destined to be built up. For every measure of land they [the inhabitants] weigh its value in gold; however, until that day comes they spend their days in hopeless delay."[85] As so often before, the speculators lost out; the leap to prosperity was an illusion.

Carmel families raised rye, buckwheat, corn, and vegetables as well as some cattle and poultry. The majority, however, became increasingly dependent on the sewing machine, making shirts for big city contractors. Tailoring was no crime, Moses Klein protested to the fault-finders in comfortable Philadelphia; after all, the "farming tailors" had large families to support as well as rental or mortgage payments on their homes, for in 1889 W. H. Miller, the original land promoter, still owned many of the homes in addition to the synagogue, post office, library, school, and butcher shop.

Among the rural tailors of Carmel radicalism seemed to flourish more than in the other colonies, perhaps because so few succeeded as farmers. They developed a reputation as intellectuals imbued with the ideas of Russian nihilism, atheism, and even—some said—free love. Bold individuals among them tried to deliver inflammatory socialist lectures in an imperfect English on the main street of Bridgeton, but they were chased off by the constabulary. A few experimented briefly with communal living in 1910—the same year the kibbutz Degania was established in Palestine. The net effect of these experiments, however, must be calculated in terms of the colony's image among its neighbors, rather than in total number of radicals or significant ideological developments. Perhaps, if they had not been strangers in the country, their efforts would have appeared more like populist self-help. A consumers' cooperative, a farmers' cooperative for the purchase of seed and equipment, ephemeral producers' cooperatives (shirt and dress factories) in the 1890's, all were oddments of quasi radicalism in a setting of individual enterprise. Not surprisingly, the building and loan associations and the big-city manufacturers with local branches showed little patience toward this radicalism, particularly in its later expression as strikes of the garment workers. In the struggle for a balance between farm and factory, the latter would eventually prevail.

Yet another sensitive area brought scorn from the Jewish press of Philadelphia: some of these colonists seemed to lack a proper concern for the religious education of their children. Nonetheless, despite economic adversity and criticism, Carmel grew to 1,250 Jews by 1909. Its fine new synagogue Beth Hillel was dedicated in 1908, proving a commitment also to provide religious training for the children of the congregation on a par with other colonies.[86]

Life in the country offered pleasures as well as problems. The pioneers and their children, in Carmel as in the other colonies, enjoyed a sense of kinship with their brethren in the close-knit community: many participated in discussion groups, amateur concerts and operettas such as the Yiddish *Bar Kochba,* or simply hiking and singing along the road. Years later they recalled the hayrides to the Maurice River and Parvin Lake, the swimming in Mill Creek and Lebanon Stream where Skudivitch built bathhouses open to all for two cents' admission, the boyish filching of ripe watermelons and grapes from Weissman's vineyards, and even the long ride to high school via Rovner's cart and the Bridgeton-Millville trolley. Mail was carried by Max Ettinger's horse and buggy from Rosenhayn's Post Office to Carmel's where Postmistress Lizzie Levenson took over. And on the steps of the post office, many joined to watch Halley's Comet, during those nights in 1910 when nature's splendors still aroused awe and apprehension.

On a lesser scale were the gayer man-made spectacles, such as the annual Simhat Torah torchlight parades from Columbia Hall community house to the synagogue. In Carmel, as in the other colonies, laymen led informal religious services first in a small building off Irving Avenue then, with the aid of Carmel's Independent Order of B'rith Abraham Lodge 246, in their fine new Beth Hillel synagogue (after the Hebrew name of local manufacturer and philanthropist Henry Dix). And on Friday afternoons, those of the faithful who could afford it prepared for the Sabbath by taking the traditional steambath built by farmer Tudras, which was complete with hot stones, misty alcoves, and birches.

As if in token of Americanization, other spectacles sometimes lit up the skies over the colonies: great bonfires burned on election nights and New Year's Eve when "even outhouses were not spared."

Jewish agrarianism in America: Dream and expediency

On the Fourth of July the pageantry included a baseball game between the mighty Carmel Athletic Association and the Valmars, a club of Jewish students from the University of Pennsylvania; it was capped by traditional fireworks and dancing. In those halcyon years, the Girls' Athletic Club wore ankle-length skirts and shirtwaists during their tennis matches.

Election year (1912) saw citizens of Carmel taking part in still another great American tradition. Annie Goldstein presented a bouquet to candidate Theodore Roosevelt, and Jake Sobelman greeted him on behalf of the people of Carmel. In that era, Taft and Wilson also stopped to campaign along the Bridgeton-Millville pike, but with apparently less impact on the local residents.

Not politics, however, but livelihood, was really uppermost in the citizens' minds during those years before the emergence of the welfare state. In Carmel especially, manufacturing and farming seemed perforce to blend with the rural setting, and nearly everything that happened reflected the close community life. Part-time factory workers drove their cows down Irving Avenue, the verdant strip between Morton's and Dix's factories leading to Miller's pasture. At the end of day, the cows were claimed again from the common enclosure, though the strays had to be redeemed for a dollar a head. In what might have proved a tragic incident, all factories shut down for several days so that everyone could search for three-year-old Ralph Borofsky, feared lost in the Lebanon Swamp; the boy was finally found safe on the far side of the stream.[87]

More Factories and Farms in the Wilderness

A clear combination of industry and agriculture, at the outset at least, was Norma, a new village off the southeastern end of Alliance. At first its existence was precarious, its farmers dependent on their own meager resources. In the 1890's it had a reputation among Vineland's natives as the dirtiest of "Jew towns." Its main street, right on the way to the area's popular lake resorts, presented to passers-by a picture of slovenliness and poverty, contributing to the occasional hostility shown toward all the colonies.

Norma had advantages, however, which required only some capital to develop. Among these was its location on the Central Railroad of New Jersey at what was originally called Bradway Station, just three and a half miles from Vineland. The necessary boost came first from Philadelphia philanthropist Maurice Fels, whose enlightened interest extended far beyond the family soap factory. He established at Norma a large model farm to service all Jewish colonies in the area, emphasizing such crops as asparagus and sweet potatoes as well as the various fruits which could be profitably grown.

More significant still was the Allivine Canning Company of Norma founded by Fels in 1901 to cope with the vagaries of agricultural over-production which often forced emergency dumping of farm produce on the distant city markets. Fels's initiative inspired also the active cooperation of the newly organized Jewish Agricultural and Industrial Aid Society, an offshoot of the Baron de Hirsch Fund. The Society erected a large building used initially for a waistcoat factory, thus supplementing the independently owned garment-producing units and helping to provide employment as machine operators for the majority of Norma's breadwinners. By 1908, the population of 549 (almost all Jewish) could take pride in a balanced economy as well as such community institutions as a post office, library, synagogue and a religious school, a growers' association, and several fraternal lodges.[88]

Opposite Norma at the northeast corner of Alliance lay Brotmanville. Almost separated from the mother colony by cultivated fields, it was developed by Abraham Brotman, an enterprising New Yorker whose plan included not only farm sites but also a large factory. The latter became a nucleus for the virtually all-industrial community. In 1908, the village numbered just two hundred people, mostly living in homes owned by the Jewish Agricultural and Industrial Aid Society. Although the Brotman family retained a local residence, they followed a path similar to other trailblazers and innovators in ceding their commercial property rights, including land and factory, to the Society. Lighted by electricity generated on the premises and powered by steam, the modern factory seemed to symbolize Brotmanville's betrayal of the agrarian ideal, or at least so it appeared to the farmers of Alliance. The *schneiders* (tailors) and the farmers looked upon each other with contempt, their objectives pinned on differing values. In effect, Brotmanville's operators lived always in a kind of company town (though a benevolent one), lacking the idealism of the Am Olam, the dream of tilling one's own soil, the spirit of communal development.[89]

As if to fulfill the ancient promise that the seed of Abraham would become as the stars of heaven, other satellite colonies developed, including Garton Road, Six Points, Estellville, Hebron, Mizpah, and Zion. They were small and generally short-lived. Garton Road was founded by a Russian immigrant in 1888 and lay about two miles west of Rosenhayn along the Jersey Central Railroad. It remained entirely agricultural, partly because the soil was somewhat better than in the other colonies. Its population (almost all Jewish) soon grew to 145, and, although it was not a distinct political unit apart from Rosenhayn, it too had its own religious school, public school, lodges, and even a number of telephones.[90] Six Points, in turn, was a satellite of Alliance founded by the Jewish Agricultural and Industrial Aid Society in 1907, as the tide of immigration continued to crest. The first 20 families received farms of about 25 acres each, a more realistic size when compared to the smaller lots assigned to the earlier settlers of Alliance.[91]

On the other hand, settlements that lacked some outside organizational or philanthropic support seemed doomed to failure. This was as true for the small Jewish colony (1891) near Landisville, across the Atlantic County line from Vineland, named Hebron after King David's capital, as it was for Halbertstown or Habberton (1891) eight miles south of Millville. Habberton was developed by a private New York syndicate which hoped to settle one hundred Jewish immigrant families in an agricultural-industrial complex including clothing and furniture factories, an ambitious scheme that ended in bankruptcy in 1899.[92]

A more rapid and tragic failure was the land development scheme sponsored by General Burbridge of Atlantic City. Early in 1882, he and his associates purchased a large tract of infertile land six miles below Mays Landing; then they built a number of frame houses and proceeded to recruit "refugee Russian Jews" for a colony called Estellville. Each family was allotted a fifteen-acre farm and rickety dwelling. Although by fall, the colony numbered eighty-six people, mostly women and children, no provision had been made to feed them during the first winter months. Some managed to find work for an incredible fifteen to thirty-five cents a day; most were reduced to accepting the barest subsistence from appeals to the commissioner of immigration and the Hebrew Emigrant Aid Society. The year's first crop failed, then a flash fire consumed one refugee family. One by one, the disheartened would-be farmers went elsewhere, usually the cities.[93]

Nor did the place called Zion succeed: a tiny Jewish settlement near Newfield, about five miles north of Vineland, it was continually torn by labor strife.[94] The drive towards manufacturing in a rural environment could not be contained, however. There was, for example, Mizpah, about ten miles east of Vineland. Strange that in Atlantic County there should be a reminder of that place in Gilead where Jephthah once pledged to defend the children of Israel and where Jacob and Laban had also made a pledge to each other! This Mizpah, however, was literally the property of Messrs. Blumenthal and Daniel, Philadelphia manufacturers of children's clothes. They founded the town as a production center where land, labor, and climate would combine more favorably than in the big city. Their workmen were "nearly all Russian Jews," on whose behalf the paternalistic firm donated a synagogue. On 31 December 1895, the new house of worship was dedicated by the Rev. Dr. J. B. Grossman, the *Jewish Exponent* noting that at least "the spiritual natures of the colonists will thus find suitable expression."[95]

The firm of Daniel and Blumenthal also had a hand in the growth of another community over fifteen miles to the south, a comprehensive agricultural and industrial planned experiment, developing into a sizeable township and sound political unit. Located in the interior of Cape May County, Woodbine developed apart from the Vineland colonies. Its broad scope and progressive features require a more detailed analysis than just the brief narrative of its founding. Most of all, Woodbine was the fulfillment of the dream of Baron de Hirsch and his American fellow philanthropists.

WOODBINE

> Haste to yonder woodbine bower,
> The turf with rural dainties shall be crowned,
> While opening blooms diffuse their sweets around.

These old lines of Pope seemed to come to life when spoken by Judge Myer S. Isaacs at the 1902 Commencement of the Agricultural School in the Woodbine colony. He admonished the graduates to remember their agrarian heritage, and indeed, the reminder was not unrealistic, for modern Jews continued to celebrate the old festivals that took their meaning from occasions in the field: Pentecost, for the first fruits of the land, and Sukkot, for the final harvest. The Book of Ruth, the Song of Songs, the weekly Torah readings, the many debates in the Talmud, all harked back to the life of the farmer.

In the Diaspora, Jews were prevented from tilling the soil; they could but dream of their own homesteads. Yet "now," the Judge maintained, "the hospitality of the American States invites these descendants of Boaz to resume their ancient vocation." Agriculture had long been admired in America, and was available to all both great and small. Like the shepherd-kings and farmer-warriors of Israel, so, it might be said, George Washington left his farm to battle for his country. And Judge Isaacs appealed to the young graduates to be "good Jews, upright men, citizens true to the Republic which knows no distinction of sect or race."[96] In an age of big business, economic instability, and limited opportunity for the little fellow, their best prospect was "an honest and a permanent livelihood out of the soil."[97]

These were the high hopes of the president of the Baron de Hirsch Fund, the benevolent organization which founded Woodbine. This model agricultural colony would demonstrate, in the words of the baron himself, "that the Jews have not lost the agricultural qualities that their forefathers possessed."[98] Somewhat less charitably, the Philadelphia *Jewish Exponent* called it "a practical experiment toward . . . teaching the Russian-Jewish immigrants, who were coming to this country in such large numbers . . . the lesson of self-support by agriculture and by following other industries, besides peddling, to which they seemed to gravitate."[99]

By far the largest colony, Woodbine was founded in 1891 on the 5,300-acre estate of Judge Moore, purchased for $37,500. Located in sprawling Dennis Township 56 miles southeast of Philadelphia and twenty-five miles above Cape May, it seemed then "simply a jungle of scrub pine." But the advance guard of 300 Russian and Rumanian refugees cleared 1,600 acres and built homes that were larger and more comfortable than those in Alliance. Here the family homestead consisted of 15 acres, with an adjoining 15 acres to be deeded in fee simple once a farmer had proved his worth to the colony. As in Alliance, the colonists were expected to shoulder the responsibilities of private property; their homes were leased on 5 year contracts with 5 percent annual interest on the original cost of $650, to be paid in graduated monthly installments. Thus, including land and improvements, each family started with a debt of about $1,000, a staggering amount to immigrants unfamiliar with middle class American standards.[100]

The trustees of the Fund, however, argued from the outset that part of the colonists' experience consisted of learning the sound business practices expected of independent yeomen; and furthermore, repayment was required for them to assist more new immigrants. Ideologically, the stress on eventual ownership of both home and land emphasized a theme stretching far back into American history, namely, only property owners have a real stake in society. It was a principle fostered both by the Fund's operating agency, the Woodbine Land and Improvement Company, Inc., and by Superintendent H. L. Sabsovich. A report to the Roosevelt Commission on Country Life sounded the keynote, "Woodbine is working out its salvation on purely American lines."[101]

But first the trees had to be cleared. And in the stuffy, moisture-laden, lonely forest, the mosquitoes "were everywhere," wrote one of the pioneers, "in my ears, nose, mouth, and even in my eyes. . . . In the Ukraine," he reminisced, "with hundreds of miles of steppe, there were no mosquitoes. . . . Nostalgia seized me for the open steppe, for flocks of bleating sheep . . . most of all, for the horizon where the blue sky meets the warm black earth." Little, if any, reassurance came from the German-born farm manager, the red-bearded Schmidt, who appeared to mock the perspiring amateurs laboring a full morning with axe and pick just to remove one tree stump.[102] When finally cleared, the sandy soil required expensive fertilizers which the "charity farmer" could little afford, especially since there seemed to be a market for neither corn nor other produce.[103]

Even in the first year, then, manufacturing was introduced into Woodbine to supplement agriculture and to provide jobs for the "Ghetto's surplus." Businessmen-philanthropists, confronted with rising numbers of impoverished immigrants, saw here a hope of assisting them toward economic independence at "considerable low expenses and small investments." Out of the cities, and the "alarming congestion," sweatshop workers could be moved to factories built in a pleasant rural environment, where good food was cheap, housing costs low, and "the disposition for strikes has no chance to develop."[104] With both direct and indirect subsidies from the Baron de Hirsch Fund, the production of clothing, pocketbooks, hats, paper boxes, and other soft goods eventually afforded employment to the majority of Woodbine's breadwinners. Industry thus provided the impetus for the increase in population to twenty-five hundred within a decade; it may also explain the *Vineland Evening Journal's* comments on the "unusual degree of prosperity" in the new all-Jewish borough incorporated in 1903 by an act of the New Jersey legislature.[105]

But providing agricultural education and setting a model for the practical guidance of numerous Jewish farmers remained first on a list of founding principles. A foremost example was the fledgling colony's Baron de Hirsch Agricultural School, established in 1894 and continuing to 1917. The school encompassed about 300 well-developed acres, and its large classroom building had a capacity for 250 students. Its orchards, gardens, nurseries, apiaries, laboratories, dairy farm, and machine shop served as a brilliant model—if not always attainable—for the entire area. Though primarily a training school for boys, one of its graduates remarked that even "full-grown, bearded men," fresh from Russia, trying to learn "the first and simplest things about how to make things grow out of the earth" sometimes attended the school.[106] But that they were there at all, seeking refuge from an old pogrom-ridden environment and new city slums, stubbornly trying to master a strange soil; that they received a unique opportunity to make such an attempt in the New World—that is perhaps most remarkable.

Greenhorn farmers and self-help philanthropy

I contend most decidedly against the old system of alms giving which only makes so many more beggars. . . . What I desire to accomplish, is to give to a portion of my companions in faith the possibility of finding a new existence primarily as farmers, and also as handicraftsmen.

Baron de Hirsch, July, 1891[1]

You know that generally I have a soft spot for Jews. Nonetheless I came here expecting only a caricature of a colony, not a real enterprise. The two days' visit proved me wrong. . . . Here a group of people were organized who love the earth soaked with their sweat. . . . In this new Palestine, the forest covering the entire area only two years ago has been cut down, uprooted, the area has been cleared and built up by the citizens of Woodbine . . . our Jews.

Russian writer Vladimir Korolenko to his wife, September 12, 1893[2]

3

Bringing Forth the Fruits of the Land

Hardship and frustration mingled with hope and joy in farming the land. The high expectations of the Jewish agrarians in New Jersey were often overshadowed by the unyielding facts of poor soil, nonexistent markets, and inexperienced labor. This land of pine barrens seemed to bear out the legend told among the natives of the Jersey Devil, a dragon with giant batlike wings who forecast calamity to farmers and woodsmen; it was a dreaded creature to be exorcised by bell, book and candle.[3]

For years much of the colonists' land remained uncleared or uncultivated in spite of their back-breaking labor. Fathers, mothers, and children struggled under the hot sun, unaided by either machinery or draft animal, to remove the stubborn stumps and choking undergrowth. Only the stunted pine and scrub oak seemed to flourish in the "thin, shifting soil, which ages ago had been sorted and re-sorted by the waves, and the ocean was chary about leaving it little besides the rounded grains of quartz," recalled pioneer soil chemist Jacob Lipman. In Woodbine, where skilled woodsmen from Dennisville could be hired to work alongside the newcomers, land was cleared more readily. The natives "were slow and did not seem to perspire so much, but produced twice as much work," remarked one of the pioneers.[4]

Summer after summer saw entire families trudging along the hard-won rows of corn and sweet potatoes or crawling in strawberry patches to hasten the fragile berries to market. Besides the work at home, many mothers and children walked miles to pluck strawberries, cranberries, and blackberries for others, using worn-out stockings to protect their arms from the jealous thorns. A family of three experienced hands could thus make three or four dollars a day in 1888. Only at the end of each hot day were weary families reunited, sometimes for a swim in the cool, shallow water of the Maurice River, much to the delight of the youngsters. Come fall and the peak of the canning season many young people left home for weeks to work all day in the canning factories of Bridgeton; there they lived in company barracks indifferently maintained by the proprietors.[5]

Competition between Jewish colonists and native farmers soon became a stark reality. "Vineland! beautiful Vineland!" of fruit farms, pure water, and "good society" had long been extolled by local publicists as a leader in fruit culture and a haven for those who would become gentlemen farmers. Yet, by 1887, the *Vineland Evening Journal* conceded that the "quality of local berries as raised by the Jews has been largely improved on, and some fruit is now grown there as fine as in Vineland proper."[6] The rivalry between the two communities was punctuated by such periodic reports as "Alliance Jews have shipped about 65,000 quarts of strawberries this season," out of 200,000 marketed from the area. The Russian Jews shipped their strawberries even as far as Boston. Taking a more philosophical attitude, the *Elmer Times* advised that "those who suppose the Jews are a worthless set pay their villages a visit. What a few years ago was an almost worthless tract of land has been transformed by the hands of these men and their wives into farms in a good state of cultivation."[7]

In a region of small-sized units and light, sandy or gravely soil poor in retention of water or fertilizing elements, competition with the western grain belts was out of the question, but small fruits

76

offered hope, as did such truck produce as tomatoes and sweet potatoes (the "Vineland Sweet"). Local farmers were continually exhorted to concentrate on a high quality of berries, vegetables, and fruit, including grapes. These latter were marketed for wine and also became the basis for the local grape juice industry founded by Dr. T. B. Welch, a Vineland dentist.

Welch, an ardent Methodist and a teetotaler opposed to the use of fermented drink even in Communion, developed a thriving business which provided a market for local grapes until the 1890's. Then, plant disease and other problems caused the Welch Grape Juice Company to move to New York State. It was succeeded locally by the Vineland Grape Juice Company, whose vineyards later became the site of a viticultural experiment station operated by the U.S. Department of Agriculture.[8]

Jewish farmers, too, participated in the production of grapes for both juice and wine. Some of the more enterprising even formed their own cooperative wine company rather than depend on the whims of the market. Reactions to such an ambitious undertaking were mixed, ranging from the *Jewish Exponent*'s praise for their "large quantity of excellent wine," to the local journal's fear of bad influence on the younger generation—granted there was more money in wine than in grapes sold on the stem and the older inhabitants were perhaps proof against the temptations of excessive drinking, but how would this incipient wine industry affect their children, "the Americanized addition to the colony?"[9] From the 1890's through the 1920's liquor remained a persistent issue in relations between the colonies and the city of Vineland, where the prohibitionists predominated.

The less glamorous berry crops, shipped mostly to New York with some also to Newark as well as Boston, continued to be a major source of income, but in times of generally low prices, only those farmers who relied solely on their own family's labor were able to more than break even. Transportation costs too were an important factor, for Vineland and other nearby towns offered but a meager market, even though their grocers frequently exhibited prize-winning berries or citrons from Alliance, and Woodbine's variety of agricultural and industrial products repeatedly captured awards at the Cape May County Fair.[10]

Striving for economic diversification, Jewish farmers developed a poultry industry without benefit of incubators, and, as early as 1888, sold spring chickens and eggs at an exchange near Six Points.[11] Samuel Spiegel of Alliance raised Irish potatoes successfully; Steinsneider of Brotmanville was reported "doing a big business in cattle"; B. Goldstein raised many hundreds of poultry near Alliance; and Rosenhayn farmers were paying off their mortgages with proceeds from tomatoes, lima beans, and strawberries. Rosenhayn, moreover, was rapidly becoming a popular summer resort for Philadelphians attracted by its nearby lakes and woods; to a lesser extent, the other colonies also drew vacationers and tourists. Even in Carmel, with its three factories for a population of 1250, the *Jewish Exponent* as late as 1909 found that "farming still has an upper hand . . . farmers seem to be enjoying prosperity" (a report that would soon prove over-optimistic).[12]

The communities also received semi-official sanction when the New Jersey State Bureau of Statistics published a pamphlet, *The Jewish Colonies of South Jersey,* prepared by William Stainsby, Bureau chief. Replete with illustrations, it told the story of the colonists who "fled, as did the Pilgrim fathers, from tyranny, and relentless persecution to a land they knew not . . . to make homes for themselves and their children." To the question "Can a Jew become a successful farmer?" the pamphlet replied affirmatively, citing such evidence as healthy stock and crops well adapted to the region. Sweet potatoes from Alliance brought twenty-five to fifty cents more per barrel in New York than did those from other areas, while the colony's total fruit and berry crop alone amounted to $40,000 in 1899. In short, the colonies were well on the road to success, at least according to this official publication.[13]

Such optimistic evaluations of Jewish involvement in agrarian life continued over the years. For example, Abe Lipitz operated a successful peach orchard of fifty acres in Vineland proper. Youngsters from Norma and Alliance won top honors in the children's gardens category at the 1908 Trenton Fair; in the same year,

78

seventy-five children won other local awards for gardening. In Woodbine, yearly poultry shows, beginning in 1909 under the newly unfurled banner of "Chickenville," attracted much attention. And by World War I, Rosenhayn alone was shipping a record 86,000 crates of strawberries. "That sounds like some money coming into a community for one crop," commented the Vineland newspaper.[14]

One of the most respected of the Russian Jews, Jacob G. Lipman, combined agrarianism with the Jewish love of learning to become a world-famous soil chemist and bacteriologist. Both he and his brother Charles, a plant physiologist, received their first training in the Woodbine agricultural school. Early in his career, Jacob Lipman also demonstrated that the lessons learned in Woodbine could be applied in Alliance and Norma. His work with the Allivine Farm, a model agricultural enterprise, set an example of scientific practices to all farmers in the area, both Jewish and non-Jewish. Another brother, Raymond, was manager of the Farm. Dr. Jacob Lipman devoted his life to the service of New Jersey and all its farmers, first as director of the agricultural experiment station in Vineland, then as dean of Rutgers' College of Agriculture at New Brunswick.[15] The Lipmans were an illustration of that rich human contribution made by East European immigrants, a contribution worth much more than the measurable products of farm or factory.

Though men like the Lipmans could supply the professional talent, it was the Fels family, those ingenious Philadelphia philanthropists, who understood the practical difficulties confronting the colonists and supplied the capital for their experiments. Maurice Fels' recognition of such problems as high transportation costs, broker's charges, and fluctuating markets brought about the construction of Norma's large canning factory. The initial investment of $25,000 was soon supplemented by expansion of the adjoining property into the experimental Allivine Farm, the entire project being supported also by the Fels Brothers, Joseph and Samuel. A much-needed boost resulted from this new combined enterprise: the canning factory represented local demand for berries, tomatoes, sweet potatoes, lima beans, and other staples, while creating production jobs; the farm provided not only a model for the care of crops and livestock, but also a private agricultural extension program. The Allivine Company consistently offered good prices, encouraged farmers to negotiate on a group basis, and supplied fertilizer at cost as part of its campaign to improve cultivation. Some of the company's profits were applied to such causes as a new school for Norma in 1906, and its continued expansion stimulated economic activity also in Rosenhayn, Vineland, and throughout the region.[16]

Unfortunately, conditions in the canning industry fluctuated. In 1915, for example, a sharp decline in fruit prices hurt both farmers and canners; ostensibly, more housewives did their own canning to take advantage of the low prices. Also, by then, the huge Seabrook Farms Company of Bridgeton was hiring local workers for their own mass production processing and shipping operations; Rosenhayn residents who had never before been inside an automobile were transported daily to and from work in Seabrook Company cars. Partly as a consequence of such changes, the Allivine Canning Company sold out in 1919, but the Allivine Farm continued with help of the Jewish Agricultural Society to become a focal point for experimental agricultural practices.[17]

The Farm remained an ideal place for the social and business gatherings of the Jewish Farmers' Associations of Salem and Cumberland counties. Manager Raymond M. Lipman acted as host at meetings; and while the men inspected the latest facilities, the women met with Mrs. Lipman for a round-table discussion on homemaking. Brief orchestral concerts added a note of gaiety to the sandwiches, cookies, and punch. At one such meeting, the guest speaker was Meyer Goldman, who himself had left Norma to study agriculture at Cornell University and had been appointed to the staff of the new National Farm School in Doylestown, Pennsylvania. Then farmer William D. Brodie dealt with the main business of the day, which was, as usual, an organizational report and an appeal for unity among the Jewish farmers' groups confronted with ever-present difficulties.[18]

Greenhorn farmers and self-help philanthropy

Hardships of Farm Life: The Process of Attrition

Colorful and dynamic in its varied activities, Jewish agrarianism was a microcosm of the forces both within and outside the Jewish community in America. But it would not prove to be a massive or expansionary movement. One measure of the strength of any movement lies in numbers, and in this respect, while the New Jersey colonies were the only ones to survive into the post-World War I period, they nevertheless showed a decline. The Jewish population of the colonies, which in 1901 was about 3,275, dropped to 2,739 by 1919 (see Tables, pages 348-350). Equally significant, many of the surviving original settlers moved away, and their children, in most cases, left for the cities in search of better educational, economic, and social opportunities.[19]

Why did so many leave? The hard times for farmers and trend towards urbanization prevailing in America were significant factors, but the special circumstances of this social experiment were equally responsible. A critical shortcoming was the unilateral manner in which the terms were defined from above. The colonists' benefactors made it clear that only those who followed the rules, those who helped themselves in the classic American way, would merit additional aid and eventually acquire title to the land. This edict soon led to charges of bad faith on both sides, as the colonists felt they were being forced into a state of near peonage, while the philanthropists feared that their plans for a healthy agrarian middle class were being subverted by idleness and the "peddling instinct." Further, rapport was made difficult by the persisting cultural gap between the cosmopolitan West Europeans and Americanized Jews on the one hand and the East Europeans only recently escaped from the provincial *shtetl* on the other. Not only did the philanthropists themselves seem different and distant from the immigrants, but their representatives as well sometimes could not speak the Yiddish *mahme loshon* (mother tongue).[20]

Only months after the founding of Alliance, a number of immigrants were expelled for failing to meet their financial obligations, for showing themselves "unfit to become farmers." One group of disaffected colonists from Estellville broke into the empty barracks in Alliance and started rioting, ostensibly for more generous arrangements. Such actions brought representatives of the Hebrew Emigrant Aid Society (Dr. Julius Schwartz and S. H. Mildenberg) to press charges before the local courts, as well as some obviously unfavorable publicity; three of the riot's leaders were jailed by the Salem County constables. Interestingly, the *Vineland Evening Journal* was critical of the colonists for creating an unlawful disturbance and for "playing sharp games" to extort funds from the "genial" agents of the Society—a reference to the hundred-dollar initial subsistence allowance given each family. The *Jewish Record* reacted with embarrassment and an emotional defense of the Society's role: given its strained resources, it reasoned, they could not have acted otherwise in the face of such ingratitude. Even the distant East European *Hamelitz* published reports from Philadelphia's young rabbinic scholar, Cyrus Adler, critical of those who sowed "dissension amongst the colonists," concluding that the few who reneged on their obligations "caused a scandal in the city of Salem, and were arrested and imprisoned, thus besmirching the name of the colony."[21]

Inadequate and unstable financing, certainly in the early period, was a major source of the problem. As the Hebrew Emigrant Aid Society proved incapable of further assistance after 1883, there was a hiatus of extreme privation relieved only by the philanthropy of Simon Muhr, Alfred T. Jones, and other Philadelphians. Then, in 1885, the Alliance Land Trust (ALT), financed partly by the Mansion House Committee of London, took over the burden. It assumed all existing obligations in return for new thirty-three-year mortgages at 3 percent interest, granted only to "the most desirable settlers, while the few unfit to become farmers were bought off." Prior to a grant each farmer was called before the distinguished trustees—then including William Strauss, Henry S. Henry, Isaac Eppinger, Leopold Gershel, M. W. Mendel, Leonard Lewisohn, Dr. F. De Sola Mendes—and questioned concerning his farm and family. If successful, he received fifty dollars to be used solely for plants or seed. Deeds were not transferable for the duration of the mortgage period without consent of the trustees.[22]

Not all settlers, however, fell into line—some were dubbed "restless . . . socialistic" spirits, spreading dissension, claiming the land had been overvalued and their own labor insufficiently rewarded. The trustees' response was additional pressure and occasional inspection tours. One visit in 1887 turned into a gala event when the dignitaries included banker Jacob Schiff and Judge Isaacs. Driving up in a large coach, they were met at the entrance of the makeshift synagogue, the community's focal point, by a delegation of farmers bearing local fruit; thence, with an air of noblesse oblige, they stopped at many a humble home, accepting petitions, granting gifts of cash and sewing machines (fifteen in all), promising travel tickets for relatives still in Russia. Nor were the community needs neglected: Mr. Schiff donated $250 towards a library building and $250 more for a permanent synagogue; and he promised to supply a Hebrew School teacher for the children as well as a night school for adults. So he and his party went, "paternally ministering to those who justly expected it."[23]

Philanthropists Eugene Benjamin, Cyrus Sulzberger, and Morris Loeb were among those who lent personal assistance to the settlers and graced their homes. One of Benjamin's favorite pioneers was William Kolman, "a fine old man who never complains of his lot, and bears his ills like a philosopher." Kolman enjoyed the title of doctor, in recognition of his extensive knowledge of Middle Eastern plant life. Yet, he too, like his neighbors in Alliance, had a hard job in developing a fourteen-acre farm to feed his family and to grow marketable crops of vegetables and fruit. The Kolman home, although only a typical three-room frame house, was a place of charm and hospitality for residents and distinguished visitors alike.[24]

Personal attention was appreciated, but it could not substitute for long-term planning or dispel the prevailing image of the "charity farmer" which tended to curb initiative and self-reliance. Eventually, the settlers' discontent and the philanthropists' generosity brought more reasonable mortgage terms. By 1888 the average farmer in Alliance owed ALT a principal of only $200, repayable at 3 percent interest over a 10-year period; this compared favorably with average principal indebtedness of $400 by those who had purchased land on their own initiative from Leach Brothers. Then, too, the colonies around Vineland became the object of an ephemeral competition between the New York philanthropists, such as Henry S. Henry and Leopold Gershel, and the Philadelphians, such as Mayer Sulzberger and Simon Muhr.[25]

A period of salutary neglect followed, some colonists not troubling at all with either principal or interest. Somehow, whether because of a language difficulty or cultural difference or a belief that it was simply unjust to make them pay for the privilege of struggling in a wilderness, these colonists considered the loan an outright gift, especially as affluent philanthropists seemed to be their devoted patrons. The axe fell, however (1905), when renewed economic prosperity encouraged the ALT to press for a resumption of payments. Numerous appeals and lengthy negotiations postponed the threatened foreclosures, much to everyone's relief.[26]

But other difficulties, equally fundamental, persisted among the daily hardships of the pioneers. The farmhouses were poorly built and the slight protection they provided against the winter's cold and summer's heat caused some suffering among the women and children. Some colonists were always close to calamity, and recurrent droughts, storms, and fires were a major hazard (one early fire in Estellville caused the death of two young children). Especially in the first years, shortages of food, clothing, fuel and other necessities had brought numerous pitiful appeals for help to the United Hebrew Charities in Philadelphia. One of these letters read: "We are in a worse condition than prisoners sent by the Russian Government to Siberia, because besides hunger and cold, we are compelled to listen to the cries of our wives and children, and to witness their fearful appearance. Do what you can, for the love of Heaven."[27]

At one point (1885), even the Leach Brothers appealed to Philadelphia Jews on behalf of the colonists for emergency relief followed by supplementary employment opportunities, possibly a planned program for sub-contracting garment work. One visiting delegation early that year reported widespread destitution in Alliance, with children unable to attend school for lack of clothing and shoes. Inevitably, the established Jewish community responded in ever-growing numbers, both individually and through organizations; yet charity was also mingled with factionalism and recrimination. Thus, in a campaign for Passover aid, the *Jewish Record* could liken the efforts of Philadelphians to the "humane consideration of father or protector" while castigating the relationship between the New York ALT and the colonists as "that of landlord over tenant." Occasionally, a successful fund-raising campaign was accompanied by veiled threats or by rumors that destitute "Russians" would march on Philadelphia's business district.[28]

The five sons of sixty-one-year-old Noy Gartman of Alliance indeed searched vainly for temporary work in Philadelphia and New York to help carry the family through the hard winter of 1885–86. With the fall's Feast of Tabernacles, another harvest had come and gone, leaving not enough cash to pay a lien of $260 to Leach Brothers. The family's own investment of $560, as well as their back-breaking labor on the farm, seemed useless. "What will God do with us?" asked old Mr. Gartman, "Will He forsake us to be thrown out into the streets?" But he was soon to recall the psalmist's consolation, *kerovah teshuatee lavoh*, ("my help is close at hand"). Through the intercession of Philadelphia's Jewish leader Alfred T. Jones, the Mansion House Fund sent a $200 draft, and the Gartman family, like many others, was given another chance. Gartman's letter of gratitude was written in Hebrew and translated for Jones and other readers of the *Jewish Record* by "Ben Yehudah," who commented "that kind words sound louder than the roaring waves of the sea."[29]

Charity had, at times, an enervating effect on the recipient. It may have encouraged idleness among some newcomers, and an attitude of expectant dependence. Much as the charitable activities stemmed from noble intentions, they seldom attained that highest level of giving recommended by both Jewish tradition and modern economics: assistance ought to enable the recipient to support himself (in twentieth century economic usage, it is a *development* fund rather than mere subsistence aid). Although the Jewish community of Philadelphia contributed substantially through its organizations, they lacked imagination in expanding the limited economic opportunities. Pleas for more practical, long-range solutions too often fell on deaf ears. One wonders about the demoralizing effect on both settled and prospective farmers of newspaper appeals "for sweet charity's sake . . . lending to the Lord," and of perennial expeditions by "benevolently disposed ladies" bearing Purim goodies for the children, as well as clothing and other personal necessities.[30]

Moreover, as is usual in such obviously paternalistic relationships, the recipient felt beholden to the giver; in effect, the colonists were made to feel that they were not merely working for themselves but rather for the cause of proving that Jews could be farmers. At the same time, it was woe to the colonists if they expressed gratitude to their New York benefactors without giving equal praise to the "good Philadelphia Israelites." One such petition of thanks pledged the colonists to prove themselves by an "unrelenting perseverence [sic] on the field of agriculture, which is our salvation and the honor of Judaism, and by the care we will exercise in teaching our children the Law, and love they owe to God and man."[31] Such sweeping commitments were not only unrealistic, but their fawning tone seemed inconsistent with the free spirit of America, as the younger people soon discovered. Individualism, materialism, equality, and self-interest were part of the New World's attractive promise; few among the youth were willing to live as dependent martyrs to a cause that seemed no longer relevant. For some of the middle-aged, too, the colonies were only a stopgap measure before resuming the occupations they had followed in Europe.

The total lack of farming experience among most of the colonists was something of a scandal. Said one Jewish pioneer: "They did not even know if potatoes grew above or under ground." Prosperous Vineland natives would sometimes hire the Russians as farm hands. One of them, so ran the local joke, mistook some choice tomato plants for weeds and proceeded to destroy them with his hoe; another, hired to lay bricks, failed to meet the simplest specifications of local masons.[32]

In the cranberry bogs, however, they were always welcome laborers. On some of the large estates, such as Isaac Hanthorn's in Vineland, gangs of as many as a hundred Russian Jews (parents and children alike) toiled each year under native overseers "who drive them up and down the bog, upbraiding them when they do not do their work well, in their eagerness to get where the picking is better."[33] The pay was only a few pennies per bucketful, so scurrying for the most fertile patches was a harsh necessity. Meanwhile, parents struggled to keep their hungry children from stuffing themselves with all the berries they could eat, for green berries like green apples would cause a terrible stomachache. Hundreds from Carmel and Alliance became virtual slaves for the short season of berry picking. And with even the kindest overseers, the blazing sun, the mosquitoes, flies, and poison ivy in an alien land made work in New Egypt, New Jersey seem not a little ironical.[34] For some, exodus was the only answer.

A few of the city-dwelling agrarians were beginning to doubt the wisdom of group colonization. Naturally, the Philadelphians blamed New York's "Gothamites" for selecting a poor location and failing to supply adequate implements or healthy cattle, and the newcomers should have been provided with more than the initial fifty dollars per homestead plus meager allowance for the first months: Vineland's "sandy, sterile soil . . . would have been the last place that a practical farmer would select." Far better the fruitful land and year-round favorable climate of the South, where "Nature is ever ready to reward industry . . . 'like a tree planted by the river of water that bringeth forth in his season.'" (Fortunately, few of the southern farmers then suffering from a decline in cotton prices read the *Jewish Record*.) And why, asked one practical critic, were so few of the colonists' homes built with a cellar for the storage of wine, fruit, or meat?[35]

Two major issues persistently divided thought on the subject. Was it necessary to settle Jews together in colonies of their own in order to preserve their social and economic identity? And, to what extent would the agrarian ideal be compromised by the introduction of industry? Philadelphian Simon Muhr, while touring parts of the South, convinced himself that an initial one thousand Jewish families could be scattered among many towns of the Carolinas alone, and there find work in the cotton mills. He too felt that the New Jersey colonies had not been located with a view to such practical considerations. Others repeated the proposals to remedy the lack of employment by establishing industry within the colonies. This was done in Carmel, for instance, where tailoring and shirtmaking became the major mainstays of the economy by the turn of the century.

After 1900, the Jewish Agricultural and Industrial Aid Society frequently encouraged this kind of diversification. But others, however, uncompromising agrarians like Rabbi A. R. Levy of Chicago, saw it as a betrayal of the cause; he founded and continued to operate a western purists' group, the Jewish Agriculturists' Aid Society. Some Philadelphians, too, agreed that only agricultural colonies could "proclaim liberty throughout the land and unto all the inhabitants thereof." Among the eastern purists was Inspector of Immigrants Joseph Ehrlich, who praised the farms of Alliance and denounced the "sweating system" of Carmel and Rosenhayn.[36]

What of the colonists themselves? Anna I. Seldes of Alliance wrote (1895) of a thirteen years' struggle "with almost barren results." Several mortgages held by the building association in Salem were recently foreclosed, she reported, and the farms sold by the sheriff. In the face of anxiety and starvation, some lost hope and moved to Philadelphia, actions which created only bitterness among their neighbors. Even with fewer people in the colonies, winter unemployment remained a problem: the cloakmaking season lasted but a few weeks that year.

The year 1895 also saw the death of a typical old-time settler, Kotzehue, who left a wife and six children as well as a grieved community. Persecuted in Russia, he became imbued with the idea of independent existence as a farmer. Soon after the founding of Alliance, he took over the land of a disillusioned pioneer who had left for the city, and in spite of ill-health labored to clear and cultivate more acres. Like many others, he stooped over a sewing machine during the winter, if there was work, and earned in spite of it barely enough to keep his family. Even when bed-ridden, he refused charity or loans, fearing that he could never repay the favor. Finally, farmer Kotzehue died in a Philadelphia hospital, leaving his family on the verge of starvation; at least three of the children were placed in a Philadelphia orphan asylum. Yet, Mrs. Seldes reported, such instances of tragedy were far from uncommon.[37]

The last years of the nineteenth century were a time of crisis for the American farmer in general, and brought to the South Jersey colonies even more foreclosures by the building and loan associations of Salem. Moses Klein, reporting as *Hatzophe* ("The Scout") for the Association of Jewish Immigrants (1897), described what he observed in parts of Alliance and Rosenhayn: there were empty houses and desolate gardens, many a farmer turned into a tailor, "and many tailors who have girded their loins and assumed their former Russian nomadic lives." But others remained and in spite of hard times held on tenaciously. Even some who could no longer meet their obligations, losing substantial investments of money and labor, managed somehow on rented or marginal land in the woods or on the outskirts of town, away from "the serpents of the building associations."[38]

For these families, farming was a hand-to-mouth existence, dependent on a remaining cow and calf, a half-hundred chickens, and a small plot of vegetables. The money received from the crates of berries shipped to the cities, subject always to the vagaries of the market and of distant middlemen, often failed to cover even transportation costs. When there was full-time work in the shirt factory (it was shut down for months in depression periods, such as 1893–1897 and 1907–1908), the head of the family could earn about five dollars a week to supplement the meager income from the land, doing his chores before dawn and in the evening after work.

In the midst of hard times, word came of a messenger from the Holy Land, even from Jerusalem. Was it perhaps Elijah, herald of salvation, coming to the oppressed of this new Carmel in New

Jersey, "sent from on high to announce the redemption of this, *their* Holy Land, from the cruel building associations"? Such, if but brief, was the grapevine's tremor of a half-serious hope. Alas, it was but an envoy of the *halukkah* distributing charity boxes for the indigent of Palestine, and the poor of New Jersey's "New Jerusalem" gave in spite of their own need.[39]

Years of drought or too much rain, insect plagues attacking the fruit, poor soil, and chronically low prices for farm products caused many to surrender to the despair and to the building and loan associations. It is ironic how the gentile money lenders of Salem and Vineland managed to become so influential. In part, it was because the colonists obeyed the commandment to be fruitful and multiply—larger families seem almost traditional for farmers— and the original small homes and fifteen-acre plots proved inadequate for growing families. New and more spacious homes cost about $1,200 and the price of land doubled during the 1880's, with periodic spurts of speculation in the real estate around Vineland causing further increases. The results, for many colonists, were heavy mortgages and high interest rates. For others, however, rising land vaues offered a chance to sell out and seek a better life in the city.[40]

Yet farms were not really much in demand during the depressed 1890's, and unfavorable publicity in the Yiddish press warned away many potential settlers. Front-page articles in *Die Arbeiter Zeitung*, official weekly of the New York United Hebrew Trades, derided the petty bourgeois speculation of South Jersey farmers. Journalist Louis Miller returned from a summer inspection visit in 1891 with few positive comments on the future of the colonists: most families averaged about $300 a year, he reported, supplemented perhaps by another $75 at the sewing machine. Yet, many stubbornly remained on their poor acres, refusing to sell any land to more efficient Jewish neighbors such as Alliance pioneer Sidney Bailey. Was it speculation, as Miller thought, or the desire to hold on to a long-sought homestead, which put a high price on inferior land? In any case, fifteen acres was hardly enough for successful farming, and local banks grew reluctant to extend additional loans for either expansion or improvement.

Most of those who held on, Miller charged, became little more than "proletarian land slaves" with the illusion of some agrarian pot of gold before them, themselves the victim of "criminal speculators." Their homesteads were barren and poor, their margin of subsistence derived from the short berry-picking season and needlework, their anguish symbolized by the swarms of bloodsucking mosquitoes. Had the philanthropists tried to settle Americans rather than refugees in such an unfortunate location and on such poor terms, they would have been "lynched," or so Miller was told by one unnamed American. Nonetheless, he had to admit that some, like Moses Bayuk and Sidney Bailey, had succeeded: these were the better educated, more efficient farmers. Even those who failed in Alliance, Carmel, or Rosenhayn were, as he admitted with a trace of condescension, "Jewish patriots who thought to solve the difficult 'Jewish problem'" by the quixotic means of colonization. Miller had more harsh words for the affluent benefactors; in the pages of their *American Hebrew* he reminded them that he had met in Alliance "the same misery and want as anywhere on the Hester Street" of the Lower East Side.[41]

Also in these issues of *Die Arbeiter Zeitung,* in a mute testimony to the persistent dream, the old Am Olam leader M. Herder of Carmel offered a typical promoter's pitch for the sale of undeveloped homesteads at a "splendid location" sixteen miles outside Philadelphia. You too can own a farm, the immigrant Yiddish reader was informed, in a hopeful new venture called *Beis Lechem* ("Bethlehem"). Apparently, however, this new colony never entered the field of competition with the South Jersey colonies, never made it beyond the dream.

Ignorance of farming was further compounded for many first generation settlers by the language difficulty. Market reports, agricultural extension services, farm journals and lectures directed to the native farmer were nearly useless to the non-English-speaking colonist. Moreover, because they were unfamiliar with the ways

91

of their newly adopted country, they sometimes fell prey to the sharp practices of peripatetic swindlers. One of these confidence men, for example, posed as a labor contractor for Delaware peach growers in need of harvest hands: he disappeared after collecting two dollars each from about fifty colonists, ostensibly to pay for the group's travel expenses, plus a small fee for himself. The disappointed harvesters, short of work and money, called on Marshal Nichols of Vineland, but the law was slower than the enterprising swindler.[42] Warnings against land speculators and swindlers would appear periodically in the Yiddish-language pages of the *Jewish Farmer,* to include particularly advice for the new-comer to check the legality of land deeds and hidden mortgages. The Jewish Agricultural and Industrial Aid Society also offered highly qualified counsel and assistance, though occasional tragic instances of swindles by land jobbers and labor recruiters were still reported.[43]

It was a hard road from the East European *shtetl* to the farm in America. Among those with the will to endure were the intelligentsia who steadily opposed the ghetto spirit and who believed in agrarianism as the salvation of the Jewish people. If one of their goals was to counteract anti-Semitism and to impress the gentile world in general, then indeed they met with a limited success. They proved that Jews could be farmers. Thus, the eminent Russian writer Vladimir Korolenko, who visited Woodbine, admitted that where he had expected but a "caricature" of farming, he had found true farmers "who loved the earth soaked with their sweat." A farmer's life, wrote Korolenko, wrought profound improvements, especially in the youth: even "their bodily structure is different; these young farmers can do the work and no distinction exists between them and the Americans."[44]

But the majority of immigrant colonists, and certainly of their children, were not of that intelligentsia imbued with an agrarian ideal. For most, the main concern was simply to find refuge and economic opportunity. They recognized also the need for education in this country of freedom, and knew that better schooling was available in urban areas. Local leaders like Joseph W. Pincus, president of the Woodbine Board of Education, warned that inadequate educational facilities were driving families from the farm to the city. Ironically, it was the idealistic intelligentsia who, in the long run, found the cultural paucity and drudgery of rural life most unbearable. In 1905, Abraham Cahan, editor of the New York *Forward,* recalled that the "first educated Russian Hebrews to come to this country were attracted neither by the American colleges nor by the access of their race to a professional career," but sought in farming a solution of "the Jewish question." Although eventually they were forced to abandon their agrarian ideals, "of the two movements which were set on foot in 1882 by the Palestinians and the Americans, the American movement seemed the more successful [then]. . . . The whole Jewish race was expected by the Americans to follow suit. . . ." Yet, Cahan knew better than Korolenko that some of the agrarian groups had to disband "immediately upon reaching New York. . . . The would-be pioneers were scattered through the Union," most turning to the professions or other non-farm occupations attuned to twentieth century America.[45]

The second generation was even less impressed by the prospect of earning the praise of a Korolenko. As one of their prominent spokesmen, looking back on the pioneering generation in unromanticized objectivity, put it: "they came here to Alliance, a couple of hundred families, made a big campaign, a moral issue about going back to the soil, but that didn't mean that every one of them was suited for it. Mostly the opposite was true."[46] This was perhaps an overcritical evaluation, certainly oversimplified, but the fact remained that by 1919 only a handful of original settlers still lived in the colonies: that year a census indicated that only 219 out of a total Jewish population of 2,739 had lived on the land more than fifteen years, and not all of these were descendants of the original pioneers. This lack of retaining power helps to explain the decline in population compared to 1901, when the colonists had numbered about 3,500. Woodbine alone lost scores of families at a time when Cape May County grew by more than 4,000 (see Appendix).[47]

Reorganizing Jewish Agriculture:
From Philanthropy to Cooperatives

If the return-to-the-soil movement eventually proved less than successful, it would never be for lack of ambitious and well-meaning organizations, of farmers as well as philanthropists. As far back as 1882, with the colonies in New Jersey scarcely under way, leaders of the Union of American Hebrew Congregations issued from Cincinnati a national appeal for a Hebrew Agriculture Society (actually organized as "The Maccabees"). The plan proposed to cope with the influx of "Israelites" by supporting them on farms for a year or two until the first harvest, and thus establishing a new independent yeomanry. With some prescient wisdom—perhaps because it was closer to the Jersey colonies—the *Record* noted the flaws in this program: it was inadequately financed, it assumed that the inexperienced could readily enter into farming, it provided no opportunity for training, and it was developed without consulting the immigrants concerned. At a convention in July 1885, the Union of American Hebrew Congregations turned down further proposals for a new American Hebrew Farmers' Association.[48]

Greater financial assistance did become available, however, from outside the United States, especially from the Jewish Colonization Association based in Paris. The JCA, however, concentrated its efforts on colonization in Argentina. Periodic disputes marked its relations with the American leaders of the Baron de Hirsch Fund who were specifically committed to aiding Jewish acculturation and farming in the United States. Both groups, though, were pledged to the Baron's objectives, "to show that the Jews have not lost the agricultural abilities which their forefathers possessed . . . and to make for the refugees a new home in different lands where they can be useful to their country as free farmers on their own soil."[49] By the turn of the century, these tasks required greater specialization: to meet such needs, in the face of the mounting new waves of immigrants, the Fund and JCA agreed to establish a third organization, the Jewish Agricultural and Industrial Aid Society, chartered in New York on Lincoln's Birthday of 1900.

Significantly, this new organization focused on the previously recognized goal of training artisans as well as farmers, attempting to establish a balance between industry and agriculture in the rural communities. The Society extended loans for land or equipment at a rate of only 4 percent interest, repayable in easy installments. Most of these loans were on a second mortgage, some on a third or fourth; they came at a time when no other credit was available to the colonists and when American farmers generally complained of excessive interest charges and tight credit. It was not until 1916 that the Federal Farm Loan Act provided more adequate credit facilities for the nation's farmers, and then at interest rates averaging about 6 percent.[50]

Among the other important functions of the Jewish Agricultural and Industrial Aid Society was assistance to farmer's cooperatives, including creameries, storage facilities, and factories, as well as the transfer of industry from crowded tenement districts. Its Industrial Removal Office relocated about seventy thousand immigrants from the slums of New York between 1901 and 1917. (After 1907, when this office became a separate organization, the words "Industrial" and "Aid" were dropped from the name of the Jewish Agricultural Society.) Jobs on the farm were secured by its Farm Labor Bureau, and beginning in 1908, the Society offered scholarships to agricultural colleges. Such scholarships were held by some of the best students at New Jersey's College of Agriculture.[51]

Agriculturists from the Society visited the New Jersey colonies periodically to lecture on new developments and to give individual assistance. At long last, starting in 1908, the Yiddish monthly, the *Jewish Farmer* offered a means of communication for the immigrant on the land, and its timely articles concerning vegetable crops, dairying, poultry, and other topics were doubly welcome because they were written in the people's language. Its columns devoted to letters from the readers helped to relieve the cultural monotony of country life. Later a page in English was added for the farm boy and girl.

Americanization services, as well as instruction in gardening and hygiene, were provided by the Society's Bureau of Educational

Activities. Its resident director for the New Jersey colonies, Louis Mounier, a humane and cultured Unitarian, and himself an earlier immigrant from France, fostered not only the practical arts but also the aesthetic and intellectual during his appointment from 1901 to 1917. Such efforts were very much in tune with the recommendations of President Roosevelt's Country Life Commission (1909), which deplored the lack of adequate educational and social opportunities in rural areas.

Moreover, self-help through organized farmers' groups in an era of powerful business combinations and trusts was also given further impetus by the Jewish Agricultural Society. In the New Jersey colonies, there were almost spontaneous movements to form fruit marketing cooperatives as early as the summer of 1889. Though such attempts were resumed periodically, no effective national Jewish farmers' organization appeared until 1909, when the JAS helped found the Federation of Jewish Farmers of America.[52]

One of the Federation's early projects was an agricultural fair held in New York's Educational Alliance, so slum dwellers could catch a glimpse of country life. This was a proud occasion, occurring quite appropriately during Sukkot Week (the harvest festival) 1909. There the country folk exhibited not only their vegetables and fruit, but also homemade butter, cheese, preserves, baked goods, and floral arrangements. Ever since the 1880's smart New Jersey farmers converted their milk to butter for New York, where *landsleit* paid more because they knew it was kosher. Including entries from the Baron de Hirsch Agricultural School, the great fair offered material evidence for the Educational Alliance's verbal descriptions and lectures on Jewish farm life, that had been accompanied in the past only by crude stereoptic slides.[53]

Among the practical benefits of uniting within the Federation of Jewish Farmers was a proposed central exchange for the cooperative selling of commodities and purchasing of seed, fertilizer, and tools. Their plans were based on high hopes for the "moral support of all Jewish communities, and, at the beginning, some financial backing," and suggested that Jewish buyers in the large cities would favor all produce from Jewish farms.[54] Such expectations eventually foundered, not only because they represented an unrealistic view of big city market conditions, but also because the number of Jewish farmers did not grow sufficiently. Nonetheless, with subsidies from the JAS, the Federation continued to increase its new programs, including local credit unions. And its annual conventions featured outstanding New Jersey pioneers, such as H. L. Sabsovich and Dr. Lipman, who also initiated its lecture series. Among its long-time officers from the New Jersey colonies were Israel Hersh Levin, A. M. Kuntz, Joseph H. Cohen, and Samuel Kleinfeld. Officers of its credit unions included George Kotinsky and Morris Zimmerman of Woodbine and Paul Rogovy and Morris Etinberg of Carmel.[55]

Relations between the parent Federation and local groups were not always peaceful, however, as indicated in the proceedings of the annual conventions, and duly reported in the *Jewish Farmer*. For example, Woodbine farmers complained that they were getting too little aid from the Federation in their struggle against the high insurance rates charged by private companies.[56] On the other hand, as late as August 1918, Joseph W. Pincus, secretary of the Federation, castigated a mass meeting of farmers from Norma, Alliance, and Six Points for their inadequate interest in the cooperative movement. With wartime earnings increasing farm incomes to record levels, Pincus maintained, almost everyone could afford to participate. Nevertheless, the three hundred families in Woodbine apparently preferred to invest in Liberty Bonds, having exceeded their fifteen thousand dollar quota by thirty thousand in a surge of patriotism.[57] Intercolonial competition, too, became an obvious impediment to the cooperative movement. For example, Carmel had its own credit union, and so declined to join with farmers of nearby Garton Road in a combined agency for small loans. The Norma Growers Association operated separately from the Carmel Farmers Association, and the Woodbine Farmers Association also managed its own cooperative buying and selling.[58]

Much good feeling, however, among Federation members was also evident. Many weeks before Passover the *Jewish Farmer* carried an urgent appeal to all readers to purchase their holiday wines

97

from the colonists of Woodbine, Carmel, Rosenhayn, Alliance, and Norma; this wine was strictly kosher, tasty, and reasonably priced. Then in its editorial, the magazine called on both brother farmers and city dwellers to do their share in the cause of Jewish agrarianism. Listed sales agents for the local associations were Jacob Crystal (for Alliance, Norma, Rosenhayn), A. Narovlavsky (for the individualists in nearby Carmel), and Joseph H. Cohen (for Woodbine).[59] Resolutions of thanks to "noble patrons" and others who toiled for the cause were also common, going, for example, to Joseph Fels and Raymond Lipman.[60]

Business, too, frequently offered pleasant occasions: a united farmers' convocation in Woodbine or in Vineland, a joint celebration of Hanukkah or other traditionally joyous holiday, a graduation ceremony at the agricultural school with specially composed songs, or an appearance by Joseph Rabinowitz, mayor of Woodbine, to announce, as in 1915, that the town's population had reached twenty-five hundred (90 percent Jewish) and to plead that next year's Federation convention be held there in honor of the community's twenty-fifth anniversary.[61] In Norma, the local farmers' institute held frequent meetings in the newly built community hall (1919), where one of the favorite topics drawing people from surrounding colonies was the problem of readjustment after World War I. Many realized that the temporary wartime spurt in demand for farm products was coming to an end; Benjamin S. Stone, editor of the *Jewish Farmer*, visited the colonies to urge a united effort to cope with postwar "reconstruction" dilemmas.[62]

It was an era of change in America as well as the rest of the world, a great transformation was taking place, given even further impetus by the Great War. The future would bring economic and political crises, and postwar quotas would begin to stop the flow of Jewish refugees precisely when they were most in need of a haven; even as early as 1914, the Jewish Colonization Conference concluded sadly that both "England and America are making effective obstacles against Jewish emigration in order to prevent further overcrowding of Jewish cities." The Conference called for new colonizing efforts in the Turkish-controlled Near East as "the only effective expedient." No more would the doors of the New World be wide open for "co-religionists in the East."[63]

This was still a decade before the restrictive National Origins Act of 1924 solidified the postwar policy of discriminatory immigration quotas, but war itself was a most effective jailer. Neither the seaboard cities nor the rural colonies could ever draw as heavily from the great human reservoir of mass immigration. Amidst the economic prosperity of war, while the cities assimilated their millions of immigrants into the sweatshops and mills, the Jewish rural colonies continued their own long process of adaptation to the ways of America.

The thorny paths of Americanization: Rise and fall of agrarian utopia

If we entertained dreams of a contented Jewish peasantry, we were soon disillusioned. . . . The immigrant was a child who must be carefully kept in his place. . . . My young dream of a righteous American community had come to disillusion.

Dr. Boris D. Bogen, on
his leaving Woodbine, 1904

4

Trouble in the Melting Pot

Because of its geographic position, New Jersey always felt the impact of a population movement, and this was especially evident in an age of mass immigration, when the spreading network of railroads spewed forth additional newcomers. New Jersey had long been a "melting pot of differing ethnic, religious, and social groups, each one clinging to its language and customs well into the nineteenth century."[1] For the Jewish farmers and tailors from Eastern Europe the South Jersey communities formed a stage on which the frequently competing forces of integration and group identity confronted one another.

Just what was the melting pot, a symbol of fusion or confusion? asked Philip Gleason, as he traced this popular concept to the era of concern over the "new immigration" and especially to the national attention focused on Israel Zangwill's play, *The Melting Pot,* first presented in 1908. Its hero, David, is a young Jewish immigrant to America whose family was murdered in the Kishinev pogrom. A musician, his great ambition is to produce an American symphony denoting the harmony of all the varied strands of America weaving inexorably into a single fabric. David's eventual marriage to a Christian settlement house worker and his determination to cast off old attitudes and loyalties reflect, in part, Zangwill's thesis that Jews faced a choice between abandonment of all distinct cultural traits or "renationalization" in a homeland of their own. In a final triumphant scene after the success of his symphony, David extolls the "glory of America where all races and nations come to labour and look forward!" How much more preferable he believes this is than the lesser "glory of Rome and Jerusalem where all nations and races come to worship and look back."[2] Old World differences would be submerged in favor of a new and better breed of men.

But the vision of the crucible in which was produced a "real American" was received less warmly in many places. So in Vineland, where as far back as 1876 "the heterogeneous population" was blamed for an increased liquor traffic, where a "colored people's festival" caused a mushrooming of "for sale" signs, and where editorials (1878) warned that "the golden shore will be overrun with Celestials." Before the end of the century, Vineland's own melting pot contained, in addition to Russian Jews, other Europeans. The town's founder, Charles Landis, was forced to reassure the citizenry that the Italian newcomers on his tract, though poor, were hardworking, loved their families, and did the kind of heavy manual labor that Americans were unwilling to perform. "Do you ever see," he demanded rhetorically," an Italian tramp . . . [or] criminal . . . [or] drunkard?" Too many local people, Landis charged, were guilty of an "erroneous . . . judgment" against these new neighbors.[3]

As in New York or Philadelphia, various ethnic groups were pressed into their own districts, a process that tended to weaken the melting pot idea. Germantown, for example, was in the southwest of Vineland's tri-county area near Chestnut Ridge; the Italians lived between Cherry Street and Seventh in Vineland and the Jews, near the Plum Street synagogue between Boulevard and Sixth. Nor did the different groups occupy themselves with harmonious fusing. Tensions rose when Jewish radicals from nearby Carmel insisted on flying the red flag in one July Fourth parade down Landis Avenue, and, in another case, the whole town was "stirred up over a fight between the Jews and the Germans [caused by a] Hebrew's cow getting into Mr. Hulzhauer's cabbage patch." Stones and clubs were cast aside only after several arrests.[4]

More important battles were yet to be fought, one of them being the struggle to learn English. Perversely, Vineland's board of education refused to provide night school programs for adult Hebrews whose petitions were left dangling for years. The Jewish welfare organizations, however, planned from the outset various language instruction classes to include adults, and, in the same year as the infamous Russian May Laws, adult refugees were being taught English in such makeshift places as a room in Philadelphia's railroad depot.

The *Jewish Exponent* crowed over the number of older colonists in Alliance who could plow through an English-language newspaper unaided, though most, it ruefully admitted, in 1888 still read "only Jewish jargon" or Hebrew books and papers. The children, of course, were breezing through *Ivanhoe, Robinson Crusoe,* and *Frankenstein.* One fifteen-year-old, Alec Yosef, who worked on his father's farm in summer and on the sewing machine in winter, attracted attention by spending his evenings reading books with "incredible rapidity." The Russians would soon be transformed to Americans. "Long live Alliance!" The *American Hebrew* relished the assurances of Cyrus Adler that the newcomers were "becoming Americanized," and that some of the children spoke English "fluently . . . not betraying even the slightest foreign accent."[5]

The peculiar attachment of even the most promising colonists to Yiddish, however, remained a constant source of embarrassment. Is this *Juedisch Deutsch* really a language and not a jargon? asked the *Exponent,* and even if it is, as lexicographer Alexander Harkavy and others maintained, then "it is of no actual utility here . . . and can but act as a hindrance to real advancement." Mingling patriotism with cultural snobbery, the *Exponent* chided that "English is our country's language . . . besides which, true culture and refinement are needed at all times." It was advice intended not only for the colonists, but also for Philadelphian George Randorf, who wanted to include Yiddish in the curriculum of his school in Alliance.[6]

The broader issues of assimilation and loss of identity were raised to high pitch by a *New York Herald* interview with Baron de Hirsch in 1889. Ostensibly, the noted philanthropist advocated the "amalgamation" of Jews within the rest of the population, wherever they lived. "Let the Jews as a distinct sect disappear" was the most painful of the statements attributed to the Baron by the *Herald's* reporter. It was all just "another *Herald* hoax," cried London's *Jewish World* in an article reprinted by the *Exponent*. The latter also inveighed against enterprising but sensation-seeking reporters, warning the community to beware of newspapers which failed to meet adequate journalistic standards. But in Vineland this advice was ignored. There, the *Journal* preferred the *Herald's* version and gave notice that "the greatest Jewish banker and philanthropist believed the true future for the Hebrew race will be found in assimilation with Christian races and religion." This stirred "all the prominent Hebrews," who almost to a man opposed such "revolutionary views," reported the *Journal* with seeming satisfaction.[7]

Exaggerated and out-of-context statements based on the de Hirsch interview soon had to be denied by the Baron's aides via messages from Isidore Loeb, secretary of the Alliance Israélite in Paris, to Rabbis H. Pereira Mendes in New York and Sabato Morais in Philadelphia. The Baron had no intention of presiding over the dissolution of the Jewish people. It was for humanitarian reasons only that he wished to see his brethren in East Europe "assimilate" like their Western counterparts the social customs, speech, and occupational patterns of the rest of the population.

In effect, the Baron's views represented the kind of "positive assimilation" taken as the watchword by westernized Jewry seeking to earn equal treatment from their fellow citizens in Europe and America. Only by adopting the ways of the world around them could the Jews aspire to the tangible emancipation which they so earnestly desired. Moreover, unlike many (probably most) of the East European Jewry, the Baron shared neither the faith in a personal Messiah nor the dream of a national restoration of the ancient homeland. Salvation would be by secular means only, and its ends were western, pragmatic, and conventional.[8]

104

Controversy over the de Hirsch interview was only symptomatic of a more serious rift between Western and Eastern Jewry, and between benefactors and aliens in the New World. In addition to the *New York Herald's* reporters, others were either confused or hostile to the results of the melting pot process. One writer for the *American Israelite* worried lest the exotic-looking newcomers become "an element of Jewish tramps and paupers, producing criminals, who disgrace the name of Israelite through the land." And in the face of growing anti-immigration sentiment B'nai B'rith leader Simon Wolf needed to assure a Congressional committee in 1901 that American Jews had "never stimulated, encouraged, desired, or wished this wholesale influx of their coreligionists. . . . [having] naturally preferred that they should remain in the countries in which they had been born."[9] Pogroms in Russia and elsewhere, however, offered no other option.

Simon Wolf, as other communal leaders, took pains to deny that Jewish organizations aided the entry of cheap labor to compete with native workers. Moreover, Wolf's efforts in opposing new immigration restrictions were more docile—"reminiscent of the operations of the court Jew," according to one writer—than Max Kohler's or Jacob Schiff's interventions on behalf of the East Europeans.[10] Yet, as trustees of the Baron de Hirsch Fund, which itself subsidized immigrant colonies, men like Schiff and Kohler were perforce sensitive to charges that the newcomers were economically, morally, or even physically unfit. Theirs they felt was a humanitarian program of training and resettlement, carried out as was stressed in their press releases, without recourse to the public purse. Providing the private subsidies, they could determine the conditions for Americanization, though in both city and rural colony it was a goal beset by contention and ambiguity. For example: "The ready assimilation of the children depended upon the rapid elimination of *chedorim* [religious schools] and the swift absorption of their pupils into the public schools of the city," even though these latter were overcrowded and otherwise far from ideal. As for the immigrant adults, Judge Isaacs saw an opportunity in offering them trade school education, so that they could, in his words, "abandon their daily vocations as *Melamdim* [religious teachers] or peddlers for the position of mechanic to which they aspire." The deed of trust of the Baron de Hirsch Fund specifically provided for training in the mechanical trades, agriculture, handicrafts, English, and "the duties and obligations of life and citizenship in the United States"; it contained no provision for Jewish religious or cultural education.[11] As early as 1893, the Fund's budget for schooling in English and in the trades totaled fifty-four thousand dollars.[12]

Such stress on assimilation and training reflected not only the divergence within the Jewish people, but also a response to external pressures; there had been repeated moves, some successful, to expel those Jewish refugees charged as paupers "unfit for work" or otherwise considered undesirable.[13] Among the early opponents of the East Europeans had been Jews as well as non-Jews, an opposition which grew ever more vociferous in the years between the founding of Alliance (1882) and Woodbine (1891). In describing the latter as a fresh haven for refugees from Russia, the *New York Sun* complained that "the exiled Jews come to us more empty-handed than the immigrants of any other nationality," a statement especially damaging as it appeared shortly after enactment of federal restrictions against assisted immigrants. Although they "confine their begging to their coreligionists, who are both able and willing to assume the care of them," the *Sun* continued, the dumping of these additional destitutes created intolerable social evils. "An English or a German Jew adapts himself to this country as readily as an Englishman or a German who is not a Jew. But the uneducated Russians . . . assimilate to us very slowly and imperfectly . . . Russian Jews are no more adaptable than other Russians," the *Sun* noted despairingly. Italians were at least more useful in the factories, even if they did bring "social or political evils." In the future, Baron de Hirsch's widespread colonization programs, especially in Argentina, should ease the burdens of "American Hebrews . . . in taking care of these wretched people," the *Sun* concluded hopefully.[14]

Indeed, from the early 1880's American philanthropic organizations were stretching their capacities to the breaking point, besides having to fear the effects on public opinion of a continued influx. Some felt that the refugees should be cared for in Europe by European philanthropies. In a cable to the Alliance in Paris, the short-lived Hebrew Emigrant Aid Society had warned: "We will not receive another refugee. Funds here are exhausted." Before the end of 1882, the Society advised the superintendent of New York's Castle Garden immigrant station that Jewish entrants would no longer receive their assistance.[15] At a conference of Jewish philanthropies in the same year, Simon Wolf, soon to become chairman of the Board of Delegates of the Union of American Hebrew Congregations, had also launched into the perennial theme of more aid by West European Jewry. "Jews in Russia," he exhorted, "were as capable of rising to the full stature of manhood as are the negroes of the South . . . the plan ought to be to first make men of them and then let them take care of themselves."[16] In short, more of the vital work of retraining and even absorption ought to take place within Europe's communities.

Criticism was directed especially against the Paris-based Alliance, which some regarded unfavorably as a foreign organization; its focus on disseminating the benefits of French civilization also irked such German-Jewish leaders as Jacob Schiff.[17] Even Judge Isaacs and Jesse Seligman, who as trustees of the Baron de Hirsch Fund had to work closely with the Paris office of the Jewish Colonization Association, warned the Alliance and its London committee to restrict the further influx of immigrants to the United States. Only those with training in the trades and some knowledge of English, only the young and strong workmen, especially those interested in farming, would still be considered acceptable. This, at least, was a more positive formula than the blanket conclusion by the United Jewish Charities of Rochester that "organized immigration from Russia, Roumania, and other semi-barbarous countries is a mistake and has proved a failure. It jeopardizes the well-being of the American Jews."[18]

Other voices, however, more dedicated and confident, were heard again in defense of the Russians. True, the task was overwhelming, the funds available a mere pittance, and the institutional framework grossly inadequate, but the responsibility could not be shirked. The new immigrant masses must be absorbed and made less glaring to the hostile eye. Appealing on behalf of the new immigrants, Benjamin F. Peixotto, leader in the YMHA movement and one-time consul in Roumania, insisted that "the Jews are not paupers, nor are they criminals, [but] come here as the Pilgrim Fathers came and as the Huguenot Fathers came, driven by bigotry."[19]

In New York also, Judge Isaacs continued to disclaim any intention of inviting "these people here," while maintaining that those who did manage to come could be made into good citizens. "They are generally industrious, moral and well behaved, and by no means paupers," he pleaded. At the same time, he tried to get the newcomers out of the cities as rapidly as possible, even if they could not be farmers: "testing their capacities for agricultural life is subordinate to the demonstration that they can live happily and prosperously outside of the tenement house sections of the city." Similarly, in Philadelphia, William Hackenburg reassured the public that the refugees would not require assistance from governmental funds. The *Press* of that city headlined his claims, "No paupers among 150,000. . . . The country need have no fears for the Hebrews."[20]

But actions spoke louder than words, as was demonstrated in the program of colonization set by the Baron de Hirsch Fund's trustees. The rural colonies, especially Woodbine, became showcases of applied Americanization. On behalf of the Fund, General Agent Adolphus S. Solomons boasted to the *New York Herald* that "our primary objective is the Americanization of our immigrants: to mix with the masses," to learn English and the ways of the country, including the respectable occupation of farming. "They can't all be pedders and merchants," he concluded. In a similar interview with the *Times,* Solomons was quoted as wishing not only to Americanize the immigrants, but also to "assimilate them with the masses and thoroughly imbue them with the American constitution and American institutions." Furthermore, in the colonies "none of the Nihilists, Socialists, or anarchist elements will be tolerated."[21] Such objectives were widely applauded, as the public relations campaign began to bear fruit. In the *New York Herald* Christians were called on to join the burdened Hebrew community "in transporting Russian refugees from our city to places where they are desired, and can become self-supporting."[22]

The waves of immigrants seemed endless. Indeed, for the hard-pressed Jewish leadership in the West, the expanded migration of the 1890's brought ever greater challenges. Diplomatic pressures and worldwide humanitarian protests failed to stay Tsarist oppression, and the magnitude of the flight made it difficult to control dispersion or even to classify immigrants en route. Jacob Schiff and other Americans continually strove to divert some of them from New York with the willy-nilly cooperation of the Alliance. In hopes of a more orderly distribution, Baron de Hirsch had provided assistance for the settlements in Argentina as well as the United States, but most yearned for the latter: the forty-two thousand immigrants in 1891 almost doubled to seventy-six thousand in 1892; this compared to six thousand for Argentina in both years.[23] The total for the 1890's was to be three hundred thousand, up one-third over the 1880's.

It seemed impossible "to control the stream of immigration forced by Russian despotism so as to do least damage to all classes of our own population," lamented Chicago's Jewish *Reform Advocate*.[24] Secretary of State James G. Blaine expressed the misgivings of some influential Americans who remained hard to convince that philanthropic resources would be adequate for the new "great influx of Russian Jews to become speedily assimilated into the body politic . . . an orderly, thrifty and law-abiding element." President Benjamin Harrison himself offered fresh doubts about "the sudden transfer of such a multitude" even if he did take comfort in the assertions that "the Hebrew is never a beggar, . . . that no race, sect or class has more fully cared for its own than the Hebrew race."[25]

Could a Schiff or Sulzberger prove untrue to this tradition? If more Easterners insisted on immigrating, they would be cared for in a rational, dignified fashion, and for the good of all. As rapidly as possible, they and their families would be Americanized and their children assimilated into the public schools and other institutions. Through training in Woodbine and the various other programs planned by the trustees of the Baron de Hirsch Fund, "a patriotic spirit would be inculcated which leads them to love the Republic and to honor the flag."[26] It was a glorious not to mention urgent undertaking, and scarcely anyone in power, Hebrew or not, thought of consulting the Russian Jews on either objectives or means.

Colonizing: Aliens vs. Benefactors

The Eastern Jews, if they had read carefully in their own Hebrew or Yiddish press, might have been forewarned. Not that events in the New World overshadowed developments on the Continent or within the rich vortex of Jewish life. But Hebrew-language periodicals such as *Hamelitz* of St. Petersburg and *Hatzfirah* of Warsaw published frequent eyewitness reports from America. They were usually, of course, colored by East European views, including concern for the viability of orthodox Judaism in the far-away land, as well as a certain antipathy to the German Reform Jews who dominated the overseas communities. America proper was depicted glowingly as a land of economic oportunity and of liberty. Far from being anti-Semitic, the American people seemed friendly and their leaders, like Secretary of State Blaine, apparently deplored the persecution in Russia.[27]

But both economic opportunity and freedom were often dearly paid for. The papers reported that some found the work too "oppressive" and that, at other times (the depression in 1884), unemployment threatened starvation. Women in the agricultural colonies were required to labor arduously in the fields. On one occasion, when they demanded to be returned to an easier life in Russia, they were confronted with a court opinion that this work was quite reasonable for "such strong and healthy women." The difficulties in the older agrarian colonies near Vineland were duly noted, although it was conceded that "in general most of the colonists are happy and they do not intend to return [to Russia]." The failure of other settlements was laid at the doorstep of prosperous German Jews who had sent the immigrants off to "deserts from whence they return in despair to the cities." There was also a lack of planning and only intermittent financial support, just to get the newcomers out of sight as rapidly as possible; it seemed that "mercifulness was turned into cruelty."[28]

Even more alarming to the East European journals was the emphasis on assimilation by both rural and city programs of the philanthropic organizations. The Alliance had been warned to notify all refugees "that a rigid adherence to the rites of Judaism will in many cases be entirely impossible." Such a warning also came from M. A. Kursheedt, secretary of the Russian Emigrant Relief Fund and scion of a prominent New York family of both German and Sephardic origin as well as a member of the education committee of the Baron de Hirsch Fund. Kursheedt echoed the complaint that too many refugees "are clerks or tradesmen" or "theological students merely." Invidiously, he pointed to "the emigrants of other faiths . . . [who were] skilled mechanics . . . or able bodied laborers . . . willing to live on almost any kind of food."[29] True, this was a land of labor and freedom, but both, claimed *Hamelitz,* threatened to sever the traditional bonds of religion.[30]

"Toil of flesh and weariness of soul" continually characterized the life of the immigrants, according to *Hamelitz.* Their traditional Sabbath conflicted with the American Sunday, and there was little other leisure in the week for peddler, farmer, or factory worker. Frequently, the children also worked, which exposed them to undesirable influences and left little time for study. Most vitriolic, however, was the criticism of Reform's religious shortcomings— departure from Torah law, synagogues empty except for the High Holidays, gentile choir members, and a symptomatic neglect of Hebrew. In one half-hearted defense, a correspondent from Trenton countered that Eastern Jews were free to desist from profaning the Sabbath, if they so desired, for this is not "a land which devours the faith of its inhabitants," he protested, "[not] a land which collects all those who forget God and abandon religion."[31]

The more rapid pace of American life tended to deepen the cultural gap between German and Russian Jews, often to the point of outright hostility. Some of the Russian intelligentsia, such as

Dr. George M. Price, suspected the motives of a few German Jewish leaders, feeling that "in America, more than any other country, a clever politician uses his philanthropy to his own advantage."[32] Partly because of mistakes made in the selection and support of the first agrarian colonies, close to eight thousand had to be returned to Europe by the United Hebrew Charities between 1882 and 1889, most on cattle steamers (a trip comparable to Hades, according to Price).[33] As the continuing crisis forced the American Jew to consider emergency solutions, he suddenly regained awareness of the "peculiar position which the Jew has occupied in history," and then became "afraid that the mass influx will delay the process of assimilation—the process of Americanization of the Jews of the United States."[34]

Price claimed a high regard for the American trustees of the Baron de Hirsch Fund—"the lawyer Isaacs; the millionaire banker Seligman; the millionaire philanthropist Schiff; the lawyer Goldman; and the industrialist Hoffman." He doubted, however, that they either knew or understood the individual Russian immigrant, or had enough time for him in their own busy careers. In philanthropy, moreover, he feared that the executive staff might be hired on the basis of social standing or forensic ability, rather than administrative expertise or intimate knowledge of a particular field. Such was the case, said Price, with the Fund's first executive secretary (1890–1903), Adolphus S. Solomons, "a gentleman without a definite calling, a former Congressman, a statistical expert, President of the American Branch of the *Alliance Israélite Universelle,* President of a Masonic Lodge . . . [but un]familiar with the needs of the immigrants. He neither understands Yiddish nor German. He very seldom sees the Russian Jews." Other candidates, such as Arthur Reichow or Herman Rosenthal, though closer to the immigrants, had not been as presentable to the elite.[35]

While disavowing personal bias, Price voiced an eloquent plea on behalf of the immigrant, "the lamb" whose succor hinged on protracted deliberations in which he had no part. "Can we ever dare to assume that . . . these luminaries of jurisprudence, these kings of finance . . . would need the advice of tattered and poor immigrants, shoemakers, tailors, factory workers?" As for the immigrant intelligentsia, it was not considered "politically dependable," even though a few were consulted on a pro forma basis. Why should the trustees "ask these agitators advice as to how to dispose of the millions of Baron de Hirsch?" Price queried sarcastically.[36]

Ultimately, the Fund did accept in large measure the new proposals for industrial-agricultural colonies presented by Price and other Russians, some with experience in the agricultural settlements of the early 1880's. Among them was Herman Rosenthal, who had led the abortive colony at Sicily Island in Catahoula Parish, Louisiana. Rosenthal, who had advocated colonization even before leaving Russia, remembered how his party of thirty families were hurt by the poor planning and unfulfilled pledges of the New York philanthropists. "A viler spot on God's Earth it would be hard to find . . . nothing thereunto pertaining save some poisonous serpents . . . and there our unfortunate, much tired co-religionists were to learn a love for agriculture," he wrote.[37] Almost ten years later (1891) Rosenthal was asked by the Fund to join their Russian-Jewish agronomist, H. L. Sabsovich, on the exploratory mission which led to the founding of Woodbine. Sabsovich remained as superintendent of the colony, to work with the newly formed Woodbine Land & Improvement Company.

This did not mean, however, that the trustees were willing to yield substantial power to the Russians in the founding or operation of Woodbine. All of the Company's directors were also trustees of the Fund, which, in turn, owned the capital stock; Julius Goldman was appointed president of the board. And even the trustees themselves were not of one mind concerning policy for employees and colonists. Schiff had to be persuaded to abandon his early idea of a simple lump sum grant of a thousand dollars to each of fifty or more families who would find themselves homesteads. Such direct philanthropy was opposed by Judge Isaacs who first favored planned settlement in "convenient suburban localities where industries exist or will be established," as well as one rural colony (Woodbine) for experiments in education, agriculture, and the trades.[38]

Suburban locations, however, were rejected by the majority of the trustees, apparently because of the feared weakening of agrarian ideals due to the settlers' commuting to the city, and the high land costs around New York, Philadelphia, Trenton, and Newark. Thus, negotiations for a large tract at Harrison, a few miles outside Newark and sufficient for two or three hundred homes, broke down at an early stage. Instead of suburbs, the Russians were consigned to the isolated five thousand-acre tract in South Jersey, where land cost only six dollars an acre. The proprietor, Judge Moore, owned Clayton Glassworks and was also a director of the West New Jersey Railroad which cut through the estate. He was interested in selling; the few people in the Cape May County area seemed kindly disposed to Russian Jews; and there were thus high hopes that the new community (1891) could become eventually "a second Vineland." Sabsovich reported favorably on soil and elevation, and Solomons, always conscious of public relations, assured the *Times* that good homes were to be built in Woodbine, architecturally "diversified, so as to please the finer senses and the better tastes of the more cultivated immigrants." The trustees did not want to give "the appearance of a charitable settlement."[39] Leach Brothers, the same firm which constructed homes in Alliance, was also the initial contractor for fifty cottages at about $500 apiece, plus a factory to provide 250 jobs.[40]

Indeed, no pauper could afford the $200 down-payment requested by the trustees. Although exceptions were made for many of the most promising settlers, the first sixty Woodbine families contributed an initial total of $3,365 towards their land and homes. Further, in their first three months of work, they chopped down cord-wood valued by Julius Goldman at $4,620.49. It was Company wood, with proceeds to go to the Company; the labor was paid the prevailing wage, a basic $7 for clearing one acre.[41] The high-pressure development work included not only homesites, but also an 800-acre town site and roads named after American presidents except for de Hirsch Avenue. As head of the Company, Goldman hoped to develop "industries that are more manly and more promising for the future than that of needlework, to which unfortunately too many of the Russian refugees have been forced to devote themselves." Here also town lots were sold at prices which "should in a few years reimburse the Trustees of the Baron de Hirsch Fund for the greater part of the money advanced to the colonists and when the colonists pay off the principal of their own indebtedness such payment should constitute a profit with which new colonies can be founded."[42] It was a comforting capitalist's dream.

For the settlers, mortgages that averaged eleven hundred dollars were a harsh reality. So was the lack of adequate housing, the back-breaking work, and the dependence on their children's wages. Before the end of the second year, subsidies virtually ceased, despite pleas by Sabsovich and Goldman for a hundred dollars more to each family for spring planting and improvements; the Fund refused on the grounds that the capital set aside for initial costs was almost exhausted and the colonists should now be self-supporting. Part of the trouble was due to overdevelopment, in the form of Company-owned factory buildings, a hotel, a modern plant for electric light and power, wide avenues, and "a Russian bath for public use . . . a wise innovation." Though such achievements dazzled visiting dignitaries, including Francis B. Lee, who reported all this to the New Jersey Board of Agriculture,[43] much of the farm land remained uncleared. One reporter denied it was merely virgin soil, "It is severely virgin. Spinster soil . . . scrub oak and pine land . . . confirmed in the old maid habits." Forty dollars for a cow and twelve-fifty for chickens, plus implements and seed supplied in the first year, could not make up for this soil.[44]

More was amiss, however, than the economics of mortgages and the rigors of nature. A series of persistent misunderstandings between refugees and benefactors contributed to the revolt of 1893 in which most of the families refused to abide by their obligations. Undoubtedly, the colonists were too soon left to manage for themselves. In May 1892, Sabsovich complained to Dr. Paul Kaplan, an old Am Olam friend in New York, of low morale resulting from the Fund's suspension of wages for such projects as clearing Company land. Many immigrants had sent cash to their families in

Russia, some for tickets to America. Now they had no money for seed or other necessities and the Fund refused emergency allowances; even the usually sympathetic Sabsovich seemed to accept calmly this "circumstance which had shown to the people that they have to depend upon themselves." Borrowing the business-oriented attitudes of his employers, he was willing to "let those who cannot exist now in Woodbine leave the place; let the fittest survive. . . . Alliance became a success after it was left to itself," he noted in a sanguine mood.[45]

The analogy was not entirely appropriate. In Alliance, mortgage obligations had been scaled down to $350 per family, but for many, starvation was fended off only by sewing and cigar-making. Their recurrent appeals for assistance were, at times, rejected outright. Thus, in response to a group petition, an ex-president of the Hebrew Emigrant Aid Society warned angrily, "None of you yet have ever paid anything, either interest or taxes on the land, and if you choose to leave it, you are welcome to do so . . . but it must be at your own expense."[46] Results of this policy were hardly encouraging, but similarly stern measures would also be tried in Woodbine.

While the trustees insisted on business standards and individual responsibility, the colonists were deluded by their excessive estimates of philanthropy's capacity. Baron de Hirsch's endowment was available only in the form of interest on the capital, not to be disbursed in toto; yet, some of the immigrant farmers labored under the impression that their land was an outright gift, with further allowances forthcoming as needed. Woodbine's population, mainly from South Russia, was selected by the Fund's representatives on the basis of putative experience on the land rather than educational or ideological background, but life in rural Russia was far from adequate experience for successful farming in America; and the East European penchant for heroic images caused many a colonist to build his castles in the clouds.

Among them, too, were a dozen families who had failed in the Argentine settlements, ostensibly because of religious intolerance. According to Sabsovich, they had become demoralized by charitable care all along the line, expecting it to continue and encouraging others to demand it.[47] Moreover, the trustees in New York remained torn between a paternalism thought necessary to achieve rapid development, and an American-style individualism. Ideally, "our interference should be as limited as possible and paternal government should not be encouraged," Isaacs counseled Schiff; nevertheless, the trustees remained wary of colonists organizing to run their own affairs. They made no move, for example, to recognize the Jewish Association of Russian Farm Workers in New York (*"Agudoth Ovde Ansche Russia"*). This ephemeral organization presented a petition in 1890 signed in both English and Yiddish by a hundred "family men," all claiming previous agricultural experience and requesting aid from the Fund to purchase suitable farm lots.[48]

The Woodbine Revolution and Its Consequences

Lack of recognized leadership in Woodbine, as well as cultural differences, made negotiation with the Fund's representatives difficult. Widespread grumbling developed into work stoppages, demonstrations, and refusals to respect even the superintendent's directions. Sabsovich, though a Russian, was Swiss-educated, thoroughly Western, and soon tagged with the taint of management. Vainly, the trustees tried to bolster his position by expressing their "perfect confidence" in him and warning those who disobeyed his "lawful directions" or engaged in "disorderly practices" or threats against company property. In a show of strength, the trustees posted public notices ruling out any "modification of the existing contracts": those dissatisfied could leave, taking with them whatever money they had paid down or earned; "agitators" and those engaged in "disorderly proceedings" could not expect company wages or allowances; and everyone could "rely with perfect faith upon the determination of the Trustees to carry out their contract . . . and to have it carried out by the farmers"; violators would be punished in the law courts. A final appeal included some familiar, if self-consciously loaded, slogans: "Be men. Be true to yourselves, to your brethren who have sought asylum in this great country, and whose cause you are damaging by your conduct. With perseverance and a little patience, you may live here freely under 'your own vine and fig tree,' but you should 'seek the peace of the people among whom you dwell. Be far removed from evil counselors.' Be men!"[49]

This mingling of paternal admonition and legalistic coercion fell on deaf ears. In 1893, settlers held more protest meetings and set fires in the surrounding woods. Sabsovich notified the trustees that he was forced to call on the Dennisville marshal for protection; private guards hired to patrol Woodbine were apparently unable to maintain order. On the other hand, farmers addressed their own telegrams of protest and warning. To trustee Jesse Seligman: "Sabsovich is provoking the farmers. If any trouble should happen it will be his fault." To agent Reichow: "Please call at once, if not—misfortune will happen." To A. S. Solomons and the company's consultant, Col. John Weber: "Sabsovich keeps Pinkertons who keep shooting every night. Yesterday, they nearly killed one of us. Come at once; if not, there will be murder." All were signed simply, "Woodbine Farmers."[50]

Sabsovich bore the brunt of the unrest, primarily because he chose to enforce the authority and wishes of the trustees. This written proposals, translated into Yiddish, affirmed the concept of loans and mortgages rather than outright gifts, and stirred indignant protests that "the bankers are bandits. They want to get rich on our sweat and tears." At meetings, men reasoned that if they had to "pay for land which produces nothing they would rather buy old farms with cleared soil instead of woods." Women stormed: "The bankers promise us cows, and there isn't even a goat to give milk for our babies. We demand cows!" As one of the pioneers recalled it many years later, the women could not be stilled. "'A resolution!' someone yelled. 'No, no, cows! cows!' the women demanded."[51]

No crops were planted that spring of 1893, and most other work was virtually halted for the year. To Sabsovich, the farmers' protest telegrams seemed "of a criminal character." Their actions, he feared, would put "the whole crowd of the Russian Jews of

Woodbine in a very bad light," as well as hurt the image of all immigrants from Russia. About a dozen "ruffians" were using terror tactics to keep people from working, he reported, so that additional hands had to be hired from Dennisville. The trustees, however, must not recognize any bargaining committee, but deal from strength with separate individuals; to do otherwise would enable "these dozen ruffians to get a lasting control over the crowd" which was already under the impression that the "agitators" had won a concession on the basic fifty dollar annual rental fee. In their hopes for the administration's *mapole* ("fall"), Sabsovich complained sadly to Goldman, they seemed "either children or fools or both together." Unless the situation improved, he saw the possibility of the Fund's having to "cut the knot of Gordius even by letting bleed strongly."[52]

It was a bitter admission for the dedicated Sabsovich. Only recently, he had declined an invitation to join the staff of Lincoln Agricultural College in Nebraska.[53] In the face of mounting crises, he grew more despondent: even those colonists who respected him refused under various "pretexts" (low wages, too burdensome, etc.) to accept assigned work. Others issued threats which worried Mrs. Sabsovich, but he refused to resign under the pressure—"even if my life would be in real danger." He was tired of playing a Don Quixote and feared the strain would bring him heart disease. To Reichow, he complained of a "very cool breeze" coming from the trustees in New York, and cited the lack of adequate funds for development and current expenses. Their vacillating policy of "kindness and quasi-firmness" would not safeguard the *"business principles"* (his italics) which they had all so frequently affirmed.[54]

A sense of alienation and betrayal seemed inherent in the settlers' periodic strikes, as well as in the "impudence" and "roughness," and their demands for Sabsovich's removal—"we prefer to starve rather than receive work at the hands of Mr. Sabsovich." They saw themselves destined to toil under the supervision of strangers or their agents, on land which might never be their own. For example, of the "punctual Prussian . . . the perfectionist [Frederick] Schmidt," who supervised the work of clearing, one pioneer wrote, "I hated to face Schmidt, who was contemptuous of us as workers. . . . In my heart I condemned . . . 'the Prussian'."[55] But this same overseer was just "Fred Schmidt, a fine-looking German Hebrew" to the New York *World*, as it described his efforts to supervise farming operations.[56]

When the surrounding community became agitated over the demonstrations at Woodbine, the trustees were upset, for they had always been concerned about relations with the neighboring population, especially in Dennisville. At first, "the natives looked down upon them [the colonists] with feelings of distrust," according to the New York *World*, "but time has worked a change. They are honest, industrious, persevering." Julius Goldman took pride publicly in "the astonishment and admiration of American farmers" when they perceived the "energy, determination and willingness on the part of the Russians to perform the hardest kind of work."[57] Such comforting views prevailed in spite of some local hard-core bias evident at the outset. For example, the Dennisville barber refused to cut the hair of one young colonist who came to him, fearing the loss of his regular customers if he served Jews. Sabsovich and the colonists were indignant at the affront, and a threatened boycott of the town's shops brought on a crisis. But before the boycott could be initiated Dennisville community leaders apologized. Anyway, the colonists' pride was "so deeply hurt" that they refused to patronize the controversial shop, and their own Mr. Shapiro, who had tonsorial experience in Russia, opened Woodbine's first barber shop.[58]

The "revolution" of 1893 was, however, a more serious matter, giving some hostile neighbors an opportunity to agitate against the hotbed of foreigners in their quiet corner of South Jersey. In retaliation, the colonists again threatened a boycott of local merchants. As before, however, Sabsovich's diplomacy helped smooth over the inter-community crisis: After all, the two societies did have mutually beneficial economic ties.[59]

In the long run, the greatest damage was the breach between the colonists and their benefactors; its extent was partly indicated by their mutual inability to speak the same language, figuratively

120

and literally. Sabsovich finally learned Yiddish many years after the crisis, when he traveled as a lecturer among independent Jewish farmers in New England. Nor could Julius Goldman speak to the colonists in their own tongue when he arrived on an emergency investigating mission; instead, he handed down the trustees' ultimatum in German, inviting his audience to stop him whenever they couldn't understand.[60]

Ultimately, the authority of distinguished outsiders became necessary. To Colonel John B. Weber, former immigration commissioner of the Port of New York, the Fund entrusted a major role in pacifying the colonists. He supplied the "needed power of a man admittedly their friend and yet a personality, a stranger, who by tact secured peace . . . [while] maintaining the authority of the Trustees." His mediation services cost $5700 in 1893 alone, almost enough to satisfy some of the colonists' major demands![61] Weber's reports cited Sabsovich's leadership as "judicious" and "self-sacrificing," even though Sabsovich seemed to resent his intervention. After calling in fifty-five farmers for individual interviews, Weber noted that most wished to work on the land, but required some supplemental employment; this need became especially serious when the factory was closed during the depression of 1893 (some told Weber they had no money for *matzos* for Passover). He finally advised that the trustees remain firmly in their original position: the idea of "partnership in the administration of the Fund between the Committee [Trustees] and the colonists must be expelled from their minds, and there must be absolute control by the Committee of its affairs"; and furthermore, he told them, "an example must be made of your authority and your control" for the sake of future immigrants as well as maintaining present discipline. Goldman too visited Woodbine again to warn the colonists that "management by the Company must be absolute, and conducted upon business principles." Negligence in work, unreasonable demands, and a suspicious attitude toward either the trustees or their staff would not be tolerated.

These confrontations between the Fund's representatives and the colonists had, almost inevitably, some dramatic consequences.

121

To "set an example" the County Court would be petitioned to expel about a dozen families who were "clearly the mischief-making element in the community." At the same time, an olive branch was extended to the general population, blaming their "demoralized and despondent condition" on the "shrewd cunning of their malcontent" leaders. The remaining families were promised more liberal treatment: fifteen-year mortgage extensions at 4 percent interest; substantial reduction in the basic price of their homes (eventually averaging under $400); postponement of interest payments until October 1894; and repairs at Company expense.[62]

Threats and concessions, however, had failed to clear the air; repercussions of the conflict between colonists and philanthropists were felt far beyond South Jersey. New York's civic reform leader Charles B. Stover, and others—social workers, lawyers, journalists, and champions of the immigrants—continued to plead the settlers' cause. Some Philadelphians even interceded on their behalf with Baron de Hirsch himself, who expressed nevertheless his confidence in the American trustees. The *New York Press* asked that justice (which was on the trustees' side) be tempered with mercy, warning that the colony's failure "would only add another agony to the perplexing problems of immigration."[63]

Justice finally came swift and cold in the courthouse of Cape May, the County seat. Attorneys for the Woodbine Land and Improvement Company stressed the need to maintain sound principles of management so that funds would be available to settle more immigrants on the land. The Company sought to instill the ways of dignified, self-supporting citizens, for "years of persecution in the countries of Eastern Europe had made *shnorrers* ['beggars'] of potentially fine human beings." The accused farmers bristled at the epithet, and the judge agreed to delete the word, though he objected to their characterizing the prosecuting lawyers as "lackeys of mighty bankers." He refused the farmers' claims that "there was never a clear indication we were to pay anything before the farms had yielded some income," and that hard times forced even native Americans whose farms were planted to abandon their holdings. In Woodbine, said the colonists, the stump-covered acres reminded one "more of crosses in a poor man's cemetery than fields for human habitation." The judge was unimpressed, concerned only with the letter of the law; "America was not built on charity," he admonished, and found no "valid excuse" for the farmers' refusal to pay all financial obligations.[64]

Eight who were considered most delinquent and intractable received eviction notices and were given ten days to move out. As an inducement to their peaceful departure, the trustees offered a refund of any monies paid by them, plus a hundred dollars on their return to New York. They also received a written scolding from the Company's officers, containing the usual reminder about everyone's duty to the "spirit of American institutions" and the need to preserve philanthropic resources for other newcomers. Their work stoppages and acts of terror had "brought upon the colony the contempt and distrust of the people of the vicinity and wrought irreparable injury to Russian Hebrews generally." The evicted rebel leaders, having been in the New World longer than most of their neighbors, should at least have recognized the significance of public opinion, so sensitive to any disturbance.[65]

In the long run, however, even the more moderate factions among the colonists, whom Sabsovich tried to encourage, were hard to reconcile. Despairing, Sabsovich complained that they seemed impressed only by "power and manifestations of power."[66] Then in the midst of the struggle, he suffered what appeared to be a nervous and physical breakdown, worsening in May, 1893, at the time of the group eviction. From his sickbed he advised Goldman to replace as many of the malcontents as possible with "new blood" who were more carefully selected; he instructed his assistant, Schmidt, to train the newcomers rigorously, without *rachmoones* ("compassion").[67]

Sabsovich's concern over the success of agriculture in Woodbine deepened after the revolt, but partly because of the prolonged conflict and unfavorable publicity, some farm lots remained vacant; turnover was high. He was forced to concentrate ever more on the industrial side of the colony's development. Ironically, although Sabsovich was to become one of the Socialist *Forward*'s favorite whipping boys, he had warned from the outset that "the greedy appetites of the employers" would be attracted by the prospect of cheap labor. The Fund's factories must not become an "infamous whip" in the hand of small capitalists seeking to depress the wages of urban workers by producing a big order locally and then returning to the city. Still the dilemma of unemployment remained, requiring desperate experiments. After all: "It does not pay for such an institution as the Fund to have a settlement with a periodically starving population." Jewish agriculturists could yet succeed somehow, he maintained, especially with incentive premiums to the proficient. Many Woodbine farmers "will not be ashamed before the American neighbors," he affirmed proudly. Still, Goldfarb needed $75 for a good horse and his neighbor needed. . . .[68]

Meanwhile the trustees' misgivings about the future of agricultural colonies were only increased by the revolution of 1893. Even before it, Judge Isaacs had warned against trying to make farmers of families whose "capacity and history are unknown." Noting the previous disappointments in group colonization, he preferred to assist individuals and cited the voluntary settlement of scores of farmers in New Jersey and Connecticut. *The New York Times* went further, viewing colonization as only a temporary stage of preparation for life in America, a useful opportunity at self-orientation; "Jews are not born into this world with the kind of brains that dig dirt for long," it concluded.[69]

In the wake of the revolution, Goldman's optimism too was shattered. He regretted that some of the more promising colonists had not been placed on abandoned or inexpensive New England farms. Moreover, he backed Colonel Weber's suggestion that the Fund concentrate henceforth on industrial expansion, rather than agricultural. With substantial insight, Weber had stressed the growing "tendency of the country to flock to the cities—all over Europe, as well as here"; only recent arrivals, as yet unspoiled by the attractions of city life, might make good farmers. More drastic still was Weber's counsel against concentrating the immigrants even in rural colonies; instead, "an American or outside element" ought to be added, especially to work in the factories, for such people would help to "Americanize the settlers already there."[70]

Thereafter, diversity of population and the new industry became not only attractive slogans for those who advocated assimilation, but also issues of more complex dimension. A number of trustees, and even Sabsovich, inclined towards the inclusion of some Christians among the inhabitants of Woodbine. This was a view maintained strongly by Arthur Reichow, Solomons's successor as chief agent and developer of ambitious if short-lived programs for industrial growth. More industry was vital, because Woodbine—unlike New York or Philadelphia—could not tolerate prolonged layoffs, for they brought not only suffering and bad publicity but recurring threats of an exodus to the cities as well.

Such unique restrictions as the closing of factories for the Saturday Sabbath, Reichow thought, could only hurt the colony's development: this practice "advocated by our present population practically excludes from our place non-Jewish elements and harms substantially the interests of our settlement." He suspected, moreover, that an advocacy of Saturday closing and work on Sunday (the six-day week being standard) was not always a consequence of religious beliefs, especially among the younger colonists. Instead, he speculated that it was caused by "a little selfishness on the part of our proteges" who were attempting thereby to exclude non-Jewish competition attracted by Woodbine's "superior educational facilities." In a community surrounded by native American settlers, employers and labor should have the option of working on Saturday. For lack of "mixed population," he warned emotionally, "we will witness the growth of an exclusive Jewish community, with all the repulsive ways and customs of a small Polish ghetto."[71] Sabsovich, on the other hand, respected the wishes of the settlers, though he did not himself follow any formal religion, and the colony's work whistles remained silent on Saturday.[72]

In the continued battle to cope with massive immigration, the apprehensions of men like Weber, Isaacs, and Reichow, coupled with Woodbine's perennial problems and conflicts, finally affirmed the doubts of the trustees regarding exclusively Jewish farm colonies, and by the turn of the century, they no longer considered large-scale group settlements on the land as either feasible or desirable. Support for Woodbine as an existing agricultural-industrial community continued for many years, but it remained "exceptional as a nursery and training school" to set an example for individual Jewish farmers throughout the mid-Atlantic and New England states. It was hoped that the colony's inhabitants would gradually show greater self-reliance, "rising superior to the servility in habit and thought created by the conditions of Russian life." Once sufficiently improved, they might be "entirely relieved from paternal government," alleviating in turn the trustees' own burden. In this modern age, the trustees assumed, it should not take forty years to lead their brethren out of the wilderness.[73]

People's University:
The Baron de Hirsch Agricultural School

In the wake of the revolution, Sabsovich envisioned Woodbine as a great "educational institution" sending out graduates to all parts of the country. Central to this idea was the People's University, to include technical training as well as advanced scientific and agricultural studies. He even hoped to interest the state government in contributing half the costs—for "New Jersey is very liberal in this direction"—and followed the Trenton newspapers avidly for any discussion of agricultural education. A school in Woodbine could include model farms to guide the adults as well as practical training for Jewish youth. It would be the first institution of this type in New Jersey. Here was a promising means of infusing fresh spirit into the colonizing experiment. Judge Isaacs, president of the Fund, welcomed this additional program, viewing it as a worthy new chapter in the epic of agrarianism and Americanization.[74]

When Sabsovich began his People's University, Woodbine possessed only two makeshift schools with an attendance of about one hundred children and a struggling night school for twenty-five or thirty adults. Before the end of 1893, the upper floor of a large barn was converted to a lecture hall. Mechanical shops were on the ground level, with farms number 59 and 60 reserved for technical demonstration purposes. At first, Sabsovich himself taught botany, chemistry, and physiology, with the applied subjects, poultry raising and dairying, given by Schmidt.

The first class of local students produced several accomplished alumni, most notably soil chemist Jacob Lipman, future dean of the State Agricultural College for a quarter-century. Another honors graduate of Woodbine and Rutgers was Jacob Kotinsky, who returned to teach in Woodbine, and later achieved eminence as an entomologist. Scientific achievement in the same field marked the career of yet another classmate, David Fink. Without Sabsovich's guidance these first sons of farming immigrants might never have fulfilled their potential.

The school's curriculum expanded to encompass such subjects as American history and mechanical drawing as well as horticulture and anatomy. By 1898 it offered a formal three-year course including advanced academic and practical instruction for about sixty students. Soon, enrollment increased again to over a hundred, including fifteen girls in the domestic arts program. A large brick school building, dormitories, assembly rooms, and study halls were constructed with substantial grants not only from the Fund, but also from the Jewish Colonization Association. The 270 acres of cultivated land, impressive stables and model dairy herds were managed by Joseph W. Pincus, another Woodbine alumnus who had continued his studies at Storrs (Connecticut) Agricultural College, his work receiving lengthy and enthusiastic praise in such farming journals as *Hoard's Dairyman*.[75]

The students, most aged thirteen to eighteen, were drawn from Woodbine and the colonies around Vineland as well as from other Jewish farm families, urban slum dwellers, and city orphanages. There were no tuition charges, and room and board were usually free or in return for chores. One alumnus, Dr. Arthur Goldhaft, noted veterinarian and founder of the Vineland Poultry Laboratories, recalled how he had wandered as a child in the "little ghetto streets" of Philadelphia when his parents were forced to leave

Alliance. Starting work at age nine as butcher's assistant, then becoming sweeper and paperboy, he was later advised by his godfather to enroll in the Woodbine school. Besides its useful instruction, "I think the first thing it did for me," wrote Goldhaft, "was to give me a feeling of self-respect, even that it was all right to be a Jew. . . . All around me, I felt the example of well-ordered lives, families living in ample houses, harmony . . . none of the constant strife and harassment that permeated the ghetto streets. Why, even Jews could live like decent Gentiles!"[76] After a well-rounded education including academic studies and farming, cultural pursuits, even sports and youthful pranks, Goldhaft could continue his professional preparation at the University of Pennsylvania.

Another fellow graduate was Samuel Goldberg, who emigrated from Russia to New York at the age of nine, with only his younger brother. Sam earned his own keep for years as a watchmaker's apprentice, while his brother lived with an uncle. Eventually, he saw an article on the Woodbine school in a Yiddish newspaper, and using his few dollars, made the trip to South Jersey. When his education at Woodbine was completed, he worked his way through Cornell Veterinary College and then went on to a successful career in animal pathology, joining the staff of Cornell University. At middle age, he resumed studies for a degree at New York's Bellevue Medical School, serving the urban community well as physician and hospital pathologist. As if to complete the circle in the next generation, Dr. Goldhaft's son married Dr. Goldberg's daughter and settled in Vineland.[77]

For the Jewish community of the 1890's, and well into the second decade of the twentieth century, the Woodbine school satisfied two significant concerns: it educated immigrant youth in the ways of their adopted country; and it created some sturdy Jewish farmers from among the East European masses. Thus, upon the dedication of a new classroom building in 1900, the *Jewish Exponent* conceded that although "agriculture among the Jews . . . has barely held its own, after years of hardship and the expenditure of treasures," the flourishing agricultural school "furnishes strong reason to believe that the movement has not been in vain, . . . that it will be of great benefit to the entire Jewish people, to whom this occupation brings new strength and moral force . . . especially to the large number of Jewish immigrants." In its optimism, the *Exponent* foresaw in the Woodbine School "an important factor in the development of the Jews of this country."[78]

At the same dedication, Philadelphia's Rabbi Bernard L. Levinthal preached this appropriate biblical exegesis: "Adam was placed in the garden of Eden not to trade or peddle therein, but to till it and to keep it, and the greatest of lawgivers, kings, and prophets in Israel came not from merchants, but from the rural population of the farmers." On this occasion, too, others recalled the first "poor and bare" shelters of the farmers in Alliance who had given "the initiative to Jewish farmers in this country." Thanks now to Woodbine and its school—which were "an honor to the State of New Jersey and a glory to Judaism," as Moses Klein put it—the land was converted from an "isolated tabernacle of *Baal Zebub* (god of mosquitoes)" to the service of *"Eloha Dagan* (god of agriculture)."[79]

The long-range educational programs, however, proved more challenging. Sabsovich experienced obstacles as well as achievement in staffing, curriculum, discipline, and public relations. Before much could be done, most of the youngsters had to be taught English, a task entrusted for a time to Solomon Jaffe of the University of Chicago. Students could then proceed to such academic subjects as botany and entomology, totalling twenty-four hours per week, along with the usual thirty-six hours of shop, greenhouse, nursery or open field work. Sabsovich took pride in the fact that much of the construction, plumbing, and steamheating work, especially on the smaller buildings, was done by the boys themselves, instructed by Simon Brailowsky, head of the mechanical department. Thus the curriculum stressed action and application as well as theory, and the school's many acres of orchards, truck vegetables, and field crops set a worthy example for professional agriculturists. Before the end of its first decade, Sabsovich could affirm proudly that the school was "the best and most lasting institution that we have yet introduced in Woodbine," adding hopefully,

"I do not doubt that many families will follow their boys and settle on farms." Its graduates brought agricultural know-how to Jewish and non-Jewish farmers throughout the land.[80]

Prizes for corn, poultry, flowers, garden vegetables, flower designs, etc., were soon won by the school at county and state fairs. Most glorious, however, was its showing at the Paris Exposition of 1900, when Americans sought to bring before the world the best of their economic and cultural achievements. The Baron de Hirsch Agricultural School won the silver medal for its pomological exhibit and, more significantly, the Grand Prix for secondary education. It "stands now as the leading institution of secondary education in the United States," boasted one of its promotional reports.[81] At the St. Louis Exposition of 1904 Woodbine won a gold medal for its botanical and entomological collections with photographs depicting the work of its agricultural students. This exhibit was later displayed at the Harvard Museum, the Capitol in Trenton, and last but by no means least, the Educational Alliance in New York.[82]

Individual staff members also made their influence felt outside Woodbine. Frederick Schmidt earned the gratitude of the state's entomologists and fruit growers, especially in nearby Swainton, by identifying a tree infestation, "the much dreaded San José scale," and following up with pertinent lectures to farm groups. The Cape May County *Gazette* periodically ran a column on agriculture written exclusively by the school's staff. Sabsovich became secretary of the County Agricultural Society from its founding in 1894 and was succeeded in 1899 by Joseph Pincus. Both lectured widely on scientific farming and dairying. But it was an alumnus, Kotinsky, who probably initiated the first lectures "in jargon" on such exotic topics as the "spraying of plants against injurious insects and fungi."[83] Jewish farmers in Alliance and Carmel as well as Woodbine would gather often on a Sabbath afternoon to listen to instruction in practical and theoretical subjects.

Graduates as well as their teachers thus contributed their knowledge to the community. It was no coincidence that the Allivine Company of Norma and Alliance sought out its farm manager in Woodbine. Raymond Lipman, alumnus of the school and instructor in truck farming, was one of a family of eight from Libau (in Russian Latvia), who had found country life preferable to New York's tenements. Still another alumnus was elected editor of the *Jewish Farmer,* the monthly journal in the language of the immigrant.

Not all the staff were immigrants or Jewish. One popular instructor was Thomas E. Gravatt, in charge of general academic courses. When he eventually accepted another position, his place was taken by the principal of a nearby public school, George A. Blake. In honor of the occasion, both men were feted at an informal yet festive school assembly. The day happened also to be the first anniversary of Admiral Dewey's naval victory, which was celebrated by songs, speeches, ice cream and cake. "Professor" Manahan led the school's brass band in tunes as spirited as on any July Fourth.

A relatively free communication between Jew and Christian seemed to increase in the positive environment of the school. It served as a meeting place for the County Agricultural Society and for teachers and children from the area public schools, especially for week-end conferences or performances. Here professional talent as well as fine physical facilities combined. Thanks to the school's influence, noted the *Exponent,* Woodbine's farms "have been looking more favorable in comparison with our neighbors"; and, with an eye to public image, it added, "credit is given to our farmers by the unprejudiced." Also the *Vineland Evening Journal* gave favorable reports of such items as, "The Hebrews of the Woodbine Agricultural College have planted seven hundred fruit trees this fall." And the *Trenton Gazette* concluded in 1904 that the "graduates of the Baron de Hirsch School have taught South Jersey a lesson . . . of adaptability to environment . . . a determination to make the best of conditions . . . the strength of overcoming racial prejudice." Where natives had failed to bring about development, "it was left to an alien people to perfect the growth in the wilderness." Both communities could work harmoniously toward a better future for Woodbine and Cape May County, for in "the principle of give and take is [found] the true method of assimilation."[84]

To Jewish boys from Russia or from the city, the school continued to offer Americanization as the goal of hard work and fun. Wearing "uniforms and capes like West Pointers," they marched, played in the band, and made a good showing in baseball contests with teams from public schools or factories. On the other hand, the religious tradition, while not emphasized, could not be ignored. The school's early promotional leaflets called attention to daily prayers in the main assembly room, as well as to religious instruction every Sabbath morning. Students performed no work on Saturday, when except for minor chores, school was out. The ever-popular Hanukkah assemblies included the traditional lighting of candles and gay sketches were performed. Celebrations of Jewish holidays, so often replete with agrarian idealism, followed forms practiced over centuries. Now safely on their own land, they could find personal relevance in Shabuot, the festival of the first fruits, and Sukkot, the harvest festival of thanksgiving. The *Jewish Exponent* remarked on the school's "adherence to strictly orthodox rites in observing the Passover holidays." At this spring holiday of freedom, the festive *Seder* embraced a kind of cultural division of labor. The Hebrew part was led by the house manager of the dormitory, and the historical, moral, and religious lessons of the holiday were explained by Sabsovich, "making an eloquent speech in English." One of the old Woodbine farmers then addressed the celebrants in Yiddish.[85]

In 1904, a compelling religious challenge was presented to the graduates in a commencement address by Solomon Schechter. Only two years before, he had come from England to assume the presidency of the Jewish Theological Seminary of America. An eminent religious scholar and author of *Studies in Judaism,* he was of East European birth like most Woodbine graduates. He reminded them of their people's ancient agricultural heritage and their prophets' concern over the temptations of large cities. He knew of the colony's and the school's achievements; they and others like them proved that Jews could be farmers. But more importantly, he asked, "Will the farmer succeed as a Jew?" Will the graduates, wherever they go, continue the Jewish tradition, devotion to Torah, Sabbath,

132

and synagogue? It was a formidable challenge, but one they could not decline.[86]

During the school year there were other attempts, not specifically religious, to deal with the challenge to Jewish consciousness. Sabbath eve programs sometimes included the reading of student essays and discussions of anti-Semitism or speakers such as A. Benjamin of New York, "who for the last 25 years has been fighting the Jewish-Christian missions." Most assemblies, however, concerned topics of general interest, including musical entertainment, literary recitals, or comedies. Two of the school's performers, borrowed from the factory, later starred on Broadway with Weber and Fields.[87]

Although laymen could provide elementary religious instruction, there was no rabbi in Woodbine, nor for that matter in any of the other farm colonies. Not until 1911 did the Fund see fit to allocate a thousand dollars, with board, for a rabbi to conduct religious services, to teach Hebrew and Jewish history, and to "exercise a good moral influence over the students" as well as the local youth of farm and factory. The advertisement in the *Jewish Exponent,* signed by the head of the Baron de Hirsch Agricultural School, read, "Wanted: Rabbi to fill position as chaplain and religious instructor; one who delivers his sermons in English." Apparently, the post remained unfilled for some time. Meanwhile the independent Woodbine Hebrew School foundered in the wake of recurring depressions and strikes; the Fund's small annual contributions were soon discontinued. One noted visitor, Claude G. Montefiore, an Anglo-Jewish philanthropist and educational authority, wondered at the limited religious program, especially the absence of a rabbi and the voluntary attendance at school services.[88] Some improvement did occur, rather belatedly, after the arrival in 1913 of young Rabbi Louis J. Haas, freshly graduated from the Jewish Theological Seminary, who, as religious and social director for the school to 1916, organized the first Sunday School and a Young Judaea group.

Thus, in the long run, Woodbine's Agricultural School only reflected the strengths and weaknesses of the community that furnished its staff, students, and support. Throughout its history, one traces the still persistent dichotomy between philanthropists

133

and immigrants, businessmen and theoreticians, laymen and professionals. The curriculum developed by Sabsovich drew criticism from the trustees as stressing too much the academic and scientific aspects; because of the elaborate and lengthy course of study, the number of graduates was too small to justify an annual budget of over $40,000 by the early 1900's. Rather than 25 to 30 graduates, they looked for 50 to 75, if not more; certainly a demand for these well-educated Jews existed, for the class of 1902 had received as many as 143 farm job offers in twelve states. Cost-per-graduate became a perennially vexing calculation for the philanthropists and their agents.[89] They had, after all other projects in operation, including a network of urban educational centers.

Representatives of the Jewish Colonization Association joined the American trustees on tours of inspection and returned with criticism of the school for trying to emulate the well-endowed agricultural colleges, rather than merely training sizeable numbers of good rural workmen. Youngsters with no real intention of becoming farmers and without adequate knowledge of English seemed to be exploiting an opportunity for free education and comfortable living. That both students and staff might be using the school as a stepping-stone to posts outside farming, was a recurrent charge in the 1900's.

Consequently, Sabsovich was forced to reduce the length of training from three years to a little more than two, and to focus on practical work in the fields. At the time of the 1901 expansion, Dr. Boris D. Bogen, a member of New York's Russian-Jewish intelligentsia, was assigned as head of the school, ostensibly to relieve Sabsovich for other more pressing matters in the colony's life. Further proposals for shortening the course of study to one year as well as other new sources of friction continued to plague the administration, and Bogen resigned in 1904. In his autobiography, *Born a Jew*, he recalls these conflicts and his own opposition to the Western philanthropists' plans for "a contented Jewish peasantry." They saw the immigrant as only "inured to the lot of the humble toiler and content, not knowing any better. . . . From their lofty elevations their benefactors look down upon [the immigrants] and built settlements for them; but in the end [they] were to settle their problems for themselves." Bogen perceived no wrong in his graduates taking positions in agricultural laboratories, or with the U.S. Department of Agriculture, or as teachers in the popular new vocational schools, or for that matter improving their lot in any honest occupation.[90]

Recurrent unrest among the students themselves, predominantly immigrants, soon became a major source of friction and embarrassment. It was sometimes difficult to distinguish between the usual pranks of boys in a resident dormitory school and protests against real grievances. One of the first strikes was caused ostensibly by a temporary substitution of jam for butter in the dining room. Sabsovich, who had been away on a business trip in Philadelphia, "trembled with anger and annoyance" when the students could give him no better reason for the disorder.[91] The malcontents were threatened with expulsion, a warning later fulfilled.

Such incidents brought unfavorable publicity in a number of journals, especially the Yiddish *Forward*. Always suspicious of capitalist-sponsored ventures, it was at first willing to run advertisements proclaiming the opportunities offered by the Woodbine school to Jewish boys from the city, but by 1900 it featured complaints by striking students of maltreatment, long hours, and poor food. It seemed oatmeal and coffee was their mainstay rather than the expected country eggs, butter, and meat, and Sabsovich was quoted by the *Forward* as admonishing the boys that a good farmer must develop the habit of eating whatever he cannot market profitably. In yet another issue, Sabsovich was charged with forming the idea of an agricultural school as a device to distract attention from the fiasco of Jewish colonization in Woodbine. A physician, Dr. Joseph Jaffee, was cited as having seen him inflict corporal punishment on "helpless children"; ostensibly, finding the sight unbearable, Dr. Jaffee quit his post at the school.[92]

From the philanthropists' camp, on the other hand, came charges that discipline was "simply atrocious." Some proposed closing the dormitories and requiring pupils to board with nearby families. Such suggestions received further impetus with the strikes of 1904, when students claimed their instructors were "tyrannous" and "incompetent." The *Exponent* reported that the trustees backed the school administration, and that five students had been expelled, with an additional twenty-five placed on probation.[93] Within the year, however, Sabsovich was promoted out of Woodbine, being named general agent in the Fund's New York office. Then, while attempting a radically new approach, the trustees appointed an outside agricultural expert, Dr. Harold H. Ballard, as superintendent of the Woodbine community and head of the school (1905). He served less than a year, and was replaced by Henry W. Geller, a graduate of Michigan Agricultural College. By then, the course of study was reduced to one year, with another year added soon after for field experience in producing marketable crops for additional revenue.

Only older teenagers who could "read, write and speak English fluently" were accepted after Sabsovich's departure from the school. Qualifying examinations were given at the Educational Alliance of New York. In addition, the school's objectives were outlined in a circular letter to rabbis, promising that candidates they recommended would receive "special preference." In this letter, however, was no indication at all of any religious considerations in the training program. Partly because of these more stringent selection procedures and curriculum changes, enrollment dropped from the 112 of 1903 to a reported 54 on 1 January 1909.[94]

Controversy continued, nevertheless. Severe problems of student-faculty relations were dealt with by Philadelphia trustees, as the *Exponent* liked to point out: Judge Sulzberger, William B. Hackenburg, and Samuel S. Fleisher generally expressed their confidence in the administration's handling of discipline, work schedules, or food. In 1909, however, an unexpected attack came from the social workers' section of the National Conference of Jewish Charities in Buffalo, where the charge was made that the training of each Woodbine graduate had cost as much as twenty thousand dollars; most painfully, this criticism was leveled by an alumnus, Saul Drucker, who was by then head of a Jewish orphanage in Chicago. The *Boston Advocate* too criticized "Woodbine

Agricultural, . . . a summer college with an Agricultural side show, . . . and the [high] cost of all these years" when too few "practical agriculturists" were produced. Similarly, the *Jewish Comment* editorialized against "expensive farmers."

Other alumni, among them practicing farmers, rose to the defense of their school, attributing their own successes to its training and inspiration. One, Samuel N. Aqua, a farmer on Long Island, asked, "How many of these critics have tasted the bitter morsel of insolence, prejudice and assault upon you and your race to the degree the young Jewish missionary of agriculture is confronted with?" Aqua's defense of both Jewish farmers and Woodbine included nonetheless this criticism of its placement policies for graduates: "turning them out on the mercy of some Gentile employer does not make farmers of them."[95] More alumni farmers wrote testimonial letters, from as far away as Dupree, South Dakota. Louis Fastman described his work for a farmer in Oregon, plowing and sowing 40 acres in the spring at $35 monthly, working in the fruit country in the summer and harvesting oats and hay in the fall from 4:00 a.m. 'til late at night. He and "a few other boys" started the Jewish Agricultural Association in Portland. Afterwards, Fastman joined another Jewish farmer in filing for a 160-acre stretch of land south of Faith, South Dakota, paying $80 down.

Morris Mayerson, too, who used to clerk in Philadelphia before he came to Woodbine, wrote of his position on a gentleman's estate of two hundred acres in New York. With the background he had acquired, he had trebled his employer's poultry flock; and his work was appreciated. He wished to correct the "prevalent feeling of students at the school that their religion would be a severe handicap to them; . . . this is altogether wrong"; it did not matter what one's background was "if one only does his work correctly. . . . But as soon as one is slovenly . . . any narrowminded farmer [especially in a fight] will blame you and your religion."[96] It was a charmingly optimistic equivocation.

Defense also came from the Alumni Association of the Baron de Hirsch School, reorganized in 1905 by Jacob Lipman, and meeting periodically in the New York headquarters of the Jewish Agricultural Society. Loyally still, the *Exponent* and its letter-writing readers stressed the virtues of good citizenship and American manhood inculcated by the Woodbine School. After recurrent reports of trouble "published in Jewish newspapers, both English and Yiddish," the *Exponent* often "made inquiries in authoritative channels" (e.g., Superintendent Geller and the trustees) and found the charges to be "erroneous." One trustee, it announced approvingly, was "indignant at the presumption of [immigrant] boys attending a free institution [and] provoking a strike in order to carry out their ideas" on school regulations and teaching methods.[97]

Before World War I, however, the mass of evidence spelled the school's demise. Most of the trustees agreed with Professor Charles S. Phelps, a consultant from Connecticut State Agricultural College who criticized the school's isolation, its absence of "beautiful scenery," its "disheartening environment," and the "spirit of discontent or of unrest which seemed to exist in the Jewish life" at Woodbine. Strikes at the factories were bound to affect the students. And horticulturist P. F. Staples noted pointedly that love for agriculture could be formed only by seeing prosperous farms and meeting prosperous farmers; because of natural and "environmental" factors, the Woodbine community had neither.[98]

Yet another investigator, Professor J. L. Stone of Cornell University, agreed that students were receiving "a distorted and depressing view of agriculture," partly due to the surroundings. He also noted unfavorably that the boys, most either foreign or of foreign parentage, were given by "the de Hirsch Colony" little opportunity "to mingle with different people." A similar theme was struck by A. R. Merrill, a new instructor of animal industry: "The farmers in the area are the poorest . . . always complaining about not being able to make a living"; bad enough that "it is not in the nature of the Jewish boy to look upon agriculture with a favorable eye," but to have the people in Woodbine continually urging him to give up farming for other lines of work is worse. The new *Breeder's Gazette* report on the school also commented pointedly on its location with "a village of some fifteen hundred people, nearly all Jewish." At the other extreme, an official investigator from the

Jewish Colonization Association could criticize in 1911 the "non-Jewish character of the school . . . the faculty [then] being entirely Christian."[99] It was true, indeed, that after the departure of Bogen and Sabsovich, almost all the Jewish staff resigned.

The JCA also reported that other agricultural schools were "springing up like mushrooms in all parts of the Union," many of them offering shorter, much less expensive courses of study than Woodbine's (estimated then as four thousand dollars per graduate). High costs as well as inadequate location were foremost among the objections accepted by Goldman and Schiff, while the support of the Philadelphia trustees, notably Sulzberger and Hackenburg, was diluted by their new role as trustees of a similar educational institution: The National Farm School. Founded in Doylestown, Pennsylvania, by Rabbi Joseph Krauskopf of Philadelphia's Keneseth Israel, it opened formally in June 1897, a mere three years after Woodbine's agricultural school. Sabsovich publicly deplored such dissipation of strength, calling on Jewish leaders "first to learn the existing sources of Jewish agricultural interests and to further these, before creating new ones."[100] The National Farm School, however, provided the agrarians with a new focus on the attractive Tolstoyan principles. Unlike Woodbine, it declared itself non-sectarian, though also intending to educate Jewish young adults. It differed in not being associated directly with either a Jewish agricultural colony, or with a multi-purpose organization such as the Fund. Doylestown, only twenty-six miles from Philadelphia, offered a peaceful rural environment, with the nearby Burpee Seed Farm to provide some practical training.

Most financial support for the new school came quickly from the same congregations and members of the established community who were attracted by the crusade to make farmers of their East European brethren. For example, Morris Tuska, vice-president of New York's United Hebrew Charities, enclosed with his contribution the following endorsement: "I feel that any enterprise which will assist in again making the Jew a tiller of the soil should have universal suport."[101] Similar endorsements were eventually given by Edwin R. Seligman of Columbia University, Philip Hamburger of Baltimore, Isidore Bush of St. Louis, Rabbis Leucht of New Orleans, Hecht of Milwaukee, Werthheimer of Dayton, and others. The first board members included such notables as Ben Gimbel, Nathan Straus, and J. J. Snellenburg.[102]

That the National Farm School was "not founded upon any sectarian principle," and emphasized applied skills, became a source of repeated praise in commencement addresses by the visiting dignitaries.[103] Though lacking specifically Jewish content, the school managed to recruit its students mainly from Jewish orphanages and foster homes. And not unlike Woodbine, National Farm continued to appeal primarily to those "all over the country who realize that in this movement, which seeks to lead the sons of Israel from the sweatshop and back to possession of the soil, lies the solution of one of the most vexing problems that confront our co-religionists."[104] Thus, the *Jewish Exponent* summarized the motives behind the almost frantic scrounging for workable rural experiments. At the same time, Rabbi Dr. Krauskopf, his son, and Rabbi Isaac Landman, his assistant at both Congregation Keneseth Israel and the Farm School, were pressing for their Utah Colonization Project, a test case which eventually failed. In 1909, however, Rabbi Landman still criticized Woodbine's curriculum as overly theoretical for the effective training of agriculturists as rapidly as possible.

Indeed, Krauskopf's school seemed in some respects a serious rival. Not only did National defeat the Baron de Hirsch School at football, but they also won the preference of some Vineland students —so young Sylvan D. Einstein attended the school in Doylestown instead of Woodbine. More crucial, however, was the definite shift in the preferences of the philanthropists: the Baron de Hirsch Fund itself began contributing to the National Farm School in 1906, and in 1911 Fund Trustee Jacob Schiff joined with Isidor Strauss, Daniel Guggenheim, Adolph Lewisohn, and others in National's campaign. Their letters praised its expanded services to "poor Jewish lads of the congested centres" who through it could "free themselves and their families from the miseries of the ghetto. It is preventive work of the highest kind."[105]

For Woodbine, the die was cast. After years of committee

deliberations, scientific samplings of the poor soil, disparaging comments on immigrant colonists, and the complaints of high costs, the school seemed doomed. First (1907), JCA demanded "active measures for closing the school" although it agreed to continue a reduced subsidy for three years and then again reluctantly for a similar period. Successive reorganizations, including attempts to hire Jewish instructors, were marred by student strikes and staff changes in the years before World War I. Ironically, applications to the school increased sharply in its last years, and some even considered expanding the school when its enrollment swelled to 119 by 1912. Significantly, in 1914 more than one-third of the applicants were American-born, as compared to only 6 percent ten years before.[106]

Seemingly favorable developments, however, were more than counteracted by other events. The war in Europe caused JCA's subsidy to be cut off altogether. At the same time, Jacob Schiff's long-standing criticism of the institution culminated in a dramatic gesture of philanthropy: in 1916, with Julius Rosenwald, he offered $300,000 to relocate the school in a more desirable location in Peekskill, New York; the Fund's trustees accepted gratefully. The remaining settlers in Woodbine were up in arms at the prospective loss of "one of its foremost attractions and inducements" to local farmers, homebuilders, and merchants, but their protests were ineffective. The last Jewish superintendent of Woodbine, Joseph A. Rosen, a graduate of Michigan Agricultural College, favored removal, as did his successor Arthur R. Merrill, former head of the Lyndon School of Agriculture in Vermont. With America's entry into the war, school applications dropped from five hundred to fifty, and it seemed a likely time to move from South Jersey. Experts boosted Peekskill as an area of fruitful soil and a more congenial, prosperous environment.

Significantly, war brought an end to large-scale immigration, and with that, pressure to draw the masses of newcomers away from the cities was removed. Directors of the Jewish Agricultural Society, such as Percy Strauss, Cyrus Sulzberger, and even Dr. Jacob Lipman, argued persuasively that now Americanization could be achieved in educational institutions with no Jewish sponsorship, that in effect, it was not philanthropy's business to operate separatist schools. The organization preferred to continue its widespread program of aid to individual Jewish farmers, wherever they might settle, and to students of agriculture in any accredited school, thus departing from the Fund's by now obsolete commitment to the Jewish colonies and a Jewish agricultural school.

Now, forced to defend his removal plan, Jacob Schiff argued that dropping the Peekskill project would be a setback to the "dignity of the American Jews." By 1919, however, inflated building costs raised estimates for a new school to a million dollars, and neither the American JAS nor the European JCA could be interested. The proposed site, moreover, reportedly suffered from poor drainage. Consequently, the idea of a fresh start in Peekskill was finally abandoned, the Schiff-Rosenwald gift returned, and the extensive Woodbine school properties donated to the state of New Jersey. A grateful legislature established there the State Institution for Feebleminded Males. The Baron de Hirsch Agricultural School, established by the Fund's American trustees and the Russian Jew Sabsovich for the children of his countrymen in the New World had outlived its usefulness.[107] Other means, perhaps better, to achieve economic and social integration and a sense of identity in the New World had been found.

Rural factories:
New economic diversification and the social response

The clothiers all, not able to maintain
The many to them belonging, have put off
The spinsters, carders, fullers, weavers, who,
Unfit for other life, compelled by hunger
And lack of other means . . . are all in uproar
And danger serves among them.
Henry VIII, 1.2.31-37

The spinsters and the knitters in the sun
And the free maids that weave their thread with bones.
Twelfth Night, 2.4.1-2

5

The need to supplement income from the land with industrial activity had become apparent within the first year of the colonies' existence. Bitter feuds were to rise between farmer and *schneider,* between mill hand and capitalist, foreign laborer and Americanized businessman or philanthropist. The lack of a common ideology caused friction over goals and methods. Nevertheless, manufacturing became an economic fact of life in the Jewish community.

It started in Alliance during the first winter, when of the three large buildings used as temporary shelters one was designated as a sewing establishment and another as a cigar factory. For many months, however, no sewing was to be found, and the average wage in the cigar factory was only $1.75 a week, bringing complaints of exploitation from the *Jewish Record.* Before the end of its first year of operation, the cigar factory was totally destroyed by a fire of unknown origin. The Vineland *Journal* suggested arson, perhaps by an employee angered at a recent reduction of wages. Soon, however, Alliance had a new boss cigar maker who employed about sixty hands, but was often unable to pay wages for weeks on end. Toil in the cigar factory gave small hope of "averting actual starvation," complained one of its workers in a letter to the *American Israelite.* Visiting Philadelphians on their missions of mercy in the winter of 1884–1885 found the new factory too cold for continuous work and the cigar makers earning only half the comparable city rates. In nearby Vineland, too, cigar manufacturers complained that local child labor was incompetent and threatened to move back to New York.[1] Clearly, this was not the path to success for many colonists, even though the sons of pioneer farmer Moses Bayuk of Alliance would go on to build a nationally known cigar firm in Philadelphia.

The colonists' sewing machines became both a burden and a blessing. Many a Jewish farm family would supplement its meager income by slaving over the celebrated Singer sewing machine or New Home or Wheeler and Wilson. In Alliance, the shirt and cloak factory provided jobs for only the first crucial years, while in Carmel by 1897 just twenty out of a hundred families had survived as full-time farmers producing food for the whole settlement, the others working as cloak operators and tailors. "Was it Providence that prevented them from tilling the ground for building associations, or was it their preference for the sewing machines . . . that saved their blood and marrow from feeding the land of mortgagees?" asked the *Jewish Exponent,* as it described industrial Carmel during one of its rare good times as more prosperous than agricultural Alliance. The two differed partly because the homes in Carmel were built at some distance from the fields, or as one Alliance farmer put it: "When I sit at my sewing machine and look out the window occasionally it seems to me sometimes as if that tree or that berry reminds me that something is to be done for its welfare, and I cannot rest. . . . I attend to my farm at once. Quite a different thing with the Carmel farmers whose land is away from their homes. How can they be expected to leave an occupation without which hunger may crawl up tomorrow, unperceived, to work on remote, uncleared land which might never be their own?"[2]

In Rosenhayn as well as in Carmel, the majority of breadwinners eventually worked as machine operators, cloakmakers, and tailors, on subcontracts for Philadelphia and New York manufacturers. They remained in the country because living costs were lower; in many cases, they owned a cottage and cultivated small gardens to supplement their food supply. To the "fault-finders [who] consider tailoring an unworthy occupation for farmers," Moses Klein reiterated his plea that such supplementary employment was common in the Pennsylvania farm regions too and was an absolute necessity for large immigrant families.[3]

Regardless of criticism, however, industrial expansion continued, stimulated by private and organizational efforts. One of the most enterprising pioneer businessmen in the area, Abe Brotman, received financial backing from both the New York firm of Rubel, Weil and Company and the Baron de Hirsch Fund. The outcome of this unique partnership was Brotmanville, consisting of small homes and clothing factories dominated by Brotman and Company —"one of the largest in South Jersey"—specializing in children's clothes. A sucessor firm, Kramer and Sons, turned out cloaks and suits with the aid of labor from Vineland as well as the colonies. Similarly, the Rosenhayn Manufacturing Company, makers of ladies' shirtwaists, as well as Joseph and Son, clothing manufacturers of the same community, tapped the area's labor supply, advertising in the *Vineland Journal* for machine operatives.

In Carmel the clothing factory built by the Baron de Hirsch Fund was turned over in 1899 to private management; the generous terms included only the major condition that the weekly payroll equal six hundred dollars. Likewise, the Fund also arranged for a Jewish manufacturer from nearby Bridgeton to occupy another factory in Rosenhayn, providing employment for about fifty hands. With the return of prosperity at the turn of the century, the old cloak factory in Alliance, too, was reopened by the Snellenburgs, Philadelphia merchants, as was the Cooper ladies' wear factory in Brotmanville. In spite of the continued emphasis on needle trades, however, Rosenhayn rejoiced also over a new glass-blowing plant (1899), and in 1906 its citizens made plans for a modern tin plate factory.[4]

The strongest consistent emphasis on industry was in Woodbine. Learning from the experience of the older colonies, the administrators of the Baron de Hirsch Fund planned in advance for a balanced economy based on manufacturing as well as agricultural employment. At the outset the town's construction program included a large three-story shirt factory; as noted by the *New York Evening World,* 250 "intelligent and industrious" immigrants would find jobs there. Moreover, the Fund's trustees proceeded to entice private business construction by offering rent-free terms on the available space and assurance of "compensation for losses incurred in the beginning." It was an early operation-bootstrap to attract capital to an underveloped, job-hungry area.[5] Within a few years of its founding, Woodbine hummed with industrial activity, including a ready-made clothing firm, a pocket factory, and a machine tool shop. A basket factory, utilizing local willows, sold its products to Wanamaker's in Philadelphia.

In 1895, fire destroyed one of the first factory buildings, injuring several panic-stricken men and women. Subsequently, the Fund ordered all new construction to be entirely of fire-proof brick ("even to the floors," exclaimed the *Vineland Evening Journal*). The material was produced in a local modern brickyard developed by an enterprising colonist who had discovered just the right kind of clay. In 1901, the Jewish Agricultural and Industrial Aid Society joined with the Fund to begin construction of yet another clothing factory for 300 workers and a knitting mill for 150. By that time, the seven existing plants provided jobs for well over 400 workers who earned an average of $7.50 a week.[6] Locally produced electric power was an aid in creating well-lighted, efficient work rooms.

Such rapid rates of growth could not be maintained. By 1908, factory employment totaled 575, of whom 450 were male bread-winners; wages, however, dropped slightly to an average of $7.34 a week.[7] Beneath the slowing growth lay the seeds of an eventual decline, to occur in spite of energetic efforts by the colonists and the Fund and its subsidiary Woodbine Land and Development Company. The clothing industry, always vulnerable to business cycles, was particularly unstable at a time of financial panics and general overproduction. Thus Haas and Company went bankrupt in 1896, leaving its local employees' association to manage the remains of the business. Thereafter, the Philadelphia-based firm of Daniel and Blumenthal (D. & B.) was granted a five-year concession on the factory. D. & B. brought with it a number of experienced employees, including a capable and popular foreman, Joseph Rabinowitz (later mayor of Woodbine).

While the payroll of the new company averaged about $1,000 weekly in the first years, there remained a nagging concern over its stability, which was reflected in perennial disputes with the Fund's representatives. Initially, D. & B. borrowed $300,000 from the Fund, paying off only $185,000 by 1903 and at the same time hinting of the need for further concessions. Woodbine's Superintendent Sabsovich was less than enthusiastic, warning that discord between the firm's partners was causing a decline in earnings; he pleaded with the Fund's trustees to bring another company into town, partly as a countervailing power against D. & B., but also to provide additional employment. "The needle feeds Woodbine now," he declared dramatically.[8] Furthermore, he had come to hope that an expanded industrial labor force might create a much needed local market for agricultural products.

Employing 220 in Woodbine, D. & B. remained its leading firm early into the twentieth century and was continually jealous of the Fund's favors. Second was Quaker City Knitting Company, for whom a new factory was built by the Fund in 1901 giving jobs to about 115 men and women. Other producers—of hats, machinery, paper boxes, metal ware, cigars—were less influential but equally demanding of parochial economic protectionism. Some, for example, would not countenance local competition, requesting that no additional plants be built; in 1908, a pledge to this effect was forced from Eugene S. Benjamin of the Fund. The latter continued, however, to supply free electric power, live steam, and water in return for business's promising regular wage disbursement, "good upkeep," and payment of low rentals ranging from next to nothing to no more than two thousand dollars a year for a factory employing a hundred people. Although ample service was offered by the West Jersey and Seashore Railroad, with two stations in Woodbine, there was pressure for the Fund to develop a comprehensive local transportation network as well: starting in Woodbine, an electric trolley was to run to the Pennsylvania Railroad Station at Millville, then connect Carmel with the New Jersey Central line in Bridgeton, and onward to Rosenhayn and Alliance at the Vineland branch of the Central. All the colonies would thus have been joined together at great cost and liability to the Fund, an impossible added burden.[9]

Thus, it became increasingly less practical for philanthropy to subsidize private business ventures as employers of one-time refugees. There were too many variables, both human and economic, and the area lacked the resources to warrant more than the most basic investments. Some businessmen, perhaps naturally, made excessive demands for financial aid of the distant New York benefactor; the Fund's harassed trustees in turn were incensed when employers failed to retain the promised working force. From the employers' point of view labor costs per unit seemed excessive in Woodbine, while employees and their advocates claimed that wages were substantially lower than in any of the nearby cities. The Fund and its local agents were caught in the cross fire of labor-management recriminations. Employers blamed the out-migration of labor on the "interference" of Sabsovich, who was generally sympathetic to the workingmen's cause and defended his position by blaming higher wage levels outside Woodbine as a prime cause for the loss of manpower.[10] In the wake of each factory shutdown, some colonists moved away, while others held onto their homesteads only by hiring out to cut wood or pick berries, with the youth supplementing family incomes by working in the tomato canneries of Ocean View some seventeen miles away.

Yet individual success stories were not lacking in Woodbine. Morris L. Bayard, for example, started out as a laborer digging wells and setting pumps for local homes; then, beginning in a simple supply shed, eight feet by ten, he became owner of a sizeable machine shop and reputedly one of the wealthiest businessmen in all of Cape May County. Still another success story was that of Joseph Rabinowitz, who moved up from factory worker to manager then proprietor of the Woodbine Children's Clothing Company (partial successor to D. & B.). Both these industrialists, however, were dependent on fluctuating orders from outside the colony, and both required occasional loans from the Fund. The Rabinowitz firm eventually decided to relocate some of its operations to Philadelphia in the years preceding World War I, causing a severe loss of jobs: in 1908, its last year of full-scale operation, the company's employees totaled 225.[11]

Sabsovich complained to Mayer Sulzberger that migrant industry impeded the colony's growth, fostering an unstable, unskilled labor force. What Woodbine needed instead was new industry requiring workmanship such as cabinet-making, that would raise wage levels and attract a "more select element of workers."[12] Sabsovich thus reflected the impatience of agrarians who had compromised on their opposition to mechanical trades not directly allied with farming. The original decision to refuse rental to those interested solely in industrial employment had been changed reluctantly but almost immediately, in favor of balanced agricultural and industrial sectors supporting each other. Arthur Reichow, head of the Fund's Agricultural Bureau, articulated the early dream of a thriving home industry among the farm families, "as is done successfully in all farming villages of France and Germany."[13] Although it was characteristic of a groping for Jewish respectability along precedents set by a gentile world, Woodbine was not the Black Forest, and such hopes did not materialize.

The Fund confronted instead a series of harassing realities, including a persistent inability to match the comparative locational advantages of urban industry. Eventually, its resources for rural development were strained to the utmost, requiring periodic emergency grants from the Jewish Colonization Association and other European agencies. Yet the "gentlemen in Paris" were not always responsive to the pleas of Jacob Schiff and fellow trustees of the Fund on behalf of Woodbine.[14]

Finding jobs for the immigrants proved at once the primary and decisive challenge. Ultimately, Woodbine's survival depended on industry, but it seemed well-nigh impossible to attract any but the needle trades, and even those were relatively weak firms whose complaints and demands matched their own precarious position. At one point when trustee William B. Hackenburg negotiated with D. & B. he telegraphed this warning: "Executive Committee must accept Daniel's proposition or close factory, which will ruin Woodbine." And usually they did accept. With time, however, the demands of D. & B. and others increased: more free home sites for imported employees, reimbursement of losses due to poor local workmanship, repair of machines, and total exemption from rental, light, and power costs. In spite of the concessions, the basic drawbacks to successful manufacturing remained; such factors as freight charges to New York or Philadelphia, and the lack of a large, mobile, and diversified labor pool continued to drive out industry. D. & B. planned to leave at the expiration of its agreement, but the Fund granted further low interest loans and other generous conditions to induce continued, though reduced, operations under Rabinowitz's management.

Eventually, the latent labor unrest burst into a wave of strikes for higher wages and recognition of an increasingly militant local Workingmen's Association. In the earlier, more peaceful phase, a major issue had been the closing of factories on the Jewish Sabbath, demanded by many of the workmen and granted by management. By the early 1900's, however, the long-felt disaffection with the low wage level combined with an antipathy to capitalist exploitation to yield more inflammatory conditions.

From the turn of the century, the Socialist Jewish *Forward* hammered away, often in front page editorials, at the manner in which immigrant labor was "taken care of" in the shops of Woodbine: the toiling workers were truly made "to taste the bitter side of a philanthropy" dominated by capitalist principles.[15] This view clashed with the *Jewish Exponent*'s bland denials of charges that the business management and general administration in Woodbine were "autocratic." The *Exponent* claimed "steady work, prompt payment of tolerably fair wages, running the factory on Sunday instead of [the Jewish] Sabbath, have contributed largely to a happy state of harmony, so that the tailors have determined . . . to give up their habitual nomadic life."[16] In 1905, the *Forward* was joined by the young United Garment Workers, as J. W. Sullivan, editor of its *Weeky Bulletin of the Clothing Trade*, followed an inspection trip to Woodbine with a scathing article attacking wage scales that were substantially below those in the large cities. He charged also that the town's administration permitted employers to treat labor as virtual serfs, especially in company-controlled housing where troublemakers could be threatened with eviction as well as dismissal.[17]

There was enough truth in these charges to cause embarrassment, even though the Fund's trustees rationalized their actions in terms of enabling immigrants to acquire home ownership in the American way and their good intentions included the usual liberal terms. The company houses now each contained five rooms and were built on ample 50 x 150 foot lots readily accessible to the factories. Of the $500 price, two-fifths was repayable without interest, and the rest at 5 percent in monthly installments over a 2-year period; thereafter were still obligations for the land of about $3 a month.[18] At the same time, living costs generally were less than in the city, compensating somewhat for the lower wage levels, which ranged (1908) from $7 to $8 for unskilled labor up to $12 for skilled. Unfortunately, most of Woodbine's labor clustered in the unskilled category with average weekly wages only $7.34.[19] Moreover, recurring depressions as well as the instability of the needle trades caused painful unemployment and wage-cutting, which somewhat undermined the Fund's defenses.

Immigrant Inspector Joseph Ehrlich still warned in the Philadelphia press against continued "tailoring in the Jewish colonies." In the small rural shops, he charged, "sweaters" still worked at starvation wages, especially during recurrent strikes by city workers. Moreover, the emphasis on tailoring caused a neglect of agriculture, and even worse in Ehrlich's eyes, tended "to attract anarchistic and socialistic leaders."[20]

In truth, the troubled colonies contained in microcosm the problems existing elsewhere. Working conditions were hard, disillusioning, and often tragic in that adolescence of industrial America. Many first generation immigrants as well as their laboring children never lived to see fulfilled the promise of prosperity. Child labor was common, as were industrial accidents. One of the young immigrant victims in Carmel's cloak factory was "pretty Bessie Weisse,"

153

a fourteen-year-old whose scalp was torn off by the machine she worked. "Bessie was a spry and active girl," the Vineland *Journal* commented, "and it is strange she should have allowed her hair to catch in the machinery as it did."[21] For her, the promise was not to be.

For many colonists, the factory became a symbol of serfdom and grinding poverty. Are we not American citizens, not to be sold into the slavery of management? Woodbine workers asked in a 1908 petition to the Baron de Hirsch Fund. They felt their rights were being violated by the two-fold system in the children's clothing factory of piece work and a $25 security deposit to remain on the job—four weeks' notice was mandatory before a worker could quit. Would not the distinguished trustees protect them from these management abuses? But the Fund's trustees were also bombarded by counter complaints from the companies and threats to move to Philadelphia or other cities where labor was more plentiful and tractable. Uncooperative Woodbine workers could be compelled to desist from strikes, reasoned management, if they were required to pay cash for all purchases and if the Fund held over them the possibility of eviction.[22]

It is not surprising that at times the companies received a more sympathetic hearing among the trustees, who were in the main businessmen, than did the workers. Trustee Eugene Benjamin was a leading New York clothing manufacturer, elected precisely because his business experience was deemed useful in guiding Woodbine's industrial development. If anything, however, it was Benjamin who demanded more favorable treatment of labor. Fearing attempts on the part of D. & B. and other large firms to corner the local labor market, he formulated the Fund's policy of refusing to intervene directly on behalf of management. Yet, the Fund's agents and representatives remained concerned, and attempted to mediate the recurring labor-management disputes in order to reduce suffering among strikers, while retaining an aspect of neutrality to avoid the wrath of management. But amidst conflicting charges of radicalism and exploitation, industrial peace often proved unattainable.[23] Then the gulf between the East European immigrants and their American Jewish benefactors seemed wider than ever.

A more militant spirit of self-help in the form of labor unionism increasingly displaced the intercessionism of philanthropy. To the Russians the shibboleths of individualism meant little in the face of poverty and injustice. Some, it is also true, were radicals from the Old Country. They were ready for unionization sooner than others. Thus, in the wake of a strike in 1900, there was formed in Rosenhayn a local of the United Garment Workers, a predecessor of the Amalgamated Clothing Workers.[24]

By 1903, when the knee-pants workers of Woodbine struck D. & B., the *Forward* hailed them in a front page story as setting an heroic example for even New York's labor. Although in September they were pictured in a victorious stand against "wage-slavery," come December, they were again embattled over the complex issue of higher piece rates for goods requiring more labor-time. It proved a harsh winter for the Woodbine strikers with no other work available, and an appeal to New York labor groups brought only the usual investigating committee. So this was the Israel-in-America? the *Forward* queried mockingly; working for D. & B. seemed more like the ancient bondage in Egypt.[25]

Labor unrest along with specific contract violations by D. & B., such as failure to maintain a minimum weekly payroll of $1800, contributed to the company's ultimate demise. Joseph Rabinowitz, increasingly an influential entrepreneur, acquired the company's local equity for a mere $10,000.[26] But in spite of the favorable terms granted by the Fund, Rabinowitz could not maintain peace with the local Workingmen's Association. More strikes followed, including a bitter six-month stalemate in 1908. The Woodbine Hat Company, too, was hit by strikes and riots in 1909. Sabsovich blamed part of the trouble on "newcomers who have not yet adjusted themselves to the conditions," as well as on young hotheads without family obligations.[27] In exasperation, the trustees heard that sometimes as little as twenty cents a day stood in the way of an agreement between the company and its workers. Superintendent Bernard A. Palitz succeeded finally in organizing the Woodbine Board of Trade to set more equitable business standards for all firms in the community, as well as an arbitration committee to deal with specific labor disputes. He even appealed for the intervention of Secretary of Commerce and Labor Oscar S. Straus, who was himself one of the original trustees of the Fund.[28]

But the economics of a highly competitive industry with low profit margins and locational disadvantages, frequently brought more desperate deadlocks between labor and management, and when operators and buttonhole makers were on strike, there was no work for pressers. The Fund was inevitably caught in the middle, while still trying to attract outside industry and to provide jobs. During strikes, when the local relief society was unable to cope with demands made upon it and the bakers and grocers refused additional credit, families would double up to share expenses and external aid had to be called in. The benevolent Fund could not shirk its responsibility even if the situation conflicted sharply with its own schemes for an independent class of yeomen and artisans. Almost surreptitiously, Eugene Benjamin personally donated $300 during one pre-Passover season of strikes because he did not consider it wise to "mix up the Fund with purely relief work."[29] Yet it was not always as easy to distinguish between outright philanthropy and development subsidies.

The Garment Workers Union was soon an active participant in Woodbine's labor disputes; the Fund's agents blamed it for much of the difficulty. The union, they maintained, failed to realize the precarious nature of employment in Woodbine which was based on facilities built by the Fund. Thus, with comparatively little capital tied up in the town, a disgruntled businessman could move his operations elsewhere.[30]

Such dire prophecies went largely unheeded even as they were proved true. Not only did industry leave Woodbine to return to Philadelphia or New York, but also to relocate in nearby Vineland. This trend began with Woodbine's short-lived cloak industry, Jonasson and Company, which left during the depression of 1893. In Vineland, as in most other places at the time, management's politics of lock-out, yellow dog contracting and company police, could be exercised with impunity, although the ever-watchful *Forward* did not fail to warn its readers of such abuses.[31]

More crucial was the continued outflow of labor from the

colonies to the cities, as well as the type of replacement brought from the cities by both old and new firms. Increasingly, the companies were required to maintain a quota of Jewish workers from Woodbine, although enforcement was not always feasible. Thus, the Fund built additions to the Woodbine Children's Clothing Company's factory in 1909 on condition that it employ "a minimum working force of 150 Jewish people." The Woodbine Hat Company's lease was renewed in the same year with provisions for an 80 percent Jewish labor force. But the latter firm, while promising "of course . . . preference" for Jews, pleaded the right to "engage other nationalities" as needed.[32]

Reports from Superintendent Palitz to Mayer Sulzberger continued to warn also that new industry resulted in an "unsteady and floating population," some of whom were also strike leaders and troublemakers.[33] In 1909, strikes followed the hat company's announcement that those not reporting for work by 7:10 woud be locked out for the day. The violence which resulted, while causing no serious injuries and only slight property damage, became another source of embarrassment for Woodbine and the Fund. From New York Sabsovich warned Mayor M. L. Bayard, successful proprietor of the local machine factory, to prevent "a repetition of the disgraceful rioting." The latter countered by requesting more funds for an "adequate police force . . . to control the striking workers."[34]

The crux of the labor problem was not simply union recognition. By 1911 the United Garment Workers was firmly established with a contract setting such terms as a fifty-eight hour week including only eight hours on Friday (Sabbath eve) and no work on Saturday, piece rates for tailors alone, and reference on outstanding issues to an arbitration board.[35] The always sensitive issue of radicalism among the Jewish immigrants persisted, however; as one of the proprietors put it, the main source of trouble was "inflammatory socialism." He suggested calling in such "Yiddish-speaking orators" as would emphasize moderation rather than class-struggle.[36]

In its years of industrial decline (1911-1914) Woodbine found it ever more difficult to attract new firms, partly, at least, because of this reputation for radicalism. For example, a Philadelphia firm claimed it had been interested in Woodbine, but feared the "anarchistic-socialistic characteristics of the people coupled with broken pledges . . . and striking on the least provocation."[37] Louis Mounier, the Jewish Agricultural Society's educational director for the Vineland colonies offered a similar plaint, blaming the "extreme anarchistic elements which the factories had invited" for the lack of progress in Carmel, whose poor seemed to him an "incongruous mixture of anarchistic beggary."[38]

The *Vineland Evening Journal,* too, reported dourly on the street-corner harangues of Socialist Nathan Lifshus from Woodbine as well as other immigrant radicals. A generation before, it had made a *cause célèbre* of a "Washington agitator" named Isaac Cohen, who purportedly attempted to create labor unrest in Vineland. Failing this, he had continued his inflammatory rallies among Washington Negroes, calling for a general labor strike. President Rutherford B. Hayes, so went the story, agreed to meet with Cohen and assured him that the rights of laboring men would not be ignored; but Cohen continued to agitate. Too bad, lamented the paper, that "the tramp (for this Cohen is scarcely more than that)" was permitted to believe in "the President's approval of his disgraceful actions."[39]

Then, in the years before and during World War I, the same newspaper reported frequently on the influx of Jewish-operated firms, some from Woodbine and the other colonies, into Vineland. Industry was, of course, welcome in this job-hungry area, but it brought with it strikes and "New York agitators" and a new working class. The latter they regarded as the less than desirable accretion of a generally positive economic growth. Among the attractions in the city of Vineland was a substantially larger labor pool and better transportation, storage, financing, and marketing facilities. The process of industrial migration started with advertisements such as The Morris Company's "Wanted—50 operators on knee pants and coats, The Morris Company, steam power, Alliance, N.J.," which resulted soon after in the opening of a branch in Vineland. Likewise, M. Joseph and Son moved their clothing factory from

Rosenhayn, to sell part of their business operations a few years later to Kaplan and Mendelson of New York; and the M. Cooper Company deserted Brotmanville for Vineland.[40] By 1913, even Brotman and Sons had moved their ladies' garment factory to Vineland; there they prospered in the boom years of World War I, opening branches also in nearby Millville and in Philadelphia. "Industrial Brotmanville" was taken over by other firms tempted there by the rent-free terms and subsidies of the Jewish Agricultural and Industrial Aid Society. Vineland's Board of Trade was not to be outdone, however, in the search for industry from near and far; even from distant Brooklyn they managed to attract a cloak and topper firm whose operations had been stalled by strikes.[41]

As early as 1890, when its population was still under eight thousand, industrial expansion had been considered a vital factor in Vineland's growth.[42] But it had fallen behind in the race for economic development because it lacked coal and other industrial resources as well as cheap power and a population large enough to create a substantial local market. The town had not been able to compete with communities served by the large new power utilities such as Atlantic City Electric. Vineland's Commercial League had been painfully aware of its disadvantages, even though its leaders did listen with good humor to their own Senator John A. Ackley as he joked about their "white sand known all over as the best in the world, and the stick-to-itiveness of the clay." Never mind, native son Ackley had told them, some day their great Maurice River might be harnessed to give light, heat, and power to a booming city.[43]

"Boost Vineland: The Heart of Sunny Southern New Jersey" became an industrial war cry early in the twentieth century for native and newcomer alike in this sprawling community whose 70 square miles made it the "largest city" in New Jersey. A significant factor in this campaign was the Bureau of Civic Promotion mobilized in New York to extol the virtues of Vineland, a "beautiful, hustling city [population 12,000 by 1914] with 200 miles of shaded streets . . . 23 different kinds of manufacturing interests . . . three

159

banks . . . greatest poultry center of the East . . . municipal-owned public utilities . . . commission governed . . . direct R.R. line to New York . . . and no saloons."[44]

Some of the new enterprises such as R. Sadowsky and Kaplan Brothers, filled the vacant floors of the old Welch Grape Juice Building. Kaplan Brothers, makers of hats, particularly pleased the board of trade and borough council by declining their proffered financial assistance. "They simply wanted a good will expression of the people of the town," the paper announced glowingly. Local entrepreneur Abe Lipitz was also given due credit for his role as intermediary and labor recruiter for the Kaplan firm.[45] Frank Schlosser and Victor Morvay received praise for installing the most modern electric-powered machines in their coat factory (Morvay was also an officer of the Farmers' Canning Company). Likewise, young John Joseph's factory, expanded to forty-two sewing machines, was "one of the most sanitary, pleasantly lighted and comfortable."[46]

Difficulties however, did attend the new factory establishments: fires represented a constant threat to their security as well as the town's. Louis Sagel and Sons arrived from Bridgeton to expand their modern candy manufacturing operations, increasing their work force within a year to over a hundred. When a spectacular fire destroyed the company's buildings and machines, there was great concern among the town fathers over the "loss of the wage output." Indignation replaced worry when rumor said that Sagel would rebuild in Bridgeton; he could not "be so ungrateful after accepting all the favors Vineland bestowed!" But it was only a rumor. With the aid of insurance money and local stockholders, Sagel resumed operations in Vineland.[47] Fire also damaged the S. J. Levy Hosiery Company's plant, stirring rumors of arson and grumbling among the unemployed mill hands. Within the month, however, the city attracted the firm of Ellis Brothers (Abraham and Maurice) of Philadelphia as the new owners. Much to everyone's relief, they promised to employ at first one hundred and eventually three hundred in the reopened plant.[48]

Far more unsettling, however, to everyone were the recurrent strikes in Vineland too. Apparently labor unrest, or radicalism as

some preferred to call it, was not a phenomenon limited only to
Jewish colonies or even to Jewish workers. It reflected the impact
of economic and social revolution in the whole country—of cutthroat competition, years of mass immigration, of low wages and
limited rights as well as an undercurrent of progressive ideas for
reform. Those firms which left the Jewish colonies, or New York
and Philadelphia, to seek labor peace on easy terms in Vineland
were to be disappointed.

Among the firms fleeing to Vineland, R. Sadowsky had been
castigated by the *Forward* as one of the "bosses who were strangling the oppressed workers" of Rosenhayn. Within a few years
Sadowsky's in Vineland experienced again a period of strikes and
violence which was resolved for a while through the influence of
the local Jewish Workingmen's Circle. By 1912, organizers from
New York helped to force recognition of the Coat Makers' Union,
thus ending temporarily a new strike dispute.[49] Girls employed in
the Cooper factory also struck for higher wages, while Mendelson's
employees demanded a fifty-five hour week. "New York agitators,"
joined by "union men from Newark," built more support with
fiery meetings in Johnson's Hall. In 1913, a general strike was
called in sympathy with the garment workers of New York.
Though far from being fully effective, it served notice of a militant
union strength.[50]

In the same year, labor violence in the Kramer plant in Brotmanville attracted the attention of Vineland. Foreman Morris Elson
was brought before Vineland Justice Moses Bayuk on charges of
having fired on the strikers. On management's side, three local
clothing manufacturers—Bloom, Bartman, and Blaustein—claimed
they had been assaulted by a Philadelphia unionist, David Gratz.
The latter was soon found guilty and dispatched by another judge to
six years in state prison. Many of Vineland's citizens regretted only
that the preliminary hearing for Gratz had been called on a Sunday,
in desecration of the Sabbath; others justified such sacrilege on the
ground that "he was considered dangerous and the people wanted
him locked up." Once the jury was selected, "it was reasonably
certain which way the case would go"; thus, the *Journal* hoped there

would be "no more cause for complaint" against "inflammatory" union organizers.[51]

Civic groups, entrepreneurs and labor did manage to agree that inadequate facilities were among the problems confronting Vineland from the outset. For example, Mendelson's fifty employees, mostly women, were crowded into a small frame building behind Queen and Company's factory. Workers complained of cold in winter and heat in summer; alarmed by the possibility that Mendelson's would move elsewhere in consequence, the board of trade assisted with a small subsidy, and a committee of leading gentile citizens collected subscriptions for better quarters. A solution was finally worked out with additional financing from New York. Other new plants were eventually constructed through the private efforts of businessmen like Abe Lipitz, who in 1913 was described favorably as owning "considerable property here, and he wants to see the town grow . . . to improve Vineland."[52]

There were others, however, who wished to improve Vineland in another way, and their influence was felt in sweatshop and farm. The "brilliant Miss Potter," a New York journalist, brought the message of "war between capital and labor . . . or how the nonproducers got the money by grinding down the poor." She especially appealed to the women not to "betray the cause of humanity" by scabbing for Philadelphia factories. Women also should organize, she pleaded, in order to protect their interests as both workers and citizens. However, among her enthusiastic audiences in Chosen Friends' Hall there were but "very few of the working women."[53] Perhaps they were too tired or uninterested to hear lectures on a Saturday night.

In nearby Carmel, Eugene V. Debs was heard early in a passionate defense of the underprivileged, and Emma Goldman preached her anarchist doctrine of "propaganda by deed."[54] Socialists in Vineland nominated a full ticket in 1909: Warren and Burgin for city council, Lerner and Diacont for the assembly, Schiner for country clerk, and Sheldon for coroner. Though they garnered under 5 percent of the popular vote, they continued to present their own ticket in following elections.[55]

Socialism was considered extremist, however, and even un-American. Much more attractive was Progressivism, a middle class movement of reform which drew businessmen, professionals, politicians, and writers, as well as farmers and labor. Outspoken Jewish businessmen in Vineland warmly embraced this means as they saw it, to "social and industrial justice." Joining the cause were John Joseph, Victor Morvay, David and Frank Kotok, Herman Lemisch, and A. M. Niggin. They pledged themselves to such Progressive principles as heavy inheritance taxes against "great fortunes," adequate workmen's compensation, abolition of child labor, restricting the use of injunctions in labor disputes, and "prevention of tax evasions by banks and other corporations." A score of years before the New Deal, they regarded "governmental interference as necessary to solve the problems of industry." To help achieve these aims, they campaigned for Everett Colby, Progressive candidate for governor in 1913.[56]

Soon, however, domestic reform yielded to the resurgence of nationalism and materialism in World War I as the threat of worsening recession gave way to an industrial boom which affected both Vineland and the Jewish colonies. In 1914, as a consequence of several business failures, Woodbine's employed had declined to only 240. The Fund reluctantly agreed to consider another loan of $10,000 for the Woodbine Children's Clothing Company, but distinctly moved towards ending all future subsidies. Bernard A. Palitz, promoted to general agent of the Fund, recommended sale of the power plant to a private firm and yielding of responsibility for future economic development to the local board of trade.[57] At just this critical juncture, there seemed to come a spectacular reprieve. Wartime orders, especially for clothing, caused an encouraging increase of employment in Woodbine, which rose to 700 by 1918 with a total payroll of over $400,000.[58]

In Vineland and the colonies around it, the impact of war on industry was felt almost immediately. As early as November 1914, Mendelson's Clothing "Manufactory" was working on "an almost limitless number" of canvas knapsacks for use by the English army. Its clothing orders had doubled by 1915, also mainly due to European demand. In 1916, it added a hundred sewing machines in order to fulfill new contracts for the government. Even the company's branches in Brotmanville, Rosenhayn, and Norma were in full production, making army tents as well as clothing.[59] Other flourishing Jewish clothing manufacturers among Vineland's hundred-odd businesses during World War I included F. Krich and Son, M. Snyderman and Son, Cohen Brothers and the Hamburger Cloak Company. In September 1916, the Brandeis Manufacturing Company announced delivery of additional heavy machinery for its enlarged factory.[60]

Vineland's labor shared moderately in the increased prosperity of the war years. For example, the employees of Joseph Brothers received presents of silverware, jewelry, and 5 percent bonuses at Christmas. The firm took pride in a good relationship with its 150 employees, achieved partly by this playing of Santa Claus each year. In 1916 beginning operators were paid $5 weekly, while experienced workers earned $8-$14; its work week was not reduced from 55 to 52 hours until 1917, after M. Snyderman and Son had set a precedent with a 50-hour week.[61] The war boom created a labor shortage, as attested by the want ads in the *Journal,* by high prices and profits, and also by governmental attempts to encourage industrial peace for the sake of national defense.

But there were still heard voices of protest and discontent. Palace Hall in Vineland resounded with labor oratory in English, Yiddish, and Italian during "monster mass meetings" focusing on the strife between the management associations and such unions as the Cloak and Skirt Makers and the Amalgamated Clothing Workers. The latter brought to Palace Hall the eloquent Socialist assemblyman of New York, Abraham Shiphakof, who stirred the local proletariat with visions of cloak manufacturers raising prices while reducing real wages, of bosses denying workers the right to organize and the leisure to enjoy music or the sweet gifts of nature.[62] Young local Jewish unionists like David Karp and Nathan Seltzer absorbed the message and prepared to act. Similarly, they applauded Socialist D. R. Tanner from New York as he attacked the

164

high cost of living and decline in real wages and the scarcity in the face of bulging warehouses—the "skin-game system of capitalism." In the spring of 1917, word came from California that radical labor leader Tom Mooney was sentenced to hang for his ostensible role in a bomb explosion. The news galvanized all of Vineland's labor; they signed petitions and held mass protest meetings led jointly by the Amalgamated Local 208, the Socialist Party, the Workingmen's Circle Local 57 and the Brotherhood of Carpenters Local 620.[63]

More commonplace grievances over wages and hours were not forgotten. Mendelson Brothers was forced on several occasions to halt work on government contracts because of strikes. Their branch plants in Norma, Rosenhayn, Mizpah, and Brotmanville were also struck. Among demands by the Amalgamated Clothing Workers led by Karp in 1917 was a flat 15 percent wage increase and a fifty-hour week in Vineland, although the union was willing to accept a fifty-three hour week in the branch plants. Workers in the colonies promptly rejected this "discriminatory" treatment.[64] Then the Ladies Garment Workers' Local 74 struck the Norma and Vineland shops of I. Eskin and Company, partly out of sympathy with the great wave of strikes in New York's clothing industry and partly to prevent strike-breaking subcontracts in the rural factories.

The greater mobility of the twentieth century thus brought not only an easy flow of workers between Vineland and the Jewish colonies, but also increasingly frequent visits of union organizers and strikers' delegations from New York. The latter found lodging at the Baker House, then rallied at Palace Hall where local bosses were castigated. Some employers complained that the unions were bent on driving them out of business, as evidenced, they claimed, by the union's willingness to "tempt" workers in Vineland and Norma with strike benefits of $15-$25 a week while their members in New York received only $2-$3. Here, it seemed, was another kind of union discrimination.[65] Bad feelings occasionally flared into public disagreements between Jewish employers and their coreligionist employees or union organizers. I. Eskin, for example, came before

Vineland Justice Frank Kotok (also Jewish) to charge two "New York strike agitators" Abe Labock and Myer Rosenberg with creating a disturbance at his factory.[66]

Far more sensational for Vineland, however, was the case of a young woman organizer from Philadelphia, Lillian Miller Levant. She spent several weeks trying to unionize the factories of Cohen Brothers and Krich and Sons. Finally, one woman employee charged —whether by instigation or not—that as she was about to board the train for her home in Rosenhayn one evening, a group of girls followed her menacingly. Among them was the lady organizer who threatened her with such abusive language as "scab" and "slacker" for refusing to agree to strike strategy. In the ensuing conspiracy trial Justice Kotok again presided before a large crowd in City Hall, admonishing the girl strikers in the audience to desist from giggling while "the lawyers scrapped all the time over aspects of the case." The respected law firm of Alvord and Tuso represented the state, and Borough Solicitor Hurd took up cudgels for the defense.

The prosecution's case was decidedly weak. Its key witness, the railroad agent, could not clearly identify who had screamed the noxious words. Another witness feigned ignorance of English, except, as the judge charged, for those things which he wished to hear and say; threatened with jail, however, and supplied by the court with an interpreter (Miss Dora Agronski of Alliance), he finally testified. Two facts stood out: this witness was the brother-in-law of Jacob Cohen, one of the struck manufacturers, and he had been in the company of the defendant at the railroad depot during the ruckus, but had not heard her utter the damnable language. When put on the witness stand herself, the defendant gently maintained that no coercion had been used, "only entreaties" to join "the rest of the girls striking for better working conditions." A bit melodramatically, the prosecution failed to press for a conviction, resting its case instead on a eulogy of court and defense. The feminist union camp had carried the day in Vineland, at least in court.[67]

Battle in the shops, however, continued and strained the resources of both sides. Even though employers deplored the "awful waste" of such economic warfare, they either refused or

166

were unable to come to terms with the union. After organizing Krich and Sons, Lillian Miller Levant left Vineland, although she continued to issue telegraphed instructions from Philadelphia and apparently ordered strikes against inadequate contracts. At one critical point, the Krich local's president took control, maintaining that "the girls were not at work because the elastics used in the underwear were not in stock. . . . Miss Miller of Philadelphia was sent for to settle the problem."[68] Only Joseph Brothers continued successfully to avoid union trouble because of their liberality, as they put it, in granting increases; their employees had "the best wages in town." Two hundred and fifty clothing workers struck the Vineland Coat Company and two other firms in 1917. Mendelson's, too, faced trouble again, this time for failing to translate into wages the higher prices on army clothing and for hiring "scabs." The firm's denials did not avert recurrent strikes and demonstrations in 1918— "off agin, on agin, Finigin," according to the *Journal*.[69]

Incorrigible Vineland employers were also given the back of the hand by the Amalgamated. For example, the Eskin shop, charged with moving from Norma to avoid unionization, refused to provide even a hearing for the organizer from New York, a Mr. Kleinman; consequently, workers from all the union shops were called out to march in protest against that establishment. "With Old Glory waving in their hands" the workers marched peaceably through the streets, though their "feelings had been aroused." As a result, most of the Eskin employees were signed up on the spot, and management agreed to negotiate. But trouble continued to brew over their failure to post wage scales, and reductions in pay were rumored. A prolonged strike seemed inevitable.

Louis Hollander came down from the Amalgamated's general office in New York to enter the fray. Soon he obtained the cooperation of Vineland's Mayor Stevens, partly on the grounds that a continued strike could hurt national defense, for this factory, as others, made military coats and uniforms. Eskin, on the other hand, claimed that union members violated a pledge to desist from strikes when government contracts were involved; he refused to rehire striking employees. To break the ensuing stalemate, Hollander also obtained the aid of Captain Lehman of Philadelphia's military arsenal, again on the grounds of national need. The Amalgamated Clothing Workers won the strike, claiming that "all points were conceded in our favor," and Local Secretary Aaron Coltun, son of Alliance pioneers, announced that "all non-union men must leave the shop" to be replaced by "regular union employees."[70]

During the same time, Hollander persuaded employees at another shop *not* to strike for slightly higher piece rates on army uniforms, citing the union policy of noninterference with government work. Then, when the war was over, government contracts expired, labor shortages ended, and the balloon burst. Within months, Eskin's was on strike again over a new issue, recognition of the New York Joint Board of Cloak and Skirt Makers' Union, represented by Louis Bulkin.[71]

During the war and after, Carmel and Rosenhayn also suffered chronic labor disputes at the Roschkin factory and at the Rosenthal-Dias plant. The latter made army uniforms too, but was stubbornly nonunion. Its employees complained of wages averaging $10 weekly for fifty-three hours, and some called for help from Amalgamated Local 208 in Vineland. An organizing committee headed by Louis Hollander and Local President William Keslow was unceremoniously ejected. The firm refused to bargain on any issue and a painful strike ensued. In Woodbine, too, post-war labor violence involving imported strike-breakers caused one firm after another to close down or move out. Within two years local unemployment was widespread. As "all those who had not left the town, were without work," it seemed, the million dollars invested by the Fund in this industrial-philanthropic experiment would prove in vain.[72]

The strikes were harbingers of worse times to come, of a post-war depression and instability long before the great crash of 1929. Idle factories scarred the rural colonies from Vineland to Woodbine, for the garment business became one of the early sick industries in the so-called prosperity decade. It suffered increasingly from the competition with more efficient producing centers both in the United States and abroad as well as from the introduction of synthetic materials, changing transportation patterns, new styles, and the technological revolution hastened by war. Its maladies deeply affected immigrant labor and immigrant bosses alike whose very livelihood and dreams of economic prosperity were planted in its success.

Was industry in the Jewish colonies a mistake, a distortion of the agrarian ideals embraced by so many pioneers in both Europe and America? In pragmatic terms, it was defended as an economic necessity. Moreover, industry—whether in New York or Carmel—sustained the new immigrants, enabling their children to become more than peddlers or workers in sweatshops, perhaps even scientists, writers, professionals, judges, or athletes, participants in a New World whose opportunities were greater than any dream of that first struggling generation.

Did the factory encourage radicalism? And what do we mean by radicalism? Writing of a nineteenth century variety, Gilbert Seldes, a native of agrarian Alliance, thought it "displayed a truly astounding 'mother fixation' . . . and, almost universally, a fixation on Mother Earth." Or in a psychoanalytic vein: "The land-hungry communist . . . wanted to creep back into the arms of his Mother Earth, to escape from complexity and the light of day into the darkness of primeval simplicity."[73] But the twentieth century radical perforce had to be different, for this quixotic dreamer had new, more mechanized windmills to conquer. At the same time he could remain in the radical tradition and among those "opposed to the system of 'make-money' . . . [who] wanted a freer society, an easier life for men and women . . . and a gospel contrary to the orthodox doctrine preached by the spade, the rifle, and the steam-engine."[74]

Acceptance and rejection in the new society: Aliens, natives, and German Jews

The honors in the High School this year go first to an Italian; second to a Cuban; third to a Hebrew, and fourth to an American. While the American was fourth, it was better than any of the other Americans could do.

Vineland Evening Journal
16 May 1912

I often convict myself of currying favor with the German Jews. But then German-American Jews curry favor with Portuguese-American Jews, just as we all curry favor with Gentiles and as American Gentiles curry favor with the aristocracy of Europe.

Abraham Cahan
The Rise of David Levinsky[1]

6

Equality was a fine eighteenth-century abstraction from the brow of singular American revolutionaries who had recalled the glories of Greece. Or so it seemed. To Russian Jews, however, whether David Levinsky in the cited novel of New York (1885-1915) or the real-life Levinskys (Lipa and Toba) of Alliance during the same hard years, the noble concept had little meaning. Though a familiar idea, social equality was a far-off goal. It was present in minutest details of Bible and Talmud, whose pages had been studied for centuries by Jewish scholars. But was there really more opportunity to achieve equality in the sweatshops of the New World than in the ghettos of the Old?

The East European immigrants lacked all the signs of status—wealth, power, and prestige. They lacked capital and training, as they also lacked a socially approved escutcheon, language, religion, culture, or political orientation. At times, indeed, it seemed their only possessions were the stereotypes created for them by a prejudice against Jews that was present even before their arrival, stemming almost naturally from the European precedents.

Jewish jokes had for long been familiar in the Vineland area.

171

Back in 1866, the *Vineland Weekly* had carried a story about a countryman's visit to New York and his encounter there with a merchant on Chatham Street in the Jews' quarter. The latter, a "dirty looking fellow, . . . clamorously urged him, . . . with the annoying custom of that street," to buy a new shirt—"the cheapest in the street, sir." The not-so-simple country visitor countered, "are they clean?" Whereupon the obsequious shopkeeper affirmed they were; at which the straight-faced countryman replied, "Then put one on, for you need it!" Truly "a clean sell," remarked the *Weekly*. The native's triumph seemed to bear out the old saw that Jews could not flourish among Yankees, who would "out-Jew" them in trading.[2] Or there is this story that appeared soon after the arrival of Russian Jews. How did they manage, one reporter was asked, to reach town so early for their morning purchases; their New Jerusalem was, after all, almost a five miles' trudge away from the shops of Vineland. "Easy," answered the bright reporter, "they 'Jew' the distance down to about a mile—as they do everything else in the stores when they come to buy."[3] Also passing for humor was this quip: when Jacob Lipitz climbed up the cupola of the Baker House hotel to light a glass bulb, people asked, was it "gas or electric? Some were sure it was an Israelite."[4]

Behind these attitudes, generally harmless, lay a traditional, sometimes subconscious anti-Semitism. It had no necessary relation to the immediate presence of Jews as customers or neighbors. Thus, three years before the founding of Alliance, the Vineland merchants were reported in favor of posting retail prices for all to see, as a means of preventing "the miserable 'jew' system of overcharging with the expectation of being 'beat down.'" This was no complaint about specific people; it was, unfortunately, only part of the idiom in an age of the small competitive merchant and retailer.[5]

Anti-Semitism was based on religious traditions, as well as semantics and economics. On the one hand, an old greenbacker would quote Congressman Thaddeus Stevens concerning greenback monetary legislation: it "produced a howl among the money changers as hideous as that sent forth by their Jewish cousins when they were thrashed out of the Temple."[6] This was but a classic

172

mode of expression. On the other hand, Reverend Harrison's sermons in Vineland could praise the "ancient Hebrews . . . the granite element in the power of what we ought to do . . . the gladness of their home and social life," without relating it at all to the modern "Jewish cousins."[7]

The culmination of this religious tradition occurred in 1885, when the *Vineland Evening Journal* restated the ugly European deicide libel which had cost so many innocent lives. Without indicating names, sources, or other cumbrous details, it reported a day before Lincoln's birthday that "the Jews are said to have murdered a prominent Hebrew in Besserabia [sic] because he sought to improve their religion. They did the same thing in Palestine 1850 years ago." William Levin, who came to Alliance as a youngster, recalled also that neighboring gentile school children during the 1880's were often unsparing in their use of "Christ-killer" and similar epithets.[8]

One must consider the persistence of an American nativism that was directed against Catholics as well as foreigners. Catholicism was attacked as an alien despotism trying to betray the nation into the hands of Rome. Catholic attempts to eliminate the Protestant tinge of Bible reading in the public schools aroused much antagonism, even to the extent of dragging the issue into politics. The Republican Party reaped some benefits in New Jersey as a defender of the public school system against the "Romish Church" and as a proponent of a constitutional amendment prohibiting public aid to parochial schools. In Vineland, which had been settled by Methodists, Baptists, and Presbyterians, the National Reform Association called public meetings to support the amendment and to "maintain existing *Christian* features in the American Government [italics added]." Even editorial pleas for tolerance were couched in cautious terms as they denied that mischievous "liberal thinkers" in the Protestant churches could keep "good Christian people" from moving into Vineland.[9] And even Jews would at times be accused of pro-Catholic sympathies when they opposed Bible reading in public schools.

In some respects bigots only repeated against Jewish immigrants the charges used before against Irish Catholics and later against Italians. But the Jew suffered an unyielding prejudice that could not be removed even by economic or cultural assimilation. To the Shylock figure was added the stereotype of aggressiveness and ostentation, which disqualified even the successful Jew from acceptance among genteel circles. As Higham put it, "in an age of parvenus . . . and general social climbing . . . the Jew provided a symbol of the parvenu spirit. Anti-Semitic discriminations subjected him to a discipline that native Americans could not so easily impose on themselves."[10] The Vineland press duly noted the fact that even "influential Hebrew families" were refused entry into certain hotels. For example, Joseph Seligman, "a wealthy, respected and highly cultured banker," was excluded from one of the A. T. Stewart establishments in Garden City as a matter of policy. Similar patterns of "Jewish persecution" were also adopted by the Manhattan Beach hotels, although the *Journal* wondered how long they could "hold out against the wealthy Israelites."[11]

Somehow, the *Journal* saw no contradiction between its bland reporting of discrimination and its invidious marveling at the "numerous, opulent and powerful Israelites" in New York City. "Some of them are exceedingly rich," it confided, "how rich, no one can tell, for they keep their own financial secrets . . . nearly all of them are in comfortable circumstances." Later, it published other wondrous anthropological reports on New York's Jews: "No class of New York's population increases faster than the Hebrew. . . . With all their fondness for money making, the domestic instinct is strong among the Jews . . . [they] marry young and their families are generally large." There were few old bachelors and old maids among them, and also few if any prostitutes—"the degraded of the female sex"—drunkards or brawlers. Many of their "attractive young ladies" worked as saleswomen for the numerous Jewish millinery shops on Division Street, waiting outside for customers, but, "exposed" as they were, they remained "always modest" and would suffer no "offensive remark." Lest its more Puritan-minded readers be overly concerned about the virtue of these women, the paper concluded its observations by remarking, "At all events, Jewish girls, as a class, are well able to take care of themselves."[12]

A morbid, prurient emphasis on the sexual mores of the stranger, became, as Gustavus Myers pointed out in his classic study of bigotry in the United States, one of the characteristics of nativism. Georgia's nativist hero, Tom Watson, at first attacked Catholics and their confessional as a place "in which a lewd priest finds out what girls and married women he can seduce," then in 1913 "the lust of the licentious Jew."[13]

Though most Americans were not bigots, it was hard to shake the clichés and stereotypes. Even Jacob Riis complained of the Russian Jews that "Money is their God." On the eve of a war to save democracy, a congregational preacher could amuse Chautauquans in Vineland with the line, there were but "two Scottish Hebrews," because it was "impossible to get anything from a Scotchman." In this category also was the statement that the first man one met in London was an Englishman—"a sturdy race," but slow—while the "first man in New York was a Hebrew." Yet, the same visiting preacher could close on a note of prevailing American brotherhood: no matter where one was born, what counted most was spirit and ideals.[14]

Such brotherhood was also present in Vineland. In their very first year, the settlers of Alliance were represented by manager Sternberg at Vineland's twenty-first anniversary celebrations. They were, of course, welcome in the stores as customers. There was also praise for their diligence in the fields; "some of the Gentiles might profit by their example," suggested Charles K. Landis, Vineland's founder. On another occasion, one anonymous fruit grower denied "the slanderous report that they will not work," testifying on the basis of his own observations that they labored on the farms and in the berry bogs.[15] Free instruction in Hebrew lore and theology for students at Johns Hopkins University, offered by volunteer Baltimore rabbis, won praise in Vineland, especially as the program was available without "distinction of creed." Local charitable impulses were also aroused at the sight of occasional colonists in distress: a poor Rosenhayn woman and her daughter drove down Landis Avenue one day with a lame and skeleton-like horse, and the good natured crowd, pitying both the woman and the horse, quickly collected enough money for a new, spry animal to hitch to the wagon, plus ample feed. Such was the rightly celebrated American spirit of generosity when brought face-to-face with suffering. To the *Journal*, Vineland seemed "inhabited by the freest-hearted people on the face of the earth." Pride mixed with generous confidence, as it proclaimed boldly, "Other Rosenhaynites, Carmelites and Israelites will please drive up!"[16] But no long lines of supplicants formed to accept the challenge.

Later, when the situation of Jewish people in the ravaged Europe of World War I grew to desperation, the churches of Vineland responded charitably. Appeals from the local Hebrew Relief Association were read from every pulpit on Sunday, January 23, 1916, and most people contributed. Three days later President Wilson reiterated a Senate resolution for relief to destitute Jews, requesting private aid to "the war-stricken people of a race which has given to the United States so many worthy citizens." Vineland's Major Benjamin Stevens issued a parallel proclamation, designating a local committee complete with proper credentials and badges to solicit from the public generally.[17]

In the same year, Vinelanders read how ex-president Taft "paid tribute to the Jewish race" in a well-publicized speech that "painted a wonderful word picture of the Hebrew farmer" as well as farming generally. Taft had been persuaded by George W. Ochs to speak at the nineteenth annual spring exercises of the National Farm School; it was only natural that he compliment the direction and management of the school, while being his genial election-year self.[18]

But these were great national figures, Wilson and Taft, and such issues as European relief remained somehow abstract and impersonal. In an era marked by swift social change, and painful adjustments, how did the native citizens interact with these strangers from Eastern Europe on a long-range person-to-person basis? Some, after all, were concerned that from 1880 to 1900 alone Jewish population in New Jersey had increased 500 percent, although the absolute figures were much less impressive—from 5,600 to over 25,000.[19]

Economic considerations tended to dominate local attitudes toward the colonists from the outset. When the paper announced that "the Russians will swell the population of the county by 2,000," the specific implications were immediately set in terms of purchases in Vineland stores. This was at least partly responsible for editorial hopes that the Vineland colonies would become more successful than their contemporaries in Palestine. (Even as early as 1882, a former United States consul general predicted confidently that the Palestine farming colonies were "lamentable failures" and any future efforts "by either Christians or Hebrews would probably be unsuccessful.")[20] There continued local pride that the focus on Jewish colonies gave Vineland "a world-wide reputation."

Yet between Christian and Jewish laborers all was not always so friendly. Although some "robust Russian Jews" were accepted as farm hands in local homesteads, there were also less sanguine reports of colonists unable to do the work properly, as well as, more seriously, Christian glass workers in Millville walking off their jobs to force the dismissal of 14 Jewish co-workers and for a wage increase of 10 cents per day. When the management (Whitall, Tatem and Company) insisted that replacements for the Jews could not be found, an "infuriated mob" of 500 strikers, armed with clubs, barrel staves, and other weapons, chased the undesirable 14 into the railroad station and out of town. For several days, Millville was a bedlam of street marches, cannonades (ceremonial), and a diversionary attack on Italian construction workers at the site of a new Presbyterian church. Rumors that a Philadelphia employment agency offered to send 120 Jews to replace all the strikers caused even more furor. Members of the Order of American Mechanics took the lead in demanding priority for native labor, and if that be inadequate, then the company should still "discriminate against the Jews in favor of other nationalities." Finally, the union's request for a wage increase was dropped in order to get the company to follow the example of the Bridgeton glass works, which dismissed its Jewish employees at the first sign of trouble.

Within a week, the Millville strike was over; apparently no Jews were among the hundreds returning to work.[21]

In the early 1890's, years of national depression, some Jews from Carmel were reportedly driven to begging for lack of work; a similar fate threatened the unemployed tailors of Rosenhayn. A number of Jewish girls traveled daily from Rosenhayn to Bosio's factory on the corner of Seventh and Landis in Vineland. Although their employer claimed to pay good wages, he nevertheless found it difficult to obtain enough labor in town, perhaps because gentile girls were unwilling to work the sewing machines alongside Jews. Finally, Bosio decided to move to a factory in one of the Jewish colonies, in a rare reversal of the more familiar trend toward Vineland. But apparently the town would not permit the exodus: even as the machines were being taken to the colony, the town's attorney and constable forced their return, ostensibly because of some chattel mortgage obligations. By coincidence, many Jewish tailors working on materials for coats, supplied by Bosio, were arrested on theft charges for failing to return the finished product.[22] Such minor economic autarky did nothing to relieve the impact of depression in the colonies.

Vineland's newspaper advertising also reflected an economic warfare, as the established gentile merchants fought the more modern retailing techniques of the newcomers. In 1896, the "oldest clothier," Granville Steelman, rose to the threat posed by six new clothing stores—"four Hebrews and two Americans"—by appealing to the public to "come to the old reliable and you won't be deceived." The new retailers, he charged, bought shoddy goods from Solomon Isaacs on Lombard Street, put new labels on old merchandise, and had been known to "cheat their creditors and skip town by the light of the moon." In one case, the newspaper reported that A. Bernstein, the new clothier near Baker House, gave notice he would leave town because of poor earnings. It was as false a rumor as the "exaggerated" notice of Mark Twain's death. Bernstein had only left for a day to visit Woodbine, much to the disappointment of his competitors.[23]

If anything, the number of Jewish merchants in Vineland

increased in spite of such early pressures, although there was no end to other annoyances, frequently still couched in economic terms. What was tragic fire for Carmel, was interpreted by insurance men in Vineland as only a curious kind of carelessness. Nor were the colonists spared when pursuing their nobler profession of farming. In 1898, as Jews labored to pick their record crop of blueberries, competitors only blamed them for the depressed prices: "The Jews have overstocked the market, and you know it's hard to 'beat the Jews,'" complained the *Journal.* Years later native observers musingly compared the Hebrew farmers on the west of Vineland with the newer Italian farmers on the east: "While the Hebrews have done extra well and some are neck and neck with the Italians, the sons of Italy show a decided lead in fine crops."[24]

Although this was no lawless frontier country, violence appeared on occasion, as perhaps it does everywhere. During the first winter in Alliance, "some unknown man" walked up to one of the colonists and shot at him point blank, injuring his left hand. The next day, a home in the colony was burned to the ground, the family losing all their belongings. It was presumed to be malicious arson, but no one was ever arrested. At Hanukkah time of 1886, "somebody" smashed in the door of the synagogue; friends of the accused provided more than an adequate number of alibis. The colonists were so incensed, crowed the paper, they wanted to punish the offender as they do "in their country—to cut him in four pieces."[25] Against this ferocious image, however, stood the figure of an inherent Jewish weakness. "The first time in the [ten-year] history of Alliance that a Jew was ever known to show fight or strike back when struck" was when a Jewish family fought to save their sewing machine from a Bridgeton bill collector.

Jews were also represented as a contentious race—much to the delight of Vineland's lawyers who made "a comfortable living out of the Russian Jew trade from Alliance and other settlements. . . . Nearly every other Jew you meet is looking for a lawyer."[26] Specific cases varied. One involved a suit for nonpayment of a match-maker's fee owed to Gerson Pitel of Brotmanville (the bride had refused to pay). Even more exciting, however, was the exposure

179

of neighborhood rows, such as the day Mrs. Moscovitz "banged J. Goldman over the head with a stick of wood"; but never mind, consoled the paper, this is "only a way the Alliance people have of passing the time." Rosenhayn, too, was depicted as fearful of letting a week go by without a "Hebrew scrap," as if Jewish contentiousness was somehow in a special category all its own. "To one who has never before seen a Hebrew quarrel settled in court the sight is a regular circus," began a lead story on one court case; it continued by detailing the passions on both sides, the respective character witnesses and their colorful gestures, and Justice Jones's performance as "ringmaster."[27]

Even horse thieves got into the act by camping near Rosenhayn, thus "giving people a chance to point the finger of scorn" at the indignant settlers. Then to make matters worse, Morris Greenblatt of Alliance brought a "horse story" of his own before Justice Coltun, who finally resolved in his favor a complex dispute over ownership with men from Philadelphia and Rosenhayn. In another case, Alliance drivers were criticized for failing to keep their horse-and-wagons to the right side of the road, and then for taking a "perfect delight in crowding bicycle riders into the ditch." A different version of roadway manners was offered by Louis Mounier: when his horse and buggy were stuck in a swampy stretch, the only one who came to his rescue was the Jewish poultry dealer and part-time matchmaker Gerson Pitel. Mounier dubbed him his good Samaritan.[28]

The school controversies also revealed a persistent bias. Jewish school children in Rosenhayn, politically part of the larger Deerfield Township, were at first segregated in a separate room. The reason was a familiar "I won't have my children sit in the room with the Jews," coupled with concern over the putative health hazard. Within a year, however, the system was abandoned for economic reasons as well as a growing tolerance. As one irate taxpayer said, it would "be foolish extravagance to pay two teachers . . . just to gratify the few who are acting solely from race prejudice and ignorance." Another argument for integration was the advantage it offered in teaching the English language to foreign-born children;

rapid acculturation was, after all, what both Christians and the established German Jewish community required of the East European newcomers.[29] Once when a young gentile girl was willing to tutor children in the "Jewtown" ostensibly for ten cents a day, some thought this would set dangerous precedents. "If the refugees succeeded in driving such bargains, they will soon be prepared to loan money to their American neighbors," so ran the prediction. And even as Rosenhayn's Jewish population declined proportionately in the twentieth century, there still came reports "that the Jews and the Gentiles have had a merry school war."[30]

Nina Morais, of the distinguished Jewish family in Philadelphia, once predicted how Jews would be accepted as an integral part of American society, "infusing into the practical life of our new republic the intellectual warmth of the sun lands." A sceptical response came in a letter to the Vineland *Journal:* It was a pretty prophecy, but when would the Jew stop "confining himself to money making?"[31]

Then as if to aid in the process of reforming Jews, mysterious "young hoodlums" engaged in occasional acts of terrorism against Jewish storekeepers in Vineland. For example, Israel Lerner and his family were harassed throughout the 1890's by broken windows, revolver shots, and brickbats. When Lerner finally collared one of the young men, the punishment was only a lecture from the mayor, for as usual, there was no real proof. The *Journal* sympathized with the Lerner family, who were confronted by bullets from midnight marauders and other similiar unpleasantness, but it failed to call for such mundane measures as lawful protection. "This is a dilemma for Mr. Lerner," the editorial concluded in a romantic understatement, "but [it] would be a small matter for a man who has the spunk to protect his property even if the result was a funeral occasionally."[32]

Even bathing seemed at one time one of the problems in community relations. The Millville newspapers complained about "boys and the Hebrews of Alliance bathing continually" in the pond used for the town's water supply. Still another complaint, that gentiles would be excluded from office in the newly incorporated Woodbine, was denied by Sabsovich as "absolutely false." The

Jewish town employed gentile teachers and welcomed "all good citizens irrespective of their nationality or religion."[33] But as usual, the denial took time to catch up with the accusation.

Almost imperceptibly, however, Jews began to assert themselves in the general community. One *Journal* reader from Alliance demanded to know "what the difference is between a Jewish Democrat and a Methodist? or is there such as Jewish Democracy?" Another time, popular rumor had it that some wily chicken thieves were "Polanders," apparently equated by many with the term Jew, at which M. Klure, a Jewish merchant, wrote in to explain that Polish people were usually Christian, "entirely different from the Jew." Another colonist, obviously far ahead of his time, suggested to the telephone company that he would subscribe to their service only if they could develop an instrument to "take the American language at one end of the line and turn it out Hebrew at the other," for he and his family were not yet fluent enough in the language of their adopted country.[34] Even the derogatory imputation of aggressiveness seemed to help, sometimes; thus, the local office of the Prudential Insurance Company advertised specifically for a "Hebrew agent . . . a hustler."[35]

By World War I, the Vineland *Journal* still resorted to Jewish stereotypes, though much less frequently. For example, the account of a robbery of merchant Harry Lipitz by two burglars in the dead of a Saturday night began, "he was dreaming of money under his pillow" when suddenly awakened by burglars. Just how the reporter surmised the dream is unknown, but Harry in Vineland might just as well have been Shylock in Venice. The two hundred dollars total grossed from the Lipitz family store at the end of a hard week was never recovered, in spite of a brave police chase in automobiles, no less.[36]

The rising strength of the Jewish community in the World War I era was clearly illustrated in the celebrated case of Abe Pitel, son of Gerson. Abe was a spry, second generation scrapper who brooked no nonsense. Though far from being among the wealthy or cultured of his own community, he carried his head proudly. Gideonlike, he defended his people's honor and his father's chicken business against all abuse, even if it came from a local power like Deputy Sheriff Charles P. Sharp. The latter was known for his anti-Jewish profanities, but Abe never feared to answer in kind. At one point, Abe seemed to be the winner, and even persuaded the judge to fine Sharp for his abusive language. But deputy sheriffs don't forgive and forget. Nursing his wounded pride for a month, Sharp finally arrested Abe on one late summer evening, with no reading of warrant, no benefit of bail, no habeas corpus, not even the right to notify his father. "I'm getting even with you now," the deputy was heard to say, and then locked up Abe for the night, perhaps indefinitely.

The Jewish community was up in arms at such police persecution. Justice Kotok fired off a letter of protest to the *Journal,* printed next morning, noting that he had remonstrated vainly with Sharp to release Pitel, or at least to bring him before Justice Florentino, who was sitting at that time. Kotok branded the officer's action "detestable," making him unfit to remain deputy sheriff. He demanded his dismissal. Although Pitel was released soon, a protest meeting was called by the still untested Hebrew Civic Club of Vineland. "There were about a hundred Jews present, and they were a pretty respectable and intelligent bunch," admitted the *Journal's* reporter.

Speakers noted previous examples of "brutal and inhuman treatment" by Sharp. The meeting's chairman, Dr. N. S. Greenwood, maintained order as speakers in English and Yiddish demanded immediate action. First generation immigrants united with the native-born over the issue. Old tailor Seidenstein held forth in Yiddish, while Philadelphia-born Dr. Arthur Goldhaft summarized in English the assembly's opposition to Sharp's abuse of Jews generally. Herman Lemisch, Samuel Goldberg, and others agreed, though Michael Mennies noted that Pitel might have provoked the officer. Goldhaft wondered whether the assembly was actually authorized to go on record with a resolution on behalf of all the Jews of Vineland to censure Sharp. Caution was urged by Messrs. Morvay, Niggin, and Mennies on grounds that this might set a harmful precedent for the future; but the counsel of the timid was rejected, and the censure motion carried. A committee of five was appointed to convey the assembly's feelings to the Sheriff, who had the power to dismiss Sharp. The conference with Sheriff Marshall the day after the protest meeting was termed "congenial," and the affair "considered closed."[37] More important than any specific results, however, was the feat of a minority standing up for its rights and uniting even in the cause of one petty tradesman.

A new era was coming in the history of minorities in America, of which the alleged "baseball riot" in Rosenhayn was also, perhaps, an omen. It occurred on Sunday afternoon, 19 June 1918. It was a shock to "the law-abiding people" and a continuing cause of unrest. The place, worst of all, was the school yard just opposite the Methodist Church. W. J. Purvis, local "law man," called it a "dumping ground for a gang of Virginia colored rowdies [who] disgraced the whole population, Jews and gentiles alike." Benjamin Schwenk, a Rosenhayn baseball player and clerk at the Mennies Young Men's Shop in Vineland, offered a rather different description of the "riot": the "colored men" were army personnel furloughed to work for Seabrook Farms Company; on Sunday, someone proposed a game between Jewish Rosenhayn and Negro Virginia: it seemed harmless, and the game was orderly; there was no riot.[38] Whose version is correct?

Christianity, Prohibition, and Blue Laws

Vineland had been good fundamentalist country since its founding. Baptist, Methodist, or Presbyterian, its people took their Bible seriously and remained faithful to orthodox interpretations. Although a small Unitarian fellowship (the first in New Jersey) had existed since 1865, such "liberal thinkers" were always regarded as a potential source of embarrassment.[39] Fundamentalists believed in an almost literal interpretation of the Bible, strict observance of the Sabbath, temperance, and missionary zeal, all subordinated to a rigid morality and upright living in a community regarded as an integral organism. Instances of immorality or crime, or simply of undesirable action, were viewed with alarm as being injurious to the entire body politic. Consequently, fundamentalists at times tended to place the moral health of the whole over the right of individuals or even groups to act according to their own personal beliefs.

These principles and attitudes have on various occasions stirred passionate controversy, and undoubtedly, debates over separation of church and state, Sunday closing, private versus public definitions of morality, can be expected to persist in one form or another. Such issues were also evident in the impact of Vineland's religious views, which were often written into the law, on relations between Jews and Gentiles during the era of immigrant settlement. One issue was temperance. Vineland had been founded on the eve of the Civil War as a model community based on widespread property ownership and high moral standards. Saloons were banned from the outset, and at every celebration of the town's anniversary a similar goal was recommended to the rest of the country. In the typical parade, "two wagons of WCTU ladies" rode ahead of the speaker's carriage, as the Sunday school chorus sought to stir all America with their rousing rendition of "Saloons Must Go." No speaker failed to praise Vineland as a "prohibition town," and frequently they urged more militant action to outlaw the wicked trade elsewhere.[40]

"Jersey lightning," however, had a fine reputation; it was even exported overseas. Soon enough, the trade involved Jewish men and women. In nearby Bridgeton, where liquor was also banned, "Rebecca Orbish, the Jewess," served one hundred days in jail for selling whiskey in 1888. Later, a Jewish moonshiner from Vineland was sentenced to thirty days in Salem county jail for operating a small domestic still.[41]

Prohibition, of course, presented a general problem of enforcement. As the *Journal* admitted, "liquor is sold illegally at numerous places in and about Vineland." And it continued, too, in spite of fifty-dollar rewards for the conviction of speakeasy operators or go-betweens bringing in liquor for "friends." Jewish violators were always carefully identified in the newspaper articles.[42] Sometimes the local Law and Order League got overly zealous, hauling in retailers who sold cider or vinegar. Jacob Cohen was convicted of selling "an intoxicant called Spanish cider." Such actions frequently led to persistent disputes over chemical analyses versus "practical demonstrations" of the effect on drinkers. In another case, a "new grape juice concoction" caused misunderstandings. On occasions before World War I there were raids against suspected speakeasies in Norma and Rosenhayn. Convictions were few, however, and the main evidence seemed to stem from the East European custom of preparing homemade wines for sacramental use as well as hospitality.[43] To many prohibitionists this seemed only another aspect of the corruption brought by the newcomers.

Understandably, many in Vineland praised Jewish Woodbine's consistent refusal to approve any liquor license applications. In 1919, the prohibition amendment was ratified, climaxing decades of agitation throughout the United States. No longer was the burden limited to local law enforcement and controversy. Once it had become national policy, even Jewish weddings followed the change. Joyfully, Vinelanders read of the first Jewish " 'Prohibition' Wedding" on 18 January 1920. The bridegroom was Herman N. Brotman, son of industrialist Abraham Brotman; the bride, Fannie Melletz. Many leading Vinelanders joined the celebration in Luber's drawing room in Philadelphia, returning home on the early morning train, undoubtedly sober.[44]

At least equally serious was the issue of Sabbath observance as part of the general moral climate. State laws against conducting secular business on Sunday were enforced strictly in the Vineland area, and borough ordinances required prior licensing for any kind of entertainment, exhibit, or concert, Sunday or otherwise. On a national level, the American Sabbath Union worked for a Sunday rest law to "preserve the Christian Sabbath as a day of rest and worship."[45] Debates on the proposed Blair bill to this effect excited Vineland in 1889 and later.

Here was a problem that directly affected both Jews and Seventh Day Adventists, for whom Saturday was the holy day. Objectors maintained that blue laws were not simply a matter of securing for the workingman a required day of rest, but the majority's attempt to enforce its own Sabbath. When some Vinelanders

186

did go into Norma for shopping or entertainment on a Sunday, others, indignant purists, claimed the Jews had given the Sabbath shoppers some kind of potion "which causes them to act 'queer'." One Sunday, a hapless "World's Fair" road show set up in Norma and was fined for creating a disturbance. Such sundry violations of the Sabbath "by a lot of Jews and a few American people" were castigated as nothing short of scandalous. In its report on the "Jew Colony" (Alliance), the *Elmer Times* noted the rare instance of a Jew unfaithful even to his own Sabbath, a newcomer who had moved into town on Saturday.[46]

Economic considerations, too, were an aspect of the Sabbath issue, especially as improved transportation eased travel to and from the colonies, for Jewish stores open on Sunday might take customers from the Vineland shops. "Much to the disgust of church members," reported the *Journal*, Christians went to Rosenhayn to buy meat on Sunday. In one instance, seventeen Jewish store-keepers from Carmel and Rosenhayn were tried before the Bridgeton judge on blue law violations, but were exonerated, possibly because they were known to observe the Sabbath on Saturday. At the same time, a Rabbi Cohen was fined ten dollars and court costs for keeping his small store in Vineland proper open Sunday when all other businesses were closed.[47]

Apparently, this was an issue on which at least Vineland's establishment would brook no compromise or exceptions. In 1914, "the anticipated has come to pass," said the *Journal:* "a Hebrew" dared ask openly foı permission to operate his store on Sunday. The humble petitioner was Mr. Scribner, whose store at 519 Plum Street was next to the synagogue. Out of respect for the worshippers, as well as for his own religious convictions, he kept closed from sundown Friday until Saturday night, but he could not afford to do so until Monday. At the hearing, Mayor Stevens flatly denied his request, while Councilman Bugbee pontificated that "those who adopted America as their home should observe America's custom." Properly chastised, Scribner could only retire with a respectful "thank you" to his elected superiors.[48]

Such Puritanical restrictions as the ban on Sunday dancing

extended even into the highly personal area of weddings. From the outset, no dancing at any kind of group function was allowed until after midnight Sunday. To insure against violations, township officials were posted at the gala occasions: so at the wedding of Sarah Berstein and Samuel Kishner, the proud father asked the band to strike up for dancing early in the course of the festivities, but was forced to hold off until the prescribed midnight hour. Nonetheless, it was a festive spring wedding, complete with the traditional religious ceremony under a canopy, friends of the bride and groom in a circle holding candles, and abundant refreshments (nonalcoholic). The bride was honored with a bouquet of flowers from the local Workingmen's Circle Branch 57, and Mr. Berstein, pleased "to have so many Americans attend," made them all feel at home, even the watchful town marshals.[49]

Far less pleasant was the continuing row over Jewish-sponsored "Sunday balls" in Rosenhayn. Nothing as sinful was tolerated within the wide triangle of Vineland, Millville, and Bridgeton. By 1912, the "church people" of Rosenhayn itself were up in arms against the Sunday night carousals, with a vigilante committee vowing to close the social dance halls. "The Americans feel that if the Hebrews do not wish to observe the laws of America they do not have to stay here," was the way the *Journal* summarized the situation.[50]

Such an attitude still persisted thirty years after the establishment of Alliance. Almost a quarter-century since the first Jewish farmers had received their citizenship papers, an angry Jewish letter writer demanded to know, "If we are not Americans, kindly tell us who are, how we may distinguish them. . . . It seems to us that if these moral and pious 'Americans' that are so shocked at harmless 'balls' would open their eyes to what some of [their fellow] 'Americans' do on Sunday they would become so busy that they would not notice the 'balls' at all." Intolerant invitations to obey or leave, he concluded, smacked too much of Russia.[51]

But the bold were more than matched by the moderate. Louis Mounier, educational director for the colonies, acted as a kind of official spokesman. He publicly chastised both extremes, but especially the Jew who had compared the blue law champions to Russian bigots. Furthermore he made it clear that "the majority must have the priority when for some reason it does not wish to compromise." The matter of Sunday dances "is not one of religion but of civics," requiring everyone to abide by the law. All minorities, he counseled, should learn the wisdom of "when in Rome do as the Romans" unless sheer necessity dictates otherwise. Even then, however, unjust laws must not be violated, though in a free country one might work for their repeal. Only in Alliance or Woodbine, still almost all Jewish, could the blue laws be ignored.[52]

Within a year, Sunday dancing in Carmel and Rosenhayn was forbidden, and events previously scheduled were cancelled. It was not, apparently, the kind of willing compliance Mounier had hoped for. But his decision to close the two community halls to such objectionable functions was "hailed [in Vineland] by all good citizens." Those who preferred to dance on their one day off were less enthusiastic, nor was there much joy among those who preferred to shop or work on Sunday. Mounier persisted, however: the Constitution may not be Christian but the nation is. Even many Jews, he noted approvingly, recognized this fact by shifting "their time-proved Sabbath or day of rest, to the Christian Sunday."[53]

Of course, the kind Mounier (Unitarian son of a French Deist) was not proselytizing; he was just trying to make peace, in his own gentle if naive manner. Many Christians, however, did see the religious conversion of the Jews as an essential aspect of their assimilation as well as their salvation: to become a "real" American and at the same time to save his soul was the tantalizing fruit dangled before the immigrant. Here too, as in sweatshops, strikes, and less than equal citizenship, the environment of South Jersey was perhaps not too different from that of the Lower East Side.[54] In fact, one of Vineland's most colorful missionaries had his main office on New York's East Seventh Street, just a short walk from the poor relief station of the United Hebrew Charities; he was Meyer Lenman (or Lerman), billed as "the oldest missionary to the Jews" in the United States.

Lenman distributed tracts and delivered sermons in Yiddish

to the Jews of Alliance, Carmel, Rosenhayn, and Vineland. On such occasions, the beneficiaries of his message were no longer merely "Russian Hebrews," but "God's own people, Israel." He was a popular speaker too at the Presbyterian Church, according to the *Journal,* "and the Jews of Vineland should hear him." And they did come out, but hearing was not believing: although Lenman's visits were termed a "great success," only three from the area "expressed a willingness to become Christians."[55]

Another "missionary lady" was also at work in Alliance, Carmel, and Norma, where the population continued to be predominantly Jewish. In Rosenhayn, however, lived a sizable number of Christian families, some of whom preceded the Jewish settlement. Here, much more ambitious missionary campaigns were conducted, including long camp meetings led by Professor Stroeter and the Reverend A. C. Gaebelein. The latter claimed the impressive distinction of having converted over six hundred Jews. In Rosenhayn also, a Hebrew Mission and free reading room was opened to serve all the colonies. The town became a center for missionaries from all parts of the country. Among them was Philip Sidersky, a converted Jew whose good work in Rosenhayn brought him also invitations to speak at the Presbyterian Church of Vineland.[56]

Other converts, such as S. K. Braun, were favorite speakers in the local churches; oddly, their topic was often the life and customs of the Jews or such ethnic subjects as the ten lost tribes. Undoubtedly, there was a natural thirst among the Christians for more information about the people of the Bible who were appearing in modern guise as familiar farmers, merchants, or labor agitators. One can only wonder both how much objective information was gleaned by a Baptist as he listened to a convert speak on the "peculiar life and worship of the Jews," and how effective convert Maurice Ruben was as he addressed a packed house of Presbyterians on the meaning of the Jewish Passover. As the *Journal* admitted, "Mr. Ruben is trying also to convince the Hebrews that they are mistaken in celebrating the passover in the way they do, that their guest [Elijah, messenger of the Messiah] arrived long ago

190

when Christ was born." But although "a good many Jews" heard these latter-day appeals, apparently none came forward.[57] Mutual respect between Jews and Christians might have been furthered by the kind of unbiased inter-group exchanges in which future generations would participate, but neither side in Vineland nor in the country generally seemed as yet ready for this approach.

Jewish religious leadership in town was initially weak, even after the first Vineland synagogues were founded in 1905 and 1906. The colonies had synagogues, but no rabbis to answer questions involving relations with church bodies or public agencies in the area.[58] Such an issue, for example, was the matter of kosher meat which had to be ordered from Philadelphia. The Vineland Council classified the visiting butcher who filled such orders as simply a common "peddler," requiring him to pay twenty dollars every three months in license fees. But to the butcher and his regular customers this seemed a punitive measure, even if it did please the proprietor of the local Enterprise Meat Market. Who would explain the laws of *kashrut* to the Council and plead on behalf of the traditionally faithful Jews who were paying more for their imported meat? For lack of clergy, industrialist John H. Joseph came forward, armed with a letter from a Philadelphia rabbi stating that ordinary butcher shops which did business on the Sabbath and sold pork were unqualified to supply kosher meat. Since the Enterprise Meat Market failed on both counts, the meat orders from Philadelphia were a basic necessity. As spokesman for the group, Joseph pleaded that the special tax be revoked. He might have quoted the great John Marshall's dictum that the power to tax is the power to destroy; but in any case, the council referred the matter to committee, where it faced an uncertain fate.[59]

It was not entirely necessary that even such technical matters remain a stumbling block to Christian-Jewish understanding. By World War I, the *Journal* was quoting the *Boston Transcript* on the wisdom of Jewish dietary and sanitary laws in general, including the prohibition of pork or other unclean foods and the ritual slaughter of permitted animals. Most of all, the full-length editorial

191

praised those far-sighted aspects of the Mosaic code that attempted to quarantine diseased animals, calling them hygienic "hints the Gentile world did not fully accept until a century or two ago."[60]

Indeed, bigotry was not a very serious problem between Jew and Christian in South Jersey. By and large, economic and civic relations tended to focus on mutual respect. Jews were often "cordially invited" to church programs, even if sometimes in the hope of converting them. Nonetheless, it was the spirit of mingling rather than segregation. Increasingly, the old vicious stereotypes disappeared as the barriers to understanding crumbled in the twentieth century.

A generation before World War I, in the year Alliance was founded, Emma Lazarus prophesied that the putative "dualism of the Jew is the dualism of humanity; they are made up of the good and bad." It was wrong, she pleaded in the pages of *Century,* to think of two kinds of Jews in terms of one as westernized and acceptable and the other as the benighted Russian, physically and morally stunted by inhuman persecution. Their "social and moral code," a heritage of all Jews whether from Germany or the Slavic countries, gave them the strength to contribute bountifully whereever they were not cramped by tyrannical restrictions.[61] It was good advice to her fellow Americans, both Christian and Jew, and especially to those who still feared the unassimilated East European immigrants. For they would prove their merit long before Arthur Goldberg, son of Russian Hebrews, sat on the bench of the Supreme Court or represented his country in the United Nations.

Reaction to European Anti-Semitism

The vast front page coverage given in Vineland to the tragic stories of Jewish suffering is in itself remarkable, for pogroms in Bessarabia, Russia, Poland, and perhaps riots even in a more civilized Berlin or Vienna, might all have seemed far-away events of little import to South Jersey. Nevertheless the sordid details of Europe's inhumanity unfolded almost daily before the local readers from the 1870's to the end of World War I.

Sometimes, the United States' role was mentioned, as in the

wake of anti-Jewish riots in Berlin early in 1881; Germans were reportedly resentful of protests by Americans, "the feeling being that Germany can tolerate no intervention in home affairs by a foreign State."[62] But more usually, the accounts concerned a range of anti-Semitic depradation, from the academic Jew-baiting of Germany's Dr. Henrici to the tightening of ghetto restrictions by Russia's General Ignatieff and the massacres instigated by Tsarist police as cossacks sent to "restore order" joined the mobs in arson, rape, and murder. In captive Warsaw too, "outrages against Jews . . . were encouraged by the apathy of the officials" (1882).[63] There were reports also of violence in the Austro-Hungarian Empire, in places where Jewish culture had flourished for centuries, like the home of the great Talmudic academy, the city of Pressburg, whence six hundred Jewish families were forced to flee.[64] Westward, French anti-Semitism was epitomized in the dramatic case of Captain Alfred Dreyfus, a Jewish officer condemned on false charges to life imprisonment on Devil's Island. Throughout the Dreyfus affair, Vinelanders were kept well informed as both Jews and non-Jews watched with agonized interest the mounting evidence of justice distorted by bigotry. Dreyfus was finally vindicated in 1906 by France's highest tribunal, but the anti-Semitic propaganda and riots accompanying the affair remained a shocking contradiction of French democracy.[65]

This kind of railroading by court-martial, "foul with forgeries, lies, contradictions and puerilities,"[66] aroused American public sympathy for the victim and his co-religionists; in the course of the French scandal, Grand Rabbi Zadok Kahn had been basely denounced as "the leader of an infamous Jewish conspiracy against France," according to an indignant *Vineland Evening Journal.* Even Henry Adams, who despised Jews for their ostensible threat to Boston's aristocracy, admitted that the whole Dreyfus Affair represented the " 'moral collapse' of 'soldiers and civilians alike,' indeed of France itself."[67]

But for moral bankruptcy and brutal treatment of the Jewish minority none was worse than Imperial Russia. In the 1890's following an extension of the May Laws thousands of Jews were expelled from Moscow, Kiev, St. Petersburg, and other cities outside the Pale of Settlement. The barbarous pogroms of the 1880's had brought protest meetings in London, New York, and Philadelphia, as well as a resolution by the United States House of Representatives and a formal denunciation by Secretary of State Frederick T. Frelinghuysen. These and other protests, though, had little lasting effect. With a worsening of official persecution in the 1890's, the Tsar was said to be "irritated by the interference of foreign priests and preachers."[68] In the New World, the Vineland *Journal* was among those that featured accounts of the atrocities, torture, and famine reported by newly arrived refugees.[69]

Again, in 1892, the House Committee on Foreign Affairs focused its concern on the worsening persecution, "as vast numbers of Jews driven from Russia are continually seeking refuge here." It was obvious, moreover, that Russia's laws were enacted against only a specific segment of her population. How would such biased policies affect the status of American citizens of the Jewish faith who may be in Russia for business or personal reasons? asked the Committee. "Our Government can make no distinction based on creeds or birthplaces of its citizens, nor can it permit such distinction to be made by foreign powers. . . . This much is due to the commercial greatness, the usefulness and patriotism of American Jews," concluded the Committee's report.[70] In the national elections of 1892, both major parties also included in their platforms expressions of sympathy for the oppressed Jews of Russia.

Such statements were a prelude to future American foreign policy in opposition to Russian pogroms. But the worst was yet to come. More than most of the American public, Vinelanders read of the tragic Kishinev massacres of 1903: forty-five men, women and children killed, eighty-four mutilated and severely wounded, five hundred injured, ten thousand homeless.[71] Unlike other newspapers, the *Journal* had no editorial on the subject, perhaps because the facts spoke eloquently enough; nor did it comment on the joint resolution of protest passed by Congress, or the personal note of deep concern from Theodore Roosevelt to Tsar Nicholas II in which the President remarked that he had never "known of a more immediate or deeper expression of sympathy for the victims . . . of horror over the appalling calamity that has occurred."[72]

But the pogroms in Russia continued, even if temporarily abated during the Russo-Japanese War. Stirred by reverses in the Far East, according to the *Journal*, a mob attacked Jewish homes in the town of Bender, "threw women and children out of the windows," and committed other atrocities. It was a Saturday, when most of the congregants were in the synagogues.[73] Such was the harrowing fate also of Jews in Lodz and Warsaw in 1905 and in the reign of terror which brought even worse new massacres to Kishinev and spread throughout Russia into Odessa, Bialystok, and countless other cities, towns, and villages. "Heads were battered with hammers; nails were driven into bodies; eyes were gouged out . . . petroleum was poured over the sick found hiding in cellars, and they were burned to death." In Kiev, reported the *Journal* (reprinting dispatches from the London papers), "children and old people have been barbarously murdered while the military and police looked on with cynical indifference."[74] The tragic catalogue of massacre, torture, fire, and expulsion reappeared over the years on the front pages of the *Journal*. Featured again and again were the heartbreaking personal accounts by refugees who had managed to escape to freedom.

The trial of Mendel Beilis, accused of so-called ritual murder, presented a new, rather sordid development in the Russia of 1913. A Christian boy's body had been found with numerous stab wounds. As the *Journal* explained in a front page article, the accusers "alleged that the blood of the boy was used in a Jewish ceremony." Only after an ordeal of more than two years was Beilis finally acquitted amidst threatened pogroms by the terrorist Black Hundred.[75] Amazingly, the Russian jury still insisted on the validity of the ritual murder charge, and government propaganda continued to use an elaborate structure of distortion for anti-Semitic incitement. In America, the highest Catholic and Protestant prelates joined in petitioning the Tsar: "in the name of our sacred faith," they prayed that such blood libels, once used against early Christians, be withdrawn.[76] It was only the confession of a Russian criminal gang that brought the notorious case to an end, and the Jewish population could breathe easier.

Vineland was treated to a dramatic rendition in Yiddish of all the melodrama and passion of "Mendel Beilis." The Lieberman Stock Company came in December to perform it in the town's Auditorium. In Carmel, too, amateur actors were organized to produce a film on the Russian blood libel case. It was Hanukkah of 1913, another season of deliverance, this time from the Pharaoh of Eastern Europe.[77]

Such was the country, as Georg Brandes noted in his *Impressions of Russia,* where "all knowledge is dreaded . . . the universities are closed at the least sign of a disturbance . . . [and] the press cannot have any political importance."[78] Even the Russian Church, as he failed to add (perhaps for fear of the censor), was intimately allied with the tyrannical regime. In the open society of the United States, however, many channels of knowledge were available to the public, including detailed press reports on the pogroms. In Vineland, as elsewhere in the United States, these were part of the informational background shaping American attitudes toward Jews, immigration, and social protest movements.

Throughout the era of persecution in Russia, the American conscience was never stilled. In Philadelphia, State Senator Horatio Gates Jones and Mayor King joined early in the relief plans proposed by the local chapter of the Alliance, led by Moses A. Dropsie and William Hackenburg. Speaking for "most of the Christian ministers," too, the Reverend R. H. Harper expressed his "horror at the treatment of the Jews" and desire to assist in the refugee relief campaign.[79] Volunteers, including many non-Jews, provided medical care, food, and employment services to the thousands of refugees.[80]

The New Jersey Assembly had adopted its first resolution in 1882 "demanding protection for the oppressed Jews of Russia." This reminder appeared in the Vineland *Journal* along with later protests from eminent world figures, such as Gladstone, who expressed his "horror at the cruelties of the Russian Government toward the Jews." Tolstoy's statement on the Kishinev massacre was also reprinted: "My relation to the Jews can only be as that to brothers whom I love. . . . [Horror and pity] mingled with perplexity at the bestiality of the so-called educated people who instigated the mob . . . the government, with its foolish, fanatical priesthood and gang of robber officials . . . hesitating at no atrocity. . . . The Kishinev crime was a consequence of preaching lies and violence which the government carries on with such stubborn energy."[81]

In response to the new Kishinev pogrom, Philadelphians held three protest meetings, while at a Baltimore meeting three thousand people heard, among other things, a statement from Cardinal Gibbons; reprinted verbatim in the *Journal,* it expressed his "abhorrence at the massacres that have carried to their graves gray hair and innocent childhood." In Atlantic City, too, Jewish Chautauquans met in protest and listened as the oppression of Russian Jews was dramatically depicted by former immigration commissioner John B. Weber, who headed a congressional committee studying causes of mass migration to the United States.[82]

Oddly, the Vineland *Journal* neglected protest demonstrations closer to home. Were the local Russian Hebrews, having themselves reached safety, now simply indifferent to the fate of their brethren? Not at all; one need only look in the *Jewish Exponent* to find full coverage of their mass meetings. The colonists did not forget: farmers and tailors, they too gathered to protest, to pray, to make collections. (But was it not all a mock tragedy, this mass scurrying of little people? In the wake of the Nazi genocide, does it not seem a Chaplinesque charade of helpless protesters?)

From all the colonies and from Vineland itself, they trooped into Carmel's new Columbia Hall "to take action regarding recent outrages." Professor Mounier presided, speaking as a "Christian sympathizer." Other speakers included Louis E. Levy, representing Philadelphia's Association of Jewish Immigrants, and George Goward, industrial agent for the Baron de Hirsch Fund.[83] In Woodbine also, the response to Kishinev was a heartfelt cry of anguish and an immediate stirring to relieve the victims. "Bravo, Woodbine!" proclaimed the *Forward,* in one of its rare expressions of praise (for such were times that united the American Jewish community). Abraham Cahan, editor of the *Forward,* made a passionate personal appeal at the Woodbine rally. Relief funds were raised and later collections continued by an emergency-aid committee. The contributions turned in to the *Forward* were impressive, and the newspaper commented glowingly on the generous response of "this Jewish town of 1,800, especially when one considers that they are almost all poor people."[84] A greater sacrifice was made not far away in Jamestown, where a protest rally of Jewish Chautauquans was addressed by a rabbi from Cleveland, who, in the midst of describing the horrors of Kishinev, suffered a fatal collapse.[85]

It was in vain, this wave of protest sweeping the United States, a futile sop to national conscience. The Vineland *Journal* considered the "embarrassment" caused to Russo-American relations by the protest petitions, as it described Jewish representatives in conference with President Roosevelt or Secretary of State John Hay trying to plan the wording of some protest or pick the most opportune time of presentation. The Russian giant, however, seemed unmoved and unmovable. The "delicate task" remained abortive as the Tsarist government refused to accept or consider the transmitted "Jewish petition."[86] Like Germany before, Russia insisted that the persecution of her Jewish minority was, in the language of diplomacy, a purely domestic matter. Revolution, World War, Bolshevism, and Civil War were to make the position of Russia's Jews chronically precarious—an entire people walked a tightrope called survival. Up until 1920, the Vineland *Journal* continued to report countless victims of pogroms in the Ukraine, estimating the total killed through most of 1919 at twenty-nine thousand.[87]

At the same time, the *Journal* highlighted evidence of the growing acceptance of Jews in America. One example that caused a sensation in 1911 was a minor, inverse Dreyfus affair in the United States army. The hero was Frank Bloom, a young American who had tried for years to enter West Point but without success. Finally, on the advice of President Roosevelt, he enlisted to work his way up from the ranks, but in spite of a good record, including service on the Mexican border, his promotion to lieutenant was blocked by Colonel Joseph H. Garrard, commanding officer of cavalry at Fort Myer, Virginia. Accompanying Bloom's application was the Colonel's reference letter damning the potential officer with faint praise: Yes, the young man was "undoubtedly honest and upright, ambitious and probably deserving, but . . . [he] is a son of Joseph A. Bloom, of Jewish persuasion . . . a tailor . . . [and therefore] I would not desire him in my command as an officer and a social and personal associate." Moreover, the Colonel concluded, he knew that Bloom and his family would be unwelcome at other army posts because of their religion, which could only result in "mortification" for them and "trouble" to higher officers. President Taft learned of the Garrard letter, apparently through Simon Wolf, pioneer leader in the American branch of the Alliance and the American Jewish Committee. As "Commander-In-Chief of the Army and Navy," Taft rebuked the Colonel, specifying: "I resent . . . such unfounded and narrow race prejudice. . . . The statements made by Colonel Garrard are not true with reference to the standing that Jews have in this country." In a long, front page Vineland article headlined "Taft befriends Hebrew in Army," the President was quoted as finding it difficult to read the Garrard letter "without condemnatory words that had better not be written."[88]

Growing acceptance within New Jersey and American society was exemplified even in overblown compliments to a declining Jewish agrarianism, such as an editorial reprinted from the *Newark News:* "In our own State there are at least five colonies of Jewish farmers, with a dozen associations and over 200 individual members [1914], and these and other foreigners are among the more successful and prosperous of the tillers of the soil." If the older native stock could no longer appreciate farming, it was only right that these "new Americans" should make such good use of the land, concluded the editorial—"even as our own forefathers did two or three centuries ago."[89] Such laudatory messages, toward those already here, hardly included the admission of more immigrants.

Closing the Door on the Immigrant

All the aspects of America's attitude towards the Old World and towards the aliens already in her midst were ultimately bound up with the single issue of immigration. To commiserate with the victims of oppression, to sign petitions, and to contribute money for their relief, even to welcome refugees with the traditional New World hospitality, all this was a hallmark of the progressive spirit. But a line had to be drawn somewhere, often at the point where newcomers seemed to threaten the natives' economic, social, or political habits. "Drawing the line" was practiced even before twentieth century restrictions, and its adherents included native and Americanized Jews as well as non-Jews.

Some early agitation for restricting the flow of immigrants came from nativist organizations with know-nothing roots, such as the American Protective Association (1887). However, this group's preoccupation with finding Catholic conspiracies everywhere soon became somewhat old-fashioned, especially with the rise of the Immigration Restriction League (1894). Originating in Boston and particularly strong among some of New England's best families, the League focused its attention on the need to safeguard Anglo-Saxon predominance from the threatening tide of inferior strangers. The latest immigrants from Southern and Eastern Europe, warned the League, were "historically down-trodden, atavistic, and stagnant." How could such people make any kind of positive contribution? An appeal was made also to organized labor to protect the "better class" of wage earners from the "horde of illiterate, unskilled laborers, . . . almost entirely in the cities of the Atlantic States . . . [who were] a menace to the labor as well as the national interests."[90] The Vineland *Journal* waxed enthusiastic over proposals in the Italian Chamber of Deputies to refuse a passport to any potential emigrant lacking funds for passage across the Atlantic and initial upkeep in the New World. Would that other European countries adopt such policies to save America from the impoverished![91]

Poverty was indeed one of the marks of Europe's oppressed. Long before the doors were closed by legislative restrictions, the

Journal reported the "sorrowful tale" of a large group of Russian emigrants wandering about the seaports of Germany for lack of means to complete their voyage to the New World. Later, when other wanderers could receive at least temporary assistance from the philanthropic societies, the *Journal* advised caution lest these "pauperize the refugees. . . . Like Oliver Twist, they will still cry for more."[92]

Informed in detail of the "horrible" situation of the Jews in Russia, Vinelanders were yet forewarned against any efforts to "unload the unfortunates on the United States." Even after Federal law had excluded aliens who might become public charges (1882) and those whose passage was paid by labor contractors (1885), the *Journal* expressed fears of inundation by the destitute. An unnamed "prominent manufacturer in New Jersey" was rumored to have attempted evading the ban on contract labor in order to guarantee employment for several hundred "exiled Russian Jews" (1891). In the same breath, the paper reported that the "Hebrews of Warsaw" were both persecuted by the Russian authorities and in control of all commerce and trade in that capital city—"very few of the Jews being engaged in ordinary labor."[93] It was the familiar, self-contradictory stereotype of people at once too rich for honest work and yet poor enough to threaten the jobs of humble workers. Jewish leaders, engaged in rescue and resettlement, perforce remained sensitive to such charges, so they followed the example of the Baron de Hirsch Fund in public disclaimers of any intent to bring paupers into the country or that those assisted were a threat to American labor.

An early example of the risks incurred in these efforts was one of the abortive attempts to settle refugees in a suburban colony, one near Hightstown, just east of Trenton. The site had been favored by James H. Hoffman, chairman of the Fund's committee on agricultural and industrial settlements, but as word leaked out, the price of land skyrocketed; the ambitious plans were abandoned and the first thirteen families were forced to seek the usual work in a nearby shirt factory. With the Fund's decision to concentrate instead on Woodbine, the local land boom was replaced by dire predictions of "Hebrew competitors," as labor and merchants "suddenly became jealous." Many taxpayers, originally enthusiastic at the prospect of investments by wealthy outsiders, now wanted the poor foreigners to go. "Sermons were preached against them," reported the *Journal*.[94]

By providing for the resettlement of immigrants, the Fund exposed itself to accusations that its pie-in-the-sky promises encouraged Jews to leave Europe "under any pretext . . . [for] they all expect to get rich in America." Many would be bitterly disappointed. Failing to find quick fortune and deceived by their benefactors, the *Journal* charged, they would apply for re-entry to Russia, where conditions were perhaps not really so bad. The authority for this conclusion was the Russian vice-consul in New York, a not unbiased source, who claimed "the secret of the Jewish exodus was that they had an idea they would get money from the Hirsch fund."[95] Persecution and pogroms took a back seat, at times, as rationalization combined with nativist expediency.

Some immigrants, however, did honestly feel deceived and disillusioned by conditions in America which in some respects were almost as oppressive as those of Dickens's England. It was an era of instability and extremes of wealth and poverty. "So wretched were conditions in 1888," wrote Moses Rischin in *The Promised City*, an epic of New York's Jews, "that 200 immigrants were shipped back to Europe in cattle steamers."[96]

Even the eloquent oratory protesting the pogroms in Russia was often colored by the facts of America's economic revolution. On the one hand, Jews were, in John Weber's words, "the sport of the rabble, the spoil of the official, the football of fanaticism, the buffer against which strikes the wrath of bigotry, intolerance and savagery." On the other, they were those "who [had] come to us crushed in spirit and impoverished in substance, entering into competition with our respected and self-respecting labor." Although Weber rejected in principle the pressures for closing freedom's doors to the masses of "hunted, terror-stricken human beings," he could not in practice accept everyone who wished to make this country his new home. While admitting that the New World had been built by immigrants, Weber claimed that refugees from Russia represented an "abnormal immigration" resulting from the Tsarist repressions; it would be preferable, he maintained, if immigration were confined to "normal causes alone."[97] Such standards of normalcy represented, indeed, a radical departure from America's traditional open door. Had they been applied previously, one can only wonder how many would have been admitted at all, from among the Irish, the Germans, the Norwegians, or even from among the early Puritans, Huguenots, or Quakers. In any case, Weber's solution was twofold: prevail upon Russia to become more tolerant; divert the refugees elsewhere. Ironically, Weber's services had been procured for the optimum development of Woodbine as an immigrant haven.

By the time of this speech (1903), there arose an apparent agreement between the Immigration Restriction League and the American Federation of Labor. Samuel Gompers, writing to Georgia Congressman James E. Watson, confirmed labor's support of proposed new literacy requirements as well as other measures to restrict immigration. Himself an Anglo-Jewish immigrant, Gompers warned that "both the intelligence and the prosperity of our working people are endangered by the present immigration. Cheap labor, ignorant labor, takes our jobs and cuts our wages."[98] Although vetoed by Presidents Cleveland, Taft, and Wilson, the literacy requirement finally became law in 1917.

Almost in vain did the Liberal Immigration League (New York) publish testimonials from many distinguished figures (including a former President) on the 250th anniversary of Jewish settlement in America citing the Jewish people as particularly "the source of all the highest conceptions of God, man, and nature; [the] industry and virtue" of these immigrants made sturdy by centuries of oppression accompanied a remarkable "facility of adaptation and assimilation." Yet, even the League pleaded that the new mass immigration was a national rather than merely a local problem requiring more equitable "distribution" throughout the country, wherever labor was relatively scarce. It took due note of the criticism by Commissioner of Immigration Frank P. Sargent, who saw the "alien communities in our great cities [as] a menace to the physical, moral, and political security of the country. . . . Do away with them [by redistribution] and the greatest peril of immigration will be removed," he advised.[99] As the ravages of World War I spread throughout Europe, the *Jersey Journal* (quoted favorably in Vineland) predicted the removal of legal disabilities from the Jews in Russia so they would no longer need to crowd American labor markets: being "frugal and intelligent above the average," they would prosper at home, resisting the old temptation to risk the "hardships of a new home among strangers."[100] Sadly, the hopeful and flattering prophecy proved less than half-right: for millions, the Russian homeland was to become a prison or a grave.

While the anti-immigration agitation could never have been anything but unpleasant to the Russian Jews, it must have been even more so when it came from their own brethren as well. Among the newer immigrants, the Russian Jews were numerous, mobile, and readily distinguishable, sometimes even bizarre in appearance; they outnumbered by far the earlier Jewish arrivals of Spanish-Portuguese and German origin, who in the face of their less fortunate brethren found it more difficult to display a distinctive communal behavior developed over years of acculturation. Meanwhile, the German Hebrews, as they preferred to call themseves, had in many cases achieved some economic success and even substantial social acceptance. Could they now disassociate themselves from the newcomers? To their dismay, by the turn of the century, any distinction between "refined Hebrew ladies and gentlemen" and "vulgar Jews" seemed no longer in vogue.[101] German Jews sometimes still contemptuously called the new immigrants "Polacks." At one of the first meetings of the Hebrew Emigrant Society, Michael Heilprin himself had to admonish such detractors by quietly reminding them, "I am a Polish Jew. I belong to that despised race."[102] But though Heilprin wrote for the *Nation,* his views were ignored by the *Hebrew Standard* and other spokesmen of the German community; in their eyes, the "thoroughly acclimated American Jew . . . [was] closer to the Christian sentiment around him than to the Judaism of these miserable darkened Hebrews." The *American Hebrew* seemed more distressed by the "un-American . . . Orientalism" of the East Europeans than were even non-Jews.[103]

Likewise, the westernized Jews were sensitive to both the newer manifestations of anti-Semitism on the Continent and the anti-immigration movement in the United States, particularly to recurrent charges that paupers were being brought into the country. Not primarily relief, but rural colonization and training for those selected as the most capable were the means to producing good and loyal Americans, well-integrated into the cultural fabric. Even friendly visitors to the South Jersey colonists continually warned them to avoid separatist ways—"not to make a Ghetto of their own."[104] Thus, the established Jewry became protectors and intermediaries in the process of acculturation to the prevailing society. Underlying the many good works of philanthropy and discernible in all the rural colonization programs, is this theme of Americanization, of adapting in every way to western society. Was this the foremost gift of the German Jews to their East European brethren?

Struggle for identity: American and Jewish

Never should it cross our minds for an instant to shrink from proclaiming that we are Jews.
Sefer Hasidim

Despise not those obliged to violate the Sabbath, but admonish them gently not to forsake the Law.
Maimonides, Iggeret Ha-Sh'mad

This synagog is our temple, this city our Jerusalem, this happy land our Palestine.
Gustav Poznanski, sermon, Charleston, S. C.
19 March 1841

7

Citizenship and Judaism

The Russian Jews who crowded suddenly onto the quiet streets of old Salem, New Jersey, and trooped along its modest thorough-fare, many still conspicuous in their East European clothes and beards, seemed an outlandish phenomenon in the town founded by colonial Quakers. Not fewer than eighty green farmers and part-time tailors from Jewish Alliance were present on that memorable 22 October 1889 to receive their final citizenship papers. Though closer to Vineland in distance and economics, Alliance was just inside the Salem County line. Historic coincidence had brought these newcomers to a place whose name was the Hebrew word for peace and whose founders had been another oppressed religious minority; before the Civil War, Quakers in South Jersey had partici-pated in the underground railroad, now their town was again a station on the road to freedom.

Salem was a friendly community. To handle the rush of new applicants, it organized a special court where the clerks were reportedly patient even with those immigrants who could not yet write. For the citizens-to-be it seemed an almost miraculous process, this final ritual of naturalization in the Land of Freedom. To become a citizen of the United States was for them a "distinction of as high importance as that of a governorship in the czar's domains."[1] One liberal Russian dignitary invited to witness the event exclaimed, "Of all the varied scenes which America affords, none can be of greater interest for the Muscovite visitor than the sight of Jewish farmers of Russian birth rejoicing under the blessings of a free citizenship of this glorious republic—a privilege for which their co-religionists of my country have so long struggled, alas! in vain." Local observers, too, wondered at the periodic mass pilgrimages. On another such occasion, one awed reporter from nearby Elmer "saw something like an army . . . Jews from Jewtown going to Salem to get naturalized."[2]

The new citizens applied themselves with a zeal to the practices of their adopted country. As elsewhere, July Fourth in South Jersey's rural settlements was a day of patriotic speeches, marching, music, and entertainment. Apparently, Woodbine's musical and theatrical celebrations of Independence Day were so notable that they attracted scores of visitors from Philadelphia and New York who then stayed on for dances sponsored by the Ladies' Aid Society. Rosenhayn's added attractions were bicycle and horse races conducted by the local Knights of Pythias, as well as the usual baseball and free ice cream.

For the younger generation the baseball squad sponsored by the Norma Athletic Association and including Alliance and Brotmanville, embodied the fun and opportunity of the New World. Baseball, "more than anything else, gripped our youthful imagination . . . [it] showed that we were really Americans."[3] On that "gallant team" were such local champions as Jake Spiegel, Isaac Lipman, Israel Levinson, "Big Izzie" Goldstein, John Levin, Moe Spiegel, and others, many of whom later served on a greater team in World War I.

The colonists became Americans almost as a matter of course, whether through the process of naturalization or, as did their children, by birth. The achievement of this cherished new status set them above the newly arrived aliens, the still lowly greenhorns. In this country they were not just permitted, but guaranteed the right to practice the religion of their fathers. In the incomparable haven of America the East European Jews could enjoy for the first time a freedom both secular and spiritual. Economic or political opportunity no longer had to be purchased at the price of baptism or servile dependence on the will of the mighty, or religious devotion and learning at the cost of ghetto imprisonment. In the Old World, one could not at the same time feel truly free both as Russian and Jew; in the New, one could be American and any religion he pleased, even no religion at all. If the shock of uprooting and migration was traumatic, perhaps equally so was this discovery of freedom which tested old loyalties and demanded new ones. With Americanization as a primary and natural objective, would Judaism flourish as well?

Except for a handful of avowed free thinkers, most of the original settlers considered themselves faithful to the religious traditions of Eastern Europe. A substantial number, among them Moses Bayuk and Isaac Krassenstein in Alliance, possessed the advanced religious education not unusual in the Old World; and for study, these two had brought with them a complete set of the Talmud, while Eli Stavitsky brought a *Sefer Torah* (a scroll containing the five books of Moses). There was no dearth of qualified men to conduct services, even though the colonies would never have an ordained full-time rabbi. Donations toward the cost of after-school religious instruction for the young were made almost immediately by Michael Heilprin and Judge Isaacs.

Religious observance among the newcomers continued to attract the attention of the established American Jewish press, which was sometimes critical, at others curious or defensive. The *Jewish Record*, for example, in July 1882 quoted favorably the first reports of Alliance's Superintendent A. C. Sternberger: "the rites of their religion have been in every respect sedulously and strictly observed, no business or labor being permitted to interfere in any way." He then detailed the observance of the Sabbath, the purchase of kosher meat from Philadelphia, and the availability of a *shochet* to perform ritual slaughter of animals locally. Such practices were made possible, in his opinion, by the combination of a shared religious tradition and the relative isolation in a rural environment. The high degree of traditional observance, boasted the *Record,* "will show our English cousins how we compel (!) the refugees to violate the Sabbath and dietary laws."[4]

Services were first held in the barracks initially built for housing the newcomers and in private homes, but within the year a committee was formed to build a synagogue. Means could not be found, however, until 1885; then the funds raised by Dr. De Sola Mendes, secretary of the Alliance Land Trust in New York and a leading rabbi and scholar, were used to refurbish the abandoned cigar factory as a house of worship in time for Rosh Hashanah. Mendes remarked on the colonists' ability to conduct their own traditional services, led by a *hazzan* (cantor) from their midst. In the same year, a *mikvah* (ritual bath) was added and the burial ground furnished with proper fencing.

With Mendes's aid, rudimentary religious instruction was made available to children in Alliance: the younger ones learned to write a little Hebrew and to read from Mannheimer's *First Reader;* older children studied the Bible, memorizing such passages as the Ten Commandments and the Song of Praise in Exodus. Their teacher, George Randorf of Philadelphia, reported to Mendes that his main objective was "to excite in the children a sympathy for our enslaved ancestors and a sense of gratitude to that increasing Providence that has shaped events to subserve most high purposes." Randorf offered instruction in English too, including in the lessons poetry recitations and the composition of moral essays on such topics as "A New Application of an Old Rule." Though classes had to be held in the evening, they usually attracted thirty to forty youngsters each night of the week.[5]

Although the colonies were always poor in funds, they were not so in people; soon their influence reached to Vineland as well. Thanks to a few Russians imported temporarily from Alliance, the first Jewish service in Vineland was held as early as 6 July 1884, when the town's Jewish families were still counted on the fingers of one hand. A visiting Philadelphian provided the impetus as he sought the requisite ten men for a memorial service.[6]

Most important, however, was the eventual founding of Alliance's first synagogue in its own distinctive two-story building of stone foundation, brick, and clapboard; it was this great undertaking which united the colonists with Jewish Philadelphians and New Yorkers, even though they could not agree on its name. To traditionalists like Moses Klein, it was *Eben Ha' Ezer*, the Rock of deliverance; to the *Jewish Exponent*, the new institution represented Congregation Emanu-El, a promising source of unity and enlightened worship; to the pioneering fraternal Lodge of the Red Men, before they acquired their own Red Men's Hall, the social hall was as important as the synagogue proper. In any case, its cornerstone was laid on the first day of Hanukkah, Sunday 11 December 1887 with appropriate ceremony. The blustery winter day was brightened by the sight of marching children, all bearing American flags. Their teacher, too, played a prominent role in the ceremonies, along with the colony's own *hazzan*. Thirty-two colonists enrolled on the spot, pledging from forty to a hundred dollars each, payable over a period of ten years.[7]

A still greater event was the actual dedication of the completed building on 29 July 1888, the anniversary of most settlers' landing in America. Reporters described the new synagogue as a "commodious" structure with an ample basement hall for social functions, lectures, or classes. The sanctuary was well lighted by double windows and boasted the traditional separate three-sided gallery for the ladies. It was a source of pride for the colonists who themselves had supplied the labor, working with plans drawn up by one of the settlers. "As the children of Israel in the past, they had erected with their own hands a tabernacle in the wilderness of New Jersey to the God who had redeemed them from Russian bondage," cheered the *Exponent*.[8]

Praise was also lavished on the New York and Philadelphia benefactors who had turned out for the occasion. Over the main street fluttered a triumphal banner proclaiming *"Vive l'Alliance Israélite Universelle!"* in tribute to all the Francophile philanthropists, if not to Jacob H. Schiff, who made the most substantial single donation. A token contribution was sent by the Alliance

Land Trust, which still held the colonists' mortgages, while trustees Leopold Gershel, Isaac Eppinger, and M. W. Mendel attended the ceremonies and made their donations in person.

Trustee Dr. Mendes initiated the religious ceremony by chanting from Psalm 118, "This is the gateway of the Lord; the righteous alone may enter." *Hazzan* Tolchinsky chanted Psalms 1 and 24 as the Torah scrolls were carried in a processional; then Mendes, again, concluded from Psalm 30, "a psalm and song at the dedication of the house of David, . . . 'Thou hast turned for me my mourning into dancing.'" Both men, the East European and the American rabbi, stood together under the *hupah* (traditional wedding canopy) holding aloft the sacred scrolls to which Israel remained wed.

In his address, Mendes reminded the colonists of their former oppression, of the hardships they endured on their new homesteads, and then of the debt of gratitude they owed to those who had settled them in the land of freedom. He expressed his hope that the sacred edifice would bring them nearer both to God and to humanity; "Cultivate not only the soil, but also your hearts," he urged. Another major speaker was the Honorable Adolphus S. Solomons, then president of New York's Alliance. Praising the children for carrying American flags and emphasizing America's friendship toward the oppressed Israelites, he recalled Jesse Seligman's telegram to President Arthur as he sought American intervention against Russian persecution, and also the asylum offered by the New World to so many refugees from the Old. In return, the colonists should respect the laws and customs of their newly adopted country, he told them, though never forsaking their fathers' religion. Solomons thanked God, too, that unlike Moses he was able actually to visit his Promised Land. At last the children's chorus struck up "the well-known song, 'Live for Something, Be Not Idle.'"

On this occasion the colonists were deemed ready to receive the deeds to their homesteads: mortgage payments were among the acknowledged badges of those preparing for roles as respectable citizens of the land. The settlers replied through schoolmaster

George Randorf, who delivered a formal address in German that contained many florid references to the ancient slavery and the preparations for freedom. He compared the selflessness of Moses to the benevolence of the modern philanthropists who were saving the oppressed from a new Pharaoh: Without doubt, Randorf told them, these were noble and humanitarian leaders, responding to "religious inspiration, comforting their brethren and sisters in dire distress." In return, he assured the philanthropists, the settlers would persevere in agriculture and educate their children in the ways of America. A note of obsequiousness entered Randorf's pledges on behalf of the colonists as he hinted that they would henceforth follow the wishes of their benefactors. Remembering past favors in the face of perennial need, he called, "In your hearts you had only love, in spite of our blindness to acknowledge it . . . unworthy as we often were."[9] Unfortunately, dependence could breed both love and hate, especially when honor was tied to mortgage strings.

Virtually no fanfare was accorded to another synagogue dedicated a year later, on 14 July 1889. The settlers called it Tiphereth Israel ("Glory of Israel"), then later Shearith Israel ("Remnant of Israel"). It was a more modest all-frame, but well-lighted building at the corner of Schiff and Gershel Avenues on an acre of park land granted by the Alliance Land Trust. No visiting dignitaries made speeches; only the colonists and officers of the institution were present, all of them older pioneers: Simcha Luborsky, president; Lazar Perskie, vice-president; Isaac Krassenstein, the *hasid,* secretary.[10]

Thus, the community built two synagogues within its first decade. The second and smaller was strictly traditional and oriented almost entirely toward prayer and study, while the larger, Emanu-El, represented more progressive attitudes. In this first synagogue were celebrated most weddings and other religious occasions; it was also the place for recreation and dramatics, for politics and social clubs, as well as the library. Its comprehensive activities formed a classic example of the community-center concept in American Jewish life, even before New York's Educational Alliance opened its doors.

Reflecting the religious tradition of almost all the colonists, both synagogues remained, in effect, orthodox. Both, for example, observed two days of Rosh Hashanah and other holidays. But a spirit of divisiveness was early recognized by such astute observers as Moses Klein, who noted (1889) that a "strong minority have already introduced innovations upon their older customs, such as some English in the service, and have arrayed themselves as 'Reformers.'" Whereas neighboring Carmel and Rosenhayn each had a common prayer service for everyone, Alliance allowed each rival sect its own. This was especially significant, Klein warned, because "the religious organizations form here, as in all primitive communities, the focus of social movement." In a personal footnote, he advised, "To me it appears that there is more *Ezer* [deliverance] and *Tiphereth* [glory] in a community worshiping The One God in one Synagogue than in a small community divided in two groups."[11]

There was a tendency to regard Emanu-El as the more official congregation. For example, it was here on the second day of Rosh Hashanah that postmaster Seldes read New Year greetings from the philanthropists. On the High Holy Days, Emanu-El was "crowded with worshipers," the *Jewish Messenger* reported. Here they could "delight" in the "sympathetic singing" of Cantor Tolchinsky, assisted by a male choir. At Emanu-El memorial services would be held for Baron de Hirsch, who died on 22 April 1896, and for President McKinley, on 19 September 1901. On such occasions Jews from the entire area united there in a service of hymns and eulogies. And visitors generally regarded this edifice as a chief attraction, built as it was on an elevated central location; thus they attended its services when possible and admired its "modern" Hebrew school and comprehensive social activities.[12]

The cycle of traditional holidays and ceremonies soon involved the whole Alliance community. On the first *Hoshanah Rabbah* of Emanu-El, the women's group presented a new Torah scroll, which occasioned festivity and speech-making as well as a small crisis. At the crucial moment for inscribing the final letters onto the scroll, no quill was to be found, and the *shochet* ruled out the use of a steel pen. "There was great embarrassment and despair on the faces of the honest colonists," reported the *American Hebrew*. The situation was finally remedied by young Benjamin Rudnik: that very evening, he related in a trembling voice, his wagon wheels had run over an object in the roadway which to his astonishment turned out to be a grown eagle. He took the injured bird, still alive, to his home to care for it. Here was the source of the quill the colonists sought! "A shout of joy was the response . . . [as] the king of fowls carried the evening on the plume of his wing." That same evening the children, too, presented a ceremonial wine goblet, and the older boys and girls, a traditional velvet curtain for the Torah ark.[13]

Among the holidays enjoyed most by the youth was Purim. Then they were allowed to hear the reading of the Book of Esther at the synagogue, and some boys reportedly celebrated by shooting off cap pistols at the mention of Haman, the villain. Groups of children in the afternoon religious school enjoyed a wagon ride through the streets of Alliance, circling the synagogue and their teacher's home and singing not only songs of Purim but also such popular American ballads as "Marching Through Georgia." Music and dancing rounded out the carefree day-long celebrations.

Throughout the first decade at least Sabbath observance in Alliance was reported as well nigh universal. Visitors remarked that no work was done on the seventh day in the fields or berry-patches, even when it meant irreversible losses due to spoilage. One correspondent for the *American Hebrew* noted "Sabbath observance so general that we could not get a farmer to begin hitching a horse until darkness set in." And he found that although Emanu-El was the less tradition-oriented of the two synagogues, its services offered none of the features of Reform congregations, and, with a trace of condescension, its library was used less as a study hall than as a theater for "itinerant companies of Jargon actors."[14]

To less severe observers, however, traditional practices in an unusual rustic setting seemed somehow more meaningful. One Jewish traveler, the wife of Charles D. Spivak, a Philadelphia community leader and Old Country Am Olam adherent, wrote glowingly of a Sabbath eve in Alliance. Weary farmers and their children hastened "to greet the beautiful bride, the Sabbath, the day of rest." A festive appearance graced the frame huts: tables were covered with white cloth and *hallah*, and the benediction candles cast a warm glow as men chanted the Friday evening prayers. In the New World, she prophesied, the Jewish people would find their old wounds healed; moreover, they would achieve "a high position among the learned of the land," obtain success in commerce, and even "as in their younger days [be] tillers of the soil." Assimilation, however, might become a danger as "neighbors, either from love or from hatred, [would] wish to obliterate [the Jew's] distinctiveness." Then he must again look to Jerusalem for inspiration and comfort. Pondering under the starry heavens of Alliance, she concluded that "Israel's history is not finished yet."[15]

What religious accomplishments were achieved in pioneering Alliance were possible in the other colonies as well, but each contained some unique differences. On the sandy soil of Woodbine, settlers and visitors alike drew sustenance from the well-springs of tradition, too. Yet, although among the colonists were men of learning and piety who could provide religious instruction, the struggle for livelihood left little time away from farm, factory, or store. The Baron de Hirsch Fund was geared overwhelmingly towards economic and secular objectives and the creation of a sturdy rural middle class adapted to the American environment. Somehow, the religion which seemed such a natural, if not excessive, part of the immigrant's makeup would survive, the philanthropists thought, without substantial subsidy or material nourishment. At a time when the annual budget of the agricultural school would run $35-40,000 the Woodbine Hebrew School languished, and especially during economic crises, when the colonists were less able to supplement the sporadic contributions of the Fund.[16]

Superintendent Sabsovich, who spoke with a Ukrainian accent and liked to tell visitors of his years in the Caucasus adapting to the life of the peasants, was not primarily concerned with his people's religion. To the liberal Russian writer, Vladimir Korolenko, Sabsovich appeared "strong and energetic . . . not like a Jew at all." His schooling had caused him to become "estranged to [sic] the Jewish environment." What a pity, Korolenko wrote his wife, that such sturdy people were forced to leave southern Russia, their places taken by "Greeks and other barbarians who are worse than the Jews." To Korolenko, Sabsovich apparently confided his own complaints about the Woodbine settlers: many were intractable and lacked true piety or learning. "You know the Jews of South Russia, don't you? They are not experts in Talmud, nor are they *Hasidim,* neither like the West European Jews."[17]

The immigrants were experts, however, in their responsibilities toward Judaism and their fellowman. Within two years of the colony's founding, there flourished an active *Agudath Achim Anshei Woodbine* (United Woodbine Brotherhood), whose aim, as stated in the 1893 constitution, was "continuing and strengthening the basis of Judaism and spreading the light of our religion, which teaches the principle of love of unity and peace, lofty moral standards, and good deeds." The association's business was conducted in both English and "the ordinary Jewish language and writing [Yiddish]." Admission requirements included a Jewish religious education as well as adherence to rules of arbitration and other aspects of Jewish law.

The president and vice-president of the Brotherhood were required to know Yiddish, and to attend services at least on every Sabbath and holiday to make sure they were conducted "decently [including orderly allocation of honors at the Torah reading], without quarrels, and in strictly orthodox manner." The religious staff, if any, would also be "strictly orthodox." Among the tasks of the *gabbai* (lay overseer of services) was "to see to it that the women live up to their duties in accordance with Jewish law," while the officers checked the work of the committees that visited, with traditional communal responsibility, the mourning and the sick. A board of trustees oversaw the functions of the synagogue, seats for the High Holy Days, the Talmud Torah (part-time religious school), the *mikvah,* and the cemetery; funeral arrangements were in the care of a special *Hevra Kadisha.*

In contrast to the Fund, whose trustees served uncontested for as long as a quarter-century, the Brotherhood was run on the principles of democracy; its general assembly met annually and all officers were elected to one-year terms by secret ballot. More than a religious institution, the Woodbine Brotherhood represented the hoary tradition of the workers' fraternal orders and mutual aid societies that was rooted not only in Eastern Europe but in the pre-trade union heritage of Britain and the Continent. Payments in case of illness or death, including funeral and burial expenses, a modest monument, and basic survivors' benefits, were provided. The folk patterns of Judaism were taken into account in this insurance program: thus if a member left no male heir to say the *kaddish* prayer in his memory, the association was obligated to find a substitute.

Presumably such potential benefits as these made necessary the investigation of each applicant for membership, including such "circumstances as whether his wife be in the family way." The sums involved were small: three dollars weekly to a sick bread-winner for four weeks, a special decision being required beyond that; annual dues were only four dollars. Almost a half-century before social security, this kind of basic cooperative protection helped ease the lot of the Jewish laborer who depended on his own two hands for the survival of himself and his family.

The Brotherhood also reflected traditional Jewish respect for governmental authority. Penalties, including expulsion by due process, were leveled against any member "who carried on a bad, disreputable way of life" or who was convicted in court of violating the law of the land. In all disputes, the board of trustees was required to provide mediation and arbitration. Perhaps also to discourage the kind of divisiveness found in Alliance and elsewhere, a member who secured some other synagogue for major family celebrations, such as a wedding or Bar Mitzvah, was subject to a fine.[18]

Though personally irreligious, Sabsovich was duly impressed by the power for good which the Brotherhood represented. He considered it "the most important" influence in shaping public opinion, "the prime mover of all public enterprises" in Woodbine, and so he told the Baron de Hirsch Fund trustees.[19] They seemed reluctant to act on the information, just as they were ever wary of an implied partnership with the newcomers who remained too noticeably different in culture, level of Americanization, material means, and even religion.

Led by their Brotherhood, prime mover of enterprises which captured the heart of Woodbine's people, the building of the synagogue emerged as the major devotional task for the colonists. Almost everyone contributed by digging, carrying locally-made bricks, and carpentry. Once, it was reported, the whole colony turned out for work on a road project to earn some very scarce cash for the Brotherhood's synagogue fund. The result was an edifice of "considerable dimensions" (forty by seventy-five feet and thirty-four feet high), all-brick, more imposing than that of Alliance and including rooms in the basement for a religious school. "Every part of the structure was made by the colonists themselves," remarked Lewis T. Stevens, historian of Cape May County, who estimated the basic cost at a minimum of $6,000. Also the *Jewish Exponent* commented, during the construction phase, on the "notable fact . . . that the work is being done entirely by Jewish colonists, who give their labor and contribute in other ways." The work continued the week round, the journal reported, except for Sabbaths and holidays, in further testimony of the immigrants' unbroken "allegiance to the faith of Israel."[20]

The land was, of course, the property of the Fund, nor could other costs be met by the settlers' own labor. As a consequence, the synagogue, like almost everything else, carried a Fund mortgage, one which was not to be paid off for another quarter-century. This did not, however, alter the festive tone of the dedication on the eve of Hanukkah 1896. It was also another opportunity for the philanthropists "to inspect the colony," as the *Exponent* reported; the visitors included New York trustees Goldman, Isaacs, and Schiff, Agent Solomons, as well as Joseph Jacobs, Anglo-Jewish historian and secretary of the British Mansion House Committee. Within the same contingent were Arthur Reichow and George W. Youland, then principals of the Fund's New York trade schools for immigrant youth. The train from Philadelphia brought additional notables of .contemporary American Jewry: Trustee Hackenburg, rabbis Sabato

Morais and Marcus Jastrow, and community leaders such as Mrs. Simon Muhr and Louis Edward Levy, a founder of the Jewish Emigration Society. Poor weather limited their tour of the colony, though not enough to prevent the visitors from remarking the evidences of "thrift and material prosperity." Wagons brought them back to a hospitable luncheon served by the colonists in the basement Hebrew School of their new synagogue; after the meal came the dedication ceremonies.

These were tactfully planned by Sabsovich to allow the diverse religious and secular spectra of American Jewry to feel at home. American flags and bunting decorated the as yet unfinished interior, and a male choir imported from the City of Brotherly Love chanted in English the traditional *Mah Tovu* ("How Beautiful Are Thy Tents, O Jacob"). The sacred scrolls of the Torah were entrusted to the hands of six members of the Woodbine Brotherhood who made the customary three circuits of the sanctuary before placing them in the new ark. One of the colony's young daughters, pretty Sophie Neustadt, presented the keys of the edifice to Herman Rosenfeld, president of the Brotherhood and pioneer editor of the Yiddish *Farmer*. Agent Solomons was honored by being chosen to kindle the eternal light above the ark, which signaled the start of the multi-lingual oratory and prayers including memorial chants for the recently deceased Baron de Hirsch. Rabbi Sabato Morais preached the main sermon in English, followed by Rabbi Jastrow's address in German and benedictions in Hebrew. Both men, leaders of the Historical School which later became the movement of Conservative Judaism, strove to preserve the essence of traditional faith, rejecting what they considered an excessive transformation wrought by the tide of Reform. Only ten years before, Morais had founded the Jewish Theological Seminary of America, which was to be a bastion of traditional learning as adapted to modern conditions. Reform leader Rabbi Kaufmann Kohler was also scheduled to address the Woodbine celebrants, as was Orthodox Rabbi Henry Illowy of Philadelphia; for some reason, perhaps sectarian, perhaps personal, neither took part in the dedication of Agudas Achim

Anshei Woodbine, as it was known to its East European member-ship.[21]

Thus, the Woodbine Brotherhood had its own synagogue as well as its program of mutual benefits and fraternal aid, limited only by the precarious economic conditions in the colony. The dedication of Woodbine's sanctuary climaxed the initial cycle of synagogue founding in the pioneer rural communities of South Jersey. Moreover, the Woodbine Brotherhood's constitution bore striking similarities to that of Alliance's Eben Ha' Ezer and Hevra Kadisha in its provisions for majority rule, secret ballot, Yiddish-speaking and religiously oriented officers, care of basic institutions to meet the spiritual needs of the community, and mutual aid in time of need.

Such institutions illustrated a pattern of growing self-assertion on the part of the East Europeans. One of these, the pioneer Yiddish journalist Moses Freeman, saw early signs of independence in the founding of Philadelphia's B'nai Abraham Anshei Russia on 1 October 1882. In Woodbine, such an identification of origin would have been redundant. The Eastern Jews, wrote Freeman, thirsted for cultural and religious inspiration and were drawn to the syna-gogue as others might gravitate towards sports or amusements. They proceeded to satisfy this traditional craving as soon as they man-aged to obtain even a meager livelihood and could free themselves from the domination of their German "elder brethren," the assimila-tionist *yahudim*. Even the humblest immigrant peddler found time for prayers thrice daily and to return home for the Sabbath no matter how hard the journey.[22]

The *Yiddishe Gazetten,* an influential weekly, also stressed this theme of the East European Jew rediscovering a sense of identity within his own institutions, whether religious or philanthropic, city or rural. Within his own institutional setting, "no matter how poor and small the building, it seems big enough and comfortable. He feels at home among his brothers who speak his tongue, understand his thoughts, and feel his heart." By contrast, the "fine offices" of the German-sponsored charities were run by men "with strict and angry faces." Sounding the call for further self-help, the journal editorialized, "It is up to us Russian Jews to help our poor country-men and not allow them to be insulted by our proud brothers to whom the Russian Jew is synonymous with *schnorer,* tramp, good-for-nothing," as they had been called in the farm colonies as well as in the urban melting pot.[23]

After perhaps too many years, the two Jewish communities would move closer in understanding, joined by their common experiences and problems in the New World as well as the tragic events in the Old.[24] But in the 1890's, the East Europeans still seemed apart, a condition felt strongly by the rural colonists whose benefactors were so overwhelmingly pillars of the Reform Judaism dominant among American Jewry in the nineteenth century. They used a prayer book based on the *Minhag America* ("American Rite") of Rabbi Isaac Mayer Wise or the German-style *Olat Tamid* issued by Rabbi David Einhorn of Baltimore, in a service cold and strange to an orthodox devotee. The differences were not only in language of worship, length of service, and role of the rabbi and congregants, but also in total outlook.[25]

Such differences, as well as the other early sources of conflict between pioneers and their benefactors, probably contributed markedly to the delayed and then relatively weak support for religious institutions in Woodbine and the other South Jersey colonies. They illustrated the broad cultural gulf between estab-lished community and newcomers, a divisiveness which occasionally flared into internecine conflict. Reform Jews criticized the orthodox practices of the Easterners as outlandish, impractical, medieval or worse. At times, intolerance seemed to undermine the humanitarian effort of absorbing the pogrom-era refugees. Vituperative letters in *The American Israelite* once suggested that the refugees "be bundled off to Alaska . . . American Russia would be the place for them. They could worship [there] among the Russians, as they were never permitted to do in their own country." Another asked that the newcomers "be admonished to leave their (so-called religious) superstitions behind them."[26]

Detroit philanthropist Magnus Butzel ascribed the "hyper-orthodoxy" of the East Europeans to the oppressiveness of their

"Muscovite serfdom." He accompanied this, however, with a typical concern for maintaining satisfactory Christian-Jewish relations, an other-directed fear of a tarnished public image: "I believe that the liberal [Reform] interpretation of Jewish doctrines as accepted and practiced by the majority of the American Israelites, finds them further removed from the *Chasidim*-ridden Russian refugees than from any of the other religious societies that exist in this country." Moreover, the Russians' religious ceremonies "bring Judaism into ridicule . . . before Christian audiences." Their ancient dietary laws, he complained, kept them from eating at the table of the very same people who helped them, even their fellow Jews.

At the same time, typically, Butzel was not all negative. These refugees had suffered, as "our ancestors" did, for the sake of Judaism; there was a kernel of religious truth "within [their] sometimes repulsive fanatic shell." All they required was the healing ointment of that perennial patent medicine, Americanization. If anything, their spiritual heritage, that mysterious force "which had upheld these people in their unspeakable woe, when reconstructed after American views, will make them all the better citizens." On this premise, Butzel subsidized the Russian Jews of a farming colony called Palestine in the swamps of Bad Axe, Michigan, one of the many short-lived experiments in bucolic Americanization.

Though religious differences persisted, at least the rural colonies of South Jersey earned praise from American Jewish leaders such as Benjamin F. Peixotto, ex-consul to Rumania, for preventing a "second Warsaw here in New York." He knew from first-hand observation the terrible plight of his coreligionists in the East and their need to escape. You "cannot keep them back," he warned a group of YMHA leaders. "This is a free country, open to all except criminals and paupers"; the Jews were neither. The people already established here had a moral obligation to help their brethren, though without being swamped or having their own position threatened. "In one word, this great inundation from Europe is not so dreadful if we meet it with colonization." Taking the Jersey settlements as an example, he saw no end to additional opportunities in the West, where the refugees could take with them their religion and culture. "I would aid them to go away," Peixotto urged, "to the great West which awaits them." He had seen one such group bound for the frontier, carrying their old Torah scroll with them. "Do you think that I laughed?" he asked his audience of sophisticated Jews. No, Peixotto affirmed with an unselfish candor, let them go ahead and "bring a new light into the great West."[27]

If there was prejudice in the German Reform Jews toward their Eastern brethren, it did not go unreciprocated. In 1894, the *Yiddishe Gazetten* bitterly rejected the complaints of Rabbi Isaac M. Wise against those orthodox immigrants who refused to recognize Reform Jews as coreligionists. Why did he and others look down on the Russians as dirty, unrefined, and uncivilized? retorted the *Gazetten*. The Russian Jews in the agricultural colonies as well as the cities were tired of being charged with beggary or religious fanaticism; their children, the journal suspected, were shunted off into special training schools so that they would not shame their affluent cousins in the public schools.

Hurt pride brooked no compromise, it seemed, on a number of sensitive issues: "We leave it to the rabbis to decide if the Reform Jews are our brothers in religion . . . let them even excise the *kaddish* . . . but from a social point of view the Reform Jews themselves have declined us all brotherly feeling. . . . No wonder the Russian poor have come to regard help from a German Reform Jew as charity from a rich *Goy*," the *Gazetten* concluded pointedly. "All talk of 'civilizing and Americanizing' is but exaggerated phraseology to insult us under a mask of friendship." Those not blinded by bias should have perceived among the Russian immigrants "many educated persons whose only vice was their poverty and by no means a lack of civilization." Using the style of Yiddish folk prayer to clinch its argument, the *Gazetten* ended one 1898 editorial thus: "Guard us, O Lord, from our own Jewish anti-Semites; from the non-Jewish ones we shall guard ourselves with our own efforts."[28]

Though neither the *Gazetten* nor others were unbiased, they indicated the mood of the immigrant community and the movement towards independent institutions that reflected its own cultural background. Some of these organizations, as Freeman admitted, were influenced by sources of division carried over from Europe, especially the rift between the *Hasidic* pietists and the *Misnagdim,* their rationalist opponents. In Philadelphia, there was even a tiny "lunatic fringe" of Russian Jewish anarchists who maligned both God and Judaism, and fought battles with Social Democrats over the true path to utopia.[29] Although less dramatic, some of the internal divisiveness was played out within Alliance too. For example, the constitution of the Hevra Kadisha required members to maintain exclusive ties with Tiphereth Israel rather than Eben Ha' Ezer (Emanu-El). And among the forty-odd charter members of the *Hevra,* there were listed none of the approximately thirty founders of the latter synagogue.[30]

Religious differences among the colonists remained a source of confusion to Louis Mounier, the Unitarian educational director employed by the Jewish Agricultural Society. He was sympathetic to some of the "free-thinking tailors" of Carmel and Rosenhayn, but what of the divided traditionalists? At one time, Mounier arranged a lecture by the renowned New York preacher, Zvi H. Masliansky, whose Yiddish oratory stirred the East Side as well as the South Jersey colonies. Mounier arranged for him to stay with farmer Bayuk of Alliance, who was an acknowledged Talmudic scholar and later the author of several interpretive works. He had thought the choice met the specifications set by the visiting reverend, but was later confounded by complaints from the local *Hasidim,* some of whom apparently considered the learned Bayuk too worldly. How could Mounier have taken "a Rabbi to an irreligious man's home?" When informed of the incident on the way back to the railroad station, Masliansky remarked wryly of the *Hasidim,* "Oh, they are stricter than God!" He had found no fault at all with his hosts. He made some general comments, however, based on his having observed the difficulties of maintaining traditional religious practices throughout America: this was not, after all, the environment of the old *shtetl.* "Many who keep a kosher home do so only in reverence to either parents or friends who otherwise would not enter," Masliansky confided.[31]

225

Mounier did not cease to wonder, however, at the strength of traditional patterns. All colonists celebrated the Sabbath and holidays in one form or another, he recalled, although few could claim that they had never violated the seemingly multitudinous Sabbath laws. He also relished desultory debates with the colonists, including one vegetarian who drew his justification from the Talmud. The latter considered even ritual slaughter, with its humane precautions, to be an unwarranted compromise to man's crueler appetites. To Mounier's rational, scientific mind, however, this made little sense: even fruit and vegetables, after all, contained the germ of life, he twitted his opponent. Moreover, was it not a "universal law of nature that life is sustained by life," with higher forms feeding on the lower? Such was the natural order of things; the "facts are right since they do exist."[32] Mounier was a Darwinist, an agnostic anti-clerical descended from French deists; though a man of cosmopolitan views, he could not quite sense the ethical imperatives of applied Judaism as a way of life.

Even the reputed radicals of Carmel clung to their Jewish heritage in their own manner, though they delayed building a synagogue. Within the new century's first decade, they too built their Beth Hillel, designed partly by Mounier and completed with a supplementary grant from Henry A. Dix, a Jewish manufacturer in nearby Millville. It was dedicated on 20 September 1908 just a quarter-century after the colony's founding. At this dedication, too, there was still visible the interplay of social forces both within and without the rural colony. It was also a measure of the relative lack of progress in vital areas. Was it the strength of radicals in Carmel or the orthodox practice of informal services in homes or the poverty of this factory-based community, which had delayed for so long the building of a sanctuary? All formed part of the explanation, with the last probably the most important. On the day of the dedication, however, the humble homes of the village were decorated with American flags and bunting in the manner reserved for momentous occasions. The parade was led by two local brotherhoods, the Independent Order of B'rith Abraham and the Independent Order of Sons of Joseph, both decked out in their best clothes, badges, and banners. Philadelphians predominated among the visitors, and especially notable was Cyrus L. Sulzberger, who delivered the keynote address.

Sulzberger urged the colonists to dream great dreams, like their patriarch Jacob on his way to a new land. American opportunity and freedom could make them come true, if the settlers would exercise their franchise "for the highest purposes." In the now plaintive tone of organized philanthropy, he admonished them to resolve soon to break away from their dependence on external subsidies, not *Leshono Habo* ("next year") but *Leshono Hazeh B'nei Horin* ("this year, we are free"), in paraphrase of the Passover refrain. A similar theme was pursued by Leonard G. Robinson, new manager of the Jewish Agricultural Society, who urged the settlers to continue their progress in self-help, for the philanthropists' patience was nearing its end.

George Goward, who almost single-handedly founded the Russian-American Association of Philadelphia (later renamed the Hebrew Literary Society), was honored as master of ceremonies and parade marshal. Joseph Gross, another Philadelphia leader and lawyer-champion of Russian Jews, warmed the celebrants' hearts with some fiery Yiddish oratory focusing on the great Rabbi Hillel's advice, "If I am not for myself, who is for me? And if I am for myself alone, what am I?" Deploring tendencies towards irreligion, he saw nonetheless a promise of spiritual regeneration through the new synagogue. There were also pleas for frequent attendance and decorum at services. It was left, however, to the colonists' resident physician to remind them that they had better plan to give their children a more effective religious education; his proposal for a Sabbath school was warmly received and implemented.[33]

Nor did the colonists forget their pioneer benefactors on such significant occasions. In Carmel, the late Michael Heilprin was eulogized. In Woodbine, all males born within a year of Baron de Hirsch's death bore his name, and a similar honor was extended the Baroness Clara after her death. Contributions were made in their names on behalf of victims of the Johnstown floods. In the schools, essays, recitations, and speeches complemented the religious services of the synagogue, and whenever possible New York's eloquent Masliansky would be invited again to preach.[34]

So it was that the cycle of Jewish holiday seasons and sacred occasions turned round from year to year in the colonies, seemingly independent of the immigrants' changing fortunes. In the Woodbine Brotherhood synagogue, students from the agricultural school attended High Holy Day services in a body, and celebrated Hanukkah in their own social hall. Festive and well attended weddings were held in the colonies, with Reverend Joseph Rosenbaum officiating in Woodbine and Reverend Jacob Margolis in Carmel.

One of the advantages of proximity to Philadelphia was the periodic impact of its spiritual leaders, including the distinguished orthodox rabbi, Bernard L. Levinthal. In 1904, he acquired a summer home in Woodbine, leading the *Exponent* to conclude that thereby this "Jewish Community would come under his spiritual supervision in matters educational, social and religious."[35] Such hopes foundered, largely for lack of institutional support. Aside from occasional contributions to the Hebrew schools in the rural communities, there was little organized concern with traditional religious education and religious programs generally on the part of the Fund, or the flexibility to forego its usual business standards regarding mortgage obligations even for religious leaders. The *Yiddishe Gazetten* had noted bitterly that the aged *shammes* (sexton) of the Woodbine synagogue had been expelled over a failure to continue payments.[36]

Perhaps the most active religious agency in the South Jersey colonies in the twentieth century proved to be the Reform-centered Jewish Chautauqua Society, which derived its inspiration from the Methodist Chautauqua's literary circles and courses for rural Sunday school teachers. Founded in 1893 by Rabbi Henry Berkowitz of Philadelphia's century-old Rodeph Shalom "for the dissemination of knowledge of the Jewish religion," it initiated a wide-ranging social and cultural program among the immigrant settlers in rural South Jersey, and stimulated such organizations as the Federation of Jewish Farmers of America to take a greater interest in education. The education of youth was given priority, focusing on Jewish history, holidays, and even Hebrew prayers. The Society's executive secretary, Jeannette M. Goldberg, appeared before the second annual meeting of the Federation of Jewish Farmers of America to report on such educational activities as were offered in the South Jersey colonies. These, she noted, could serve as experimental models for projected Sabbath schools in other isolated areas; to get such programs started, the Society would make available suitable books and course materials at minimum charge.[37] Indeed, all the conventions of the Federation of Jewish Farmers (beginning in 1909) indicated a concern with not only such practical matters as cooperative purchasing, but also the vital problems of religious education. "Awaken Jewish sentiment in American Children," read the headline of an appeal for subscriptions to *The Ark,* the "only Jewish monthly in English for the entire family" (offered at a combination rate with the official *Jewish Farmer*).

As part of the program of the Jewish Chautauqua Society, visiting rabbis gave twice weekly lessons to children in the South Jersey colonies. But what of the many other Jewish farm families who were by then scattered in isolated areas? To meet their needs, the Federation distributed printed correspondence courses developed by the Reform Union of American Hebrew Congregations; these were followed by monthly issues of the *Jewish Farmer* containing test questions to be administered by the parents. Thus, it was hoped, would arise a new generation of Jews who were "physically and spiritually healthy."[38] Moreover, the indefatigable Miss Goldberg managed to organize evening classes in history for young adults, as well as Sabbath schools in all the colonies, both with apparently encouraging results. At intercolonial assemblies, hundreds of children and their parents gathered for recitations of poetry, choral readings, quizzes on Jewish history and religion, musical programs, and lectures.

In 1912, some Chautauqua Society programs were directed by Rabbi B. L. Grossman of the Jewish Theological Seminary in New York; and the *Jewish Farmer* boasted that six hundred children were enrolled. Within two years, however, the figure declined to five hundred.[39] Even more ominous were the indications that the program was proving to be superficial and unexciting. By 1914, the new director of religious, educational, and social activities, Philip R. Goldstein, discovered that the classes were "poorly attended," the youngsters apathetic, and the older folks "indifferent."[40] It seemed as if educational quality and inspiration were not commensurate with the challenge.

Young Goldstein, who wanted to teach sociology after graduating from Cornell, found himself treading gingerly between the orthodoxy of the first generation, represented by a part-time *melamed* whom he did not wish to offend, and the indifference of the second which seldom engaged in traditional prayer or study. Except for the major holidays, synagogue attendance grew smaller; perhaps, he thought, for lack of an inspiring sermon based on moral or ethical principles, or for lack of esthetic qualities in the orthodox rite. In contrast to traditional education, the Chautauqua program was based on the latest character-building methodology, emphasizing ethics and literature, using English as the language of instruction, and focusing on meaningful religious observance. Its representatives had high hopes, in spite of the apparent difficulties.

"Although the trustees of the [Chautauqua] organization are Reform Jews," Goldstein affirmed, "they are broad-minded men and women who can tolerate and even value the habits and customs of the orthodox, so long as they lead to right living."[41] For the colonists, still mostly Yiddish-speaking and orthodox-oriented, he organized literary and social clubs in a kind of community center, thus expanding on the services provided by the Jewish Agricultural Society. In the social halls and meeting rooms of the colonies, gatherings of young and old helped to "mitigate the frictions and antagonisms which inevitably arose between two generations from two worlds." Goldstein's teaching of the Old Testament from the point of view of the higher criticism made it clear, however, how he personally felt. Most of all, he tried to emphasize the positive aspects of the blending of "Jewish values" with American "patriotism and sportsmanship."[42]

There was a brisk current of twentieth century progressivism in this work of the Jewish Chautauqua, the JAS, and the men like

Mounier and Goldstein. It focused on the middle class, optimistic, utilitarian, and pragmatic features of America in the era of the melting pot. Yet, with all its good intentions, it sometimes smacked of condescension towards the alien whose ancient religion was a universal liability and whose American brethren had found the key to success through acculturation. Goldstein at least recognized the danger of such condescension, though not without yielding also to the typical adulation for the self-made man, "I took care always not to let my efforts look like philanthropy or 'uplift' but rather . . . as encouragement to increase their happiness by exercising their own talents . . . while the furnishing of facilities was purely thoughtfulness on the part of idealists who had become happy Jews in America earlier."[43]

The American Generation: Public School, Zionism, and the City

World War I dealt a powerful blow to the idea of group settlement. And somehow the accumulated impact of Tsarist terror, exile, migration, and uplift, loosed many East European Jews in America from their traditional moorings. Was forced Americanization a cause of alienation?

To the immigrant, the New World with its vastness, wealth, and relative equality of opportunity was, after all, so different from the Old. In Eastern Europe, where life was often precarious, one tended to cling to God as the protecting Father. Judaism, embracing ethics, study, faith, and ritual, was a daily way of life. Here in an industrial, pragmatic America, however, that way of life appeared much less relevant. The law protected all, impersonally, but with little or no prejudice. And the bustling marketplace seemed like a great lottery as the wheel of fate showered its individualist favorites with the blessings of prosperity.

Most significant was the opportunity available to immigrant youth in the form of accessible secular education, a stepladder to recognition and status, if not to wealth. The drawing power of the public schools, coupled with the rigors of livelihood and integration, usually left little room for religious studies. And to both native and alien, chances of education and economic success seemed brightest in the cities. All these factors intertwined in the social development of the rural colonies.

In the environment of South Jersey, brave steps were required to provide adequate schooling. The children of Alliance at first had to trudge for miles through the woods to the unpretentious public schools of Union Grove or Willow Grove. "This was not satisfactory to our Jewish parents," recalled one of the pioneers, "with whom education of children comes next in command to the *Shema* [liturgical profession of faith]."[44] Eventually, Pittsgrove Township yielded to their insistent petitions to build a new schoolhouse within the colony. But it was not completed until 1890 and then it proved inadequate for the two hundred Alliance children. Norma had a one-room schoolhouse, largely for kindergarten-primary children and another four-room building for the rest of the elementary grades. Jewish children in Garton Road and Brotmanville attended ungraded, one-room schools; the one in Brotmanville closed down finally during World War I for lack of a teacher. Carmel boasted a four-room school plus the usual ungraded one-room cabin on its outskirts. In Rosenhayn, where the Jewish population was in the minority even before the turn of the century, Deerfield Township provided two schools of four and two rooms respectively.

These country schools offered fair-sized playgrounds in addition to the natural rustic setting, the joys of bathing in the Maurice River, and other childhood pleasures of the "good old days" remembered happily by the pioneers. There were youthful pranks, such as pilfering watermelons from Steinberg's farm or boxes of prunes from Krassenstein's store to be buried on Sam Spiegel's land, and gathering in the evening at the Alliance post office where teen-age romance blossomed. But there were also the hardships of country life in a none-too-prosperous region and the obstacles to acquiring a good education. As late as 1919, when their pupils numbered close to seven hundred (mostly Jewish), all of the above schools had no artificial lighting of any sort, no central heating—only wood-burning stoves—no running water, and no indoor toilets; none of them provided education in all the elementary grades.[45]

Supplementary instruction was virtually starved for lack of

support in the early years.[46] Libraries, lecture series, or secular classes for youths and adults did not flourish until after the turn of the century, when Mounier began his work as educational director (1901). By profession, Mounier was a painter and sculptor. He had conducted an art school in New York, but poor health brought him to Vineland in hopes of recovery. Warned that the town lacked an interest in art and culture, he managed to obtain occasional commissions to lecture in New York as well as locally. To the solid citizens he was "professor," an exemplar of Vineland's attraction for the scholarly and worldly. It was to him that Julius Goldman and Eugene Benjamin of the Fund came to offer the position of "Director of Educational Work and promoter of Americanism and Sociability" for the colonies.

Mounier had his doubts: he could not even see himself as completely Americanized, so how could he administer the process to others? One of his friends warned him, he said, that "I would be ostracized as if I were a Jew," if he associated with the aliens who were causing difficulties over the strictly enforced Sunday blue laws.[47] Shortly before, Mounier recalled, during the Spanish-American War, Alliance had received unfavorable publicity about a riot against a factory operating on the Jewish Sabbath; the Morris Company had wanted to complete a government contract for army coats, but the sound of machinery violating the serenity of their Sabbath brought angry groups of local farmers on the march. Verbal warnings soon gave way to rock-throwing, forcing operations to cease; the incident was followed by court appearances and critical comments from the press.[48]

Yet, to help these people, Mounier thought, was an opportunity not to be missed: he could "become a philanthropist without being a millionaire." He lectured to them formally on everything except religion, played the 'cello, gave lessons in art and music, organized nature study classes especially for the children, and expanded the libraries. He remarked on the eagerness of both young and old who attended his illustrated lectures on botany and astronomy. For example, among those who met in a dilapidated Brotmanville shop were one old Jewish farmer who had walked two-and-a-half miles to hear the same lecture twice and a "keen-eyed, attentive little boy" named Morris Greenblatt, who would become a prominent Vineland attorney. One of his young pupils in an art class, Ben Scribner, later studied architecture to become a pioneer in the construction of modern commercial buildings.[49] With time, too, a few of the native public school teachers took the colonists' youngsters under their wings to teach them not only English but also "refinement . . . [an American] mental and spiritual pattern." Some students were able to complete their elementary education with honors and soon to proceed with higher studies away from the colonies.[50]

The nearest high school was across the county line in Vineland, another farther away in Bridgeton. Although the Jews of Carmel did band together in the school district elections of Deerfield Township to press for a local high school and more support for education generally, an issue on which they sometimes overcame native opposition, little was accomplished. Consequenly, sending a child to high school entailed appreciable hardship and sacrifice, including payment of tuition and transportation costs. Farmer Eli Bakerman's son John was the first Alliance pupil (1907) to graduate from the high school in Vineland, where he achieved a notable record, later matriculating at Oberlin College.[51]

Two pioneer women, Mrs. Rudnick and Mrs. Bailey, once made up their minds that their daughters also would receive the benefits of a high school education. By both Old and New World standards, and especially in rural areas, this was a radical venture. Good neighbors attempted to dissuade them from needless sacrifice, but to no avail. Mrs. Bailey walked the two girls two-and-a-half miles each day to the railroad station in Norma; then she operated a small store in Vineland to make it possible for her daughter to attend high school there. Such sacrifices, as others, proved well worthwhile. Young Margaret Bailey, later Mrs. Herman, went on to the Medical College in Philadelphia and began a life-long career in the same city as a physician serving the poor and underprivileged of the urban slum. Elizabeth Rudnick returned to teach in Alliance, as did some of the other girls from the colonies.[52]

In Woodbine, planned by the Fund as a model community, at least elementary education was less of a hardship. After the first pioneering years when the children had to walk to Dennisville well over a mile away, three public schools were built in locations that were within a mile of most homes. Nevertheless, for over a score of years, youngsters had to travel to Millville for their secondary education. And the elementary schools totaled but eight rooms for an enrollment of four hundred children in 1902-1903, so that Sabsovich had to count on renting one room in the Talmud Torah and another in the synagogue basement. There were but ten teachers, working in "overcrowded" conditions, he complained, "quite busy teaching this small army of future American citizens." The colonists were hard pressed for the necessary tax revenues to support their own schools, since they also paid taxes to Dennis Township, Sabsovich noted in his annual report of January, 1903, and they had just expended $2,600 toward finishing their Talmud Torah building. He hoped their situation would improve with the state legislature's endorsement of separate incorporation for the proposed borough of Woodbine.

These expectations materialized, though perhaps too many years late, over a decade beyond the colony's founding. Woodbine achieved independent status as a separate incorporated borough in 1903 and immediately organized its own school district and board of education, headed by Sabsovich and Bogen. In 1904, the inadequate elementary facilities were finally replaced by a consolidated school in a modern, ten-room building, and bus transportation was provided for children living two miles or more away. Adjacent was the planned four-room high school, dedicated at long last on Columbus Day of 1914, to offer a full four-year course locally. The new schools contained a well equipped plant, including kindergarten rooms, manual training shops, and playgrounds. More fortunate than their contemporaries in the colonies around Vineland, the Woodbine children enjoyed central steam heating, electric lighting from the pioneer plant constructed by the Fund, and indoor plumbing. Here, at least, the outdoor water pump and outhouse were banished in the twentieth century's first decade. Adult classes in English, a library, and a reading room further enhanced the colony's cultural environment.

Relations with Cape May County governmental authorities were good, largely because of the Fund's impressive investments for economic development and public education which benefited the entire area. The incorporation of Woodbine also eliminated a source of conflict with nearby Dennis Township. This was one of the advantages accruing to "The First Self-Governed Jewish Community Since the Fall of Jerusalem," as Woodbine was proudly described by David Blaustein in *Circle* magazine (1907).[53]

Woodbine's schools became also the locus of related activities: sewing classes, a girls' club for "mental and general culture and social enjoyment," a mothers' club to discuss parental duties, and an area Teachers' Conference Society to deal with pedagogical problems including how to foster good citizenship. For the young men, Sabsovich had formed a civic club that they might "imbibe the American spirit [including] ways of self-government" and rights and duties of citizens under the Constitution, in order to study American history and celebrate national holidays, with appropriate patriotism. The colony took pride in one of its own alumnae, Mary Freedman, daughter of a local pioneer, who returned to teach in Woodbine's primary grades. And the *Jewish Farmer* regularly reported with satisfaction on the hundreds of children receiving a fine American education in Woodbine.[54] By 1920, a clear majority of the youngsters were going on to high school.[55]

Ironically, the striving for education weakened the rural colonies. Most of Woodbine's high school graduates did not remain on their parents' farms or in the local factories. Whether or not they went on to college and into the professions, they usually sought their fortunes in the cities, especially Philadelphia. Likewise, this was also a trend in the colonies near Vineland, whence entire families were attracted by the opportunity for a better education as well as economic advancement in store or factory. These colonies, unlike Woodbine, never had a high school of their own. As early as 1902, the annual report of the Fund warned against this tendency "among the more intelligent farmers" in the Vineland colonies to send their children to the city; it was getting ever harder to keep the young generation on the land.[56]

As a result of the steady influx from the colonies, the Jewish community within Vineland proper flourished in numbers as well as religious and cultural activities. Carmel's *mohel* had performed the first circumcision in Vineland, what the somewhat uninformed *Journal* of 1898 called "a grand christening event . . . where refreshments were served in great abundance." By 1905 the first congregation held regular prayer meetings in Hoffman's Hall with a Torah scroll donated by local Jewish women. Rabbi Bernard L. Levinthal brought fraternal greetings from his Philadelphia congregation and formally "completed" the new scroll at ceremonies on 27 August of that year, but it was an Alliance baker who won the first letter in the traditional bidding for the remaining letters to be inscribed ino the Torah parchment. All guests, including his Honor, Mayor Conwell of Vineland, enjoyed the unique celebration, the speeches, the music and the ever-abundant "refreshments . . . both liquid and otherwise."[57]

Soon after, the new congregation organized officially as the Sons of Jacob, and moved into the old German Lutheran church building on Grape Street. On 20 October 1905 Vineland was treated to the spectacle of an outdoor procession led by the city's own Silver Band, as the scroll of the Law draped in an American flag was carried from Hoffman's to its new location. The main speaker, the Reverend Alpert of Alliance, contrasted the freedom in Vineland with Russian brutality and called on everyone to be forever loyal to America, the land of liberty. A similar theme was sounded by the spokesman for Allivine Farm, with all joining in cheers for the USA and President Teddy Roosevelt.[58]

Divisiveness, however, seemed as unavoidable in Vineland as in Alliance. Was it a specifically Jewish or American trait, or just human frailty? The *Journal* thought "the Hebrews of the town are becoming Americanized enough to divide into factions the same as Americans do," as it reported the formation of yet another synagogue, Ahavas Achim, under rival lay leadership. Formally organized in 1906 with twenty-six charter members. Ahavas Achim immediately proceeded to establish a Hebrew school in an old building on Plum Street adjacent to the city's high school. At the same location they completed before the end of the year a new sanctuary and *mikvah,* a combination the *Journal* described as "a fine . . . commodious-looking church" with attached "Turkish bathhouse or swimming pool."[59] Thus, Vineland had two synagogues, both orthodox, both with services during the same hours.

The kosher meat shop that opened in October 1905 on Sixth Street reflected yet another aspect of orthodoxy's influence on the community. At first, the city council had looked askance at the idea of permitting outsiders to compete with exising butcher shops. How would he like it, they asked local shoe merchant Goldberg, who defended the application, if out-of-town dealers came in to sell shoes to his customers? What was wrong with Vineland meat? Goldberg explained that the kosher meat imported "from Jewtown" (Philadelphia's ghetto section) was prepared according to Biblical and Talmudic requirements, and as proof, he presented rabbinical certificates of *kashrut,* in Hebrew, to the puzzled councilmen. Permission was eventually granted. Before World War I a movement led by a prominent Hebrew to establish also a kosher restaurant in town was reported.[60]

Brief explanations of the major Jewish holidays were included regularly in the *Journal,* accompanied by a list of store closings. "The Hebrew holidays are being carefully kept by about all of the Jewish residents," the *Journal* reported in 1914; then "only occasionally will you see one doing business of any sort." The year before, Ahavas Achim had built another and larger synagogue on Plum Street and celebrated with a full-blown dedication, including an outdoor procession down Landis Avenue, the main street. Then not to be outdone by their rival, the Sons of Jacob proceeded to build their own *mikvah,* or "Turkish bath and baptismal pool in the rear of their church."[61] At the same time, news came that a splinter group from the old congregation in Rosenhayn had appeared, which in 1914 led to the construction of a second synagogue in that colony too.[62]

238

A more difficult problem than the appearance of splinter groups, however, still begged for attention: the religious education of the young. Not so surprisingly, perhaps, the Vineland Hebrew Ladies' Society launched a campaign that culminated in the Hebrew Free School as an adjunct of the Sons of Jacob Congregation. The school opened its doors in October 1909 with daily classes being given by "the far-famed teacher, Mr. Goodwin of Philadelphia." Ahavas Achim apparently had a less formal school based on the desultory lessons of the traditional *melamed*. Every so often, however, came demands for a more effective education than was offered in either synagogue. Much enthusiasm was evident when Rabbi Levinthal pleaded before a capacity gathering in Palace Hall for a community-wide full-time day school. That was in 1914, but no such institution was established in the Vineland area until 1953. Fluctuating community interest—occasionally aroused, but usually apathetic—was at the core of the problem.

During the war years additional meetings were held in an attempt to develop more viable, even if only part-time religious instruction; then the newly formed Hebrew Civic Club joined in the campaign to support Jewish education. At one such mass meeting a record six hundred dollars was raised to subsidize the recently expanded educational program of Ahavas Achim.[63] Unfortunately, neither administrative nor financial support was provided on a continuing basis. At the same time, even in "all-Jewish Woodbine," Mayor Joseph Rabinowitz had to warn the Fund that the local Hebrew School Association was about to discontinue its good work for lack of adequate support. And the orthodox *Jewish Daily News* revived complaints that food in the agricultural school was not prepared according to religious dietary standards. Although these charges were entirely true, retorted the new superintendent, he knew of "no student who left the school on account of *kashrut*": it was impractical to conform to these ancient laws; besides, there were other ways, he affirmed, in which the school tried to foster the spirit of Judaism.[64]

The Fund's trustees were fully aware of these difficulties. Years before, while replying to criticism from the European agents of the Jewish Colonization Association, Eugene Benjamin had admitted that "there is no strong religious spirit in the institution." This was due to no "fault of the institution itself, but rather of the conditions that exist with practically all the younger Jewish generation" and result in their lack of concern with religion. Citing the school's good influence on future farmer citizens, he insisted that "it is absolutely Jewish in spirit . . . [its] very existence" serves to impress the American public with the Jewish community's moral intent "to induce newly arriving Jewish immigrants to take up farm work systematically."[65]

Perhaps it was this kind of reasoning that added to the confusion of the younger generation. What they did grasp readily and what was always made abundantly clear was the need to learn the ways of the New World including the value of educational achievement. Jewish children in Vineland, for example, figured early on the public school honor rolls. John Daniels, an observer of the Americanization process, commented in his *America Via The Neighborhood* that while the focus of the "Bohemian community [was its] freethinking society, and that of the Dutch community the church, in the case of this Jewish community the center is the public school."[66] This evaluation, stemming from Daniels' interest in Woodbine, might perhaps have been applied as well to almost any other Jewish immigrant community in melting-pot America.

Jewish parents in the Vineland area as elsewhere took pride in the educational progress of their youngsters, probably above anything else. For example, in 1906, Elwood Unger and George Seldes of Alliance attracted attention in Vineland High School's annual debate where they defended the affirmative on the question, "Resolved, That a citizen should stand by his country, right or wrong," against a duo of native boys.[67] Soon, honor roll graduates from the high school included numerous youngsters from the immigrant settlements. College was the next step, and by 1913 of the Vineland graduates accepted at various colleges and universities one-fourth were Jewish. One, Ben Shanefield, won prizes in Roman law and went on to Yale Law School after service with the Army, and two girls continued their education at the State Normal School in Trenton. Another of the boys passed the necessary civil service examinations and began a noted career in the Department of the Interior in Washington.[68]

Such young people were the protoytpes of the growing number of successful second and third generation Jews in America who were educated, professionally oriented, and progressive. Many of them tended to reject external ethnic characteristics or the notion of there being any distinction between Jew and Gentile other than a somewhat abstract religious group loyalty in the larger context of America.[69] As the American-born son of Alliance pioneers put it, his contemporaries were among those "modern young people who did not go to synagogues . . . [but who] tried to maintain a sort of almost kosher home when mother was around . . . (to keep things quiet)."[70]

Yet, there was also an ambivalence of feeling, for this "unreligious" young generation recalled by Dr. Goldhaft lacked a conscious, clear-cut break from the past; they "scorned the orthodox religion of [their] parents," but felt as out of place among Philadelphia's Reform Jews as in the churches or missions. Where did they go, these immigrants' sons who left South Jersey to seek education or business success?

To some, the ethical culture movement seemed somehow both a continuation of their heritage and a break with the past: "The Ethical Culture Society gave us a gathering place, and though we debated socialism and utopian ideas and women's rights, and though it was non-sectarian, there was still something Jewish about it, perhaps not only because of the attendance but because after all the Jewish religion is concerned with moral ideas; people around a synagogue are always arguing about what is right and what is wrong; so we felt comfortable doing the same thing in another setting."[71] As a student, Jacob Rubinoff of Vineland was also attracted to the Ethical Culture Society, serving on the executive council of its University of Pennsylvania branch. At the same time (1914) he became president of the University's new Menorah

Society, a pioneering extra-curricular organization originally begun at Harvard in 1906 by Horace M. Kallen and others to foster Jewish culture, history, and ideals. Another active chapter had been established at Cornell by Philip Goldstein, soon to become educational director in the South Jersey colonies and doctoral candidate at the University of Pennsylvania. There was also the Jewish fraternity, Sigma Alpha Mu, originating at the City College of New York, and having its Beta chapter at Cornell again founded by the ubiquitous Goldstein.[72] Such organizations represented part of the response to the external and inner pressures that were transforming the immigrants and their children; it was a groping, experimental kind of metamorphosis. There were, after all, no easy solutions to the dilemma of Americanization versus religious-ethnic heritage, of melting-pot amalgamation versus group identity.

The challenge was only increased by the resurgence of the centuries-old dream of a return to Zion. Secular prophet and intellectual, Theodor Herzl, published his call in 1896 in a small book entitled *Der Judenstaat* ("The Jewish State") in which he advocated nationhood for his long-suffering people. Within two years, political Zionism was launched as the First Zionist Congress proclaimed to the world its objective: "to create for the Jewish people a home in Palestine secured by public law." Indeed, the idea of redemption in the Promised Land had always been at the very heart of traditional Jewish religion and culture. And years before Herzl's call, the Love of Zion movement had created fifteen pioneering agricultural colonies in Palestine. Before the end of the nineteenth century the conception of making East European Jews into sturdy farmers was still bold, but hardly unprecedented. Baron Edmond de Rothschild aided some of the first Palestine colonies; Baron Maurice de Hirsch subsidized grand colonization programs in the New World. What Zionism now offered was not merely settlement, but the goal of a restored national sovereignty.

In May 1895 Herzl had obtained an audience with de Hirsch and addressed him with blunt accusation. "This philanthropy debases the character of our people. . . . You transport Jews as plough-hands. They naturally feel that henceforth they have a claim on you, and this certainly does not promote the will to work. Whatever such an exported Jew costs you, he is not worth it." Instead, Herzl proposed political means to revitalize and unify the Jewish people, with the migrants building their own sovereign state. And the dream of a Promised Land would not be fulfilled unless the people first became "strong as for war, filled with the joy of work, penetrated by high virtues." Never forgetting this audience with de Hirsch, he wrote in *The Jewish State,* "No human being is wealthy or powerful enough to transplant a people from one place of residence to another. Only an idea can achieve that. The State idea surely has that power."[73]

Herzl failed to win Rothschild or de Hirsch—or the acculturated philanthropists generally—for the cause of Zionism, which seemed no more than intellectual fantasy to some, smacked too much of political agitation to others. The emancipated Jews of the West saw in it a risk of disturbing their longed-for accommodation with the dominant majorities. It might also disrupt the more practical work of rescue and rehabilitation, and perhaps even impugn the motives and patriotism of those who supported the philanthropic endeavors. From the religious point of view also objections were raised. At one extreme, some of the orthodox were convinced that restoration could be achieved only by the coming of the Messiah, while many Reform leaders regarded Zionism as a threat to their doctrine of divinely ordained permanent dispersion for the world's spiritual good. Judaism, they insisted, was a religion pure and simple without the complication of ethnic or national distinctions. And the irreligious left scorned the bourgeois-nationalist aspects of a return to Zion, while many, if not most of the young American generation, were simply indifferent to this new crisis of identity.

Although such divisiveness was starkly evident in the American Jewish community when the Federation of American Zionists emerged in 1898, yet there predominated also the massive, if amorphous, center group of immigrant sweatshop workers, peddlers, pioneer farmers and intellectuals whose still vivid memories of European brutality merged with the deeply ingrained, inherited prayer for Zion's restoration. Perhaps, many wondered, the time had come for the homeless to be reunited in their own land; had they not already suffered their full measure of pain?

Moses Klein, of the *Exponent,* working so closely with the South Jersey colonies, was one of the first in America to raise his voice on behalf of the new Zionism and the "transplanting of outcast Israelites from barbarous countries to the Land of the Covenant." Even back in the 1880's he had envisioned both the United States and Palestine as "the two refuge-places" for Jewish agricultural colonization, neither incompatible with the other. In the 1890's, he warned, there were signs of a new era in America—an era of immigration restrictions, violent labor disputes, and over-burdened hospitals, schools, and orphanages. What, too, of declining Sabbath observance, mounting conversions, and other symptoms of a breakdown in the Jewish community? All these factors, he argued, bespoke the need for Zionist inspiration and achievement. American Jews, he pleaded, must embrace Zionism and so resist "the odium cast upon it by the [Reform] rabbinical fraternity of New York." In sarcastic tones, he called on "these divines" to halt their irresponsible opposition. "You teachers in Israel protest against the creating of a *Juden-Staat,*" he mocked in the spring of 1897, "and prefer to leave the Sphynxes [to] solve their own riddle [of Jewish survival]."[74]

If Zionism continued for some years to draw but lukewarm if not hostile, responses from Reform leadership, it nevertheless enjoyed substantial success among the Jewish farmers and factory workers of South Jersey. The Vineland colonies were represented by J. C. Reiss at the Federation of American Zionists' convention in Philadelphia in 1901. Soon, the United Zionists of Norma were holding regular sessions, featuring cultural programs and addresses, some at mass meetings in Alliance Hall. The new Zionist medal, struck in 1902, was featured in a Vineland *Journal* story stressing its motto, "the Divine message in Hebrew: 'Behold, I will take the sons of Israel from among the Gentiles, and I will bring them into their land.' "[75] In Woodbine, socialist labor competition delayed the institution of an effective Zionist program until 1907. Once off the ground, however, it operated successfully. A Junior Zionist Society was centered in the agricultural school, with delegates from the National Farm School in Doylestown also attending.

Two events of 1908 afforded further stimulus. First, the national Zionist convention was held in nearby Atlantic City, with Bernard A. Palitz, Woodbine's superintendent, serving as presiding officer and the colony itself receiving favorable attention. The other was a visit by Israel Zangwill, the Anglo-Jewish novelist who championed the principle of Jewish nationality (even if on some territory other than Palestine); his appearance stirred the entire Vineland area as well as Woodbine. At subsequent meetings in the Woodbine agricutural school, Palitz urged the young people to excel in farming studies as part of their preparation for Jewish national rebuilding. It was a radical departure from the usual emphasis on Americanization as the supreme goal. As if in response, ardent young Zionist students organized in 1909 a Hebrew journal, *Haikkar Hatzair* ("The Young Farmer"), that included reports from Jerusalem by Dr. Arthur Ruppin, director of Zionist settlement. And at agricultural school assemblies recitations in Hebrew and Yiddish were heard more often than before.[76] The peak of youthful Zionist enthusiasm in Woodbine was reached in March 1914, when *The Jewish Farmer* reported that the young men of the Zionist Society, mostly recent graduates of the agricultural school, met in the social hall bedecked with the banners of America and Zion to sing the songs of the movement, some specially composed for the occasion. Student and adult speakers lauded the cause of national restoration.[77] Little did they realize that the coming war would hasten the demise of their school, and, even more significant, drastically affect both the world's and Palestine's future.

Zionist activity in South Jersey was always influenced by the city, and it inevitably shifted from the farm colonies to Vineland. Then Philadelphia became a vital source of inspiration in the form of leaders like Rabbi Levinthal or Dr. Benjamin L. Gordon, who lectured to the farmers of Alliance and Norma on his trip to Palestine, illustrating his talk with stereopticon views of conditions in the Jewish colonies that he had seen there. It was, perhaps, an idealized version of the "natural life" in the historic homeland. Reportedly, there was great interest on the part of these Jewish farmers in the welfare of far-away Palestine's pioneers.[78] Also from Philadelphia came attorney A. E. Hurshman to speak on "The Emancipation of the Jew" before Vineland's Hebrew Educational League. By 1915 the Vineland Zion Camp, too, had been formed with the aid of Isaac Carmel of New York. He described vividly the new tragedies of World War I and warned that Jews would be the losers no matter who won unless they could control their own destinies. At yet another meeting, Philadelphian M. Katz, editor of the *Jewish World*, discussed the cultural contributions of famed literary figures, specifically Heinrich Heine and Georg Brandes, whom "the Hebrew nation [had] produced," but who were known to the world as German or Dane, not Jew. The "great national movement," he concluded, would provide a much-needed sense of identity in a world of numerous nationalities.[79]

"We, the Jews of Vineland, N. J., assembled on Sunday, September 19, 1915, in Red Men's Hall" express our concern for the depths of suffering by brethren in all the countries at war and call for organized efforts to "ameliorate and normalize" their condition through a two-point program: 1) full and equal civil, political and national rights for the Jews wherever their rights are limited, and 2) a politically secured home in Palestine as a national center for the Jewish people.[80] It was a bold and energetic declaration, the culmination of organizing efforts by three local leaders—Max Krich, Hyman Cohen, and Frank Mennies. More than that, it reflected the sense of urgency which the World War had created within all of American Zionism, as well as the spark of the new captain at the movement's helm, Kentucky-born Louis D. Brandeis. To those who feared dual allegiance Brandeis replied, "Multiple loyalties are objectionable only if they are inconsistent. . . . To be good Americans we must be better Jews, and to be better Jews we must become Zionists."[81] Such was the counsel of a future Justice on the United States Supreme Court. But the debate was far from finished.

Eventually, much of the Jewish labor movement also swung over to the Zionist idea, forming a kind of left wing, and its eloquent champion, Dr. Nahum Syrkin of New York, addressed the Vineland Zionists on more than one occasion. He preached in favor of a national labor commonwealth in Palestine as well as a democratically elected American Jewish Congress to provide adequate representation for all shades of opinion, not just the wealth and social status.[82] Syrkin found a sympathetic audience among the poverty-ridden Jewish farmers and factory workers in South Jersey.

But the gentle, nonpartisan message of Mary Antin, author of *They Who Knock at Our Gates* and *The Promised Land,* had an even wider impact. The writer whose books so poetically described the travails of the immigrants and their stubborn faith in their new homeland had herself been one of the young refugees from Russia in 1894. She chose to speak in the Alliance-Norma colony in 1916 to a large audience composed of her own people from the entire area, and "a surprising number of prominent Gentiles." Though she still believed that the immigrant had to become Americanized, she embraced Brandeis's concept that one could be an even better American by being a better Jew. In short, Mary Antin now championed the "Zionist movement as an Americanizing force." The people who had brought the Ten Commandments to the world, she pleaded, must maintain their traditional values; they should remain in America where their good, well-disciplined home life would be a deterrent to juvenile delinquency and crime. For Jews in other countries, however, where they were harried and persecuted, Palestine was by right the homeland, although the cause of Zionism and the Palestine colonies deserved broad American support as well for their example of both spiritual and material progress. Her address concluded with some warm words in Yiddish, much to the delight of older Jewish Chautauquans who determined to rename their group the Mary Antin Circle. Young and old had been effusive in their enthusiastic reception.[83]

Mary Antin's message, however, also stirred the local opponents of Zionism into public debate. Professor Louis Mounier issued an open letter in which he found the "conversion of Mary Antin . . . to an ardent advocate of Zionism to be greatly deplored." Did this not violate her own beliefs, and those of all "liberal-minded people," in the primary goal of "Americanization and sane assimilation?" Why give comfort to divisive influences by "advertising one's origin or belief [while] in the ordinary walks of life?" There ought to be no references, Mounier maintained, to a "Jewish farmer . . . Jewish Judge of the United States Supreme Court [Brandeis's nomination had just been approved in spite of some virulent testimony] . . . French artist . . . German chemist . . . Catholic . . . [or] Methodist." He granted that there was a "certain deterioration" in the family life of immigrants as a result of new American values and social pressures but eventual absorption was worth all costs, even if "meanwhile the [foreign-born] parents must suffer the loss of certain ideals, customs, language, etc." Mounier's talk of ethnic divisiveness as well as his reference to "hyphenated-Americans" was undoubtedly influenced by Theodore Roosevelt's colorful attacks in the close, war-atmosphere campaign of 1916.

Soon, the local Zionists' rebuttal was presented by Max Krich. As a delegate to the Zionist convention in Philadelphia a few months before, he had heard Brandeis uphold the obligations of American Jews. Besides, Krich asked, who had attempted to single out American Jews from the rest of their fellow citizens if it was not the same type of bigots who had oppressed their brethren in Europe? They, not the Zionists, were divisive, he claimed. Next came Philip Goldstein's round in the battle of words. He outlined in a calm, expository manner the mutual relationships of state, group, and individual. Across the seas, he maintained, a great war was being fought partly because monolithic powers refused to respect ethnic and cultural diversity. In a free America, however, "good citizenship does not demand from the Jew the sacrifice of his religion, tradition and historic memory." Who could be charged with disloyalty for furthering the biblical prophecy, "For out of Zion shall go forth the law, and the word of the Lord from Jerusalem?"

Mounier returned again, however, to cite the evils of diversity, recalling even the bloodshed of the American Civil War. Moreover, "would the Lusitania horror have remained unpunished, if there had not been hyphenates?" he asked, in obvious sympathy with TR's bellicose anti-German stand. A friend had warned him that

Mary Antin's Zionist address had incited "racial or religious prejudice" in the community where he, Mounier, had spent fifteen years
to foster harmony. Her defense by Goldstein, "the genial and brilliant teacher from the Jewish Chautauqua Society," glossed over
the central objective for which all good people strove, that is "perfect Americanization." In substance, these two professional Americanizers of Jewish South Jersey disagreed on ultimate objectives:
the older man defended the still fashionable melting-pot theory,
while the younger looked ahead to the pluralistic society.

Dr. Arthur Goldhaft, spokesman for the native generation, also
made his views felt in press and public meeting. His attitude
reflected a combination of humanism and pragmatism as well as
the fashionable social gospel. Settlement houses and social centers
could do a more effective job of making good citizens out of "children of all nationalities" than could their "alien parents." If the
two generations drifted apart, the remedy was not, as Mary Antin
would have it, to teach the "old folk songs and traditions" to the
children, but rather to move the parents forward to the level of
their offspring—"Let them learn all American customs . . . make
them real chums, and the children will not be ashamed of the
old-fashioned ways of their parents." As for the problems of delinquency and vice, Goldhaft preferred to attribute these to low wages
and economic instability rather than to a weakening of traditional
family ties. Zionism interfered with the process of "undiluted . . .
Americanizing," so he opposed it: "no broad-minded person can
serve two masters." At the same time, he called on his fellow citizens to press for "universal brotherhood and ever-lasting peace.
Working for the welfare of our [Jewish] class of people while many
others are suffering is a selfish motive," he pleaded.[84]

Dr. Goldhaft was to live a long useful life and to learn the
tragic lessons of Jewish agony and mass death in the 1930's and
World War II. He was to find the new Israel (reborn in 1948) a
thrilling emotional experience, visiting it, working with its officials
to modernize its poultry production, and delighting in the proud
discovery of a cousin, Rabbi J. Newman, who wrote his doctoral
dissertation on "Agriculture Among the Jews of Babylon." He

labored for Histadrut and UJA; and local Hadassah meetings were held in his Vineland home in those later years.[85] His original opposition to Zionism in the World War I era had stemmed partly from fear that it might follow other national movements in Europe into dissension and bias. Moreover, as a leader in the local Ethical Culture Society, he had eschewed any sectarian or particularist movements.

Standing against him at public meetings in those early years, Philip Goldstein denied that Zionism necessarily involved compulsion or that it required that more than a small fraction of world Jewry settle in Palestine. Alliance pioneer Sidney Bailey also argued that Zionism could do much to alleviate anti-Jewish prejudice. He chose to embrace the movement for such secular reasons, describing himself as less than traditional in religious practice. Disagreeing with Bailey, however, one local Jewish socialist restated the typical doubts that Zionism could end Jewish suffering. On the contrary, he complained, under international capitalism all strangers were disliked, whether they had a homeland or not; he blamed the class strugle for such repressions of Americans by their own countrymen as in the violent Colorado miners' strike (the Ludlow "massacre" of 1913). Zionism, especially if in bourgeois form, would not alleviate the suffering of either Jewish or other labor throughout the world, he concluded. Still other debaters and speakers on this popular controversy included Philadelphia lawyer Herman D. Levinson, whose exposition of "Universalism and Zionism" was sponsored by the Hebrew Educational League of Vineland.[86]

The wide-ranging debates had their positive aspects. They focused on the continuing search for identity and even tended to unite the Jewish community, especially at critical or dramatic occasions. Such were the mass meetings held to raise relief funds for the victims of World War I. Local Zionists presented the speeches and organized programs of music, recitations, and drama. Also, memorial meetings for Theodor Herzl drew wide participation. One of these, held shortly after America entered the War to Save Democracy, was organized by the new Vineland Lodge of B'rith

Sholem, whose national grand master delivered the main address. A large audience gathered in Lubin's Grand Theatre and responded enthusiastically to the stirring defense of Zionist aspirations; reportedly Max Krich was able to sign up an astounding 235 new members for the local Zionist Society that very evening. Even the Plum Street Hebrew school became a nonpartisan beneficiary of Zionist enthusiasm when the Society decided to raise funds for improving educational facilities.[87]

Moreover, demands for democratic representation within the Jewish community joined the cause of Zionism in bringing slow but sure efforts to form the American Jewish Congress. It was a movement spearheaded by East European intellectuals, the Yiddish press, moderate Jewish labor union pioneers (notably Joseph Barondess), and "general" Zionists. In large measure, they were united by their lack of confidence in the group of wealthy leaders who controlled the American Jewish Committee formed in 1906 as a kind of self-perpetuating establishment. Its members were mostly in the acculturated, Reform stratum of the deeper-rooted German rather than East European migration. These, who still did not consider the latter sufficiently Americanized or responsible, had intended to keep control in the hands "of the most conservative men . . . [to uphold] the standing of the Jews in the American nation," lest their organization "fall into the hands of radical theorists whose vagaries will then be accepted by the American nation as expressive of . . . the whole Jewish community."[88] Such condescension was nothing new to the South Jersey colonists, or to the East European immigrant in Vineland, New York or Philadelphia.

Vinelanders responded eagerly to the rebel call of the *Jewish Nation's* editor, Abe Goldberg, and others who urged democratic representation. It was not inappropriate that the first conferences of the American Jewish Congress were held in Philadelphia, America's "cradle of liberty." From Vineland, Dr. N. S. Greenwood and Max Krich were nominated; from Rosenhayn, Philip Goldstein; from Alliance-Norma, Charles Reis; from Carmel, M. Weinberg. In early June 1917, elections were held in all the colonies, including tiny Brotmanville. Reis and Krich won. By November, many were also buying the *shekel* for twenty-five cents as a kind of voluntary poll tax or contribution for voting in Zionist elections.[89]

Within the same momentous year, the Turks were driven out of Jerusalem. The front page accounts in Vineland's newspaper described the celebrations throughout the Western world, and even the special services of thanksgiving held by the Jewish legionnaires trained in England. Jerusalem's liberation was also the theme of a Christmas week sermon by Dr. Thomas S. Brock in the local First Methodist Church. Speaking on "The Jew and Jerusalem," he presented a brief history of God's "chosen people . . . repository of the Divine truth." The time was now near, Dr. Brock predicted, when the Jews might be "witness as a nation to the Messiahship of Christ." With Jerusalem in the hands of the British, who were known for their "fair play and tolerance, the hope of the Jew's returning to what may be a Fatherland is brighter than ever before," the minister concluded optimistically.[90] Dr. Brock presumably knew of the Balfour Declaration made just the month before, in which Britain regarded "with favor the establishment in Palestine of a national home for the Jewish people."

Jews in the Vineland area rejoiced after their own manner. At yet another mass meeting, Max Krich reminded his numerous audience that the Turkish surrender took place on that day of Hanukkah on which the Maccabees had liberated Jerusalem almost twenty-one centuries before. He called for and received a rousing vote of approval for the Balfour Declaration. Visiting Rabbi Samuel Fredman, of Philadelphia's Beth El Synagogue, proclaimed, "The Zionist idea is now a fact. The Jewish State does not [yet] exist, but the Jewish nation exists and has been recognized by Great Britain." Then he proceeded to expound a relevant Jewish interpretation of the chosen theme: "Through Israel, God gave the Law, and what makes our people unique is the fact that our secular and religious history go hand in hand."[91]

Excitement continued to mount in the months to come, arousing support from some unexpected quarters. Suffragette leader Mrs. Anna Lowenberg of Philadelphia had helped to organize Vineland's Young Women's Zionist Association early in 1918, with a memberhip of over sixty "young Hebrew women." Some of the most eligible girls in town were officers, and one of their projects was the door-to-door collection of contributions to the Jewish National Fund for land purchase and reforestation in the Holy Land. Men and women, young and old, native and newcomer, could also follow the progress of the Jewish Legion as it helped to free all of Palestine. One of the battalions consisted of several thousand volunteers from America, mostly noncitizens, including the exiled David Ben-Gurion and Isaac Ben-Zvi, labor leaders of Palestine who had found welcome refuge in the New World. Among them also were such American Jews as Jacob Epstein, renowned sculptor from New York's Lower East Side.[92]

Long before Henrietta Szold founded Hadassah, the Women's Zionist Organization of America (1912), she had almost despaired of the wide gulf marking the immigrant "Russian Jewish element [which] defies analysis . . . [in] their tendency toward grouping and segregation" apart from their acculturated German and Sephardic "predecessors". She was confident, however, that as a social by-product of the good works of Zionism and its cooperative program a greater unity could be achieved within the diverse American Jewish community.[93] This faith was sustained, in large measure, through the years of crisis.

In Vineland, Mayor Stevens, too, participated as a friendly guest at some of the Zionist rallies cosponsored by the Hebrew Civic Club. He shared the platform with such Zionist publicists as Charles A. Cowen of New York and Philip Raskin, the Yiddish poet. And by April 1920, when it seemed to local leaders that a Jewish commonwealth was imminent, the Zionist flag was displayed even in Vineland's city hall. As if to clear up any misapprehension over the "Yiddish flag," the *Journal* saw fit to note that "not more than five percent of the Jews contemplate going back [to Palestine]."[94]

The newspaper's concern, if such it was, turned out to be premature. Israel's time of redemption was not yet at hand. Nor was it clear that the lives of young Americans, including the sons of Jewish farmers among so many others, had not been given in vain on the battlefields of Europe. The end of World War I did not bring peace, justice or democracy to a suffering planet. While the United States pursued the illusions of normalcy, Jews in America concentrated on their future as Americans.

Within American society: Toward democratic pluralism

As newcomers, we have not had the privilege of fighting for the freedom granted us here, but as Jews, the underlying theme of our political life is equality.

B. A. Palitz, Commencement Address
Woodbine, New Jersey, 1908[1]

Thou favorest man with knowledge, and teachest mortals understanding . . . and insight.

Daily prayer service

8

Self-reliance and Integration in the Progressive Era

The impressive participation by Jewish immigrant communities in America's causes, traditions, and politics added weight to the praise the US Immigration Commission lavished upon them in 1911. Its exhaustive report on "Hebrews in Agriculture" lauded the Russian Jew's civic virtues, his pride in citizenship, and his active involvement in its duties and responsibilities, ostensibly "in marked contrast to the incoming Italians in New Jersey, who have little care about the prerogatives of citizenship."[2] Even if such comparisons proved premature and essentially unfounded, it is significant that the report minced no words in singling out the Jewish immigrant as "likely to become a citizen sooner than most East European immigrants and to take a more intelligent interest in politics." Few among the Jews were illiterate; almost all of the second generation and those minors who had been in the country for some time could "speak, read and write English." Moreover, the evaluation continued, ownership of a farm in South Jersey furthered the Russian Hebrew's "independence, self-reliance and self-respect."[3] Success, it seems, crowned the years of arduous Americanization as the colonists developed "a desire for representative government, democratic institutions, an educated electorate, equality of opportunity and the free agency of the individual."[4]

At the same time, the official report included a theme apparently inconsistent with the melting-pot and integrationist tendencies of the twentieth century. When the immigrant Jews were clustered within their own settlements, the report maintained, they developed unique institutions useful to themselves and to their neighbors. The voluntary ghetto had its compensations. Thus, where the colonists were "segregated with sufficient compactness, their leaders have originated social, educational and recreative enterprises for the benefit of the community."[5] By way of documentation for this statement, there followed chapters detailing the growth of the South Jersey synagogues, schools, libraries, meeting halls, mutual aid societies, lodges, fraternal orders, and remarkable associations such as the Woodbine Brotherhood, literary clubs, and active units of the Federation of Jewish Farmers.

Civic initiative was perhaps the most striking in Woodbine, whose independent incorporation earned it that grandiose title of "First Self-Governed Jewish Community Since the Fall of Jerusalem."[6] Even before 1903, it possessed a Village Improvement Association, its own board of health and volunteer fire department, and an Educational Alliance serving both children and adults. Alfred Cooper, editor of the *Cape May County Gazette,* wrote of Woodbine, "From its earliest inception I have always maintained that the colony was of incalculable benefit to Cape May County. . . . The schools of Woodbine are doing wonders for the schools of our other towns."[7] The community of Jews was thus in various respects a significant model.

Yet, conflict over school aid and the distribution of tax funds had become precisely the issue that lent impetus to the movement for independence from Dennis Township. In petitioning the state legislature, "the people of Woodbine" affirmed that theirs was the only part of Dennis Township which is progressing steadily." Unfair assessments, they claimed in words reminiscent of the American Revolution, forced them to bear "the main burden of taxation . . . without adequate returns and representation." By electing their own council and mayor, along with their own board of education and other agencies, they could look forward to more efficient use of revenues in "the best interests of the community." To set the pattern for independent government, a mass meeting of citizens named a committee of twenty-five, representing farmers, workingmen, business, factory management, "liberal professions," and the Fund's Woodbine Land and Improvement Company.

As in any transformation, there were those suspicious of independence, those who, according to Sabsovich, had "an axe to grind"; and "timid residents" asked whether this was not merely a new device to place greater control in the hands of the Company and the New York philanthropists. Would Company properties and those of various business enterprises be subject to at least the same tax rates as individual homesteads? Sabsovich, always the man in the middle, reassured the farmers and homeowners that any new revenue provisions would not be detrimental to their interests; eventually, one of the incorporation clauses spelled out the principle of nondiscriminatory taxation for both Company and individuals.

At the same time, Sabsovich had to reassure the New York trustees that the influence of the local registered voters, who were 114 substantial, property-owning citizens, would outweigh any extravagant spending schemes by the 59 who owned little property. It did not seem overly significant at the time that most of the voters without taxable property were gentiles, of whom only a handful possessed any material stake in this Jewish community.[8] Moreover, registered voters in all categories represented a minority of the 2,500 population (over 400 families), a fact of political life accounted for by the large numbers of children, women, and newly arrived immigrants. The population turnover caused by instability in agriculture and light industry continued to be high throughout Woodbine's history.[9]

Nonetheless, the day of independence dawned on 3 March 1903, when the incorporation bill declaring a "body politic and corporate in law by the name of the Borough of Woodbine" was signed by the governor. In mid-April, elections were held, with Sabsovich

257

winning unanimous backing for the office of mayor. As such he was empowered to appoint committees on taxation and other matters, with the approval of an elected six-man council. Also elected were an assessor, a collector, a justice of the peace, and three commissioners of appeal (for tax cases).

"And notable was that day," Dr. Boris Bogen reminisced expansively, "when the Borough of Woodbine was established—the first all-Jewish political unit in America and, for that matter in the [modern] world. . . . The banner of political purity was forthwith raised," representing a break, according to Bogen, with the occasional corruption of previous election campaigns. With a Jewish administration installed, "the politically untutored Jew proved he was as good as any in all the techniques of politics, save that he conducted this election with clean hands." To help celebrate their newly won sovereignty came notables like Abraham Cahan, editor of the *Forward,* Joseph Barondess, labor leader, and Yiddish dramatist Jacob Gordin, as well as "sociologists and social reformers and soul-savers," among whom was even Booker T. Washington.[10]

Yet in truth, it was not a utopia that was born here, no socialist commonwealth for a minority group. It was, rather, a Jewish immigrant community giving life to the progressive philosophy of middle class America, focusing on such virtues as clean government, private enterprise, the absorption of newcomers into the prevailing culture, and public education as "more essential for our form of government than any other."[11] Among the borough's first ordinances were pure food regulations, provisions for testing of milk, prevention of contagious diseases, and sponsorship of a Home-Seekers' Club to provide housing on easy terms.

After Sabsovich's departure to New York to become the Fund's general agent, political leadership in Woodbine devolved upon the local businessmen, notably M. L. Bayard and Joseph Rabinowitz. Both employed large numbers of factory workers and were involved in disputes with both labor and the trustees. Although they offered effective management practices in government, they were scarcely impartial or uniformly popular. Also, the Fund's large-scale investments, through the Woodbine Land and Improvement Company, in farm and town sites, the light and power plant and other facilities made its political intervention almost a necessity. Citizens complained of domination by large-scale philanthropy as well as the private business interests. Worst of all, the persistent decline of industry after 1911 made economic survival the paramount issue.[12]

Nonetheless, the progressive theme of self-improvement through education and enlightened group action was strikingly present, probably to a greater degree than in the cities. It seemed a self-conscious response to the fact that Woodbine was Jewish, when its citizens resolved to "not only keep up the good name it has won by reason of frugality, hard work, soberness and moral character, but that it will prove, like any other American community, that it is worthy of . . . self-government." Woodbine's civic club of about sixty active members was praised by the *Exponent* for being ever on guard against potential "corrupting influences" and political bossism of the type so common in the big cities. Liquor licenses were frowned upon from the outset, partly because of the area's prohibitionist sentiments, but also because "Jewish colonists were not drunkards" and they did not want their town to become "a mecca for objectionable elements."[13]

As early as 1903 the Mothers' Club had launched projects for beautification of homes and streets; it provided newcomers with instruction in improved child care, housekeeping, even current affairs and music. Factory girls were also organized into a club of their own, featuring social and cultural programs "to make the rural life, otherwise so devoid of interest for young minds, more attractive." This thirst for cultural attainment was likewise reflected in such events as five hundred men and women turning out to hear an evening lecture on "Life and Literature" in the three-hundred-seat auditorium of the agricultural school.[14]

Was it Jewish tradition or the American environment of the colonies which caused them to favor equal rights for women? In 1915, Woodbine voted more than two to one in favor of women's suffrage.[15] Years before, the Progressive Club in Vineland, led by Mrs. Traiman, Mrs. Eisenstein, and the wife of farmer Samuel Stern, worked for women's rights, making such noninflammatory appeals as "Take Care of Your Mother When She Is Old." The Hebrew Educational League packed as many as two hundred into their forums on votes for women, with the "great majority" of both men and women usually in favor of the question. Among their guest speakers, Anna Lowenberg argued passionately that "the mother element is necessary in politics," charging that American men were too preoccupied with making money.[16]

Moreover, Jews in Vineland participated in other elements of the progressive impulse. In 1909 they formed a cooperative insurance society. And Mrs. Joseph Fels, widow of the Philadelphia philanthropist, stirred the Hebrew Educational League with her pleas for national reform through the single tax program: the proper valuation and full taxation of land would cut back the profits of speculators and relieve the misery of the laboring class, she explained. At another meeting, Mrs. Samuel Fels championed the cause of the Consumer's League demanding factory inspection, shorter working hours, and improved conditions for working women. Progressive Party candidates received warm backing from the Vineland Hebrew Civic Club, too, in the crucial years of 1912–1914. "Whatever may be said of his agriculture [not always favorable], the Hebrew farmer is a thinking, protesting citizen," the immigration commission observed; he was able to voice "intelligent protest" against such abuses as discriminatory railroad rates, exorbitant express charges and marketing fees. Especially in the South Jersey colonies, he excelled in a high level of social participation and self-government.[17]

Although New York's *Forward* glowed as it reported the fifty-seven socialist votes cast in Vineland as early as 1901, before and during World War I little headway was made by local candidates Abe Warren and George Burgin or by the street-corner harangues of Socialist Nathan Lifshus from Woodbine.[18] Instead, Jewish settlers tended to join the mainstream of American political life, especially the progressivism of the middle class. Like their neighbors, they often felt strongly about nonideological matters: Carmel held meetings to protest poor mail delivery; in Alliance and Norma, citizens were incensed at county authorities who permitted roads so hazardous that even by 1912 the ASPCA ruled them the ruin of any healthy horse.[19] In Vineland, some Jewish merchants joined in backing fellow businessman John Ackley for mayor on a platform of efficient management and integrity. Ackley, a Democrat, won this campaign, and in 1913, was elected to the state senate, defeating the Republican candidate Morris Davis, who happened to be Jewish. By that year, the newly formed Hebrew Republican Club, led by merchant Jacob Rubinoff, was active in politics, though Jews were not at first especially successful. Michael Mennies suffered defeat in a contest for a seat on the board of education, when the economy-minded electorate turned down proposals for a new high school. And those who backed Roosevelt on the Progressive ticket were to find themselves on the losing side. Abe Lipitz, at least, enjoyed ephemeral glory when the visiting Republican candidate, President Taft, shook his hand and recalled seeing him in Atlantic City. In that heated presidential campaign of 1912, a Roosevelt-Johnson Club was formed even in little Alliance, though all three candidates, including New Jersey's own victorious Woodrow Wilson, were well represented in the final tallies of local voters.[20]

After 1914, progressivism became increasingly overshadowed by the problems of a tenuous neutrality, as Jews, like other citizens, were torn by the conflict between hatred of Tsarism and love for democracy along with all the Old World predilections. "New Jersey, with its polyglot population," noted one authority, "was especially beset with ethnic strife" in these divisive years.[21] During this same period, however, Frank Kotok, a Hebrew Republican, was elected justice of the peace in 1915, "the first Hebrew ever elected to office in Vineland." By then also, Joseph B. Perskie, son of Alliance pioneers and son-in-law of preacher Masliansky, was assistant district attorney in Atlantic City, later rising to associate justice of the New Jersey Supreme Court. Kotok, Perskie, Mennies, Abe Brotman, John Joseph, Abe Lipitz, and Victor Morvay joined together to revitalize the Hebrew Citizens' Republican Club. Somewhat invidiously, the *Journal* noted that the "Hebrews are getting warmed up in politics," an asssessment that was soon borne out by their outspoken support for various local candidates. And among triumphant Republicans invited to the inaugural of Governor Walter E. Edge appeared John Joseph and Michael Mennies.[22]

Political activity, especially in the colonies, was one of those things that lent color and excitement to a sometimes drab rural existence. Even Vineland remained sparsely populated, with some farming homesteads far apart within its vast expanse of sixty-eight square miles. In Alliance, the periodic tug-of-war between Republicans and Democrats brought joyful quarreling among farmer friends and neighbors. Politicians would supply the herring, crackers, and beer—the requisite sustenance for parched and speech-weary voters. On at least one occasion, the colony's urchins made off with the herring and crackers before the end of a momentous rally, causing some ill-humored mutterings among the electorate. That time the candidates, both local Jewish Republicans, barely managed to turn almost certain defeat into victory and then only after considerable beating of drums. The Alliance Republican Club, operating under the slogan of "Organization and Education," dated back to at least 1892, when it first met in Alliance Hall. Then its officers signed their names in Yiddish only and were all charter members of Eben Ha' Ezer.[23]

The strength of Republican loyalties among the Jews of South Jersey was probably the result of several factors combined. At the time of colonization and for decades after, the GOP was the dominant national party and seemed more clearly American to the immigrants and their business-oriented benefactors. Under its wings one could seek protection from nativist sentiment at home and the Tsarist oppression abroad. Its program reflected a moderate, if not conservative, consensus which it was quite safe to support. Perhaps also, like the Germans in New Jersey, some Jewish settlers found Irish politicians too deeply entrenched in the Democratic Party. Moreover, the banner of Theodore Roosevelt represented a strong appeal for reform and progressivism in the bolder twentieth century years; and the immigrants also felt gratitude for Roosevelt's personal intercession on behalf of Russian Jews.

But political allegiance was hardly a status function in the rural colonies. Class distinctions in the relatively homogeneous society that lacked extremes of wealth or poverty were minimal. As noted by official observers, "there is little class or caste among the Hebrews in the settlements. The rich and poor meet together on terms of amicability and good feeling."[24]

To Make the World Safe for Democracy

World War I broke harshly upon the American preoccupation with the task of absorbing its millions of immigrants into a constantly changing society. By the spring of 1917, the period of maneuver and debate was over, and the New World and the Old were joined together in war. The land of immigrants, of "hyphenated" Americans who were riven by loyalty for one or another of the belligerent mother countries in Europe, united in the interests of national security and international idealism. World War I disrupted and temporarily seemed even to reverse the trans-Atlantic human tide, as American doughboys crossed eastward, among them countless thousands retracing their journey over the ocean to Europe again. Immigrant Americans fought alongside their native comrades for a common cause that included, in the words of their President, "the ultimate peace of the world . . . the liberation of its people . . . the privilege of men everywhere to choose their way of life." They fought to make the world "safe for democracy," or perhaps only to "Halt the Hun!" proclaimed a Liberty Loan poster. The relatively untested Jewish communities in South Jersey pitched in with a will. There was no doubting their allegiance.

Among the first to volunteer for service was Joseph I. Scribner of Rosenhayn, who joined the Navy as early as 1915, "with a determination to get into the war" even during this period of uneasy neutrality for the United States. The same was true of Ben Kravitz of the Sandy Point Farm near Vineland, and of David Joseph, son of the Vineland manufacturing family, who joined the early ranks of local sailors. The name most prominent among the area's Zionist leadership, that of the Krich family, was soon represented in the US infantry by sons Benjamin and Herman. When they left, they were the lone delegates from Vineland on the train for Fort Dix. It was a wet and cold morning, too inclement to call out the band, but they did receive farewell copies of the New Testament from the Reverend Watson, who headed the official send-off committee. George Bloomenstein, Jacob Lihn, and Rube Mennies enlisted in the coast artillery, and Ervin Levy in the engineers. Soon it was Michael Mennies' turn, along with Isidore Morvay, Max Pitel, and many others. Some families had more than one man in the armed forces: for example, Dr. William Mennies, a dentist, was the third of his brothers to join up, enlisting in the Navy; Israel Kotok gave up his fruit business to follow brothers Louis, Myer, and Herman into the service; there were, too, Jacob and Harry Lipitz, Gilbert and Samuel Brotman, and Mortimer and Nat Liebman.[25]

Some who left were leaders in the Jewish community, and these were honored with appropriate farewell ceremonies. Michael Mennies, for example, who joined the pioneering aviation corps, had been founder and first president of the Hebrew Civic Club. He was reminded of his role at a gala banquet attended by many of the then hundred-odd club members. Justice Kotok presided over ceremonies which included friendly speeches by Mayor Stevens and other distinguished well-wishers. A similar send-off was given to Vineland's Attorney M. J. Greenblatt, also active in the Hebrew Civic Club, as well as the Hevra Kadisha of Alliance and other communal causes.[26]

Soon, the letters from "over there" started coming. Lieutenant Robert ("Rube") Mennies of the Second Trench Mortar Battalion wrote from France expressing with good humor his disappointment at not having sighted any submarines while crossing "the big pond." France was "interesting," but he regretted not arriving sooner than the spring of 1918. By chance, he met Morris Melletz, also a local serviceman, who had arrived in February. The latter served in the new tank corps, and his correspondence concentrated more on the blood and hell of the fighting—keeping the "Boche on the run." Nat Liebman wrote his parents from France of his hope that "God may spare you to me until we meet again, when our flag has triumphed in the cause of Liberty and Humanity."[27]

Harry Lipitz wrote to his wife and parents from "no-man's land" in the winter of 1917–1918, promising to be "home by Xmas at the latest" and enclosing a poem he composed in honor of the Army engineers, his outfit. He had volunteered in the spring of 1917, in hopes of joining the young aviation corps in France or, he half-threatened, of returning home in time to pick the first peaches that year. He eventually realized it would take much longer to say "good-bye, Kaiser," in spite of his poetic "we're tough enough to beat the Boche, as you can plainly see."[28] Lieutenant Jack Rubinoff fought in the Eleventh Machine Gun Battalion, handling the latest weapons of the time including the still novel hand grenade, a lethal device to be cast expertly at the "Hun trenches" lest they "throw it back" before the fuse exploded it. By the summer of 1918 he was writing to his mother on the farm that the "Germans seem glad to surrender." To his brother David, he described the furious cannonades and repeated attacks on hilly gun positions before the enemy retreated. Come Rosh Hashanah, he cabled "New Year's greetings to all" from France.

Within a few months, as others were being discharged, Lieutenant Rubinoff remained with the American Expeditionary Force, then in far-off Russia which was torn by internecine war in the wake of revolution. From the wintry port of Archangel, he wrote of meeting the Pines family, ardent Hebraists and Zionists with whom he felt "very much at home." Occasional discussions with the head of the family, "a doctor of philosophy and a very learned man" in secular and religious areas, provided a welcome opportunity to "brush the dust off my brain." Thus wrote the immigrants' son who had returned as a soldier to the land of his parents' oppression. It was not until the end of July 1919, long after the armistice, that Rubinoff marched back home with the AEF.[29]

In their own various ways, these men contributed to the war effort. Sergeant Jack Berstein managed a vaudeville and moving picture show for the troops in France. Although Vineland's Sam Gassel stayed on the job as borough recorder, he also found time to write the morale building war song, "Good Bye, Sammie; Gee I'm Glad To See You Go." It was a catchy tune in two-four time with lyrics glorifying liberty and the doughboys who would push the Kaiser down to where he belonged. Its Philadelphia publishers saw it selling well.

Some of the local men died in the war. One doughboy was

Infantry Corporal Lou Gassell, who wrote from France that there was a big job to be done and he hoped mother wasn't worrying about him. To his brother Sam, he promised a "Dutch" helmet or similar souvenir as a sure sign that all was well, but he died leading his squad in the Grand Pré offensive. After the Great War, memorial trees were planted for him and the others by Vineland's City Beautiful Committee.[30] Earlier, there was also sorrow for a Woodbine boy, Ben Wolfson, reported lost in action on the battlefields of France. He had had a large number of warm friends in Vineland, reported the *Journal*, "not only among his own nationality, but [also] among other races of people."[31] Even at that late date, and having died a hero in his country's cause, it seemed he was not yet considered to be fully American.

At the other extreme perhaps was farmer Philip Helig, arrested by Sheriff C. P. Sharp on charges of maligning the United States' leadership and mocking the doughboys' fighting prowess. Reportedly when "reminded that he was earning his livelihood from [fellow] Americans by selling the products of his farm, . . . he replied that the Germans had bought as much." Witnesses "Billy Moore and his barber" vowed not to let the matter be hushed up, though Helig was released by the mayor after a few days in jail.[32] The country was at war; there were widespread, sometimes exaggerated, fears of subversion, and especially the foreign-born, or those considered by some as tainted with alien characteristics, were watched suspiciously.

Shortly after American entry into the war, the American Jewish Committee set up an office of war records to gather data on the number of Jews in the armed forces. Official figures added up to 225,000, well above their proportion of the total populace; the same was true of casualties and service in the combatant branches. Ironically, the proportionately greater number of Jewish soldiers stemmed not only from a higher ratio of Jewish volunteers, but also from the fact that relatively fewer Jews were engaged in farming, where exemptions were usually granted on grounds of national need.[33] Nonetheless, the *Jewish Farmer* periodically listed names of farm boys in the service, such as these from Woodbine:

Nate Greenstein with the coast artillery in France, Max Benzino-wich on the Mexican border, Morris Cohen and the two Letwin boys in the infantry.[34]

On the home front, Jews in South Jersey, as elsewhere, partici-pated in many activities then encouraged. For example, the Red Cross flourished in Rosenhayn under the leadership of Mrs. M. Schecter, with periodic drives and community meetings. At one of these, Dr. Joseph Conwell of Vineland, regional chairman, compared the hand of healing and service held out by Rosenhayn's Red Cross to the hospitality shown by the Jewish patriarch Abraham. The war would bring an end to autocracy in Russia as well as Germany, he concluded, so that those of the "Hebrew race" who wished to return would be able to do so.[35] Patriotic prayer services for the cause of the United States and the Allies were held on such occa-sions as Memorial Day at Vineland's Ahavas Achim and other synagogues. These first and second generation Americans also lent their enthusiastic support to the national crusade for Liberty Bonds. Woodbine rallied around a flag whose thirty-seven stars represented recent graduates from the local high school then in the armed forces, all but three of them volunteers. When the *Jewish Farmer* pleaded that everyone support the bond drives, its editors pointed to Wood-bine where each of the three hundred families managed to buy at least one bond. "Have you done your duty?" they demanded of their Yiddish-speaking farm readers, as they lauded the patriotic example set by this small Jewish community which had thrice exceeded its bond quota, purchasing $45,000 worth before the end of 1918.[36]

In Rosenahyn also, Zionists led successful campaigns for Liberty Bonds, while in Vineland, the ready enthusiasm of the Hebrew Civic Club brought this pragmatic editorial praise in June 1917: "The members are strong for their adopted country and are willing to put their money and young men into service."[37] Maurice Fels was a favored speaker at Liberty Loan rallies. Even Boy Scout Troop 9 of the Ahavas Achim synagogue labored in the drive to obtain bond subscriptions along with other troops and adult committees and auxiliaries in town, both Jewish and gentile.[38] It was a struggle which unified and excited the people at home.

267

Amidst the responsibilities of citizenship and the beckoning opportunities, Jews never lost their sense of obligation to their brethren abroad in the Diaspora of bigotry. This was abundantly clear in the World War I era, when the immigrants and their children held mass meetings in Vineland's Red Man's Hall, in Rosenhayn's Franklin Hall, and in Alliance Hall, to protest East European pogroms and raise relief funds for victims of war and religious fanaticism. Everyone joined in these drives—Republicans Morvay and Kotok, the Zionist Krich, and the universalist-minded Goldhaft. A conference of local organizations was formed, including the Hebrew Benevolent Society, the Workmen's Circle, the B'rith Sholem Lodge, the synagogues, and the Hebrew Civic Club, to labor jointly for the American Jewish Relief overseas operations. Before the end of 1919 well over $3,000 had been collected in various drives, including a Yom Kippur appeal.[39]

Ironically, the victory of democracy at the end of the war heralded still more tragic pogroms in newly independent Poland, herself recently freed from Tsarist terror and suppression of Roman Catholics. As part of their protest, Jewish shops throughout South Jersey closed early, just as all work had stopped in the wake of the Kishinev pogrom fourteen years before. On June 10, 1919 Vineland witnessed a mass meeting at which Mayor Stevens affirmed that "the town was a unit in voicing a protest against the massacres in Poland." Along with him, the Reverend Dr. Thomas S. Brock stepped forward to "add his protest to that of the Jewish race," praying that it would bring action by the League of Nations. The chairman, Dr. N. S. Greenwood, asked how long the world would continue to tolerate the rape and murder of Jewish human beings. Also A. H. Fromenson of New York stressed everyone's shock that "a nation which had shed blood for liberty and had won should seek to kill another people who wanted the same liberty." Appropriate resolutions were drawn up to be sent to Washington, and the Reverend A. Stokes Watson concluded with a sympathetic address on the Jews' "hour of grief." Later, Governor William N. Runyon, too, lent his support to the American Jewish Joint Distribution

Committee's overseas relief work on behalf of the victims of violence.[40]

The Jews of America learned to give on a scale unmatched by any other voluntary effort. In this, too, the Jewish community was not only helping its own, remaining loyal to its humanitarian traditions, but it was also taking part in that great-hearted American campaign to feed, clothe, and rescue the victims of World War. At the same time, like most of their fellow citizens upon the return to peace and normalcy, Jews tended to draw back even more zestfully into the prewar goals of Americanization and economic success, including the shibboleths of education and assimilation. Almost inevitably, the war seemed to mark the parting of ways between the foreign-born and native generations.

Was there no means to bridge the gap between the greenhorn culture and the Americanized second generation? The former was clearly on the decline, and the strangling postwar restriction of new immigrants was only one of the reasons.

The New American Generation

Somehow, the social cards seemed stacked in favor of the younger people and their achievements. Perhaps it was because of America's characteristic bias for youth and conformity. "The Hebrew children rank well in the public schools," commented the prewar official report on rural Jewry, "and frequently [they] advance more rapidly than those of American parentage." Hardly any of them suffered from that typical children's disease known as truancy.[41] Acculturation, as rapid as possible, was what society demanded of them. Not only the New York and Philadelphia philanthropists, the Chautauquans, the social workers and civilizers, but also their own parents yearned for them to achieve the kind of education and success which they themselves had never possessed.

This ultimate good inevitably spelled the breakdown of old cultural patterns and misunderstanding between the generations. Even Dr. Arthur Goldhaft saw his own father Tevia, as a kind of "displaced person . . . who couldn't adjust himself to the new life"

269

either in Alliance or Philadelphia. He was an *edeleh mench,* a cultured, gentle man, not particularly pious, yet, oddly, an inveterate synagogue-goer, who could find success "neither on land nor in the shop." Perhaps one had to face the "plain fact" that "Dad didn't like to work," although in Russia he had traveled far and wide selling tobacco. Inter-generational contrasts going beyond religion were noted also by Woodbine's eminent son Jacob Lipman. Taking pride in the "progressive" tone of the community, he focused likewise on Sabbath observances reflecting the typical older settler's orientation. "Dressed in his Sabbath clothes and wrapped in the Sabbath mood, he looks into the outside world and judges it according to his light. . . ." With factories closed, it was a day for rest and traditional studies. "It is otherwise with his children. . . . They are Americans," Lipman concluded, acculturated in language and life-style apart from their Yiddish-speaking parents.[42]

Traditional matchmaking and parental consent were among the early casualties of acculturation. In the Carmel colony of 1883, eighteen-year-old Jacob Sobleman fell in love with Leah Levenson and announced their intention to marry. Their parents, from old Kishinev, disapproved, partly because of their insecure economic position, but also because there was no rabbi in the area, not even a synagogue as yet. "You would not be married by a *shochet,* would you?" they queried. The young people saved their pennies from farm labor and sewing machine, scheming secretly for an elopement while feigning indifference. Their chance came on the second day of Passover, when all were engaged in celebrating the holiday of freedom. To elude potential pursuers, they avoided the roads, mapping out a route over two miles through woods and swamp to the South Vineland railroad stop. Initial fears were overcome. They boarded the train for Philadelphia, thence to Baltimore, where the young man found a job in a factory and married his Leah. Unlike most others, however, they later returned to Carmel and lived there for over fifty years more; they had fourteen children, reported the bemused Mounier, always a friend of the two families.[43]

Marriage fequently took young people away from rural South Jersey to the city, often because it was the home of their betrothed, but more usually because of its wider range of economic and cultural opportunity. Louis Traiman, well known in Alliance and Vineland later a prominent auctioneer, married a Philadelphia girl, with a "party of Alliance young men" joining in the Philadelphia wedding. Likewise, many "popular belles in Alliance" wed men from the City of Brotherly Love. Some at least had their wedding in the home colony, as did the Bakerman boy, when he returned from graduation with honors at Oberlin College. Over a thousand people, it was estimated, gathered in and around the Alliance synagogue for the Bakerman-Steinberg wedding. Such local traditions as Carmel's outdoor candle procession from the bride's home to the rustic sanctuary, the playing of bittersweet violins, the flowery, embroidered *hupah* (wedding canopy), and other marks of an East European wedding were not easily forsaken. Still, a Jewish farm leader of the second generation insisted it was almost no use to train more young men in the agrarian arts because "they cannot find Jewish girls who would be willing to share with them their lives on a farm."[44]

Indeed, most of the young people did not stay in the area after school or marriage or attaining professional status. Among the exceptions, however, was Jacob Crystal, who remained a farmer in Alliance almost his entire long life. He met his wife, a Philadelphia girl, at his sister's wedding. "She was the finest and best-looking girl there," he always recalled, even though at first she had thought him a rough countryman. Eventually, she agreed to marry him and settle on his farm. Although it took three months for the new plaster in their home to dry, for it was a cool and rainy spring, country life proved good to them and to their children, who relished such simple treats as fresh rye bread out of the old Russian wood-burning stove and did not mind the kerosene lamps or the other rural hardships.

Young Jacob had saved up $100 by "working to death," and bought some uncleared land next to his father's farm. Then he borrowed $400 more from Mr. Durgin, a local mortgagor who liked him personally, though he was leery of investing in "wild land." There was also a $250 mortgage on the house from the Jewish

Agricultural Society. Young Mrs. Crystal vowed, "Jake, I'll do every-thing I can to help you pay it off." Happily, they paid off both mortgages, and in good years they felt like "millionaires" as they made $1,500 on their sweet potatoes; they also grew tomatoes, lima beans, string beans, and green peppers, the latter fairly new to the area.[45]

But most of the colonists' children loved farming "even less than [did] native American young people," noted the 1911 report of the Immigration Commission. Except for some moderate suc-cess in the South Jersey farm colonies, praised for their husbandry over other Jewish farmers, it ruled the return-to-the-soil movement a failure in its strictly agrarian aspects. Here, too, the report tended towards premature and exaggerated judgment, but not without a measure of truth: "The rural Hebrews as a whole have given little to American agriculture either in the way of [new or improved] crops, culture [cultivation], management, or marketing; with a few notable exceptions, their agriculture is but mediocre or unsatis-factory."[46] It cited once more the mistakes of the past—poor loca-tion, inadequate training and financing, and so on. The young people, it predicted, would not stay but, like other American youth, would leave for the city in their discontent with "meager returns for labor expended, the isolation, [and] the absence of social con-veniences" such as higher education and other urban community facilities. Yet, perhaps more was the pity, the report also noted, for in the colonies there was very little crime or intemperance, but rather a sacredness in family relationships, a generally high moral level setting an example for nearby communities, and even, in Woodbine specifically, a remarkable kind of "political honesty."[47]

Did such virtues of family life and citizenship grow out of a farming existence, or were they a function of the cultural and religious heritage, which the Jewish immigrants carried with them into the New World? The latter seems a more reasonable explana-tion. There was a thriving Jewish life in the rural colonies, some-thing like that of the immigrants on New York's Lower East Side early in the twentieth century. But could this mode of life survive, in spirit if not in form, the double onslaught of Americanization and dispersion, especially among the children of the second and third generations?

Jacob Crystal, William Levin, Simcha Helig, and others who stayed. on in Alliance through old age, contemplated the youth going off to the cities, especially in the sharp postwar depression of 1920–1921. Depressions had a way of clinging to farm areas throughout America. Gradually, the youth group activities declined, and sometimes there were not enough people even to keep the synagogues open daily. Old Eli Bakerman stayed to care for Eben Ha' Ezer as its volunteer *shammes* (sexton), but his sons were gone. Moses Bayuk remained on the family farm, but his three sons left early to build their fortune in Philadelphia manufacturing cigars. They even paid for their father's scholarly-scientific expedition to the Holy Land in 1912.

Other native sons who left made their contribution in the wider society. Thus, Gershon Agronsky, who read from the Torah scroll as a teenager in Alliance, had served abroad in the Jewish Legion in World War I and returned to work in Philadelphia as a journalist. Later, he migrated to Palestine, eventually becoming editor-publisher of the *Jerusalem Post* and then mayor of Jerusalem. His nephew Martin remained in the United States, carving out a career as noted news commentator. Jacob Perskie, brother of the State Supreme Court Justice, won renown as a portrait photographer of great men, including Franklin D. Roosevelt. Another family, the Konovitzs, who were farmers and peddlers in Alliance, left to become founders of Wildwood, on the South Jersey shore.

Among the newer families who migrated to Alliance just before World War I were the Golders. They settled on land so poor and earned so little that other Jewish farmers regularly delivered bread at their humble home. It must have been the kind of tragically hopeless soil that the government report on "Hebrews in Agriculture" found existing in some parts of the colonies in South Jersey— "a bed of sand almost worthless for agricultural purposes . . . responding but feebly to large applications of fertilizer."[48] From this

273

desperate situation, young Ben Golder went on to study law at the University of Pennsylvania, and in the 1920's became the first Jewish congressman from Philadelphia.

Most outstanding in the American humanities, however, was the contribution made by Gilbert Seldes, whose father was a pioneer Alliance farmer and whose mother helped by managing its first post office. Born in Alliance in 1893 and graduated from Harvard in 1914, Gilbert was first a war correspondent, then a sergeant in the American Expeditionary Force. After the war, he tried his hand at editing *The Dial,* a brilliant new magazine of the arts. His pioneer work in the field, *The Seven Lively Arts,* was followed by *The Stammering Century.* This social criticism of nineteenth century American utopians deals with the fabric of "idealistic dreams not unlike those" of Alliance, as Arthur Schlesinger, Jr. pointed out in the foreword to a new edition of the book, calling it "a work of continuing vitality and interest."[49] Its author achieved eminence, too, as dean of the School of Communication Arts at the University of Pennsylvania. George Seldes, his brother, was a respected journalist and writer as well.

Virtually unknown, however, was a gifted young "wanderer-poet-philosopher," Vineland's George Kotok, seventh son of Russian immigrants. At age fifteen, he determined to enlist in the US cavalry but was turned down, whereupon he made his way to Belmar, Texas, and there joined under the assumed name of George Karvel. For a year, 1916–1917, he took part in skirmishes along the troubled Mexican border; then he was badly injured and honorably discharged. He returned home to complete the course at Vineland High School; he was also a "four-minute" orator for Liberty Bonds and even spoke before several thousand people from the same platform as the Governor of New Jersey. College was the next logical step for a bright boy—first George Washington University and then a Harvard B.A. in 1924. Yet he remained restless, traveling in search of literary inspiration through the Southwest, the Pacific coast, the northern Great Plains, and Canada—sometimes working on road gangs and, whenever he could, writing essays and poetry. Contemporary society, he observed, was replete with imperfections that stood in the way of man's happiness; therefore he embraced "socialism, atheism, and free love [as] the holy trinity of his new faith." Kotok's poems, published after his early death in 1927, reflect the scenes of America and the themes of inner conflict. In one poem, he reassures his mother that he will sometime cease his wandering, quiet the struggle in his heart, and bring her joy, not grief. The pedestrian virtues of home and success were not for him.[50] Frank Kotok, an older brother, remained in Vineland as a respected judge. Brother Edward, however, also traveled west, staying on in California's forestry service as director of its Forest and Range Experiment Station. He became an authority on the control of forest fires, erosion, and the utilization of water resources.

Even more far-ranging was the life work of Joseph A. Rosen, last headmaster of the Baron de Hirsch Agricultural School in Woodbine. His "Rosen Rye," a variety which could be grown in soil of limited fertility, won prizes at Chicago grain exhibits for over a decade. More significantly, however, his expertise was applied in aiding the new Jewish farmers of post-revolutionary Russia, where Rosen worked under the auspices of Agro-Joint and ORT (American Jewish Joint Agricultural Corporation, cooperating with the Jewish Colonization Association and the Organization for Rehabilitation and Training). Later, in the Hitler era, Rosen would direct similar settlement programs for Jewish refugees in the Dominican Republic.[51]

For those who remained in South Jersey, often moving into Vineland proper, life changed in many ways. Jacob Rubinoff advertised one of his good gray horses for sale because he planned to buy a truck. In the automobile age, the area changed its ethnic composition more appreciably, as large numbers of Italian settlers arrived. But Sam Goldberg was dubbed by the *Journal* as "king of the Jews, Italians and Americans combined," when he drove through town in his fine 1916 Packard.

Movies were becoming a significant adjunct of the new generation, too. *Joseph in the Land of Egypt* was the title of one new movie billed as the "greatest of educational and historical pictures." Or for five cents one could see the more controversial *Damaged*

Goods, if, that is, one were over sixteen or accompanied by parents. A number of distinguished Christian and Jewish laymen pleaded in print that the film was indeed sufficiently virtuous and even contained valuable moral lessons for those over sixteen, especially young men. Other Jewish progressives joined in a successful attempt to foil local censorship early in 1916.[52] Motion pictures, the car, then radio, all tended to melt the boundaries between farm and town, while helping to make the latter ever more attractive.

The Old Jewish Farmers and the New: Reappraisal in the 1920's

Between 1901 and 1919 the total Jewish population of the colonies in South Jersey, not including Vineland proper, declined from 3,527 to 2,739. Moreover, among the latter were many unabsorbed immigrants and nonfarmers who were primarily workers in the local garment factories or small subcontracting shops.[53] Significantly, the Jewish Agricultural Society also shifted its attention, in the form of loans and other assistance programs, almost entirely towards "privately owned individual farms," wherever they appeared feasible, in New York, New Jersey, Pennsylvania, New England, or even the Midwest. By World War I, the Society had learned well the lessons of precarious group colonization, although it still felt constrained to "assist the chronically ill colonies in South Jersey" so that they might at least "survive with its help."[54]

Even the Yiddish immigrant press embraced the concept of private enterprise farming rather than group colonization, cooperative living, or other utopian programs. *Zukunft* (The Future), the influential Socialist monthly of New York published by the *Forward* Association, compared the new agrarian generation favorably with the old. The latter was perforce dependent on philanthropy, always hoping for some external deliverance from their hardships, which were albeit real. "Martyrs" they were, the *Zukunft's* B. Gorin admitted: they had been handed a wilderness to develop, as even hardy German farmers had failed to; they had to stoop over the sewing machine by day and tend their land by night. Yet, to what end, Gorin asked, if not for the notion that Jews must cease peddling and embrace farming as a defense against anti-Semitism. It was a mistaken, self-conscious philosophy, he charged, shared by some leaders of the Russian *Haskalah* (enlightenment) as well as by wealthy western philanthropists. Thus the New World had been turned into a "great cemetery of Jewish farms" in a vain attempt to disprove some old canards.

In contrast, the new generation of American Jewish farmers bore no burden of guilt, defensiveness, or misguided idealism, no overriding concern with their image before either Jew or non-Jew. They were self-reliant and proud of their success, even if it was limited by the realities of a hard life. They entered agriculture because, like other individual farmers, they thought they could earn there a better livelihood or because they personally preferred country to city life. They did not believe they were finding salvation for the whole of the Jewish people. Even the Jewish Agricultural Society's loan program, at four percent interest, drew implied praise from Gorin as helping to foster a new kind of individual initiative throughout the eastern states; after all, these rates were far lower than the often exorbitant levels prevalent in the private farm-credit markets which, he remembered, had hastened the demise of the Crémieux colony in South Dakota in 1889.[55]

Gorin's articles in the *Zukunft* appeared first in January of 1915, another year that marked a watershed between the old-style farmers and the new. In that year, Sabsovich died on 23 March in New York's uncertain springtime, working to the end as the Fund's general agent. With his death an era ended, even though his successor, Bernard A. Palitz, continued as the last general agent for another seven years.

Sabsovich was remembered. There were eulogies by some of the agrarian-minded American Jewish leaders with whom he had worked, and also warm tributes in the pages of the *Jewish Farmer*. He was brought to eternal rest in his beloved Woodbine, where all stopped still in mourning—schools, shops, and even the farmer in his toil. At the dedication of Sabsovich's memorial, virtually the entire community from borough officials to the humblest tiller and machine operator gathered at the graveside to hear a eulogy by his former student, Dr. Jacob Lipman, then director of the New Jersey Agricultural Experiment Station at Rutgers. Many recalled what they owed to his leadership: "Only the actions of the just/Smell sweet and blossom in the dust."[56] The dust was not only on the grave of Sabsovich but also upon Woodbine as the agrarian colony declined.

Debates over the significance of Jewish group colonization, in which Sabsovich had played so prominent a role, did not die down for many years. Moses Freeman, the Yiddish journalist-historian of Philadelphia, reaffirmed during the 1920's Sabsovich's leadership of the Am Olam agrarians. He had been the movement's theoretician, Freeman explained, supplying the ideological basis and strategy as founders Moses Herder and Aaron Bakal seemed intellectually unsuited to do. Both were small-town populists unfamiliar with socialism or modern philosophical structures, and were impelled only by the needs of their people to find an escape from pogrom-plagued Russia. It was Sabsovich, educated at Odessa University, who had offered the program of communal land ownership as a major goal. "Why struggle and sacrifice to assure others the right of private property?" asked Sabsovich of his Am Olam followers in Odessa, including Freeman himself.

Freeman also recalled his own experience as a settler in Alliance for two years in the 1880's. Life there had been especially difficult for him and his wife because they had had no children to help with farm chores or to earn a few pennies at the sewing machine. He described how he and other Am Olam intelligentsia had been dispersed by the New York philanthropists to distant places like Lisbon Falls, Maine, to work in the woolen mills or other factories, far from their fellow immigrants in the urban centers. Yet, though Freeman defended Sabsovich's personal convictions and leadership, he failed to disprove the contentions of those who claimed that the Am Olam had almost ceased to exist once all their six or seven groups arrived in America (1882). Nor could he dispel the image of Sabsovich in league with the mistrusted capitalists.

Among the persistent sceptics and detractors with whom Freeman continued to tangle was Dr. K. Farenberg of the Yiddish *Day*. In 1928, the paper stated categorically, "The Am Olam was a *mish-*

278

mash, a unique, almost incredible chaos, from the beginning. Its short life-story was one series of misunderstandings, disappointments, and failures." Bitter memories of South Jersey colonization persisted also in the historical essays of the influential Yiddish writer, Abraham Sachs: the settlers had been told "to build pyramids without clay or straw," and when they failed, the hand-wringers branded them unfit for the farmer's noble calling.[57]

It was indeed true that Sabsovich and the small Am Olam groups had been forced to compromise with necessity. Those few of a more doctrinaire and radical persuasion founded such communistic farm colonies as New Odessa in Oregon, which endured only three years partly because of ideological factionalism. Could, then, Sabsovich or the more pragmatic colonists of South Jersey, or even the philanthropists for that matter, be judged by some yardstick of ideological purity? A number of other Am Olam people compromised too, by joining the short-lived Essex Street Commune (founded by immigrants from Vilno), while awaiting the call that never came to join colonies in Arkansas or Missouri.

There were so many lives to be saved, and massive Jewish immigration compelled immediate, pragmatic, and sometimes excessive, accommodations to the realities of the New World. Sabsovich knew this well. By presiding over the revision of his old Am Olam goals, he appeared a pawn in the hands of the mighty who subsidized Woodbine, while attempting to forge a solution for his storm-tossed people. Errors were committed, but at least some allowance must be made for the unprecedented crisis, the lack of experience in colonizing, and the pressures of the era.

Moreover, in administering the affairs of Woodbine, Sabsovich had pioneered on a grand scale in professional Jewish social service, a field which continued to draw his guidance and energy in the last decade of his life. His unflagging concern with this approach to the needs of the immigrant was expressed in his work as founder and officer of the Jewish Immigration Committee as well as president of the Society of Jewish Social Workers. Along with one of his former staff members at the Agricultural School, Joseph W. Pincus, he preached the need for a variety of social service activities—

agricultural extension programs and education generally for adults as well as children, library services, lectures, citizenship training, clubs of all kinds—not only in the South Jersey colonies, but also among the new breed of individualistic Jewish farmers scattered everywhere. Typically, such plans did not encompass a positive program for the survival of religious traditions, although Pincus went further than Sabsovich in at least deploring the "woeful neglect" of religious education by most farming communities, and insisting that "children of Jewish farmers are entitled to religious education as much as a city child."[58]

In 1910, there were 5000 widely dispersed farm families, but twice that number by the early 1920's as some postwar immigration from Eastern Europe resumed briefly. With the practical guidance and loans from the Jewish Agricultural Society, individual farming often seemed to thrive where group colonization had failed. The shift was eased by a significant economic breakthrough during the prosperous World War I years: increasingly, it was recognized that poultry farming could support a newcomer and his family without requiring such costly expedients as subsidized manufacturing to supplement income from crops. In New Jersey, there were pioneering Jewish poultry farmers in Vineland as well as some newly dispersed in Toms River, Lakewood, and Farmingdale.[59]

The departure from group colonization brought a mixed bag of blessings. Jewish farmers perforce had become more professional and self-reliant; their cooperative purchasing bureaus, credit unions, and fire insurance companies from Sullivan County, New York, and the Vineland-Woodbine axis to the Midwest fulfilled specific economic needs. The Federation of Jewish Farmers grew from thirteen branches to sixty-three, even in its first five years (1909–1914). Its publications included articles on good farming practices, lists of the nearest agricultural experiment stations, and such helpful advertisements as the one for "Norwich's automatic feeder, the greatest money saver you've ever placed in your chicken coops," or for Prairie State incubators or Pratt's patent animal feed and cures (all phrased in a rather homey Yiddish). There were appeals to subscribe to familiar journals such as the *Russky Viestnik,* the

Yiddish *Day,* and *Das Tageblatt,* and Jewish farmers were urged to buy Columbia's new double-disc records of Cantor Joseph ("Yossele") Rosenblatt, or exhorted to join the Workmen's Circle.[60] The new-style individual, often isolated on his homestead, generally suffered from a meager cultural environment as compared to that of the city or the old Jewish rural colonies of South Jersey. Annual conventions of the Federation, usually held at the Educational Alliance in New York, presented one opportunity to meet fellow Jews, farmers and non-farmers. Distinguished speakers addressed them: Louis Marshall, president of the American Jewish Committee, Jacob H. Schiff, the Honorable Marcus M. Marks, president of the borough of Manhattan.[61] But then when the farmers went home, they dropped back into the old ways with little else in Jewish cultural activity or social ties than the liturgical chants of the renowned Cantor Rosenblatt played on the strange talking machine.

In Vineland, on the other hand, "the Hebrews" still thrilled to Yiddish drama played periodically by a crack Philadelphia company. Israel Zangwill, in America to look after the presentations of his popular play, *The Melting Pot,* visited Woodbine as well as the Vineland communities. On one such occasion during the fall season of holidays, he was pleased to see students at the agricultural school taking their meals in the *sukkah* made of red foliage and green firs. The make–shift hut was decorated with locally harvested products, he noted with pleasure, and the ornamental electric lights were in the shape of David's Star. Zangwill presented short, informal addresses during which he stopped frequently for discussions with young and old.[62]

Settlers in and near Vineland continued their periodic cultural inter-colonial assemblies. The Hebrew Civic Club discussed with Rabbi Louis Newman, assistant to Rabbi Stephen H. Wise of New York, his views on The Jew in Literature, and some of the youngsters read from Sholom Aleichem's works. Philadelphian Leon Savadge analyzed Sholom Asch and his Drama for members of Vineland's Hebrew Educational League, while literary programs in Alliance Hall also honored Isaac L. Peretz's Yiddish classics. Rosenhayn's library, as did Vineland's, counted among its treasures the new fifteen-volume *Jewish Encyclopedia* (both sets were donated by Jacob Schiff).[63]

East European social groups, in their rich variety, had come a long way by the 1920's. Back in the early years, the colonies had only the German-Jewish Red Men's Order—*Stamm* 1, Alliance, New Jersey, *des Freien Ordens der Rothmanner*—and for the ladies, the *Frauen Hilf's Verein.* Although the women were content at first with these organizations and such limited projects as raising funds for the synagogue, the men quickly rebelled against the requirement that German rather than Yiddish be the language of minutes and other records. In Alliance the Independent Order of Baron de Hirsch, in Woodbine the Brotherhood and the Order of B'rith Abraham, and in Vineland the Hebrew Civic Club and Hebrew Women's Benevolent Society, as well as various other religio-cultural-social organizations, all soon indicated the growing associational independence of the immigrant.[64]

The Socialist *Forward* had at first sneered at the Benevolent Society as being patterned after the "rich society ladies" of the National Council of Jewish Women. But it was placated, as Vineland too organized an active branch of the Workmen's Circle, the labor-oriented Jewish family benefit organization, with a ladies' auxiliary helping to further its expansion into the postwar era. A Workmen's Circle had been formed also in Alliance-Norma, led by farmer Jacob Crystal.[65]

Altogether, the wealth of cultural and social facilities for both Jewish life and Americanization proved hard to match in the areas of settlement by thousands of individual farmers, whether in New England, the Midwest, Pennsylvania, or even the Catskills of New York. At the same time, the cultural stimulus of additional immigrants was almost dammed up by the stop-gap restrictions of 1921 and the National Origins Act of 1924, both of which effectively discriminated against all people from Eastern and Southern Europe. Whereas before the war, European arrivals had numbered close to a million or more a year, an immense source of human wealth, they averaged just slightly over one hundred and fifty thousand in the second half of the 1920's. In the depression of the '30's, a mere twelve to sixty thousand entered annually. It would seem as though America in this new era of "boom and bust" was less the land of opportunity, less responsive to the suffering of millions abroad, more xenophobic and intolerant at home. Times were bad in many ways during the uneasy armistice between two world wars.

Between two world wars: Years of "normalcy" and crisis

Seek the peace of the city whither I have caused you to be carried away captive, and pray unto the Lord for it; for in the peace thereof shall ye have peace.

Jeremiah 29:7

9

Bigots in New Jersey

Young Tevis Goldhaft, named for his grandfather Tevia, who had over a generation before made the long journey from Russia to Alliance, watched a strange parade of men in white hooded uniforms. Down the streets of Vineland they marched every Saturday evening, and the boy began to nag his father, Dr. Arthur Goldhaft, for a similar "nightshirt ghost" outfit; perhaps his mother would make one for him out of an old bedsheet. The father explained that these were members of the Ku Klux Klan, "ignorant, prejudiced people who were against Jews, Catholics, and Negroes"; and anyway, wasn't it a bit silly for grown men to masquerade thus?

The Knights of the KKK rode the crest of the postwar Red scare, appealing to extremists throughout the country as defenders of the old-style 100 percent Americanism—rural, white, and Protestant fundamentalist. They were four-square against aliens as well as "niggers," Jews, Catholics, radicals, alcohol, the new-fangled road-houses, flappers, and any hint of sexual immorality. In South Jersey, with its heterogeneous population, agrarian as well as industrial, there was a hangover of anti-Negro bias, and the KKK struck fertile ground. By 1924, the Vineland *Journal* could report an outdoor regional conclave of as many as six thousand Klansmen in a field at Malaga and Oak Roads. Many drove "new and costly cars . . . showing that [they] were men among men in the business world."[1] Cross-burnings, symbolic of the aroused KKK, took place in various Vineland locations including the Italian neighborhood and even the high school grounds. Robed Klansmen, marching en masse, were welcomed at Sunday services by the pastor and members of the West Baptist Church.

Early in 1921, the Grand Theater, acquired by a Philadelphia chain, adopted a policy of segregating Negroes. Jews were targets too. Harry Morris's billiard parlor and Mike Levy's bar were shut down under pressure from the KKK, while Sharp's billiard hall remained open. In this atmosphere, David Rosenthal, a Jewish clothier, undertook to run for a vacant seat on the board of education. He was nominated by a small coalition of minorities: "ten Catholics and two Jewish citizens," dared to sign the petition on his behalf. But within a few days, the cross-burning in front of Rosenthal's house had spread its warning, and Rosenthal withdrew. The reason cited by the *Journal* on Lincoln's Birthday of 1924 was to end the anti-Jewish sentiment stirred by his nomination.[2]

Sensitivity to local prejudices was noticeable too in the growing concern of the Hebrew Civic Club with the subject of anti-Semitism. Philip Goldstein would drive from his Rosenhayn home to Vineland to address the Club on his idea of the basic causes: Christian Sunday school instruction focusing on Jews rather than Romans as the crucifiers of Jesus, and the stereotyped Jewish image prevalent in literature such as the *Merchant of Venice*. On a somewhat similar tack, businessman Frank Mennies pleaded with the Vineland Chamber of Commerce to find some means of creating better understanding between local farmers and merchants; the latter were too often castigated unfairly as "money grabbers."[3]

As for the fresh canard tying Jews with Bolshevism, the *Journal* reported happily the story of a rabbi in Poughkeepsie, New York, who rejected his prospective bride because her radical views clashed with his Americanism. The patriotic rabbi was almost lynched, the *Journal* clucked sympathetically, by the

Bolshevik comrades of his erstwhile Russian bride who, incidentally, committed suicide.[4]

As the KKK grew in numbers and their impressive conclaves were held openly in the Vineland region, some local citizens considered counteraction by an informally organized group. KKK cars streamed through Vineland on their way to such spectacular meetings as the one in the spring of 1924 in nearby Millville where fifteen thousand reportedly gathered.[5] Then the citizens' group, including Dr. Goldhaft, took down license numbers of the cars in processions or parked at rallies; ministers and other community leaders would try later to reason with the unmasked riders of mostly lower middle class origin. In any case, national prosperity and unfavorable publicity in the urban newspapers, which focused on the occasional acts of violence and the money-making promoters, soon spelled the decline of the KKK from a membership of between four and five million to about one hundred thousand on the eve of the Great Depression.

Yet, in the 1920's there were other sources of bigotry, such as the notorious Jew-baiting of Henry Ford's *Dearborn Independent.* And near Bound Brook, New Jersey, was the headquarters of fundamentalist Bishop Alma White, who damned the Jews for allying themselves with the "Scarlet Mother" (Roman Catholicism) to "crush out the Protestant religion" by opposing Bible-reading in the public schools and by showing movies on Sunday. "The Jew is indissoluble and indigestible . . . a menace to Christianity," White preached, "especially when he is in alliance with the old papal machine."[6]

In the 1930's, as depression deepened, New Jersey was again confronted with a revitalized KKK. Vineland was stirred in 1933 by reports of cross-burning and bomb-throwing at nearby Mizpah, which, though founded as a Jewish colony, now also had a substantial Negro population. Maurice Aaron barely escaped injury when a bomb was tossed at him while he was extinguishing a cross near the railroad station. He thought that "the cross was burned to keep colored voters from the polls."[7] The emergence of new racist groups such as the Silver Shirts and the American Nazi Bund

(*Amerika-deutscher Volksbund*) was another harsh reality confronting the country as a whole. The Bund had three camps in New Jersey (at Andover, Bloomingdale, and Griggstown) and a large membership spewing forth bigotry. Native-centered demagogues, such as Gerald L. K. Smith and Father Coughlin, were not far behind.

Against this tide stood various civic organizations, including American Legion units, Jewish War Veterans, and the Minute Men organized by Nat Arnold of Irvington, New Jersey. A legislative attempt to curb those inciting group hatred, the so-called Rafferty Bill, entered New Jersey's statute books in 1937, but proved difficult to enforce, if anything, the extremists seemed to welcome the publicity. The issues became clearer only after Dunkirk and Pearl Harbor.

Wealth and Poverty Away from the Family Farm

There was much at stake, indeed, for Vineland's Jewish community in terms of impressive economic and social achievements. Its prominent citizens marched proudly as leaders in the American Legion. Michael Mennies was elected commander of the Roosevelt Post over three gentile opponents in 1920; his brother Robert, an officer too, coached its acclaimed basketball team. Popular attorney M. J. Greenblatt was elected as the Post's county delegate.

Jewish merchants in town prospered, by and large, since A. Levy had first opened his men's clothing shop on Mechanics' Block in 1882, selling cut-rate Philadelphia merchandise.[8] The majority of these Jewish businessmen came from the colonies nearby. For example, the Brotman, Eskin, Joseph, and Pressman families all moved their manufacturing and sales activities into Vineland. Hyman Mennies came from Alliance in 1895 to take over the old Levy store; his sons succeeded him in a business which the family operated until 1959. The Bernsteins manufactured clothing for their own retail outlet, while A. F. Leavitt's Pioneer Dry Goods Store preferred to buy the latest styles in New York. H. Seidenstein advertised as a "ladies' and gents' tailor," as did N. Zager and Max Rubin; and Levantman offered the services of his new-style fur shop.

Business was not all just suits and cloaks, however. A. M. Niggin prospered by selling seed, flour, hardware, and farm implements. So did Harry Coltun of Norma, for a while. But it was Jacob Rubinoff's Feed Mill, founded in 1907 as Shenberg and Rubinoff, which eventually developed into the largest of such enterprises in the eastern United States. Another farm-oriented business was that of Louis Traiman, who by 1920 regularly traveled West to buy horses and cattle for local farmers. And the Lihns of Alliance-Norma founded the Tri-State Transportation Company, a pioneer trucking firm, while their competitor, National Hauling Company, was operated by Bernard Brown, whose family had come to Vineland in the early 1900's originally dealing in barrels and crates.

Services and retailing predominated, covering a variety of enterprises, and competition among them was always brisk. In the World War I era, Gordon's ran "monster sales" on its ready-to-wear stock, partly to meet the competition of M. Lipman's Bargain Store. In 1908, Mennies clothiers first gave customers S & H green stamps. Myer and Herman Kotok surpassed J. D. Selinsky in the fruit and vegetable trade. And Abe Forstein of Plum Street ran a milk delivery for the Salem County Dairy Company.

Recognizing business opportunities in the new automobile, Myer Kotok used his car for a taxi service, Louis Kotok retailed the new half-ton capacity VIM delivery trucks, W. A. Kronheim dealt in auto supplies, and Levenberg bought and sold used cars. In Vineland, as did others in the colonies, Mr. and Mrs. Joseph Halfler prepared for the new-style summer boarders from the big cities by opening a family hotel. In a still bigger way, the Lipitz family moved into the buying and selling of real estate, acquiring a part ownership in the Baker House and the enlarged Lyric Theater.

Not everyone was uniformly successful, of course. Lazar Klure, who had donated land and building to the Sons of Jacob Congregation in 1905, was declared bankrupt ten years later, and the city receiver placed on public sale his estate of eight work horses, five heavy wagons, various farm implements, hardware, and other goods left over from his supply business on Sixth Street. Sometimes partners disagreed, as did Louis Fisher and Ben Rudnick. Then, an unofficial Jewish court of arbitration was created by community leaders in order to resolve the problem. Though conditions changed, though instability came from war and business cycle, by and large the Jewish commercial community grew.[9]

The boom years of the World War I era enabled many to expand their physical plants. Joseph Brothers, for example, moved into a larger factory building. Shenberg and Rubinoff's purchased additional property after their improvement of the old Malaga flour mills. Myer Kotok took over the Elias Jones Building. The old Welch's Grape Juice Building passed from Klure to Mennies Brothers, as did the store and stock of R. E. Williams, which caused the *Journal* to remark that they now owned as many as four outlet locations. At times commercial enterprise expanded across nearby homes; then, the *Journal* would seem especially pained as some gentile residential or farm real estate changed hands, noting mournfully that "another good citizen will leave Vineland" after selling to a Jewish purchaser.[10] Such changes, some initiated by broker Abe Lipitz, included the transfer of Hitchner's sixty-three acre farm to Abe Spiegel of Alliance-Norma, as well as smaller farms to other newcomers. Even a Jewish migrant from Brooklyn moved into Vineland, buying the old Allen place on Landis Avenue.[11]

Jews had made their mark in local professions, too, by World War I, although of course most of these were of the second generation able to grasp the chance for higher studies. N. A. Cohen, the Wildwood pharmacist, was well-known in the Vineland area even back in the 1890's. Of the younger local set, however, were the following: attorney Greenblatt, who served as borough recorder; Dr. Arthur Goldhaft, who pioneered as a veterinary surgeon, founding member of the animal hospital, and founder of the Vineland Poultry Laboratories; dentist William Mennies, who strove to set up a free dental clinic and who was joined later by Dr. M. E. Cohen, "well known in South Jersey as the painless dentist." Among those who entered nursing was Rebecca Rubinoff, who left for Philadelphia to pursue her career. In the public schools, the first Jewish teachers included the Misses Cohen and Goldsmith, employed in 1915–16. Freda Scribner, who started in 1920 and worked her way up to curriculum coordinator for the Vineland school system, continued her long career into the 1960's.[12]

Yet in the professions, as well as in commerce and industry, Vineland Jews remained a minority. Even though they suffered the kind of visibility characteristic of majority-minority group relations, they could not well be described as controlling major areas of business or professional activity. In the latter sphere, a significant achievement for the entire community was the Leuchter family's founding of the weekly *Evening Times* in 1925, which merged with the *Vineland Evening Journal* in 1942. Jewish businessmen could not compare, however, to J. J. Newberry's in retailing, Kimble Glass in manufacturing, or Kimball and Prince in lumber and building materials. Nor were they represented in the Vineland National Bank and Trust Company and the major real estate and insurance firms. And in such fields as retailing, services, or the garment industry, they competed not only with the natives but also with others of the new immigration, especially the Italians. All were hard hit by the cycles of inflation and depression.

In the prosperous years of World War I, it had seemed as if the most lucrative economic activity was garment manufacturing; yet this was also the most unstable during the era of normalcy which followed. Aside from the brief but sharp postwar depression, the clothing industry was hurt by the new foreign competition as well as the appearance of synthetics and radical changes of fashion. Labor troubles seemed chronic. In 1921, the Amalgamated Clothing Workers' Vineland local was forced to accept a 15 percent wage reduction which led to riots and the closing of several factories. Union men from New York shut down those local plants charged with filling scab orders. Some of the conditions for settlement, a five-day week and shorter hours, were met only after much wrangling.[13]

But the economics of a chronically sick industry forestalled any substantial recovery. Moreover, Vineland's liabilities in clothing manufacture proved only slightly less than those which had always

291

plagued the Jewish colonies in the area—distance from the big city markets and suppliers, limited buying capacity of local farmers and townspeople, lack of diversification, and a small, relatively unskilled labor pool that was insufficient in boom times and excessive in bad. Runaway producers from New England or New York sought ever cheaper labor and raw material costs in the South. Then the Great Depression delivered a knockout blow to an industrial situation long rife with instability. Vineland's Palace of Depression, built in 1929 of old lumber, rusted auto chassis, and other discarded materials, caught the nation's eye and symbolized her mood.

For a while, some industry returned to the outlying colonies, partly, it seemed, to evade strict labor union standards. With the new five-day week, work on the Jewish Sabbath was no longer an issue. Thus, following a merger which formed the Norma Clothing Company (1932), Benjamin Barish, president of the Rosenhayn Chamber of Commerce, announced the promised opening of another clothing factory to employ a hundred or a hundred and fifty persons.[14]

Such sanguine developments were wanted desperately in Woodbine, too. Shortly after the war almost all its factories stood still, bringing unemployment to almost one thousand workers in this small town. Many had no alternative but to leave. Failing still to attract outside business interests, a score or so of the older settlers and of the unemployed eventually were able to pool their own resources to start up work in the Fund-leased factory on a semicooperative basis. With such self-help, they succeeded in providing jobs for as many as four hundred in good years at their Woodbine Borough Clothing Company, while a children's clothing manufacturer and a hat maker employed one hundred more.

More hopeful still seemed the introduction of a rubber goods manufacturing firm in the 1920's, the innovative Bradstone Rubber Company, which at last promised to relieve the excessive reliance on needle trades. One of its two cofounders was I. V. Stone, himself the son of a Woodbine colonist and a graduate of the agricultural school who had attained a high executive position with a national rubber manufacturer. Stone received rent-free facilities plus a relatively slight subsidy from the now weary Fund. Also, a 1923 lease provided that both land and building would become Bradstone Company property after it had paid out a total of $500,000 in wages. In an age of business giants, the small rubber manufacturer floundered, however. And even before the great crash of 1929, the Fund decided to sever all economic connections with the borough. In that year, it sold the power and water plant to outside private interests with the proviso that light, heat, water, and steam services be maintained for homeowners as well as industry.

With the onslaught of depression, the town barely managed to survive. Woodbine Clothing Company, previously torn by dissension within its management, then hit by lack of contracts, laid off almost four hundred workers for several months in 1932. The plant reopened only to fill a sudden large order for the New Jersey Department of Agencies and Institutions. It was an almost miraculous respite, though company president Harry Feit could not promise full-time work for more than a few months. In the next year, the depression's trough, a smaller contract came through from the federal government—special outfits for reforestation workers.

Perhaps encouraged by this news, labor in Woodbine struck for and won, with the backing of Mayor Nathaniel Rosenfeld, a 10 percent wage increase. Later, more strikes ensued, spreading to other colonies as well. The issues were recognition of the Amalgamated, further wage increases, and a reduction of the work week from fifty-five to forty-five hours to achieve parity with Vineland factories. They won. In the changed pro-labor New Deal climate, even retroactive and compensatory payments were made to strikers in Woodbine as well as Norma, Mizpah, and Millville (where the Woodbine Borough Clothing Company owned a branch).[15] But it proved a Pyrrhic victory. The clothing manufacturers' competitive position was weakened further, and the hoped-for recovery failed to materialize. For lack of local freight business, the Central Railroad of New Jersey threatened to close its stations at both Norma and Rosenhayn. If anything, the end of 1937 witnessed a setback in economic conditions.

In the hungry winter of 1937–1938, the jobless clothing workers

293

of Woodbine chopped timber in order to survive. Some were paid by the Amalgamated's relief service, which then distributed the firewood to needy urban union members for seventy-five cents a load. During the next months, new wage reductions in Vineland caused further strikes in the garment shops. Leading citizens pleaded with young people to stay in their hometown and not to desert to the big city. In the spring of 1938, Vineland and Woodbine labor delegates could draw only slight comfort from South Jersey Day, declared in their honor by the Amalgamated's convention in Atlantic City that year, where John L. Lewis intoned about a brighter tomorrow.[16]

The travails of industrial Woodbine, though relatively unknown, became part of a larger array of rural subsistence communities founded to provide jobs and homes for displaced proletarians. In Woodbine, the settlers were either immigrants or their children, but during the Great Depression, when so many millions were out of work and thus removed from the economic abundance of America, the New Deal subsidized similar rural settlements for native Americans. The communities grew to ninety-seven altogether, each with government-financed factories, a community center, small shops, a school, a central water system, and modest homesteads on five-acre plots. They might have been, in some respects, almost latter-day imitations of Woodbine. Located in economically stagnant, infertile regions, these experimental communities were also intended to plant the seeds of a better life for the poverty-stricken and disadvantaged.

In 1938, President Roosevelt delivered a commencement address in the clapboard gymnasium of one such community in West Virginia. His speech, beamed to the nation by radio, noted the progress made by these rural projects and hailed an "awakened social conscience" as the "outstanding contribution" of the New Deal. Yet, most of the planned resettlement colonies—one named Eleanor in honor of the First Lady—turned out to be expensive failures. In a substantially free economy and society, individuals still moved in response to the forces of markets and self-interest. The bustling cities, once the crisis began to fade, offered more of the opportunity and excitement of modern America. As Paul Conkin stated in *Tomorrow a New World*, "the whole community program had been repudiated" by the time of World War II.[17] Nonetheless, it was indeed an expression of social conscience, just as Woodbine and the other Jewish colonies were, even a half-century before. In that era before the welfare state, the largesse had to come from Baron de Hirsch and other philanthropists. They suffered their experiments to last a long time. Then, when all seemed almost over, new efforts at resettlement would be required as a consequence of rising totalitarian racism in Nazi Germany.

Strengthening the Social Foundations: New Assets and Liabilities

The mainstream of America was not represented by either the KKK or the bigots of the Nazi Bund, or even by the genteel college administrator who warned Tevis Goldhaft's father-in-law, a noted pathologist, that he could "never become a professor here because of [his] race and origin."[18] On the contrary, in Vineland, at least, the participation of Jews in various civic causes seemed to be generally recognized and welcomed.

One such area was public health. Even before the World War I years, John Joseph served as a respected member of the board of health; along with Dr. Goldhaft, he fought for improved local sanitary regulations, including meat inspection. Frank Mennies was elected president of the Vineland Hospital Association, which succeeded in modernizing the existing facilities while laying the groundwork for a new edifice. Through the 1920's and '30's, Dr. Goldhaft headed advisory committees of professionals and parents to deal with the occasional epidemics of children's diseases. Nearby Norma developed its own "baby-keep-well" health clinics. Within the colonies, such efforts had helped to keep down fatalities from the widespread postwar influenza epidemic. And the Jewish community's general concern with mental health as well was illustrated by Samuel Fels's substantial endowment of research at the New Jersey Training School, a state institution for feeble-minded children operating in Vineland.[19]

295

Social acculturation and integration was evident, too, in varied activities. Community-wide talent shows, including benefit performances for the Vineland hospital, engaged the eager participation of young adults and children, notably Ahavas Achim's Boy Scout Troop 9. Jewish amateur athletes joined enthusiastically in the ten-mile bicycle races and inter-group baseball games for all ages. "Jake" Spiegel's team from Alliance-Norma early achieved a vast popularity throughout the region. But also some of the leading citizens of Vineland, its businessmen, politicians, and professionals, ignored ethnic or religious distinctions to play regular exhibition baseball, with proceeds going to charity. Dr. Goldhaft always made a good showing on the "Fats" team, which usually vanquished the "Leans."[20]

Even in Woodbine, the national sport gradually superseded such older and more serious competitions as the periodic plowing contests, occasions that had been witnessed by dignitaries like the assistant secretary of agriculture, representatives of the Jewish Colonization Society, and professors of agriculture. Plowing contests, not baseball, had been wont to fill out the earnest front pages of the *Jewish Exponent*. In contrast, the *Jewish Farmer* seemed less obsessed with agrarian prowess and more generous toward the popular game. It featured, for example, articles in Yiddish on the achievements of immigrant farmers' sons in all the colonies who united in the sport; also, there were proudly displayed photographs of the teams and the building they themselves constructed to serve the Norma Athletic Association.[21] For well over a generation after its founding in 1904, the Norma Athletic Association flourished and its functions expanded. Even in the depression era of the 1930's— Gilbert Seldes's "years of the locust"—the NAA socials brought together hundreds of rural settlers from Alliance, Brotmanville, and other villages. These were not only opportunities for amiability and recreation, but also for NAA leaders like Spiegel and Sylvan Einstein to make their perennial appeals for a greater effort on behalf of the spiritual and moral welfare of local Jewish youth.[22]

A pioneer in the drives for civic betterment, Spiegel also founded the Norma Chamber of Commerce to work towards making the community more attractive to business and residents. Moreover, as a Democratic politician, he proved a potent vote-getter, serving four terms as Pittsgrove Township committeeman and two as head of the New Jersey Association of Committeemen. As if to show that sturdy citizens and erstwhile heroes of youth and sports fans eventually receive their reward, in the first year of the New Deal Spiegel was appointed deputy collector of internal revenue for Cumberland and Salem counties.[23]

This appointment was also symbolic of the long-range shift in voting patterns among Jewish colonists from Republican to Democratic, a move hastened by the depressed state of agriculture even in the 1920's. Along with Spiegel, such Democrats as George Schalick and Joseph Alterman successfully challenged the Republican exhortations of older native sons. Rousing Democratic rallies foreshadowed the sweep in 1932, which included not only a victory for the national ticket headed by FDR, but also for the local slate of candidates, and was followed in 1933 by an antiprohibition landslide. By 1938 Woodbine's popular Republican mayor Rosenfeld was able to win re-election to a fourth term only with the aid of sympathetic Democrats. In the same year, Democrats made a clean sweep of all the offices in Pittsgrove Township (embracing Alliance-Norma). The old Alliance Republican Club, Jewish pillar of the local GOP, seemed little more than a memory.[24]

Besides these frankly partisan elections, Jewish candidates did well too in contests for the school board and other less political posts. Solomon Aaron was re-elected president of Deerfield Township's board of education in 1933, along with Milton Statler. In the larger Vineland system, Jewish chairmen of the board of education included Dr. William Mennies and later I. C. Schwartzman and Dr. Tevis Goldhaft. Hyman Goldstein and other Jewish commissioners pioneered in the electrification programs of the Deerfield Township Lighting District, being re-elected both in 1929 and 1933; it was only a short time before (1928) that the people of Norma had celebrated the installation of electric street lights with its biggest Saturday night parade on record. Yet, there remained those perennial demands that united poor rural districts on a quite apolitical basis, such as pleas for the county to improve the roads connecting the colonies with Vineland and Millville.[25]

School operations were fraught with difficulties in this "boom and bust" era. On occasion, as in 1932, teachers' salaries were delayed when harried Alliance-Norma farmers failed to keep up with their tax payments. In Woodbine, the board of education was forced to cut salaries by 5 percent in spite of vociferous objections by parents and teachers. Yet, the Jewish concern with good public education continued to be strong, as was exemplified by the lobbying team of George Schalick of Alliance and attorney Orville Schalick in Salem, the county seat and source of much-needed school aid. The names of Jewish youngsters continued to appear among local students winning highest honors, and even the grownups of the Alliance-Norma PTA were honored in 1938 as the most active unit of the Salem County Association.[26]

Thus, more was involved in the processes of citizenship than simply the act of naturalization. Participation and acceptance were among the goals achieved in large measure by the Jewish community of first and second generations. Personal success stories, given the disadvantages of the immigrants and their children, were surprisingly frequent and occasionally spectacular. One which held Vineland's fancy in the 1920's was the continued progress of the Golder boys, once alien dirt farmers in Alliance. Almost true to one of Horatio Alger's rags-to-riches stories, Ben Golder, who at thirty-three was still the youngest congressman of the time, married an heiress. The Vineland press was hard put to determine which was the more significant achievement, but gave eager coverage to his humble origins and persistent democratic leanings, as signified partly by his inviting twenty-five of the old Alliance pioneers to attend the rich Philadelphia wedding.[27]

Certainly no less striking was the record of his brother Frank A. Golder, his senior by many years, who graduated from Harvard with a Ph.D. in history and become a leading expert on Russia. He served on President Wilson's panel at Versailles, the so-called Inquiry, and then joined Herbert Hoover's postwar European relief mission. In 1923, he accepted a professorship at Stanford University and added further to his list of publications. At Professor Golder's death, early in 1929, President-elect Hoover extended an impressive eulogy: "His loss is a heavy one, not only to Stanford but those who have known him as a friend, and to humanity generally. He was a man of high character, infinite industry, and genuine scholarship. His place cannot be filled."[28] The Vineland *Times* was intrigued also by the fortune which this "son of Alliance pioneers" bequeathed to orphaned children of college professors.

The *Times* reported proudly on other successes, including the distaff side. Naomi Opachinsky (Opack) of Norma made good as executive secretary in the federal government; moreover, she was selected a number of times to represent New Jersey at White House garden parties and was even greeted personally by Mrs. Hoover.[29] Thus, the daughter of humble Alliance pioneer Israel Opachinsky met the first lady of the nation, having found acceptance in the highest official circles. The local folk saw in this yet another fulfillment of the American Dream. Later, old Mr. Opachinsky, after fifty-six years of farming, retired to Washington to spend his remaining years with his daughter.

Unfortunately, successful acculturation combined with the long-range dispersal to create an unfavorable effect on at least one set of local institutions—the religious. Through the decades following World War I, the youth groups and choirs of Alliance's Eben Ha'-Ezer virtually disappeared. For those of the newer generation, less traditionally oriented or just indifferent, the automobile was a convenient means of attending an occasional service at some synagogue away from home, in Vineland or even Philadelphia. Moreover, the language problem, in both secular and religious life, was only one aspect of the growing alienation between immigrants and their children who looked down on the old country ways.[30]

Although old *hasid* Krassenstein still persisted in calling the community to rise at midnight for the traditional *S'lihot* (penitential service) before the New Year, each fall the response grew weaker. Pioneer Eli Bakerman stoked the coal fires of the synagogue in winter, carried water to the diminished congregation and, each day, rounded up volunteers for the thrice-daily *minyan*. At least the *hasidim* and *mitnagdim* (Talmudists) were drawn closer, even if only by necessity. On *Simhat Torah, hasid* Alterman and friends would lead in celebrating the Torah's annual completion and beginning with prayer, dance, chant, and even drink, to express the congregation's boundless joy in God's gift; while Simcha Helig, like the typical Vilno *mitnaged*, celebrated the same occasion with more scholarly restraint.

Some of the remaining farmers, even those who had never before considered themselves religiously disposed, pitched in during these years of decline. Jacob Crystal, for example, was persuaded by his wife and a few pious neighbors—the former the more decisive influence—to return to the synagogue on a regular basis, helping keep it open every day. The wife of another farmer was recruited to provide some instruction for the children. For a few years, Crystal served as president of the congregation, but he could not halt its decline. Part of the blame, he maintained, was laid during the hard 1930's at the door of Communist agitators, "rotten liars" who put the synagogue to scorn. On the other hand, there was some outside aid in the sphere of religious education, especially through the tireless efforts of Sarah L. Leibert, supervisor of Jewish education for the Department of Farm and Rural Work of the National Council of Jewish Women.[31]

The influx of German refugees in the 1930's stimulated a partial though temporary revival in Eben Ha'-Ezer. A few of the newcomers were orthodox, even to the point of building their own *mikvah*, an act which some native Jews now regarded with resentment as a regression to ghetto life.[32] Moreover, divisive influences caused the formation of such separatist institutions as *Anshei Oesterreich* (Austrian congregation). It was a tendency continued to some extent by Polish and other refugees of the post-World War II era, many of whom did not settle within Alliance or choose to join one of the Vineland synagogues. Even before the close of the 1940's, Eben Ha'-Ezer ceased to exist: its timber structure was dismantled, and the proceeds went to the Hadassah Hospital in Jerusalem and other charities. Its several *Sifrei Torah*, so long and so lovingly cared for, but open to desecration in the abandoned structure, had already been distributed among nearby synagogues.

In these decades of crisis, however, the smaller Tiphereth Israel synagogue of Alliance, though equally venerable in years, never ceased to function. It was sometimes called the Bayuk synagogue after its learned leader, Moses Bayuk, and some local purists considered it to be part of Brotmanville rather than Alliance. Yet, on occasions such as Hanukkah, children from the entire area met for joint community programs in old Alliance Hall, now under the auspices of the National Council of Jewish Women. Leaders of area synagogues joined here also for addresses by visiting rabbis.[33]

By contrast with the decline of Alliance and the other outlying colonies within Vineland, fresh sources of religious strength caused the founding of a new synagogue, Beth Israel (1923). An outgrowth of the population shift from farm to town, it also represented an attempt to reach the younger generation through programs geared to their interests, as well as the newer Conservative forms of worship. There was an emphasis on the current and meaningful in Jewish tradition, whether by the congregation's celebrating together the Festival of Lights, or by hearing a concert recital of Jewish songs by a noted composer. Joint congregational ceremonies, led by Rabbi Krueger, sometimes substituted for the declining individual observance of religious ritual. And not only was the Friday evening sermon introduced as a featured aspect of the service, but it was at times preached by non-Jewish guest clergy, such as the Reverend Johnson, honored by the synagogue board of directors for his inter-faith work in Vineland.

Further, the cycle of activities among Beth Israel Sisterhood and Men's Club, so typical of twentieth century synagogues, ranged from fund-raising suppers to lectures by religious and political luminaries. For example, Jacob de Haas, Zionist pioneer and leader in the American Jewish Congress, spoke eloquently on the continued need for religious faith; he pleaded especially for greater harmony between older and younger generations. Revealing yet another viewpoint, Socialist Norman Thomas later appeared to preach the ethics of a noncapitalist commonwealth.[34]

Nor were the young neglected. Beth Israel's religious school attempted to reach the children through such means as Purim performances and other holiday programs. When the *Vineland Evening Times* described Jewish festivals, it was more often than not in terms of the rites at Beth Israel rather than at the older two synagogues, the orthodox Sons of Jacob and Ahavas Achim. Attention also focused on the yearly confirmation ceremonies at Beth Israel, which included brief addresses presented by the honored youth. Then, at the springtime holiday of Shabuot, teenage boys and girls were encouraged to prepare a talk on some appropriate religious or historical theme.[35]

Zionism also survived the urgencies and excitement of World War I as well as the normalcy which followed. True, in the later period, the local group often made the front page with such items as "Zionists Defeat Continentals," describing the prowess of its basketball team before friendly audiences in Cusci Hall. But at the same time, Vinelanders were also excited by reports of two messengers from Palestine, young farmers Joseph Saphir and David Sternberg, who sought financial help to develop B'nai Benjamin, a pioneering colony in the Holy Land.[36] The following decade (1937) all the congregations of the area joined at Vineland's Beth Israel to hear Isaac Ben Zvi, Zionist publicist and one-time representative at Versailles. They could not know that their speaker would be President of the as yet unborn state of Israel; however, they responded with sympathetic concern to the reports that Jewish settlements in Palestine were threatened by the "trouble-makers" among the Arab leadership. A substantial sum was quickly subscribed, to aid in the land purchase and reclamation work of the Jewish National Fund. Other lecturers at Beth Israel's forums, such as Maurice Samuel speaking on "Palestine Today," reflected the Jewish community's continued interest in the ancient Homeland.[37]

It was a sentiment to be given even further impetus by the unspeakable tragedy of the impending European holocaust as well as by the birth pangs of Israel, one to follow the other as if in fulfillment of some awesome prophecy of retribution and salvation. By mid-century, Vineland would possess active chapters of the

Zionist Organization of America, Hadassah, Mizrachi Women (religious Zionists), Pioneer Women, and Labor Zionists. The latter even included among their activities a radio program of Jewish news and music broadcast over the local station to serve both town residents and farmers.[38]

Refugees and Land: The Ideology of Crisis between Two World Wars

Most ideology, when viewed in the context of its time, represents a response to some urgent necessity, to a set of internal or external pressures which seem to threaten the very survival of a particular society. So it is with the periodic resurgence of Jewish agrarianism and rural colonization in twentieth century America.

For many a Jewish refugee, whether from Russia or from Nazi Germany, the intrinsic drawing power of land ownership was based on deeply felt needs, which stemmed not only from his cultural tradition of Bible, Talmud, and folk literature, but also from a desire to attain that which had been withheld from most Jews for so long—the sense of belonging and achievement associated with agrarian pursuits. There was always more at stake, however, than just plucky individuals attracted to an industry which happened to be in decline. Return-to-the-soil continued to represent for the anguished, oppressed, and self-doubting minority, a new way to security; rejected by the Old World, they were hopeful of acceptance in the New. External threats brought self-conscious echoes from within, along with defensive reactions in the twentieth century as in the nineteenth.

In democratic England, as in the United States, farming had been upheld as an answer to anti-Semitic slanders and a means of salvation for oppressed Jewry. The Reverend Simeon Singer preached at London's West End Synagogue the doctrine of "return to more natural methods of living" than peddling or shop work. His sermons, heard at the threshold of the twentieth century, only reiterated a persistent theme. "Take the Russian Jew from his Russian town, or from Whitechapel for the matter of that, and set him in the midst of an open, rolling country," Singer advised, "and you place him on the high road not merely to independence, but to dignity." In a later address entitled "Jews in their Relation to other Races," Singer tackled the associated problems of absorption and acculturation: "It is not surprising to those who know how to read the Jewish character," he opined, "that among the many races and religions contained within the limits of the British Empire there is none that has more completely identified itself with the national sentiments and aspirations than the Jews."[39]

It was a theme strikingly similar to the defense of immigrants settled in Woodbine. Such colonies were given as living "proof of the trustworthiness and courage of the [newcomers] in directing their affairs intelligently and judiciously." In this example the American public could find assurance "that the new immigrant, like his elder brothers, is becoming a useful part of and a contributor to the growth and welfare of his adopted country." Jewish farmers' achievements, even if limited by inexperience, should be sufficient, it was hoped, "to convince the anti-Jew that the Jewish conception of social life is not only commerce, but also the beautiful, the quiet and natural."[40]

This was no mere public relations rhetoric, but a response to immediate threats. For example, even in the year that Woodbine was incorporated as a self-governing borough, the commissioner-general of immigration had joined the chorus of alarm over the rising alien influx. As the annual totals reached close to the million mark, he wondered whether so many could "assimilate with the people of this country and thus become a source of strength for the support of American institutions and civilization instead of a danger in periods of strain and trial." If only they could be "removed from the sweatshops and slums of the great cities" and given some property of their own, he suggested in a mingling of despair and hope, the foreigner's radical notions might be transformed into a conservative support for "those institutions under whose benign protection he has acquired and can defend his household goods."[41]

Indeed, what the commissioner-general had recommended had for some time been the goal of those Jewish organizations which were struggling to keep the doors open. Their defense of liberal immigration policies served all the millions who managed to enter the land of freedom, not just the Jews among them; these were the teeming masses who streamed across Ellis Island, enduring an ordeal which dealt harsh blows to individual dignity. When Aaron Levy of the Federation of Jewish Organizations and union leader Joseph Barondess criticized the maltreatment of immigrants, the official retort was that "we have some of the dirtiest people in the world to deal with." Congressional hearings made it apparent that over-zealous immigration officials continued to deport numerous migrants who had not met the test of adequate funds or promise of employment, especially if they were headed for the more congested areas of America.[42]

Mary Antin was among those who persisted in upholding the ideal of the open door in the face of growing pressures against it. She joined her fellow Jews and Americans in proclaiming "that here, in the trial at Ellis Island, we are put to the test of the fiery furnace." America could not renege, she pleaded, on her promise of human dignity and "the law that the hungry shall feed where there is plenty." Referring to current invidious comparisons between the older immigration and the new, she castigated those among both "the thoughtless poor and the thoughtless rich" who resorted to such catchwords as "the scum of Europe" to describe Italians and Slavs. Of course, a Sicilian was unlike a Scotsman, but was he not just as much "a man, a creature made in the image of God?"[43] Among the newer immigrants were those—about a million of them during the first decade of the 1900's—classified officially as the Hebrew race, "that race which for nineteen centuries has sacrificed its flesh in the service of the spirit." Mary Antin was eloquent, though far from neutral, as she reminded Americans to judge the immigrants in a historical context: "It takes a hundred times as much steadfastness and endurance for a Russian Jew of today to remain a Jew as it took for an English Protestant in the seventeenth century to defy the established Church." The variety of new groups entering America, she pleaded, represented not only a fulfillment of the nation's destiny, but also a source of potential human enrichment. "America is not God's last stand," she replied to those who saw the masses thronging to the cities as a menace to established rural, Anglo-Saxon, Protestant values.[44]

Appeals on the grounds of justice, humanity, or mission would not be sufficient, however, to halt the restrictionists or to deal with the real problems of the newcomers. In the midst of postwar normalcy, William Kirsch's *The Jew and The Land* revived the agrarian panacea in new form. It outlined a specific program to wean Jews and other immigrant groups away from the city through special education and training and suggested farm tenancy as a kind of internship. A bridge to farming would thus be created, especially through the "socialization of certain existing institutions such as the credit system" to help finance the program. Federal and state aid would further ease the process of adaptation. After all, as noted in the introduction to Kirsch's book, the lack of Jewish achievement in agriculture was the result of historical disabilities, not any inherent "anti-rural proclivities." In the book's preface, progressive economist Richard T. Ely likewise expressed his faith in the use of governmental machinery to develop land policies for the improvement of Negroes as well as Jews and other minorities.[45] Humanistic progressives, too, both Christian and Jewish, united in the Amos Society to further the "social and peace gospel of the Hebrew prophets." Among its leaders were Isidor Singer, editor of the *Jewish Encyclopedia,* and Edward A. Filene, the latter proclaiming that "Jews individually have done magnificent service for America and the world." One of those singled out for their praise was "the peasants' apostle," David Lubin, a Polish Jew who migrated to California and organized an international farmers' clearing house to disseminate agricultural information in the interest of world peace.[46]

Conservative prophets proved the more influential. Preparatory to new immigration restrictions, Congress heard Dr. Harry H. Laughlin of the Eugenics Record Office (Carnegie Institution) warn of "racial deterioration" stemming from the pseudo-scientific fact that "the recent immigrants, as a whole, present a higher percentage of inborn socially inadequate qualities than do the older stocks." Future laws, he proposed, must consider "the element of family history or biological pedigree, if we are to improve the American human stock by immigration."[47] In the 1920's, America's melting pot was analyzed and found to contain too much dross among the human metal. The work of Laughlin and others who painted a frightening spectacle of Europe dumping "its undesirables" onto America's shore made a durable impression. Along with depression and another World War, fear of the foreigner would bar millions from the gates to survival.

Jewish immigrants would no longer be classified officially as a distinct race, but neither would they be considered a nationality at a time when quotas were assigned on the basis of national origin. The first was a victory of sorts for Jewish secular leaders like Simon Wolf, even though Solomon Schechter had defended the cultural concept of race as common heritage; rejection of the concept, even vaguely defined, "leads to assimilation, which is more dangerous to Judaism than any device the anti-Semites may invent."[48] Yet, lacking a national status, the Jewish people concentrated in Eastern Europe were not only subject to discriminatory American quotas but also to the vagaries of political instability and officially sanctioned oppression in countries like Poland, even before the Nazi onslaught. Those in America, too, having managed to find safety within, did not cease to be troubled by their own status as well as by the plight of their brethren. For both, agrarian colonization would remain a favorite panacea, periodically revived.

" 'Back-to-land' is veritably becoming a mass movement among the Jews," wrote Michael B. Scheler in a 1930 issue of Chicago's Jewish monthly, *The Reflex*. The oft-repeated labels of usurer and speculator were as false as ever, he affirmed, outlining a summary of Jewish agriculture over the centuries in Russia and Poland, whenever the authorities permitted, as well as in the United States (Palestine was neglected as an example). American Jews, now notably Herbert Lehman, assisted numerous Jewish farm colonies, even in the Soviet Union. The honest toil of the agrarian was not "new and unnatural for the Jew . . . [who] is only too eager to pursue all normal functions of civilized society whenever and wherever opportunity presents itself," Scheler concluded.[49] If this was an apologist's interpretation, it nonetheless represented the precedent set in the American Jewish community.

In the Depression's trough of 1933, when the farm economy was especially hard hit, a guide to Jewish agrarianism was developed for the National Federation of Temple Brotherhoods by Dr. Jacob B. Menkes. Titled *Judah's Sons of the Soil*, it offered historical case studies of Jewish farmers in biblical and Talmudic times, the Roman Empire, Spain, France, Poland, Russia (especially Kherson province), Palestine, Argentina, and Canada. Citing the colonists in South Jersey as well as those in the rest of the United States, Menkes praised their "decidedly individualistic and healthy imprint" on the New World. In this new defense of the Jewish agrarian tradition generally, he quoted numerous biblical passages and noted that the entire Talmudic tractate *Zerayim* ("Seeds") dealt with farm life. The rabbis, Menkes recalled, preached that "a small measure from the field is better than a large measure from the warehouse"; nor did they limit their references to the Holy Land: "And even if one bought land in Syria, it was as if he had bought it in the precincts of Jerusalem." His instructional guide included also questions for discussion as well as a bibliography for further study. It was especially pertinent in such hard times for every Jew to be able to respond to charges that he was not "productive . . . [not] living by the sweat of his brow, but a contemptible drone living on the toil of others."[50]

In return to the soil ideology and public relations, the perennial leader remained the Jewish Agricultural Society. The years of worldwide depression and Nazi persecution made its task more urgent: "To reduce the disparity between Jewish urban and Jewish rural life . . . to prove that Jews possess primary productive capacity, that they can work with brawn as well as with brain—if there ever was such a time, it is today [1938] when the tide of anti-Semitism is rising." Its annual reports continued with the pathetic certainty that so often characterized humanitarian causes: "There is hardly room for argument that an active Jewish movement farmward will have a wholesome and mitigating effect on anti-Jewish prejudice."[51]

The exhortations were coupled with practical assistance, as far as possible. Youth conferences, consulting services, farm loans, and various educational programs, actualized the JAS ideology, but with the limited resources available, its settlement efforts were directed mainly to those with some funds of their own (averaging about $3,000 per farm) and a willingness to risk the family's savings and labor. In 1938, of eighty-four families settled on farms only twenty-eight were European refugees, although the organization asserted that even one such family settled in New Jersey, "became the nucleus of a group of twenty persons living on four farms, with other relatives still to come."[52]

Although many others of course, managed to make their own way, the JAS did hold out the possibility of departing from "orthodox [business] principles" in the future handling of the refugee problem; farming would keep them out of the city where the competition for jobs was so keen that "every new storekeeper, every new professional, every new worker adds to the pressure." Clearly, return-to-the-soil was embraced again for its "salutary effect not only on the refugee but on the Jewish position in general."[53] It was a limited defensive action at a time when even the great were fearful, a time of Munich, of the Evian International Refugees Conference aborted by platitudes and the immutable immigration laws of the United States; even the meager quotas were left unused through the Roosevelt administration's reluctance to offer sanctuary. In the words of historian Merle Curti, "had the United States and other governments been more resolute in helping Jews . . . hundreds of thousands might well have been saved from Hitler's crematoria."[54]

To the last hour, Jewish agrarianism persisted in its desperate struggle to foster colonization as a means of rescue. The Freeland League for Jewish Territorial Colonisation, based in London, came before the Evian conferees with a program for compact agricultural settlements in any of the sparsely populated areas of the world, such as Australia, which required labor for economic development. Its memoranda and futile pleas in 1938 prophesied that the Nazi terror would spare "neither young nor old, man, woman, or child. We are dealing here with the deliberate and planned extinction of a community."[55] After the war's outbreak, the publications of the Freeland League continued to beg for some "one of the empty spaces of the world." Pointing to the example of thousands of Jewish farmers in the United States, it attempted to bolster the world's weak will: Jews could work hard, assimilate readily, be loyal citizens, and become an "integral part" of any country that would accept them. They appealed in vain, failing to find asylum even in Palestine, long-promised as a Jewish homeland. Although as many as two hundred thousand had found refuge there between 1930 and 1936, the Freeland League was painfully aware that the British government was closing that door too on the eve of the holocaust. It seemed an endless road to "free Jewish land as an integral part of a Free World."[56]

Agrarian sympathizers in the New World, including Vladimir Grossman and other Canadian liberals, also pleaded for large-scale land settlement as a means of regenerating the beleaguered Jewish people. In his book, *The Soil's Calling* (1938), Grossman attacked the inadequate planning and occasional past indifference of the Jewish Colonization Association; reviewing the history of many old Jewish farm colonies in Eastern Europe as in the Americas and praising the modern agricultural training programs of ORT on a worldwide basis, he called for a massive new self-help campaign. "Let us ourselves remove from the cities the excess of population" to the ample lands of Canada, "so far removed from *Goluth* ['exile']." The same kind of spirit as was shown in Palestine he hoped could be exhibited in New World colonies. To the heads of Jewish organizations concerned over virulent Nazi propaganda in Quebec as in New York, Grossman addressed the assurance that additional immigration was vital for the cultural survival of their own communities.[57] Nevertheless, return-to-the-soil was a dream of rescue to be realized in only small part and in only few places, while another kind of ground had already been prepared—long and perfidiously—for the holocaust of World War II.

Dream and livelihood in South Jersey: New farm communities, new Americans

I will send such as escape of them unto the nations . . . to the isles afar off.

Isaiah 66:19

10

For the particular American Jewish agrarian communities during the interwar years, changing circumstances required social
innovation and response. It was necessary for those already on the
land to attain secure means of self-support and even to assist in
the absorption of additional settlers, objectives which could be met
only by adapting to unstable economic conditions. For example,
poultry farming was emphasized more, and newly specialized communities were created as the old ones declined. Beyond the economic response, however, the immigrants developed a greater sense
of identity, unique cultural institutions, and a will toward independent action. Throughout, they maintained their ties with
brethren laboring in the cities and with those who remained in
the Old World, subjected to the rise of totalitarianism. Thus, both
internal and external concerns continued to influence the varied
patterns of Jewish community life in the twentieth century.

In Ocean County about fifty miles northeast of the old pioneering Vineland colonies and ten miles from Lakewood, clusters of
new Jewish farmers flourished, especially at Toms River. They had
been first guided there by the Jewish Agricultural Society during
the brief depression which followed World War I, and by the
mid-1920's fifty to sixty families had organized the Toms River

Community of Jewish Farmers. Though many received JAS loans, they remained economically independent operators who risked their own savings and united mainly for such specific objectives as cooperative purchasing. At the same time, as a Jewish community of farmers they were bound to the historic worldwide agrarianism of their people including such diverse contemporary experiments as those in Palestine and the Soviet Union.

The community's founder was a graduate of the Woodbine Agricultural School, Aaron Pincus. He had worked on farms from Maine to Colorado, saved from total assimilation, he said, only by faithfully subscribing to the Yiddish press. Even at the Woodbine school, he recalled, the future Jewish farmers had been introduced to "the sterile world of assimilation." Traditional prayers and Yiddish songs were fostered only by a small group of fellow students "not yet poisoned by the militant Americanism then dominant among the *'yahudmisher'* administration" which included the English-speaking rabbi.[1]

Under Pincus's leadership (1925–1948), the community supported the thriving Scholem Aleichem Folk School within its impressive Community Hall, in addition to the Hebrew School of Congregation B'nai Israel. The folk school concentrated on teaching the Yiddish *mahme loshen,* the mother tongue which united the Jewish masses but was denigrated by the established German-Jewish leadership. This was the language of the heartfelt correspondence in 1930 between Toms River and the colonists of *Freileben* ("Free Life") in far-off Biro-Bijan, the "autonomous" Jewish region of Soviet Siberia.

The warmth of these letters is evident in spite of a mutual resort to slogans and fear of Soviet censorship. Pincus wrote on behalf of Toms River to his "dear brother colonists" that all Jews took pride in the achievements of their fellow farmers in building new economic foundations for their people despite the hardships. "Like you, we left the city with its *luft* [vain, unproductive] occupations, cutthroat competition, and capitalist exploitation to seek creative productivity on the land in healthful work in the lap of mother

314

earth, to earn our bread with the sweat of our brow rather than the double-dealing of the marketplace."

A delegate from the Toms River community, Miss Weiman, journeyed all the way to the U.S.S.R. to bring greetings to a mass meeting in *Freileben*. Their letter of thanks expressed delight at the success of Jewish farmers in America, gratitude for the aid of Agro-Joint and other organizations, and hope for a time when every farmer could live "each under his vine and fig tree." Such biblical allusions came with "brotherly regards" from the chairman of the Jewish Farm Workers' Collective, Moshe Rocker, who also permitted himself a comment on the difficult conditions in Russia at the time.[2] Yet neither Miss Weiman nor Rocker mentioned the Palestine colonies, perhaps because of their bourgeois connections. Communication was soon halted by political crisis and war.

The Toms River Community of Jewish Farmers eventually prospered, with a peak membership of 360 families including refugees of the 1930's and of World War II.[3] But in Toms River, even during the Great Depression, the sense of responsibility for brethren abroad was never lost, whether in the form of aid for the Palestine *Yishuv*, collections for the Joint Distribution Committee, or protests against anti-Jewish boycotts in Poland. The National Labor Committee and the Poale Zion (Labor Zionists) were as active in Toms River as in Vineland where Dr. Arthur Goldhaft headed the local drives of the United Palestine Appeal; and the Norma Athletic Hall resounded with benefit dances on behalf of incoming German refugees.[4]

The years of depression, however, had bred yet another kind of self-help Jewish agrarianism, one that focused primarily on domestic economic problems and the persistent unemployment in the city trades. Founded in the spring of 1933, the Provisional Commission for the Establishment of Jewish Farm Settlements in America boasted a membership list that read like a Who's Who of American Jewish leaders of East European origin: Dr. Chaim Zhitlovsky, the socialist ideologue, David Dubinsky, president of the ILGWU, Joseph Schlossberg, general secretary of the Amalgamated Clothing Workers, David Pinski, president of the Jewish National Workers' Alliance, Jacob Weinberg, president of the Workmen's Circle, J. Tygel, executive director of the Federation of Polish Jews, Louis Lipsky of the World Zionist Organization, and many others. None of the older Jewish establishment was included, and the socialist-labor orientation seemed dominant. It was the turn of the proletarian leadership, at long last, to show what they could do for Jewish agrarianism.

Zhitlovsky's address at the opening conference struck a familiar note: "We Jews must reconstruct our lives, and function not only with our brains but as normal, wholesome human beings in all fields of constructively productive endeavor—particularly as TILLERS OF THE SOIL" (his caps). The details were left to two experts— Jacob S. Joffe, graduate of the Woodbine Agricultural School and professor at the New Jersey College of Agriculture, and Benjamin Brown, one-time leader of the short-lived Clarion colony in Utah and now executive chairman of the Commission. Joffe's solution for the problems of jobless urban workers was to give them factory employment in a rural setting, with agricultural work to act as an economic cushion.

At the same time, he sought to avoid the pitfalls of Woodbine, which he knew well enough. Each family would receive just a one-acre homestead, preventing both urban overcrowding and rural isolation. All would be close enough to medical, educational, and other social services while each family could have its own garden to tend. The really effective agricultural production would take place on a large-scale communal basis, allowing for mechanization and the most modern farm practices as well as advantages in the marketplace. Rather than each individual owning a single cow and run-down barn, why not, he asked, one hundred cows in modern stalls or flocks of poultry in central coops? Villagers would take turns working in the communal garment factories and in the mutually owned farming sector.[5]

Undoubtedly, Joffe could draw from the example of new agrarian forms in the Palestine *Yishuv* as well as the Soviet collectives. Yet, he also hoped that the close village settlement, rather than individual farming, would enhance the chances for a "full-blooded" Jewish cultural atmosphere (not necessarily in a religious sense, but focusing on language and history). The question had been put succinctly by an eastern friend of the short-lived Utah colony: "I hope you build a new home there, but will it be Jewish?"[6] The answer was ever subject to doubts.

Implementation was to be provided by the newly formed Association for Jewish Farm Settlements which acquired a thirteen-hundred-acre tract near Hightstown, New Jersey. Press releases announced the imminent construction of two hundred homes as well as some public buildings. Albert Einstein, among others, hailed these plans "to return some of the Jewish masses to the original means of production . . . in the interests of the Jewish community as a whole."[7] Yet, Joffe was also hard pressed by some critics (like Farenberg of *The Day*) who could not forget the errors of Woodbine and Alliance. As an expert, Joffe insisted he would not trade one acre of Hightstown soil for ten of Woodbine's mosquito-ridden, infertile sandy ground; besides, he noted, in the proposed colony, the factories would be owned by the workers themselves, not by capitalists. Moreover, this and other colonies to follow would be "as near large Jewish centers as possible," thus accessible to the older proletariat as well as the new refugees.[8] Where would the funds come from? Joffe and the Association talked bravely of an agro-industrial bank with shares owned by settlers, Jewish labor organizations, and concerned individuals. But the hard times were not conducive to finding people with money to invest, especially in a sector of the economy which showed little promise. Circular letters and a search for solid citizens interested in communal agro-industry brought inadequate response.

The federal government had money, however, and the President had always thought people better off in the country than in the seemingly hopeless cities.[9] Although M. L. Wilson, chief of the Subsistence Homestead Division, kept close touch with the plans of Joffe and the Association, funds for basic land clearing and improvement were provided by the Civil Works Administration instead.[10] Finally, this particular proletarian self-help venture was absorbed by the New Deal, becoming only one of the numerous homestead communities throughout the country, this one to be known as Roosevelt. Although most of the settlers were, indeed, Jewish factory workers from the big city, the cooperative village envisaged by Joffe was never realized. Yet, also at Hightstown, young Labor Zionists (Hashomer Hatzair) set up agricultural training camps in preparation for life on Palestine *kibbutzim* (communal villages).[11]

Years before the New Deal program of subsistence homesteads, the Jewish Agricultural Society had developed plans of its own for agro-industrial settlements. Unlike the old South Jersey colonies or Joffe's Hightstown proposal, they would not have attempted to bring factories into new rural communities, but rather they would have settled workers near some large industrial center, permitting them to commute. They would tend their farms in their spare time and slack seasons, counting also on the family to pitch in. In spite of misgivings based on previous colonizing misfortunes, the JAS proceeded to implement this new concept at Bound Brook, New Jersey, about twenty miles southwest of Newark. By 1929, within three years of its founding, the colony boasted a total of forty families on developed farms ranging from four to fifteen acres, successfully combining city jobs with farming. The depression crisis, however, continued to hit hard at both ends of this economic balancing act. Another project, combining industry and agriculture at Piscataway Township, near New Brunswick, New Jersey, also failed to make headway, even though the first families had paid one to three thousand dollars apiece.[12]

In the long run, private enterprise farming on a full-time basis seemed to hold out the promise of more adequate rewards to those families who were willing to take the risk and toil together on the land, although individual farmers could still join in voluntary self-help groups with no outside domination. At Toms River, for example, Aaron Pincus had organized a Jewish Poultryman's Cooperative Association (1928) as well as the larger Ocean County Farmers' Federal Credit Union and the New Jersey Federated Egg Producers' Cooperative Association (1932), in all of which Jewish farmers were the mainstay. Especially during the depression years, such cooperatives, whether for marketing or for purchasing feed and fertilizer, could look for vital assistance from the JAS. After all, its loan services to individuals and farm groups preceded by many years those of the federal government, and some of its experts had helped draft the first Farm Loan Act.

Yet, the new Federal Land Banks did not prove a very effective source of aid to Jewish farmers. Prospective borrowers had to be approved first by the local Farm Loan Association, consisting often of conservatively oriented native farm leaders who tended to be suspicious of big-city greenhorns. The banks, moreover, followed a rigid policy, particularly painful to Jewish farmers in the hard 1930's, of disallowing loans to those who supplemented their income by boarding guests, a practice common in New Jersey as well as in the Catskills. But even more serious was their prejudice against poultry farming as overly risky and requiring an excessive investment in basic facilities.[13] Yet, this was precisely the area in which Jewish farmers were to meet with their great success, albeit unstable, in the twentieth century.

Poultry Farming for Economic Survival and Absorption

Poultry farming, which saved Jewish agrarianism in an age when American agriculture generally was in decline, presented important advantages. Most notably, its modest land requirements made it feasible in those relatively well-settled areas of high-priced land which offered adequate public services, including transportation to big city markets and contacts with fellow Jews as businessmen or consumers. At least some income return was available almost immediately, even if the poultry farming was done on only a part-time basis at the start—a significant factor for families with small savings. Nor were the natural hazards such as drought or storm as dangerous as in other types of farming, and, undoubtedly, neither was the physical labor as back-breaking as that for "real dirt farmers." With aid from JAS, Jewish poultry farming flourished between the wars and beyond, from Toms River, Vineland, Farmingdale, and Freehold in New Jersey, the Ulster-Sullivan county area (the "Jewish Mountains") in New York, and Colchester in Connecticut, to Petaluma north of San Francisco.

Vineland, which had boasted back in 1911 that it was "very cosmopolitan . . . politically, religiously, and socially," reported even then, large shipments of eggs and "early chickens, the product of the incubator."[14] Endowed with a relatively mild climate and sandy soil for drainage, it had already been on its way to its position as, first, "Egg Basket of New Jersey" and, then, "the Egg Basket of the East."[15] Egg grading had started there soon after the turn of the century, as more careful breeding and hatching procedures were developed gradually by such forward-looking leaders as Dr. Jacob Lipman. A further spur to local initiative came from Max Fleischer and Dr. Arthur Goldhaft, who drummed up support for regional contests. And Jacob Rubinoff, who staked everything on the future of the local poultry industry, expanded his farm supply business after World War I to manufacture his own feed formula, the first in New Jersey, and developed with the aid of state poultry specialists. Before his death in 1948, when he was succeeded by his son Edward, the Jacob Rubinoff Company could claim it was not only the largest but also the most modern operation of its type east of the Mississippi.[16]

As early as the 1918 annual convention of Jewish farmers, representatives from Woodbine as well as the Vineland area were reporting notable earnings from poultry. Some of these older farmers found it a useful means of diversification, in addition to truck vegetables and small fruits. In 1917, from its newly opened Philadelphia office, JAS was able to intensify its extension aid and other services to poultry farmers in South Jersey. During the relatively prosperous 1920's, some additional city families were attracted to Woodbine, making modest down-payments on fifteen-acre homesteads, complete with dwellings, hen houses, and combination barns, prepared by the Society; the newer settlements such as Toms River were, however, much more popular with those who had substantial savings.[17] Outbreaks of poultry disease, especially in older colonies, temporarily marred the expansion. In 1925, Vineland attorney Morris Greenblatt had to lead a delegation to New

York to appeal a blanket embargo. During the crisis, the Woodbine Poultrymen's Association and other farmers' groups, with the aid of JAS, set up poultry clinics to demonstrate preventive techniques and even administer vaccinations.[18]

The critical condition brought notice to the pioneer work of Dr. Goldhaft in developing successful new fowl-pox vaccines as early as 1921. Their use spread steadily, making possible sharp reductions in the price of these medicines. Before the end of the decade, Goldhaft further expanded his Vineland Poultry Laboratories, an enterprise which achieved an admirable reputation for the production on a national scale of improved vaccines and drugs. Among Goldhaft's later scientific accomplishments were the cultivation of viruses inside the egg to produce as pure a vaccine as possible, the development of advanced poultry breeds, and the application of hormone pellets to create heftier capons. A humanitarian always, Goldhaft preached that farmers in other countries could also succeed in developing poultry flocks as a weapon against hunger. His last years (the 1950's) were devoted to outlining such proposals before the Food and Agriculture Organization. An ardent Zionist then, largely because of the Jewish tragedy, he traveled to Israel several times to assist personally in the development of the young nation's poultry industry.[19]

Goldhaft's optimism was based mainly on his own observations of the ebb and flow of life in the Vineland area during decades of prosperity and depression. At the beginning of the 1930's, farm commodity prices were down to the lowest level in fifteen years, and farm bankruptcies stood at several times the pre–World War I figure. In these critical circumstances, JAS vowed to maintain at least the previous gains, with the aid of additional subventions from the parent Baron de Hirsch Fund.[20] Yet some Vinelanders were heartened by government reports that the movement to the cities had been stemmed; in bad times, cities seemed less attractive, and if anything the movement was reversed by small storekeepers and jobless factory workers seeking respite in the countryside. As a result, the number of Jewish farm family units, about sixteen thousand in 1930, continued to rise.[21]

Equally significant, if not always successful, was the stubborn resistance of older Jewish farmers against the onslaughts of depression. In Rosenhayn, the Farmers' Cooperative Marketing Association, headed by Morris April and Dan Goldman, provided a central auction for local producers; it encouraged also improved grading and packing standards. The result was a higher return, especially for vegetables and berries, than had been previously available to individual farmers selling on consignment in the New York markets.[22] With the persistence of depression, Alliance-Norma farmers founded the Farmers' Protective Association of New Jersey, seeking governmental relief as well as mutual aid. Led by William Springer of Alliance, they joined in protest of "farmers having been harder hit than any other business people." Their demands included such remedies as price levels set at 10 percent above costs, lower property tax assessments, and no sheriff's sales of farms where the inability to pay "is not the farmer's fault." However, their plans for a fifteen-day strike and mass march on Washington had to be abandoned and their efforts concentrated instead on the approval of federal codes to cut back production and set minimum prices.[23]

The local poultrymen's groups also moved under the stress of falling prices to unite with the newly formed New Jersey Poultry Association. At an organizing meeting in Toms River that included Jewish delegates from Carmel, Vineland and Woodbine, they pledged a common effort to protect their market position. Organization, product improvement, and advertising became the slogans of self-help throughout these harsh years.[24] Not that the foreclosures ceased—there were twenty-four listed by the *Vineland Evening Times* in May, 1934 alone, mostly Jewish names. In the 1938 season, damaging rainstorms forced the Rosenhayn Market to close before the end of summer. But the depression's effects were mitigated at least by such membership agencies serving those who managed to hang on; for example, also in 1938, the Woodbine Cooperative Poultry Association boasted a new store and warehouse, and a business of eight thousand dollars monthly, paying "patronage dividends" to its one hundred members.[25]

More than ever, the farmers' organizations became also the

focus of social activity, often cosponsored by JAS, and offering serious lectures and panel discussions as well as picnics. At a typical Alliance-Norma farmers' annual outing speakers would include Gabriel Davidson and George Goward of JAS, plus the county agricultural agent; there were also non-agriculturists such as Jacob Ginsburg, editor of the *Jewish World.*

Old Home Day reunions at the colonies attracted hundreds of celebrants, and the fiftieth anniversary of their founding brought together about a thousand in 1932. Among the speakers were eminent native sons of Alliance like Joseph and Jacob Perskie and surviving resident pioneers such as Mr. and Mrs. Sidney Bailey. Arrangements for the gala event included the publication of a jubilee volume of reminiscences, *Yoval,* edited by attorney Herman Eisenberg. Its dedication to the pioneers focused on the theme of the Psalmist, "They that sow in tears shall reap in joy." The Norma Athletic Association followed up with one of its most successful dances, and on the more serious side, further exhortations to plan for the spiritual and moral welfare of the youth. The social was never without its sober moments in the Jewish farm communities.[26]

New Poultry Farmers: German and Polish Refugees

In that decade of depression marked by the jubilee of the first East Europeans and their children, German Jewish newcomers arrived in substantial numbers to settle alongside them. As Alliance pioneer William Levin put it, "German Jews helped us back in the 1880's, and now it's our turn to help them."[27] They were mostly professional and business people who knew little about farming, nor were they welcome to compete for jobs in the city. Some were older men seeking a tranquil rural location. Many who had once been affluent now required some financial assistance, which was usually provided in the form of JAS loans to enter poultry farming and supplemented by occasional grants from the newly formed National Refugee Service as well as other aid by HEAS and the National Council of Jewish Women.[28]

Some Germans arrived in South Jersey, where land was least expensive, with no more than "a suitcase, a violin," and a little cash.

In 1940 the JAS property in Bound Brook was opened as a training farm for refugees, giving them at least a few months of basic preparation. Soon, there were over a hundred such families in the Vineland area, some of them settled on abandoned farms. These "newcomers from Hitler's Germany," Dr. Goldhaft noted—and he was a shrewd observer—"actually revived the poultry business in Vineland."[29] He admired their educational and cultural background, their interest in scientific matters, their punctiliousness and hard work. Sympathy with their sufferings brought him, at last, a greater understanding of his own parents' tales of beating and murder in Tsarist Russia.

Others, however, including some descendants of those earlier migrants from Russia now among the "first families," worried about the influx. How would the refugees affect the local economic picture, especially with an industry plagued by periodic surpluses? Socially, they seemed aloof, or was it merely an effort to hold on to their own self-respect? Some talked like opportunists who wanted only to get rich fast. Generally, they did not resemble the traditional image of the diffident, ghetto immigrant of the previous era. And because of their cultural background they adapted quickly to their new environment—a virtue which some considered a fault.

Inevitably, the community at large recognized the industriousness and honesty of family men like Sali Mayerfeld, who turned an abandoned gentile homestead into a prosperous farm and became a board member of the Vineland Marketing Cooperative. Nevertheless, Mayerfeld's orthodox ways caused raised eyebrows among some of the Jewish citizenry. Indeed, a number of the German immigrants were traditionally pious, creating a revival of religious life not only within the old Tiphereth Israel in Alliance but also the Sons of Jacob and the relatively young Beth Israel in Vineland. Yet, they represented varying shades of religious persuasion and tended over the years to drift into the prevailing practice of infrequent synagogue attendance. Moreover, they were soon absorbed into the activities of such established secular organizations as the Hebrew Benevolent Society and the newer Poultryman's Club (noted for its active membership, mostly of German-Jewish background); and as soon as they had even a little money to give, they participated in the tradition of charity for various communal causes.[30]

The process of adjustment was soon overshadowed by the demands of World War II. "Food Fights for Freedom" became a national slogan, in time reflecting the vast expansion of all agricultural production and the doubling of cash farm incomes between 1940 and 1943 alone. JAS could report virtually no losses on its settlement loans, unlike the recent depression, even though it was called on increasingly to help cope with such new problems as shortages of labor, machinery, and poultry feed. Land prices became inflated, making it more difficult to select appropriate new farm sites, but due to prosperity, the draft, and a virtual cessation of new immigrants until the postwar years, the number of applicants dropped sharply.

The patriotic dedication of Jewish farmers at the onset of war was symbolized by the official letter to President Roosevelt from the Toms River Community of Jewish Farmers citing the service of their young people in the armed forces and pledging the home front to strain in expanding production and purchasing government bonds. Yet, in these years, too, JAS noted that old, persistent problem: "insidious propaganda has widened the spread of the poison of anti-Semitism." In almost traditional fashion, it saw its own responsibility as continuing to dispel the "common misconception" of the Jew as "exclusively a city product," partly through new joint efforts with the Christian Rural Fellowship and the Catholic Country Life Association. There were twenty thousand Jewish farm families at the end of World War II, JAS was pleased to report.

Moreover, after the war, JAS made its own contribution to the portrayal of American Jewry's role in World War II. It called attention, for example, to the fact that 7.5 percent of Jewish farmers from eighteen to forty-four had been in the service, as compared to 6.2 percent of all farmers; it cited too the outstanding instances of individual bravery.[31] Among the many high-ranking officers was Rear Admiral Lewis L. Strauss, honorary president of JAS.

On a knoll a few miles from the center of Vineland, in the well-maintained Alliance cemetery, a handsome monument was built for the sons of that pioneer community who had given their lives in battle: Ditmar Friede, Milton Goldstein, Herman Green, Louis Katz, Lester Kotok, Barney Lihn, Jacob Moscowitz, Howard Rothman, Earl Spiegel, Gilbert Wolf. They died for America as had others before them in World War I, for a cause and for ideals which had perhaps changed little from their fathers' time.

War's end revealed what had been known before by the world's great leaders—the horrors of genocide, the culmination of German anti-Semitism. Perhaps in partial response, the United States Government at long last relaxed the old quota limitations which had been unfilled before the war, in large measure because of over-zealous enforcement by consular and other immigration officials. In 1948, President Truman signed a bill to admit some of Europe's displaced persons, including Germans expelled from frontier areas as well as survivors of the concentration camps. At the same time, he bluntly condemned certain provisions of the act as still discriminatory against Jews and Catholics. A second act, in 1950, removed these inequities and expanded the numbers which could be admitted, although remaining restrictions still made many refugees ineligible.

Of the thousands of Jewish displaced persons who did enter the United States, many were either already interested in farming or guided into it by the JAS or some referral agency. In a sense, this was the third wave of immigrants onto the land, following the Russian colonists of the late nineteenth and early twentieth centuries and the relatively small German Jewish immigration prior to World War II. These most recent newcomers were largely East Europeans, especially from Poland; they were comparatively young and some seemed hardy, having managed somehow to survive the terrors of war, yet they had been deprived for all these years of education or the normal amenities of society. For a semblance of order, these truly underprivileged had to grope back to their memories of 1939, before their world had been destroyed by Nazi barbarism.

In some respects, the problems of these newcomers repeated

the experiences of those who preceded them, in others they differed. The number of "farm aspirants" seeking the extensive services of the JAS doubled between 1945 and 1948 to 1160, each requiring some instruction and guidance and the inspection of prospective farms; most of the 157 families actually settled in 1948, especially the new refugees, needed loans as well. Some went as far away as California, Florida, Michigan, or Ohio, but most stayed in the East. Those in New Jersey went to the burgeoning poultry centers of Farmingdale and Flemington (Monmouth County), Toms River, and naturally the older Vineland area. As in the 1930's and before, Vineland had the attraction of less expensive land, and established Jewish life and institutions.[32]

For South Jersey, which had seen Jewish farm colonies since the 1880's, this latest wave of settlers was the largest of all. Coming in individual family units rather than in groups, a thousand of them had settled in and around Vineland by the early 1950's. Their uniqueness was recognized. More than any others before them, they had undergone years of unbroken suffering—in the concentration camps, among the partisan fighters of the East European forests, or in some cellar hiding place. Yet, they proved remarkably resilient and stable in their efforts to learn the ways of their adopted country.

In many respects they seemed as strangers even to fellow Jews because of their Yiddish speech, their lack of business procedures, their manner of dress, and, sometimes, their inordinate piety. When a newcomer ran up a big bill with a feed supplier and thereupon switched his business elsewhere, some native tongues wagged, although others would accuse the dealer of sharp practices against the inexperienced new poultry farmers. Such incidents were as often as not the result of language barriers or cultural differences. In one case, a novice farmer's whole flock died because he misinterpreted the medicinal dosage to be added to the water: the prescription advised a tablespoon quantity of the American variety, not of the family's European heirloom, which was at least thrice as large.

To bring them more effective assistance, and in renewed recognition of New Jersey's large number of Jewish farm families, JAS opened a branch office in Vineland (while closing the one in Chicago). In spite of the organization's earlier misgivings, only the struggling colonies in New Jersey had survived to become what now seemed a "providential" base for the settling of displaced persons. How things had changed! the JAS reports proclaimed, since those years of the 1880's when the first refugees had come to their wilderness farms, inadequately financed, ill-equipped, with little but their axes and grub hoes to clear the pine barrens. Since World War II, the reports boasted, the number of Jewish farmers had risen substantially at a time when the farm population generally declined, and thanks in large measure to Jewish poultrymen, this industry had become New Jersey's "most important" agricultural enterprise.[33] Not only immigrants, but also veterans, former defense workers, and small businessmen joined in a return to the land.

Among the newly settled veterans were native-born and naturalized Americans alike, such as Karl Kleeblatt from Seligenstadt near Frankfurt. Landing in New York in 1938 at the age of seventeen, he found work with a household accessories firm and attended night school. Then came World War II and service in the armed forces. In 1947, Karl joined his father-in-law, Morris Aaron, in Vineland, on a twenty-acre farm of which ten acres were in asparagus, tomatoes, and cucumbers, and ten for the poultry. They managed eventually to expand from fifteen hundred chickens to ten thousand. Karl also added to the family's savings by working part-time for Pogust's Feed and Farm Supply in Vineland. He became a member of the Garton Road synagogue (Beth Israel), and later his young sons received instruction from Rabbi Baruch Schwartz of Norma while the oldest celebrated his Bar Mitzvah in the venerable Tiphereth Israel of nearby Alliance.

Of an older generation among the newcomers was Frederick S. Fernich, who migrated from the Rhine area in 1938. (His daughter and son-in-law, a gardener, had found refuge on an agricultural settlement in Palestine.) In New York, Fernich worked for years as a factory salesman, but was not happy in the business world. In 1947, on the verge of a nervous breakdown, he began to look for a farm; he finally settled on Vineland where he had relatives who would help him get started with five acres and fifteen hundred chickens. Within less than ten years, he had increased the earnings from the farm enough to allow sufficient proceeds to be set aside for retirement. Once even moderately established, he participated actively in local community affairs, including B'nai B'rith, the German-Jewish synagogue (Shaare Tikvah), and the Poultrymen's Club, which he served as director.

Typical too of the numerous postwar East European immigrants was Sol Paull (Podchlebnik) of Poland, who arrived in 1946. He stayed in New York until 1949, trying his hand in business and the trades, but came to Vineland at the behest of friends engaged in poultry farming. There, Paull became a successful farmer and outstanding community leader. More notable still, is the story of Miles Lerman, also of Poland. When war erupted, young Miles, still a student, joined a fighting partisan band. After the war, he sought in vain for his family, then, fleeing westward with other displaced persons, he met his future wife, a survivor of the concentration camps. They made their way to New York, where he progressed from clerk to manager. However, they yearned for country life and eventually bought an old house on a neglected farm in Vineland. It was so dirty and run-down that Miles didn't dare show it to his wife before he did some intensive cleaning and repainting. After initial failures, the Lermans achieved prosperity and a prominent position in the Jewish community.

As in the past, the JAS organized a program of educational and cultural activities on behalf of such newcomers. Hundreds of farmers attended the annual poultry conferences sponsored by JAS to hear addresses by Jewish experts in a variety of specialties: Abraham Dobin of Freehold, New Jersey, on cooperative purchasing and marketing; Dr. Tevis Goldhaft, like his father, on poultry medicine; Harry Rothman, Cumberland County agricultural agent on the broad range of extension services available to the modern farmer; and Samuel Lipitz, of the old Vineland family, on the sales program of FARMCO, a major egg marketing cooperative which he headed. Americanism also was not forgotten. At Vineland's annual meeting of Jewish farmers in 1952, some eight hundred celebrated the anniversary of the ratification of the United States Constitution. County Judge Horuvitz was the chief speaker on the subject of good citizenship, followed by a number of leading farmers, including recent immigrants.[34]

In 1951, the most recent newcomers to Vineland formed their own self-help institutions under the broad umbrella of the Jewish Poultry Farmers' Association (JPFA). To some extent, this resulted from separatist tendencies and socio-cultural differences among the three components of the Jewish community—the natives, the German, and the new East Europeans. Above all, however, the latter organized their own institutions not because they were barred from the existing ones, but because they wanted to recapture the richness of a Jewish life which they still remembered. Among them there were intelligent, capable leaders such as Miles Lerman, who was first president of the JPFA and who saw in its founding an opportunity to revitalize the existing community and to set an example for others. "The Jewish spiritual centers in Europe have been destroyed, but it is our duty, that of the saving remnant, to create new spiritual and cultural bastions here in America," he proclaimed, "for the sake of this greater part of our people now living outside of Israel."[35]

To relieve the "spiritual drought" implicit in a community where but a few had been active, the JPFA launched varied programs of mass participation. Some of its older members were able to draw on their knowledge of specific Jewish institutions in Europe. Among those activities which called forth widest notice was its Mutual Aid Society (Gemilas-Chesed), modeled on those of the Old Country and providing interest-free loans to distressed farmers (the aid was especially useful in the wake of the 1954 hurricanes). Another was its welfare committee, which extended medical and various personal services to needy families on a confidential basis. Even more unique, was a court of their own peers organized by the new farmers to settle disputes and arbitrate grievances without resort to governmental machinery. Nor was the practical realm neglected: farmers' education programs and attempts to stabilize market conditions by working with the ever-popular cooperative associations, both involving many of the former displaced persons.

The newcomers' unique contributions, however, remained in the realm of culture. They revived the use of Yiddish locally as the language of their meetings and records; they returned to town Yiddish theater and concerts and even sponsored weekly radio programs in the old mother tongue. Their celebrations of holidays, their memorial programs for the martyred Six Million, brought back "nostalgic feelings to many Jews who have never seen, or who had forgotten, the real side of Jewish life." Even some native and German Jewish farmers, attracted to that type of " 'Yiddishkeit' from which they had unfortunately been more or less estranged," joined JPFA.[36] Such was the estimate of Judge I. Harry Levin, a son of Alliance pioneer William Levin, and one native American who saw good in the newcomers and sensed most clearly their historical kinship. He worked closely with them in all their religious and secular endeavors: "In his devotion and good counsel he has always been to us as a father," said one of the JPFA officers on its tenth anniversary.[37]

Among the newcomers were many devoted to the orthodox tradition who considered driving to Sabbath services a violation of its law and spirit. Consequently, within ten years of their arrival they had built five new synagogues in various locations readily accessible even to those in the outlying areas. These were relatively small sanctuaries, offering a sense of kinship in religious devotion and study. Typical were such names as Congregation Shearit Hapleita (Saving Remnant) and Congregation Agudath Achim (Brotherhood). To assure a similar orientation for their children, they founded in 1953 a *yeshivah* (day school) which was attended by 120 to 140 pupils.

Many, however, were soon also active members of the three long-established congregations—Sons of Jacob, Ahavas Achim, and Beth Israel, whose new edifice on Park Avenue was completed in 1958. The latter, with Dr. Martin I. Douglas its spiritual leader, became the largest congregation in Cumberland County: under its roof were brought together many of the diverse elements in the community. A part of the Conservative movement, Beth Israel was guided by the words of Sabato Morais, "We must work to preserve historical Judaism, [even] though for its sake, concessions for which we are unprepared may be demanded."[38] (After many years of devoted service, Rabbi Douglas was succeeded by Rabbi Paul Katz, then by Rabbi Murray J. Kohn.)

Cultural pluralism within the Jewish community persisted, almost inevitably representing the immigrants' multi-faceted origins and ideological persuasions. A few of Vineland's German Jews, complaining of second-class treatment, quit Beth Israel to rejoin their own congregation, Shaare Tikvah. Their new edifice on Iowa and Helen Avenues was dedicated on 3 March 1957 in ceremonies hosted by the community's spiritual leaders: Rabbis Douglas, Efron, and Eisenstein and Cantor Garfinkel, with Judge Levin as master of ceremonies. The program was praised as one befitting an orthodox synagogue and included the traditional "Adaun-Aulom" done in the German-Jewish style. Although they had no formal rabbinic leadership of their own, the gap was filled by congregational members schooled in the Jewish tradition, such as Mr. Loewy, a graduate of the Würzburg Seminary.

Other synagogues serving orthodox congregations of Polish, German, and native Jews opened with little or no fanfare. Along the rural roads of Salem and Cumberland counties, where one least expected it, a traveler in the 1960's would chance upon a red brick, frame, or stone synagogue, an unpretentious meeting house for prayer and study. These supplemented the much older institutions of the Vineland area, such as Alliance's Shearith Israel, where orthodox services were still held regularly.

In Woodbine, too, the all-brick Brotherhood Synagogue (Agudath Achim Anshei Woodbine) still stood firm and almost none the worse for its nearly seven decades. Its high ceiling, walls, traditional ark and small front platform, and elevated central area for Torah reader and *hazzan* were all in excellent repair. Above the long benches for male worshipers were spacious side balconies for the women. The tall arch windows provided ample natural light, though hanging electric bulb fixtures were available also; along the walls memorial plaques served mute testimony to the dedication of those gone by. Here, also, as in other orthodox synagogues, the prayer book was Philip Birnbaum's *Hasiddur Ha-Shalem* and Dr. A. Th. Philips' *Mahzor* translation.

Yet, Woodbine as a community never regained its Jewish character as lack of viable industry, poor soil, population shifts, and secularization wrought their damage. Some of the surviving pioneers were bitter over its decline, blaming, in part, the discontinued support of the New York organizations. A degree of inner divisiveness stemmed from a feeling that the rabbi, Morris Garfinkle of Monsey, New York, was ultra-orthodox and too unbending on such issues as Sabbath observance. At the same time, most who stayed on continued to cherish memories of those who preceded them, immigrant pioneers now at rest in the well-maintained cemetery on Belleplain Road.

The wide spectrum of religious and cultural institutions persisted more successfully in Vineland and its surrounding communities. In the city itself, Beth Israel continued to flourish as a center for Conservative Judaism—modern in outlook yet dedicated to the historic tradition. Sons of Jacob Congregation increasingly embraced a "modern orthodox" approach under the leadership of Rabbi Mordecai V. Efron. An innovation was a late Friday night service with no separate seating for men and women, somewhat like the Conservative practices, with the customary traditional Sabbath morning rites based on the De Sola Pool prayer book. Both synagogues offered daily services also, as well as religious youth activities such as the Tephilin Club. An active Va'ad Ha-Kashruth continued under the direction of Rabbi Simon Eisenstein of Ahavas Achim Congregation.

Continuing also to be a unifying force between old and new traditional elements in the greater Vineland area was the Jewish Day School, Yeshivah Yesod Ha-Torah. On Orchard Road between Oak and Wheat, the ten-room brick building still rose above the countryside where a *yeshivah* might least be expected. Under the leadership of Rabbi Baruch Schwartz, the school offered a combined program of secular as well as religious studies from the primary through eighth grades. Its religious curriculum included Bible and

333

Talmud, preparing graduates for admission to higher *yeshivot* in Philadelphia, Baltimore, and New York. And a lively sense of patriotism was always present: a 1967 Yearbook was dedicated by the boys and girls to the "memory of the three departed astronauts . . . who courageously gave their lives for the advancement of modern science."

The day school's success was one of the achievements cited most proudly in the elaborate Tenth Anniversary Journal of the Jewish Poultry Farmers' Association (1962), which noted that most of the pupils were children of JPFA members. This, too, they affirmed, was a way to plant on the soil of Vineland the Jewish word and folk-spirit. With mutual economic aid and education, Yiddish plays, Yiddish radio programs, and a journal called *Der Neigekumener*, they hoped thus to unite and to give expression to those who had arrived on these shores "with fear in their eyes, bewildered, as if bereft of speech itself." Philip Alampi, New Jersey's secretary of agriculture, referring to their success in overcoming "barriers of language and customs," called them "modern day Pilgrims." More to the point, however, was editor Ben Leuchter's praise that "their desire to become 'Americanized' had not caused them to forget their own noble Jewish culture and heritage."[39]

But while poultry farming offered a basis for cultural and economic adaptation, it proved to be no royal road to wealth. Americanization brought with it also the inexorable facts of rural life in this century. Farm population in the United States declined from 30 percent in 1920 to 15 percent in 1950 and less than 7.5 percent by the early 1960's. The total number of farm units dropped from 5.4 million in 1950 to slightly more than 3 million in 1966. In New Jersey, employment on the farm declined by two-thirds between 1950 and 1968 (see Table, page 357). Farmers' share of the gross national product fell in the years since 1920 from 13 to little more than 3 percent, while the average size of surviving units rose to over 350 acres.[40] To the relatively new poultry industry, the late 1950's brought painful instability resulting from the cumulative effects of mechanization, automation, high labor costs, competition from the South, and even reduced egg consumption from fear of cholesterol in the diet; at the same time, the cost of feed grains was maintained at relatively high levels through government price supports.[41]

After mid-century, the trend toward big business farming resulted in the phenomenon of giant, fully integrated egg producing firms. Where once a family farm would prosper with ten thousand layers, the new integrated producers might have several units of a hundred thousand or more, combining all operations from raising and breeding hens to mechanical processing and packaging of the eggs for direct delivery to supermarkets. Ownership of feed mills reduced costs further, while automatic feeders, egg grading machinery, and other assembly line devices cut down on the need for labor. At the other extreme, specialization enabled large breeders to turn out ever more efficient lines, with the small farmer reduced to raising fowl on a contractual basis: he was no longer independent but merely a link between the hatchery and feed dealer at one end and the big dressing plant-marketing operation at the other. Especially in the face of general over-expansion and declining returns per unit, the family farm could not meet the competition. Moreover, excessive concentration within small areas fostered the spread of poultry disease, and rising land values also meant higher taxes. In the decade following 1956, according to JAS estimates, half the Jewish farmers in New Jersey were forced either to leave their farms or to sell their equipment and remain only as residents.

Those who managed to adapt successfully to the changed conditions were notable exceptions. For example, the respected and devout Sali Mayerfeld, who had arrived in 1938, developed one of the largest poultry and vegetable enterprises in South Jersey. With sons Bernard and Henry, he expanded the family farms to include about one hundred thousand poultry as well as substantial acreage irrigated for tomatoes, beans, and other crops.

Post–World War II late arrivals, however, who lacked the cushion of financial reserves, were especially vulnerable; some had over-extended their credit not only for incubators but also for the household luxuries which seemed so much a part of the American way. Lack of diversification literally left these farmers with all their eggs in one basket at times of sharply falling prices. By the recession year of 1960, more than half of the formerly prosperous homesteads of the Toms River Community of Jewish Farmers had to be abandoned, and conditions in the Vineland area were only a little better. There, even old poultry farmer Jacob Helig, then mayor of Pittsgrove Township, summarized opinion generally when he spoke of hopeless austerity for the small operator. For months and even years, as in 1959, "the average New Jersey poultryman received nothing for his own labor, no return whatsoever on his capital investment, and either failed to meet all of his current expenses or went in debt for a portion of them," stated one official publication.[42] About twelve miles from Vineland, the once-thriving Jewish community of Dorothy with a newly built synagogue in the early 1950's was on the verge of collapse by 1960. Ruinously low egg prices and heavy mortgages drove most of the settlers off the land. New Jersey's egg industry, having risen from nineteenth in 1940 to sixth among the states in 1957, dropped to fourteenth by 1964 (see Table, page 356).

Jewish farmers, as did all farmers, suffered from the economic instability; many drifted from their hard-won homesteads with heavy hearts. The younger generation, as before, went away to college and thence into professional or business ranks in the city. Yet some did stay on. They banded together for mutual aid and a strengthened cooperative movement. Such had been the patterns of America. Within these, the uniqueness of Jewish agrarianism is measured in lives, not in cultivated acres or output alone (although JAS announced in 1966 that Jewish farmers still accounted for three-fourths of New Jersey's egg production).

Were not these recent poultry farms, like the older colonies of New Jersey, mainly an instrument for the adaptation and transition of immigrant groups, a means of defense against their critics? Since the days of Baron de Hirsch, the noblest function of Jewish agrarianism was to save lives, then to enable these survivors to maintain themselves with dignity and self-respect. At the same time, agrarianism formed a bridge on which the disparate Jewish communities from East and West met and mingled, even if the partnership was uneasy and not devoid of mutual recriminations. Among the significant aspects of this mingling was the confluence of philanthropy by the established Jewish community and self-help by the newcomers. Governmental assistance thus played almost no role at all in settling the Jewish refugees. That last great wave after World War II gratefully accepted the aid of HEAS, JAS, the Association for New Americans, and other organizations of their brethren, although soon they formed their own self-help associations.

Above all, the impact of the newcomers was reflected in their focus on *Klal Yisrael*, the age-old ties connecting all Jewry. These immigrants brought with them the last infusion of culture from the wellsprings of Jewish civilization in Eastern Europe. Rabbi Mordecai V. Efron, of Vineland's Sons of Jacob, recognized their role in enriching the American environment with the spiritual traditions of the Jewish past. Perhaps, he speculated, the transplantation of culture might yield in this soil the kind of religious-intellectual wealth which had once created the Talmud.[43]

Inherent in *Klal Yisrael* was devotion to Israel, and the newcomers remained at the forefront of all Zionist activity, as well as the United Jewish Appeal and Bonds, while the Labor Zionists (Poale Zion) among them founded Vineland's own *Hechalutz* farm to train the youth preparing to settle in the old-new land. Now, the pendulum of Jewish life hung between two dynamic and free communities, both relatively young. In the most direct expression of this new relationship, some Vineland families even resolved to settle in Israel. What more logical source for pioneers on the ancient soil was there than these experienced farmers, some of them descended from the Am Olam agrarians of the 1880's? This interest was sparked, partly at least, by a visit of veteran Israeli colonist Lieberman to his Vineland relatives. Lieberman, a member of Nahalal, Israel's oldest cooperative farming village (*moshav*), evoked an eager response among his hosts. Some neighbors knew of the work done by Eliezer Yoffe, a graduate of the Woodbine agricultural school who had gone to Palestine back in 1911. There, he had settled on the land and formulated a blueprint for the smallholders' cooperative village to be first tested at Nahalal: each family would possess its own home and plot of land, though all would cooperate in marketing, purchasing, and use of machinery.

The *moshav* type of organization offered an attractive alternative to both individual land enterprise and the collective *kibbutz*. Its emphasis on agricultural cooperatives was no novelty to Jewish farmers in South Jersey who had participated in such organizations in the early 1900's. Thus, at the end of 1950, twenty Vineland families joined together in a group called *Haikar Haoved* ("The Working Farmer") and prepared to settle in Israel. Almost all were members of the American Labor Zionist movement, some had belonged to *Hechalutz*, the pioneering youth organization; at the dedication of its Vineland training farm, in 1949, the speakers' roster had featured none other than Moshe Sharett, foreign minister of the State of Israel. In 1953, moreover, *Haikar Haoved* was joined by an additional score of families, some recently arrived from Europe.

The actual cooperative village in Israel, first known as *Be'er Tuvia Beth,* then *Orot,* attracted only about twenty American families, of whom half stayed on permanently. Foremost among these was Jacob Brodsky of Alliance. Although their major land purchase was subsidized by the Jewish Agency, each family had to make a substantial investment in its own home and farm. There were also debts to be repaid for the livestock, irrigation piping, and equipment. The village's further development was augmented by the arrival of other families from English-speaking nations, though much work still remained to be done in both economic and cultural spheres.[44]

Altogether, relatively few from the Vineland area had settled in Israel. Nonetheless, its challenge of rescuing and rebuilding lives continued to be a unifying force even beyond the usual fund-raising efforts. "We saw it bringing the whole community together, the synagogue Jews and the non-synagogue Jews, the old-timers, the German refugees, and the Polish refugees," wrote Dr. Arthur Goldhaft, deciding also to have his own look. He took pride in his travels to Israel (three times in the 1950's) as a consultant on agricultural training and research. His contribution, along with others', was reminiscent of the instructional services, grants of equipment, scholarships, and other forms of aid that had been offered for so many years in America by the JAS. Before ceasing publication in 1959 (partly because its Yiddish-language message was no longer deemed necessary) the *Jewish Farmer* also brought to its readers frequent and detailed accounts of their brother farmers in Israel.[45]

The *Orot* experience did not represent as sharp a departure from the development of the South Jersey communities as might at first appear. It was faithful, of course, to the dream of building the Jewish State on the ancestral soil. Yet it was, too, a small offshoot of that great, almost century-old movement of agrarianism as a hopeful means of saving the Jewish people that had seen them settled, often as forlorn refugees, in all manner of wilderness at all corners of the globe—the South Jersey pine barrens and Utah, or Palestine, the Argentine pampas, the Dominican Republic, and Surinam. Everywhere, they had been confronted with the problems of adaptation, assimilation, and the need to build their institutions anew. Everywhere, they had been forced to experiment, to engage in a battle of ideas, even among themselves, to face failure more often than success.

In groups and as individuals they had sought to make their own way, guided partly by their ethnic-religious background and the helpful prodding of their more established brethren. The latter had been justifiably moved by the external threats, but within the uprooted and mobile minority there soon developed in the process of acculturation a need for autonomous leadership and goals. For these immigrants, and certainly for their offspring, the ethnic community with its focus on agrarian self-help had often been a corridor leading to success within the more diversified and affluent urban society.[46] The old dream of a landed peasantry had become hopelessly outdated, but it had served its purpose.

Conclusion: The mystique of migration and survival

*For as the new heavens and the new earth, which
I will make, shall remain before me, saith the Lord,
so shall your seed and your name remain.*

Isaiah 66:22

*Blessed shall you be in the city, and blessed shall you
be in the field.*

Deuteronomy 28:3

11

A nonscientific tradition in Jewish history maintains that for each major instance of oppression threatening survival itself, there has appeared a parallel source of refuge for the harried People of the Book. Over the centuries, migration has been, indeed, an historic phenomenon in the postexilic life of the Jewish people. Thus it was that in a given epoch their centers of culture and achievement flourished in Palestine and Babylon, or Spain and North Africa, Germany, and Eastern Europe. Before nation-states were created, as well as after, Jews thought and acted in universal terms, as citizens of the world carrying with them a culture seemingly unconfined by limits of soil or social environment.

In the half-century from 1880 to 1930, almost three million Jewish immigrants entered the United States, resulting in the largest, most prosperous, and influential Jewish community that has ever existed in the Diaspora. In the New World, they found not only a haven of refuge, but also an unparalleled measure of freedom and opportunity in the economic, cultural, and political spheres. As in the case of other immigrants, however, there was a gap between achievement of equality and the right to strive for it, a never-ending contest, especially for minorities. Though the immigrants were poor, in most cases they were neither peasants nor illiterates. They came to stay in the new land with their families; they carried with them also a collective consciousness, even if it consisted of varying strains, religious and secular. In an age of crisis and decimation in Europe, their shift of population to the New World turned out to be vitally significant, far more so than for other immigrant groups.

The character and development of the American Jewish community defy rigid generalization, just as perhaps the very survival of the Jewish people too remains an enigma. Yet, it is clear that in many ways Jewish immigrants proved entirely compatible with their adopted country. Their emphasis on the individual's responsibility to self, family, and community, their pragmatism, optimism, drive for improvement, and other middle class values, complemented those of an industrial America becoming a middle class society. Most of them stayed on in the cities at a time when America was becoming increasingly urban and sought jobs in industrial trades and commerce as economic conditions required massive labor expansion.

Moreover, the pluralism and diversity within the Jewish community reflected the larger pluralism of America. The traditional patterns of the old East European towns and cities had already begun a process of transformation in the 1880's, but for the immigrants these forms of communal constraint virtually ceased at the first frontier crossing. In an era when the dream of emancipation was coupled with the reality of oppression, the desperate, almost free-for-all search for solutions encompassed a range of economic, religious, and political ideas. Some of the approaches represented internal and ideological conflicts: a revival of national values conflicted with universalist integration, as well as religious tradition with secularism, socialism with the opportunities of market capitalism, utopian idealism with materialism, and urbanization with Tolstoyan agrarianism. At the other end of the migrant's journey, however, the very compatibility, freedom, and attractiveness of the new American environment—not to mention its emphasis on conformity—served to restrict cultural separatism.

With the decline of the old authorities, the weakening of

342

communal cohesiveness, and the lack of unifying leadership, the massive migration from Eastern Europe had threatened to run out of control. To fill the gap, to develop positive objectives, to protect and guide the migrants into utilitarian channels, became the major undertaking of the Jewish businessmen-philanthropists of western Europe and America. The Rothschilds, Baron de Hirsch, Jacob Schiff, and organizations such as the Alliance Israélite represented the requisite authority and possessed the necessary noblesse oblige. Naturally, they defined the objectives in the light of their own economic and social success coupled with their acute awareness of persistent hostility in the gentile world. They were, perhaps, not as sensitive to the cultural gulf separating them from their own coreligionists. Nor were the latter permitted an effective, independent leadership of their own. Nonetheless, the goals of rescue with dignity and eventual self-support created a bridge between the otherwise alienated communities of East and West.

Conflict over goals, means, and control was inevitable. From the onset of the massive Russian migration the Western philanthropists continued to favor settlement on the land, partly as a means of reducing the painful visibility of the "huddled masses" in the cities of England and America. They were convinced that a healthy rural proletariat and perhaps even a landed middle class would prevent the kind of social imbalance among Jews which their detractors pointed out with scorn. Doubtless, also, they were aware of the human misery in the city slums, burdened with shortages of housing, medical facilities and jobs, so they offered instead their model communities in the countryside, notably in New Jersey. To some extent, the East Europeans also yearned for land ownership, a happy state denied to so many of them; some were agrarian ideologues of the Russian Jewish Am Olam movement. Yet, tensions and frustration inevitably arose out of an attempt to mold the communities in a Western capitalist image, to insist on isolated rural settlement when modern trends were in the opposite direction, to practice paternalism in the midst of a relatively open society. Agrarianism without adequate support or incentives could not remain a realistic option. More significantly, the communities of South Jersey turned into a testing ground for the multiplicity of forces within the Jewish and American worlds. In both, there arose comparable inconsistencies: the opposing virtues of individualism and cooperativeness, innovation and conformity, tradition and rationalism, self-help and philanthropy, democracy and élitism.

Another seeming anomaly in the South Jersey communities was the persistent emphasis on Americanizing the immigrants, whether of the 1880's or the 1950's, while in effect encouraging their separation into relatively autonomous communities. A remarkable early example was the all-Jewish town of Woodbine, even more so than Alliance or the other Vineland colonies. It might be concluded that the pains of the melting pot were thus minimized, while providing substantial opportunity for cultural pluralism. Moreover, in such separatism with freedom there was always ample contact with external influences, both Jewish and non-Jewish. Acculturation and religious-ethnic needs could be satisfied alongside each other, although official support was for the former. The overwhelming emphasis on Americanizing contrasted with the minimal aid given to the inherited culture. Yet, independent institutions of all kinds could develop here from pioneering stages to maturity, and each new wave of immigrants was able also to make its own imprint upon the institutional landscape.

As recurring crises stimulated additional humanitarian efforts to absorb the refugees, those who had arrived previously responded to the call of their brethren. The farming region of South Jersey thus became a sort of mainland Ellis Island for the training and adaptation of successive Jewish immigrant groups—first the Russian, then the German, the Polish, and others—in a setting that was close to other ethnic minorities as well as the native American population mix.

The goal of acceptability which the Western philanthropists strove for was substantially achieved. Even the restrictive immigration laws, which they fought so hard to prevent, eventually gave way to more equitable regulations in the 1960's. Ironically, however, it was too late for most of European Jewry; the sources of Jewish immigration were cut off by Nazi genocide and Soviet repression. The Jewish community in America, overwhelmingly of East European origin, could no longer rely on such periodic infusions as in the past to strengthen its cultural institutions. In partial compensation, ties of ethnic affinity and mutual necessity developed with the reborn Israel. There remained, however, the persistent questions of identity and direction yet to be resolved out of the multi-patterned heritage of the American Jewish community.

Appendix

FIRST SETTLERS
OF ALLIANCE, 1882*

Eli and Ethel Abramovitz

Eli and Feigeh Bakerman

Moses and Ethel Bayuk

Abraham and Channah Leah Berman

William and Beckie Cohen

Hersh and Jennie Coltun

Joseph and Rachel Diamond

Jacob and Rebecca Ecoff

Chaim and Bessie Goldman

Nissan and Molka Greenspan

Abraham and Duba Grutsky

Simcha and Sarah Helig

Joseph and Yenta Kleinfield

William and Lizzie Kolman

Zurach and Esther Konowitz

Hersh and Rivka Kutzibow

Isaac and Golda Krassenstein

Labe and Bayla Kuden

Simcha and Pearl Luborsky

Israel Hersh and Esther Levin

Lipa and Toba Levinsky

Berel and Leah Levinson

Labe and Toba Riva Levinson

Henry and Rose Levy

Sholom and Pearl Luberoff

Chaim and Sarah Mennies

Labe and Rachel Moyd

Israel and Feigeh Opachinsky

Lazar and Mindel Perskie

Jacob and Golda Rosenberg

Yonah and Anna Rosenfeld

Jacob and Anna Rosinsky

Joseph and Feigeh Rothman

Joseph and Deborah Rudnick

Solomon and Frima Salonsky

Moshe and Ruchel Serebrenick

Chaim Hersh and Sima Liba Silberstein

Hersh and Rose Silberman

Lazar and Bessie Staver

Eli and Riva Gitel Stavitsky

Moses and Bayla Strasnik

Pesi and Brucha Tolchinsky

Naphtula and Deborah Yoseph

Joseph and Rose Zager

* From *Yoval: A Symposium Upon the First 50 Years of the Jewish Farming Colonies* . . . (Philadelphia, 1932), p. 10.

SURVIVING PIONEERS, ALLIANCE, 1932*

Mr. and Mrs. Sidney Bailey, Sr.

Mrs. Rose Bakerman

Mr. and Mrs. Abraham Brotman

Mr. and Mrs. M. Brotman

Mr. and Mrs. William Cohen

Mr. and Mrs. Aaron Coltun

Mrs. Jennie Coltun

Mr. and Mrs. Jacob Crystal

Raphael Crystal

Nathan Diamond

Mr. and Mrs. Abraham Dittus

Mrs. Fannie Ecoff

Mrs. Anna Eisenberg

Mrs. Tillie Gass

Mr. and Mrs. Joseph Golder

Mr. and Mrs. Jacob Greenblatt

Mrs. M. Greenspan

Mrs. Anna Halbert

Mrs. Rebecca Heisen

Mr. and Mrs. Isaac Helig

Simon Helig

Mr. and Mrs. David Hoffman

Mr. and Mrs. Julius Jacobs

Mr. and Mrs. Samuel Kleinfield

Mrs. Esther Konowitch

Mr. and Mrs. Max Kraft

Mr. and Mrs. Coleman Krassenstein

Mr. and Mrs. Nathan Krassenstein

Mrs. Minnie Levin

Mr. and Mrs. William Levin

Mr. and Mrs. Mendel Levinson

Mrs. Rose Levy

Mr. and Mrs. Michael Lipman

Mrs. Pearl Luberoff

Israel Opachinsky

Mrs. Rachel Oxenberg

J. H. Perskie

Mr. and Mrs. Charles Rice

Mrs. Hannah Rosenfeld

Mr. and Mrs. Samuel J. Rothman

Mrs. Anna Rothman

Aaron Rovinsky

Mr. and Mrs. Benjamin Rudnick

Mr. and Mrs. Harry Rosinsky

Mr. and Mrs. Meyer Salonsky

Mrs. Schrieber

Mr. and Mrs. A. Sclansky

Dr. and Mrs. Charles Silberstein

Mr. and Mrs. Henry Silverman

Mr. and Mrs. Samuel Spiegel

Mr. and Mrs. John Steinberg

Mrs. Dora Steinsnyder

Mrs. A. Tenenbaum

Mr. and Mrs. Joseph Zager

Mr. and Mrs. Nathan Zager

* *Ibid.*, p. 43.

COMPARATIVE STATISTICS, VINELAND'S JEWISH COMMUNITIES AND WOODBINE, 1901*

	ALLIANCE–NORMA	ROSEN-HAYN	CARMEL	GARTON ROAD	TOTAL
Adults	151	64	55	27	297
Children	345	158	133	94	730
Children at home	295	112	97	82	586
Children away from home	50	46	36	12	144
Married children	27	31	15	4	77
Farms	78	33	30	13	154
Acres owned	1,886	964	905	504	4,259
Acres cleared	1,354	611	661	390	3,016
Acres in field and truck crops	720	335	428	181	1,664
Cows	107	67	54	34	262
Horses	65	28	21	14	128
Poultry	7,705	3,580	3,435	2,043	16,763
Value of poultry	$5,711	$2,925	$2,275	$1,833	$12,744
Value of tools and wagons	$5,950	$2,425	$2,330	$2,328	$13,033
Value of farms	$135,250	$53,600	$47,400	$26,000	$289,250

WOODBINE, 1901*

Total population	2500
Percentage of Jewish inhabitants	90%
Jewish farmer families	52
Individuals comprising the 52 families	400
Average acreage of farm	15
Total acres owned by 52 families	785
Acres under cultivation	500
Value of farms	$50,000.00
Acreage of Baron de Hirsch Agricultural School	300
Number of acres under cultivation (School)	121
Average individual income per week	$7.30
Average annual earnings per family	$675.00
Number of cottages	175
Number of cottages owned by the B. de H. F.	14
Average cost of construction per cottage	$1000.00
Estimated total cost of all cottages	$157,450.00
Amount paid in by home-owners	$58,200.00

* These tables are adapted from Philip R. Goldstein, "Social Aspects of the Jewish Colonies of South Jersey" *(Ph.D. diss., University of Pennsylvania, 1921),* Pp. 18, 22.

STORES, 1919*

	Rosen-hayn	Carmel	Garton Road	Norma	Brot-manville–Alliance	Wood-bine	Total
Stores for general merchandise	2	2	0	1	1	3	9
Groceries	8	3	0	2	1	6	20
Butcher shops	3	1	0	1	1	3	9

* Adapted from Goldstein, *op. cit.,* p. 40.

COMPARATIVE STATISTICS, POPULATION, 1919*

	Rosen-hayn	Carmel	Garton Road	Norma	Brot-manville– Alliance	Wood-bine	Total
Jewish families	87	69	30	75	40	280	581
Non-Jewish families	78	20	24	45	21	70	258
Total Jewish Population	388	321	140	375	185	1330	2739
Under 5 years	36	38	16	55	25	156	326
From 6 to 10, inc.	52	57	15	52	20	170	366
From 11 to 14, inc.	39	49	15	45	15	112	275
From 15 to 16, inc.	21	19	8	15	11	64	138
17 and over	250	158	86	208	114	798	1614
Born in the U. S.	190	177	66	195	118	638	1384
Born abroad	198	144	74	180	67	692	1355
Naturalized	146	92	51	131	46	512	978
Declared intentions	13	11	3	6	4	48	85
Aliens	39	41	20	43	17	132	292
Lived in community over 15 years	28	24	10	35	27	95	219
Foster children	3	35	2	0	2	3	45

* Adapted from Goldstein, *op. cit.,* p. 29.

SOCIAL LIFE OF THE COLONIES, 1919*

	Rosen-hayn	Carmel	Garton Road	Norma	Brot-manville– Alliance	Wood-bine	Total
Community Hall?	Yes	Yes	Yes	Yes	Yes	Yes	
Number of organizations in colony	8	5	2	7	2	10	34
Organizations meeting in the community hall	4	3	2	3	1	6	19
Kind of playground	School play-ground only	School play-ground only	School play-ground only	School play-ground only	School play-ground only	School play-ground and public play-ground	

* Adapted from Goldstein, *op. cit.,* pp. 29, 53.

INDUSTRIAL CONDITIONS, 1919*

	Rosen-hayn	Carmel	Garton Road	Norma	Brot-manville–Alliance	Wood-bine	Total
Total number of factories	4	3	0	3	3	8	21
Active factories	2	1	0	2	1	6	12
Nature of factories	Clothing, bricks	Clothing		Clothing	Clothing	Clothing, hats, rubber, machine apparatus	
Employees	41	25	0	53	25	236	380
Dependent poor	0	0	0	0	0	0	0

* Adapted from Goldstein, *op. cit.*, p. 41

RELIGIOUS LIFE, 1919*

	Rosen-hayn	Carmel	Garton Road	Norma	Brot-manville–Alliance	Wood-bine	Total
Synagogues	2	1	1	1	3	2	10
Number attending synagogues regularly	34	24	15	35	42	94	244
Jewish children receiving Hebrew and religious instruction	65	78	24	75	12	66	320
Adults receiving a Jewish education	33	38	15	28	7	—	121

* Adapted from Goldstein, *op. cit.*, p. 50.

PUBLIC SCHOOL EDUCATION, 1919*

	Rosenhayn	Carmel	Garton Road	Norma	Brot-manville–Alliance	Woodbine	Total
Elementary schools built	2	2	1	3	2	1	11
Elementary schools used	1	2	1	3	1	1	9
Rooms in elementary schools in use	6	5	1	6	2	10	30
High schools	—	—	—	—	—	1	1
Rooms in high school	—	—	—	—	—	4	4
Teachers	6	5	1	6	2	14	34
Ungraded schools	—	1	1	—	—	—	2
Artificial lighting of schoolrooms	None	None	None	None	None	Electricity	
Heating of schoolrooms	Steam heat	Stoves in each room	Stove	Stoves in 2 schools and pipe-less heat	Stoves in each room	Steam heat	

Playground?	Yes	Yes	Yes	Yes	Yes	Yes
Type of toilets	Outdoor	Outdoor	Outdoor	Outdoor	Outdoor	Outdoor
Water supply	Pump	Pump	Pump	Pump	Pump	Piped from artesian wells
Number of pupils	261	158	25	175	38	415	1,072
Percentage of Jews	36	72	96	66	79	85	72.3
Number of Jewish pupils attending high school	19	18	7	18	7	55	124
Number of Jewish pupils attending college	2	3	1	2	2	8	18
Frequency of agriculture classes?	Once a week in 7th & 8th grades	Once a week in 7th & 8th grades	None	Once a week in 7th & 8th grades	Once a week in 7th & 8th grades	Once a week in 7th & 8th grades	
Manual training classes (on a regular basis).	None	Yes	None	None	None	Yes	
Domestic science classes?	None	None	None	None	None	Once a week	
School library?	Yes	Yes	No	Yes	No	Yes	

* Adapted from Goldstein, *op. cit.*, pp. 44–45.

ECONOMIC CONDITIONS: THE BASIS, 1919*

	Rosenhayn	Carmel	Garton Road	Norma	Brotmanville–Alliance	Woodbine	Total
What is soil best suited for?	Truck farming	Same	Same	Same	Same	Same	Same and Poultry
What are chief market products?	Strawberries, beans, peas, corn, peppers, tomatoes, sweet potatoes.	Same	Same	Same	Same	Same	
Jewish farm families.	44	46	30	28	29	26	203
Jewish non-farm families.	43	23	—	47	11	254	372
Jewish farmers with own farm & home.	42	41	30	27	26	26	192
Jewish non-farmers with own home.	28	15	—	30	7	122	202
Average acreage of farms.	35	32	50	30	42	20	34-5/6
Average value of farm.	$4500	$3000	$5000	$4000	$4200	$2000	$3771.50

Average value of farm implements.	$400	$300	$500	$300	$450	$400	$391.67
Jewish farms free of mortgage	13	13	4	10	14	7	61
Jewish non-farmers' homes free of mortgage.	20	12	—	17	4	17	70
Average net income of farmers in 1919	$1200	$900	$1500	$1200	$1300	$1000	$1183-2/3
Average wage income of non-farmers in 1919	$1800	$1600	—	$2000	$1500	$2100	$1800
Do many homes have modern improvements?	Many have gas, one home has electric lights and few homes have sanitary plumbing.	Most homes have gas, but have no other modern improvements.	None have gas, one has electric lights and few homes have sanitary plumbing.	Many homes have gas and few have sanitary plumbing.	A few homes have gas, but no other modern improvements.	Most homes have sanitary plumbing, and electric lights, and 10% have heating plants.	

* Adapted from Goldstein, *op. cit.*, p. 35.

NEW JERSEY'S EGG INDUSTRY, 1940–1964*

Year	Average Number of Layers on N.J. Farms[a] (in thousands)	Annual Rate of Lay Per Bird[b]	Total Eggs Produced in N.J.[c] (in millions)	Production as Percentage of Consumption[d] (percentage)	N.J. Rank in U.S.[e]
1940	4,653	173	805	69	19th
1945	6,271	172	1,079	61	19th
1950	11,382	185	2,110	112	10th
1955	12,899	189	2,433	123	6th
1956	13,712	192	2,629	129	6th
1957	13,068	195	2,553	126	6th
1958	12,532	194	2,433	120	7th
1959	12,101	196	2,377	114	9th
1960	10,409	193	2,012	99	11th
1961	10,014	194	1,941	96	11th
1962	9,720	192	1,864	91	12th
1963	9,267	196	1,815	87	13th
1964	8,214	199	1,632	n.a.	14th

SOURCE: The New Jersey Poultry Industry Steering Committee, New Jersey Department of Agriculture.

[a] The number of layers increased more than 100% from 1945 to 1955; it has been decreasing about 4% per year since 1956.

[b] The rate of lay increased sharply between 1945 and 1955. More high-density production and changes in management programs should increase the rate further.

[c] The trend in production follows changes in number of layers and rate.

[d] In 1963 about 87% of the eggs needed by New Jersey consumers were produced on New Jersey farms. The trend is toward an increasing deficit because population is increasing and egg production is decreasing. The New York City–New Jersey–Philadelphia market, with a population of over 20 million, receives about 30% of its egg supply from New Jersey.

[e] Alabama, Arkansas, Georgia, Indiana, Mississippi, North Carolina, Ohio, and Texas have moved ahead of New Jersey in egg production, thus accounting for the drop from 6th position in 1955-57 to 14th position in 1964.

AGRICULTURE, NEW JERSEY, 1950–1968*

Year	Number of Workers on Farms	Cash Receipts from Farm Marketings		
		Total	From Livestock and Products (Poultry, eggs, etc.)	From Crops
	(thousands)	*(thousands of dollars)*		
1950	66	292,430	188,694	103,736
1951	65	348,831	229,976	118,855
1952	61	342,447	215,156	127,291
1953	58	346,187	223,750	122,437
1954	59	314,259	194,605	119,654
1955	58	307,674	200,178	107,496
1956	53	330,372	202,117	128,255
1957	51	314,627	193,991	120,636
1958	51	304,569	191,946	112,623
1959	45	286,467	169,690	116,777
1960	44	295,411	167,222	128,189
1961	42	286,167	156,180	129,987
1962	41	278,001	146,024	131,977
1963	39	271,135	138,904	132,231
1964	37	252,632	123,334	129,298
1965	33	269,520	117,995	151,525
1966	27	273,625	119,938	153,687
1967	23	251,976	101,807	150,169
1968	23	258,100	106,157	151,900

SOURCE: Economic Policy Council and Office of Economic Policy, State of New Jersey, *Second Annual Report* (Trenton, 1969), p. 131.

Notes

Notes to Chapter I: "Give Me Your Tired, Your Poor . . ."

1. Ismar Elbogen, *A Century of Jewish Life*, trans. Moses Hadas (Philadelphia, 1946), pp. 144–145; Howard M. Sachar, *The Course of Modern Jewish History* (Cleveland and New York, 1958), pp. 225–227.

2. Elbogen, *op. cit.*, pp. 21ff., 168ff.; Sachar, *op. cit.*, pp. 68, 113, 237–238.

3. Quoted in Simon Dubnow, *History of the Jews in Russia and Poland*, trans. I. Friedlaender (Philadelphia, 1920), 3 vols., 2:379; also quoted on p. 80 of Mark Vishniak's background essay, "The Russian Jews and the Pogroms of the 1880's" in *Geschichte fun der Yiddisher Arbeter Bavegung in die Fareinikte Shtatn* ("History of the Jewish Labor Movement in the United States"), ed. Elias Tcherikower (New York, 1943), 2 vols., 1:72–87 (Hereafter cited as Tcherikower).

4. Quoted in Sachar, *op. cit.*, p. 243; Solomon Grayzel, *A History of the Jews* (Philadelphia, 1948), pp. 638–639; "Pale of Settlement," *Jewish Encyclopedia*, 9:468; for detailed accounts of pogroms in Kiev as well as Kherson provinces abetted by the authorities see Dubnow, *op. cit.*, pp. 247–258 *passim*.

5. Both quotations on p. 212 of Abraham Menes, "The 'Am-Olam' Movement," which includes a detailed survey useful throughout, in Tcherikower,

358

2:203–208; see also, Mark Wischnitzer, *To Dwell in Safety* (Philadelphia, 1948), pp. 60–61; Arthur Goldhaft, *The Golden Egg* (New York, 1957), pp. 29–30, 42 (memoirs of a second generation New Jersey pioneer whose father belonged to the Am Olam in Kharkov).

6. Menes, *op. cit.*, quotations on pp. 206, 217; for more background on the *Am Olam*, written by a participant, see Moses Freeman, *Fuftsig Yohr Geschichte fun Idishen Lebn in Philadelphia* ("History of Fifty Years of Jewish Life in Philadelphia") pp. 198ff.; Leon Kobrin in a chapter on the Am Olam admires their attempt to lend order to the massive Jewish migration, *Meine Fuftsig Yohr in Amerike* ("My Fifty Years in America"), (New York, 1966), pp. 147–150.

7. Salo W. Baron, *The Russian Jew Under Tsars and Soviets* (New York and London, 1964), p. 96; *The Jewish Encyclopedia*, 9:255. Dubnow, *op. cit.*, 2:72; 3:10, 24–25; also he devotes other chapters to a discussion of Jewish agriculture in Eastern Europe, especially 2:chapters 19–29. He wrote: "Many Russian-Jewish intellectuals dreamed of establishing agricultural and farming colonies in the United States" (2:298).

8. Moses Klein, *Migdal Zophim* ("The Watch Tower"); *The Jewish Problem and Agriculture As Its Solution* (Philadelphia, 1889), p. 15.

9. Quoted in "Jewish Agriculture in America" (Yiddish), *The Day-Jewish Journal*, Jan. 18, 1959; *Yoval: A Symposium Upon the First Fifty Years of the Jewish Farming Colonies of New Jersey*, pp. 12–13. (Hereafter cited as *Yoval*). For other details, see "How the First Jewish Farmers Founded a Colony in New Jersey" (Yiddish), *The Day-Jewish Journal*, Jan. 25, 1959; Goldhaft, *op. cit.*, pp. 32, 42–43, 50–51.

10. Quoted in Menes, *op. cit.*, p. 226 (an entry dated New York, October 17, 1882).

11. *Vineland Evening Journal* (Hereafter *V.E.J.*), for example, March 29, 1880; May 16, 1881; May 19, 1881; June 18, 1881; May 9, 1882. For an account of the government-approved pogroms at Balta and elsewhere see Dubnow, *op. cit.*, 2:299ff.

12. *Ibid.*, January 23, 1882; Dubnow, *op. cit.*, 2:287ff.

13. *V.E.J.*, February 21, 1882.

14. Myer S. Isaacs, *The Old Guard and Other Addresses* (New York, 1906), p. 8; Dubnow, *op. cit.*

15. *Jewish Record* (Philadelphia), February 17, 1882; *Jewish Exponent* (Philadelphia), February 15, 1895. For the *Alliance* in America, including charges that it was assimilationist, see Zosa Szajkowski, "The Alliance Israélite Universelle in the United States, 1860–1949," *Publication of the American Jewish Historical Society* (PAJHS), vol. XXXIX, No. 4 (June, 1950), pp. 389–443.

16. Statement of principles quoted in the *Jewish Record*, April 24, 1885.

17. Bulletin of the *Alliance*, quoted by Tcherikower, "On the Way to America . . ." in Tcherikower, ed., vol. 1, p. 160. This chapter (10) has been useful, along with his chapter 6, "Tsarist Policy and Its Effect on Jewish Emigration," vol. 1, pp. 88–112.

18. *Jewish Record*, October 14, 1881; Dubnow, *op. cit.*, 2:268f., 297.

19. *Hebrew Messenger* quoted in Tcherikower, vol. 1, p. 162; Board of Delegates in the *Jewish Record*, April 24, 1885.

20. Quoted in the *Vineland Evening Journal*, July 9, 1881; the theme is developed capably in studies such as John Higham's *Strangers in the Land* (New Brunswick, N.J., 1955), pp. 98–103, and Oscar Handlin's *Adventure in Freedom: Three Hundred Years of Jewish Life in America* (New York 1954), esp. pp. 191–193.

21. *V.E.J.*, August 1, 1882.

22. *Jewish Record*, April 24, 1885; Goldhaft, *op. cit.*, p. 23; Klein, *op. cit.*, p. 41; Philip R. Goldstein, *Social Aspects of the Jewish Colonies in South Jersey* (New York, 1921), pp. 11, 13 (hereafter cited as *Social Aspects*). On the refugees at Brody, see Dubnow, *op. cit.*, 2:268–269. Tcherikower, vol. 1, p. 170, describes the hardships of the immigrants and complaints by some that they were "treated like cattle," yet warned by the *Alliance* agents against voicing their protests.

23. Obituary, *V.E.J.*, April 22, 1896.

24. *Ibid.*; Klein, *op. cit.*, p. 14; short biography in the *Jewish Exponent*, December 17, 1901; Dubnow, *op. cit.*, 2:415ff; Samuel Joseph, *History of the Baron de Hirsch Fund: The Americanization of the Jewish Immigrant* (Philadelphia, 1935), p. 73.

25. Leonard G. Robinson, *The Agricultural Activities of the Jews in America* (New York, 1912), pp. 48–50, 64; *Social Aspects*, pp. 20–22; Klein, *op. cit.*, p. 63, Goldhaft, *op. cit.*, p. 91; biographical sketch in the *Jewish Exponent*, December 16, 1910; H. L. Sabsovich, "Report on Woodbine for the Roosevelt Commission on Country Life," November 19, 1908, Papers of the Baron de Hirsch Fund (microfilm).

26. Specific figures cited in reports of the President and Treasurer, Hebrew Emigrant Aid Society of the United States, *Jewish Record*, January 12, 1883. See also, *Ibid.*, July 21, 1882; Robinson, *op. cit.*, p. 45; Gilbert Osofsky, "The Hebrew Emigrant Aid Society of the United States (1881–1883)," *Publication of the American Jewish Historical Society*, vol. XLIX (March, 1960), pp. 173–187, offers a succinct summary of this organization's brief life.

27. Quoted from the *Jewish Record*, May 5, 1882.

28. For an effective summary of reactions within the existing American Jewish community, see the section on "The Impact of Russian Immigration," in Moshe Davis, *The Emergence of Conservative Judaism* (Philadelphia, 1963), pp. 261–268.

29. *Ibid.*, Supplementary Documents, pp. 388–392, "Plan of Action Adopted by the Central Executive Committee of The Jewish Alliance of America with Regard to Russian–Jewish Immigration."

30. Myer S. Isaacs, "Baron de Hirsch," address of October 1, 1891, in Isaacs, *op. cit.*, pp. 172, 175.

31. Gustav Pollak, *Michael Heilprin and His Sons* (New York, 1912), pp. 3–7.

32. Heilprin quoted by Pollak, *ibid.*, pp. 205, 208–209.

33. Heilprin, *ibid.*, p. 207.

34. Heilprin, *ibid.*, p. 218.

35. Heilprin, *ibid.*, p. 219.

36. Heilprin, *ibid.*, pp. 208–209; for Heilprin's influence on the leadership of the Baron de Hirsch Fund, see Pollak, *ibid.*, p. 220, and Samuel Joseph, *History of the Baron de Hirsch Fund*, pp. 13–14.

Notes to Chapter II: Jewish Agrarianism in America: Dream and Expediency

1. Anonymous farmer quoted in John D. Hicks, *The Populist Revolt* (Minneapolis, 1931), p. 57.

2. *Ibid.*, pp. 55–56, *passim;* Fred A. Shannon, *The Farmer's Last Frontier* (New York, 1945), pp. 291–295; David A. Shannon, *Twentieth Century America* (Chicago, 1963), p. 10.

3. Thomas C. Cochran and William Miller, *The Age of Enterprise* (rev. ed.) (New York, 1961), pp. 215–225; Harold G. Halcrow, *Agricultural Policy of the United States* (Englewood Cliffs, N.J., 1963), pp. 221–224; Fred A. Shannon, *op. cit.*, pp. 72, 291, 314, 418.

4. John D. Black in Seymour E. Harris, ed., *American Economic History* (New York, 1961), p. 500. For data on destitution among farmers of the Great Plains, see Gilbert C. Fite, *The Farmers' Frontier, 1865–1900* (New York, 1966), pp. 55–74, 126–131, *passim*.

5. Arthur C. Bining, *The Rise of American Economic Life* (New York, 1955), p. 452; Fred A. Shannon, *op. cit.*, p. 294.

6. Black, *op. cit.*, p. 518. See also John D. Black, "Agriculture in the Nation's Economy," *American Economic Review*, vol. 46, no. 1 (1956), pp. 1–33; by the same author, *Introduction to Economics for Agriculture, passim*. For farm population and income statistics to 1900, see Fred A. Shannon, *op. cit.*, pp. 352–353.

7. Harold U. Faulkner, *American Economic History* (New York, 1960), pp. 384–385; Bining and Cochran, *The Rise of American Economic Life* (New York, 1964), p. 404.

8. Kennan later wrote a book on the Tsarist police terror, *Siberia and the Exile System*. He was a cousin of the grandfather of the twentieth century ambassador to the Soviet Union by the same name; cf. John Gunther, *Inside Russia Today* (New York, 1958), p. 121.

9. *Jewish Exponent,* July 5, 1889.

10. *V.E.J.,* July 17, 1885.

11. Charles S. Bernheimer, "Jewish Agricultural Colonies," a paper read before the Hebrew Literary Society of Philadelphia, printed in the *Jewish Exponent,* Dec. 30, 1887.

12. *Ibid.*

13. Moses Klein, open letter in the *Jewish Exponent,* April 19, 1889.

14. "The Lesson Taught," *Jewish Exponent,* July 5, 1889.

15. Riis article cited in the *Jewish Exponent,* Dec. 14, 1900.

16. Report by Rabbi A. R. Levy of Chicago, in the *Jewish Exponent,* Oct. 27, 1899.

17. *Jewish Record,* May 5, 1882; *Jewish Exponent,* May 28, 1897.

18. *Jewish Exponent,* May 29, 1908.

19. Landman in *Jewish Exponent,* Sept. 27, 1912. The mixed feelings of American Jews on the related issues of immigration and rural colonies are analyzed by a scholarly contemporary, Dr. George M. Price, in *Russkie Yevrei v Amerike,* "The Russian Jews in America," sections translated by Leo Shpall in *Publication of the American Jewish Historical Society,* XLVIII, no. 1 (Sept. 1958), pp. 28–62; XLVIII, no. 2 (Dec. 1958), pp. 78–133; Price's "Memoir," also translated by Leo Shpall, in *PAJHS,* XLVII, no. 2 (Dec. 1957), pp. 101–110. For details on the Clarion, Utah colony, see the YIVO collection on Jewish Agriculture in America.

20. *Jewish Exponent,* Aug. 5, 1904; *Social Aspects,* p. 30.

21. John Higham, *op. cit.,* p. 239.

22. See an analysis of Edward A. Ross, Joseph Lee, and other New England authors in Barbara M. Solomon, *Ancestors and Immigrants: A Changing New England Tradition* (New York, 1965), pp. 170ff.

23. *Jewish Exponent,* Nov. 17, 1899.

24. *Ibid.,* March 9, 1906; "Back To The Soil" (editorial), March 23, 1906.

25. Goldhaft, *op. cit.,* 88; David G. Ludins, "Memories of Woodbine: 1891–1894," *Jewish Frontier* (June, 1960), p. 9 (footnote).

26. Judith Solis Cohen, *Milly: A Jewess of Today* (1909), serialized in *Jewish Exponent;* see especially issue of Aug. 27, 1909, dealing with life in the colonies.

27. Bernard A. Palitz, "Jewish Charity *vs.* Jewish Agriculture," *Jewish Exponent,* Oct. 1, 1909.

28. Eugene S. Benjamin, President of the Baron de Hirsch Fund, in Foreword to Katharine Sabsovich, *Adventures in Idealism* (New York, 1922), p. viii. This is a reasonably objective and well-written biography of "H.L." published by his wife in 1922.

29. Katharine Sabsovich, *op. cit.*, chapters 1–4.

30. *Ibid.*, ch. 5. See also the very sympathetic account of Sabsovich by the liberal Russian writer Vladimir Korolenko, who met Sabsovich on a tour of the Jersey colonies, especially his letter of Sept. 12, 1893, "Korolenko in Woodbine: Vladimir Korolenko's Letters About the Jewish Settlement," *Hadoar*, XXXVII (May 31, 1957), pp. 230–235.

31. *Social Aspects*, p. 9; Dubnow, *op. cit., passim;* "Agriculture," *Jewish Encyclopedia*, first edition, 1:252.

32. Gabriel Davidson, *Our Jewish Farmers and The Story of the Jewish Agricultural Society* (New York, 1943), pp. 194–204; Jewish Agricultural Society, Inc., *Report for the Period 1900–1924*, historical introduction, pp. 5–6; Moses Klein, in his *Migdal Zophim* ("The Watch Tower"), published in 1889, looks back nostalgically to these utopian experiments (pp. 38–39) and cites for further reading on Major Noah such works as Henry S. Morais, *Eminent Israelites of the Nineteenth Century* and Isaac Markens, *The Hebrews in America*.

33. Sabsovich, *op. cit.*, chs. 6, 19, *passim;* Davidson, *op. cit.*, pp. 256–259; *Social Aspects*, pp. 22–25; biographical sketch in *Jewish Exponent*, Feb. 4, 1896.

34. H. L. Sabsovich, "Jews in Agriculture," *Jewish Exponent*, Dec. 20, 1907; Sabsovich, *op. cit.*, ch. 14, *passim.*

35. *Jewish Record*, Nov. 4, 1881. An excellent recent monograph on the colonization in Argentina is Morton D. Winsberg's *Coloniá Baron Hirsch: A Jewish Agricultural Colony in Argentina* (Gainesville, 1964).

36. *Jewish Record*, April 21, 1882.

37. *Jewish Record*, Nov. 4, Dec. 9, 1881; April 21, 1882; *Jewish Exponent*, Aug. 2, 1889; Davidson, *op. cit.*, "Pioneers in the Land of Cotton," pp. 204–213.

38. Davidson, *op. cit., passim;* Cincinnati *Enquirer* quoted at length in the *Jewish Record*, Dec. 9, 1881. See "A Colony in Kansas—1882," including Isaac M. Wise's "An Humble Plea for a Russian Colony," from *The American Israelite*, June 30, 1882, a diary of a colonist, and a report by M. H. Marks, all printed in *American Jewish Archives*, vol. XVII, no. 2 (Nov., 1965), pp. 114–139.

39. *Jewish Exponent*, May 26, 1882.

40. For the California colony, see *Jewish Exponent*, especially May 14, May 28, June 11, July 2, July 23, July 30, Sept. 17, 1897; for Utah, and Colorado, *ibid.*, Jan. 11, 1895, Aug. 18, Sept. 1, Sept. 15, 1911; Davidson, *op. cit.*, pp. 234ff., *passim;* for Beersheba, Kansas, see *American*

Jewish Archives, op. cit., as well as YIVO collection, "Jewish Agriculture in America."

41. *V.E.J.,* May 8, 1911; *Jewish Exponent,* Oct. 20, 1911.

42. *Forward* (Yiddish), Feb. 21, Aug. 25, Nov. 20, 1902; Feb. 8, 1903.

43. *Ibid.,* Jan. 31, 1900, Feb. 22, 1901; for other criticisms of the colonizing efforts see issue of May 15, 1903.

44. *Ibid.,* Dec. 29, 1897; Jan. 23, Feb. 6, Feb. 13, 1898; Sept. 13, Nov. 4, 1899; March 25, 1901; Jan. 1, 1903.

45. Davidson, *op. cit.,* p. 230.

46. Jewish Agricultural Society, Inc., *Report . . ., op. cit.,* p. 6; Davidson, *op. cit.,* p. 150.

47. A. Whitney Griswold, *Farming and Democracy* (New Haven, 1952), p. 37; chapter 2 discusses "The Jeffersonian Ideal," with other useful references throughout the book. Elias Boudinot, director of the U.S. Mint in Jefferson's Administration, proposed to set aside 4,000 acres in Pennsylvania for colonization by European Jews as an "asylum of safety" where they might consider the advantages of Christianity. He died in Burlington, N. J., in 1821, leaving a will which specified the use of his estate (if feasible) to "aid and assist in promoting the settlement of a body of Jews . . . so as to supply each family with 50 acres." See Albert M. Friedenberg, "The Jews of New Jersey from the Earliest Times to 1850," *Publication of the American Jewish Historical Society* (No. 17, 1909), and a copy of the Boudinot will, quoted by Joshua O. Haberman, "The Jews in New Jersey: A Historical Sketch," Ms, New Jersey Collection, Rutgers, The State University, pp. 4–5, Appendix II.

48. Robinson, *op. cit.,* p. 45; *Social Aspects,* p. 14; Louis Mounier, "A Descriptive Account of the South Jersey Colonies Situated Near Vineland," January 22, 1908.

49. John T. Cunningham, *This is New Jersey* (New Brunswick, 1953), pp. 161–164; Goldhaft, *op. cit.,* p. 20; L. Mounier, "Founding of Vineland," Jan. 22, 1908.

50. *Vineland Weekly,* Sept. 23, 1865.

51. *Newark Courier* and the *State Gazette,* quoted *ibid.,* June 23, 1866.

52. *Vineland Daily Journal,* Aug. 9, 1878, Sept. 22, 1880; Goldhaft, *op. cit.,* p. 20.

53. *Vineland Daily Journal,* April 12, 1878; July 16, 1880; Nov. 19, 1886.

54. "Traveler" quoted *ibid.,* Nov. 24, 1886; copy of "Vineland of the Azusa," advertisement supplied by Dr. Max Vorspan, Los Angeles.

55. *Ibid.,* July 16, 1880; July 30, 1880; Aug. 19, 1885.

56. *Jewish Record,* July 7, 1882 and Jan. 12, 1883; *V.E.J.,* Sept. 22, 1880, Nov. 21, 1882, Nov. 11, 1890; *Yoval,* p. 13. Contemporary observa-

tion in Harshberger's *Geography,* quoted by Arthur D. Pierce, *Iron in the Pines: The Story of New Jersey's Ghost Towns and Bog Iron* (New Brunswick, 1957), p. 46.

57. *Jewish Record,* July 7, 1882, Jan. 12, 1883; *V.E.J.,* Jan. 19, 1883.

58. *Vineland Daily Journal,* July 24, 1878.

59. Charles K. Landis, letter published in the *V.E.J.,* Nov. 11, 1890.

60. *Ibid.*

61. Moses Klein, *op. cit.,* p. 41.

62. *Jewish Record,* July 7, 1882; *Yoval,* p. 13; *Social Aspects,* p. 14.

63. *Jewish Record,* July 7, 1882.

64. *V.E.J.,* May 12, 1882; *Jewish Record,* July 7, 14, 1882. A. C. Sternberger to the *Jewish Messenger,* Vol. L (July 21, 1882), p. 3.

65. Sabato Morais to the editor, *Jewish Record,* July 14, 1882.

66. *Jewish Record,* Dec. 9, 1881.

67. Louis Mounier, *op. cit.,* Jan. 22, 1908.

68. *Ibid; Yoval,* pp. 34–35; Klein, *op. cit.,* pp. 41–43, 76.

69. *Jewish Record,* Aug. 4, 1882; Feb. 13, 1883.

70. *Ibid.,* Jan. 19, 1883.

71. *Ibid.,* Feb. 13, 1883.

72. Gertrude Serata, "Jewish Agricultural Settlement in the U.S. with Special Reference to the Alliance, N.J., Colony" (unpublished paper by a native of Alliance), Jan. 1961; *Social Aspects,* pp. 14, 38; Goldhaft, *op. cit.,* p. 53.

73. *V.E.J.,* April 19, 28, May 25, 27, June 15, Oct. 4, 1882; Oct. 4, 1883, Sept. 25, 28, 1886; *Yoval,* p. 14; Robinson, *op. cit.,* p. 46; *Social Aspects,* p. 14.

74. *Jewish Record,* August 4, 1882.

75. "New Jerusalem," *V.E.J.,* June 22, 1882, Aug. 4, 1882; *Jewish Record,* Aug. 4, 1882.

76. Goldhaft, *op. cit.,* p. 36.

77. *Ibid.,* p. 37.

78. *V.E.J.,* July 31, Oct. 20, 1882.

79. *V.E.J.,* June 17, 1880; May 15, 1883; Mounier, *op. cit.,* Jan. 22, 1908.

80. *Mercury* quoted in the *Jewish Exponent,* Nov. 1, 1889.

81. *Jewish Exponent,* Jan. 22, 1909.

82. Klein, *op. cit.,* pp. 81–83; Mounier, *op. cit.,* Jan. 22, 1908; *Jewish Exponent,* Nov. 1, 1889.

83. Philip R. Goldstein, *Centers in My Life,* pp. 26–27.

84. Mounier, *op. cit.*, Jan. 22, 1908; Klein, *op. cit.*, *ibid.*; Robinson, *op. cit.*, pp. 48–49; *Jewish Exponent*, April 19, Nov. 1, 1889.

85. *Hamelitz*, vol. XIX (no. 25), translation by Dr. Joel Geffen, The Jewish Theological Seminary of America.

86. *The Day-Jewish Journal*, Jan. 25, 1969; *Jewish Exponent*, Aug. 9, 1895, May 19, 1899, June 25, 1909; Goldhaft, *op. cit.*, pp. 50–51; *75th Anniversary and Rededication*, 1908–1958, *of Congregation Beth Hillel of Carmel, N.J.* (Journal), Aug. 31, 1958.

87. For life in Carmel, *75th Anniversary . . . op. cit.;* also interviews with Harry and Rose Sobelman, I. Harry Levin, and other native sons.

88. *V.E.J.*, Feb. 11, April 11, 1901, May 22, 1902, Jan. 29, 1903; Robinson, *op. cit.*, pp. 65–66; *Yoval*, p. 16; *Social Aspects*, p. 15, *passim;* Mounier, *op. cit.*, Jan. 22, 1908.

89. Mounier, *ibid.*

90. *Ibid.;* Robinson, *op. cit.*, p. 66.

91. *V.E.J.*, Feb. 18, 1907.

92. *Ibid.*, Feb. 28, June 25, 1891, May 16, 1892; *Jewish Exponent*, Aug. 4, 1899.

93. *V.E.J.*, Dec. 21, 23, 1882; *Jewish Record*, Aug. 10, 1883.

94. *V.E.J.*, Aug. 23, 1892.

95. *Jewish Exponent*, Dec. 20, 1895, Jan. 3, 1896.

96. Myer S. Isaacs, *op. cit.*, p. 182.

97. *Ibid.*, p. 178.

98. Baron de Hirsch, in *Forum* (August, 1891), quoted in *Social Aspects*, p. 20.

99. *Jewish Exponent*, Dec. 4, 1896.

100. *Ibid.;* Goldhaft, *op. cit.*, p. 90; *Social Aspects*, p. 20–21; *V.E.J.*, Sept. 16, 1891; *Elmer Times,* Oct. 31, 1891.

101. Report prepared by Bernard Palitz, for the Roosevelt Commission on Country Life, forwarded by H. L. Sabsovich, Nov. 19, 1908, Baron de Hirsch Fund Papers (on microfilm).

102. David G. Ludins, "Memories of Woodbine: 1891–1894," *Jewish Frontier* (June, 1960), pp. 8, 10.

103. *Ibid.;* see also Robinson, *op. cit.*, p. 69; *Social Aspects*, p. 21.

104. Report of the Baron de Hirsch Fund, *Jewish Exponent*, Feb. 10, 1899.

105. *Jewish Exponent*, June 9, 1899; *V.E.J.*, Nov. 7, 1905; Robinson, *op. cit.*, pp. 69–70; *Social Aspects*, p. 22.

106. *Jewish Exponent*, *ibid.;* Goldhaft, *op. cit.*, p. 230.

Notes to Chapter III: Greenhorn Farmers and Self-Help Philanthropy

1. Baron de Hirsch quotation from his article, "My Views on Philanthropy," *North American Review* (July, 1891), in Herman J. Levine and Benjamin Miller, *The American Jewish Farmer in Changing Times* (Report of the Jewish Agricultural Society, Inc., 1966), p. 2.

2. Letter of Russian writer Vladimir Korolenko to his wife, September 12, 1893, trans. in *Hadoar*, vol. XXXVII, no. 28 (May 31, 1957), pp. 230–235.

3. The legend of the Jersey Devil, or the Leeds Devil, still persists. See Henry C. Beck, *The Roads of Home* (New Brunswick, 1951), p. 232; "Folk Lore and Legends of Our Country," illustrated map, Esso Standard Oil Co., 1960.

4. David G. Ludins, "Memories of Woodbine: 1891–1894," *op. cit.*, p. 10; *Social Aspects*, pp. 36–38; Jacob G. Lipman, "The South Jersey Colonies," in *The Russian Jew in the United States*, Charles S. Bernheimer, ed. (Philadelphia, 1905), p. 378.

5. *Yoval*, p. 31.

6. *V.E.J.*, Feb. 9, 14, 1885, June 1, 1887; *Jewish Exponent*, Sept. 26, 1888.

7. *V.E.J.*, June 6, 15, 1887; *Elmer Times*, Nov. 27, 1886. On soil conditions and farming practices, correspondence with Harry Rothman, long-time Agricultural Agent, Cumberland County (Bridgeton, N.J.).

8. John T. Cunningham, *This Is New Jersey* (New Brunswick, 1953), pp. 161–162; Herbert Lee Ellis, *New Jersey, The State and Its Government* (New York, 1967), pp. 54–55; *Vineland Evening Journal*, June 21, 1890, April 6, 1908.

9. *V.E.J.*, Jan. 11, 1894; *Jewish Exponent*, July 23, 1897.

10. *V.E.J.*, Oct. 18, 1887, May 25, 1893; *Jewish Exponent*, Sept. 24, 1897, Oct. 20, 1899.

11. *Jewish Exponent*, Sept. 26, 1888. The first poultry incubator, demonstrated in Newark in 1879, led to fears that chickens thus hatched would always smell of kerosene. John T. Cunningham, *New Jersey, America's Main Road* (New York, 1966), p. 211.

12. *V.E.J.*, July 25, 1905, Aug. 17, Nov. 12, Dec. 10, 1906, March 12, 1907, July 9, 29, 1910; *Jewish Exponent*, June 25, 1909.

13. William Stainsby, "The Jewish Colonies of South Jersey" (1901), *passim* (New Jersey division, Newark Public Library); *Jewish Exponent*, May 17, 1901.

14. *V.E.J.*, July 1, 1916; Sept. 22, Oct. 14, 1908; Sept. 12, 16, Nov. 28, 1916; *Jewish Exponent*, Feb. 25, 1910.

15. *V.E.J.*, Aug. 27, 1906, April 23, 1910, June 24, 1915; Davidson, *op. cit.*, pp. 181–182, *passim;* Cunningham, *New Jersey, America's Main Road*, p. 232.

16. *V.E.J.*, Feb. 11, April 11, 1901; May 22, July 7, Nov. 5, 1902; Jan. 29, 1903; Dec. 28, 1904; Jan. 6, Feb. 27, 1905; March 23, Aug. 3, Nov. 3, 1905; Feb. 9, 28, 1906; Oct. 9, 1907; *Jewish Exponent*, Feb. 15, 1901, Feb. 16, 1906; Goldhaft, *op. cit.*, p. 46.

17. *V.E.J.*, Sept. 23, 1915, May 25, 1916; Louis Mounier, "Retrospect . . ."; Goldstein, *Social Aspects . . .*, p. 15. Charles F. Seabrook expanded the family farm to 2,000 acres by 1920 and later developed quick-frozen vegetables sold on a mass distribution basis under the Birdseye label.

18. *V.E.J.*, Aug. 12, 1919. Raymond Lipman later acquired ownership of the Allivine Farm, still operated by his son Aaron in the early 1960's.

19. *Social Aspects*, pp. 18, 22, 29–30.

20. *Jewish Record*, Jan. 22, 1886; Morton D. Winsberg, *Colonia Baron Hirsch . . .*, p. 34.

21. *V.E.J.*, Jan 31, Feb. 1, 6, 1883; Aug. 18, 1885, "Russian Jews have all left Estellevile"; *Jewish Record*, Feb. 23, 1883, March 27, 1885; Report by Cyrus Adler in *Hamelitz*, Oct. 28, 1884, trans. by Dr. Joel Geffen; also, Cyrus Adler's analysis for the Philadelphia *Ledger*, quoted at length in the *American Hebrew*, vol. XIX, no. 13 (Aug. 8, 1884), p. 200.

22. *Jewish Record*, March 27, 1885, Feb. 26, 1886.

23. Reports from Bayuk, *Jewish Exponent*, Sept. 2, 9, 1887; Goldstein, *Centers*, p. 42.

24. Visitors to Kolman home described in Louis Mounier "A Discovery" (unpublished ms.).

25. Letter from Bayuk, *Jewish Exponent*, Sept. 2, 1887; *ibid.*, Sept. 26, 1888.

26. *V.E.J.*, March 4, 12, April 15, 1909.

27. *Jewish Record*, Feb. 13, 1883; Dec. 5, 26, 1884.

28. *Ibid.*, Jan 9, 16, 23, 30, Feb. 13, 20, 27, March 13, 20, 27, April 3, 1885.

29. *Ibid.*, Oct. 23, 1885.

30. *Ibid.*, March 12, 19, April 2, 1886. See also, *American Israelite*, Jan. 22, 1886.

31. *Jewish Exponent*, Aug. 31, 1888.

32. *V.E.J.*, June 22, July 6, 1883, Nov. 13, 1885; *Social Aspects*, p. 11.

33. *V.E.J.*, Sept. 15, 1888.

34. *Ibid; Yoval*, p. 14.

35. *Jewish Record,* Nov. 13, 1885; Sept. 26, 1888.

36. *Jewish Exponent,* Oct. 19, 1888; July 5, 1889; Jan. 11, 1895; Aug. 13, 1897; March 25, 1904.

37. Anna I. Seldes, "The Condition of Alliance," *ibid.,* Jan. 25, 1895. Mrs. Seldes was married to farmer-postmaster Ceigi Seldes; their sons, Gilbert, literary critic and later Dean of the School of Communications, University of Pennsylvania, and George, also eminent as a journalist.

38. *V.E.J.,* April 17, 1897; Moses Klein, *Jewish Exponent,* Aug. 13, 1897.

39. Klein, *ibid.;* Louis Levy, *ibid.,* Dec. 3, 1897.

40. Klein, *ibid.;* Klein, *Migdal Zophim* ("The Watch Tower"), p. 65; *V.E.J.,* April 20, 1889. On continuing financial problems, including new mortgage obligations, see the *American Hebrew,* vol. 61, no. 18 (Sept. 3, 1897), pp. 518–519.

41. Louis Miller, *Die Arbeiter Zeitung,* Aug. 7, 14, 1891 (Yivo Institute for Jewish Research); Miller reports in the *American Hebrew,* vol. 48, no. 7 (Sept. 18, 1891), p. 141.

42. *V.E.J.,* Aug. 20, 1889.

43. *The Jewish Farmer,* July, Aug. 1908.

44. "Korolenko in Woodbine," *Hadoar,* vol. XXXVII, no. 28 (May 31, 1957), p. 235.

45. Pincus in *Jewish Exponent,* Feb. 19, 1909; Abraham Cahan essay in *The Russian Jew in the United States,* Charles S. Bernheimer, ed., (Philadelphia, 1905), p. 37.

46. Goldhaft, *op. cit.,* p. 232.

47. *Social Aspects,* pp. 18, 22, 29; Theodore Levin to Bernard A. Palitz, Sept. 5, 1915, Baron de Hirsch Fund Papers.

48. *Jewish Record,* Dec. 15, 1882 (letter from Cincinnati group, plus editorial); *American Hebrew,* vol. 23, no. 11 (July 24, 1895), p. 165.

49. Quoted in Goldstein, *Centers,* p. 27; Davidson, *op. cit.,* p. 10; Robinson, *op. cit.,* p. 50. Baron de Hirsch's plans were developed with the assistance of Dr. Wilhelm Lowenthal. See Bernard D. Ansel, *American Jewish Historical Quarterly,* vol. LIV, no. 2 (December, 1964), p. 213.

50. *Jewish Exponent,* July 15, 1910; Robinson, *op. cit.,* p. 52; Hicks, Mowry and Burke, *The American Nation* (Boston, 1968), pp. 372–373.

51. Goldstein, *Centers,* p. 26; Robinson, *op. cit.,* pp. 55–56; *Jewish Exponent,* July 15, 1910; July 28, 1911.

52. *V.E.J.,* July 22, 1889; *Jewish Exponent,* Jan. 10, 1909; Dec. 9, 1910.

53. Davidson, *op. cit.,* pp. 42–43; *Jewish Exponent,* Sept. 26, 1888; "The Jewish City" (Woodbine), lecture by Boris D. Bogen, instructor at the Baron de Hirsch Agricultural School, *Forward,* Aug. 19, 1903. As early as 1883, produce from the Vineland colonies was exhibited in New York's

Temple Emanuel and other synagogues, *American Hebrew,* vol. 16 (Oct. 5, 1883), p. 85.

54. "Farm Exchange Proposed," *Jewish Exponent,* July 15, 1910.

55. *Ibid.,* Dec. 9, 1910, Feb. 17, 24, 1911, March 15, Nov. 22, 29, 1912.

56. *Jewish Farmer,* Feb. 1913, p. 40; Aug. 1914, p. 209; June 1915, p. 154; Oct. 1915, p. 238; Jan. 1917, p. 212; June 1918, p. 167.

57. *Ibid.,* Aug. 1918, p. 212; June 1918, p. 167.

58. *Ibid.,* Feb. 1909, p. 27; June 1916, p. 158; Aug. 1918, p. 212.

59. *Ibid.,* Feb. 1912, p. 39.

60. *Ibid.,* Jan. 1912, p. 10.

61. *Ibid.,* Jan. 1914, pp. 13, 17; Feb. 1914, p. 50; Aug. 1914, pp. 209–210; Jan. 1915, p. 7.

62. *Ibid.,* Jan. 1918, p. 6; April 1919, pp. 99, 103.

63. "Jewish Colonization Conference of 1914" (Report), in Baron de Hirsch Fund Papers (on microfilm), henceforth cited as B.D.H.

Notes to Chapter IV: The Thorny Paths of "Americanization": Rise and Fall of Agrarian Utopia

1. John E. Bebout and Roland J. Grele, *Where Cities Meet: The Urbanization of New Jersey,* p. 12; see also pp. 42, 45, 80.

2. Quoted in Philip Gleason's incisive analysis of "The Melting Pot: Symbol of Fusion or Confusion?" *American Quarterly,* vol. XVI, no. 1 (Spring, 1964), p. 26.

3. *Vineland Daily Journal,* Feb. 25, June 5, 7, 1876, Aug. 9, 20, 1878; Charles K. Landis, "Italian Immigration," *V.E.J.,* July 24, 1890; see also, *ibid.,* June 10, 21, 1897 on Italians and Germans.

4. *Ibid.,* July 30, 1900, Oct. 23, 27, 1913.

5. *Jewish Record,* March 3, 1882, Sept. 26, 1888. Cyrus Adler's reports to the Philadelphia *Ledger,* quoted in the *American Hebrew,* vol. XX (Aug. 8, 1884), p. 200.

6. *Jewish Exponent,* Oct. 26, 1888, Jan. 31, 1890.

7. *New York Herald,* Feb. 11, 1889; London *Jewish World,* Feb. 15, 1889; *Jewish Exponent,* Feb. 15, 1889; *V.E.J.,* Feb. 16, 1889.

8. *Jewish Exponent,* Feb. 15, 22, 1889; Baron de Hirsch, "My Views on Philanthropy" (Appendix A), "Deed of Trust of Baron de Hirsch Fund" (Appendix B), in Samuel Joseph, *op. cit.,* pp. 275–282; see also *ibid.,* pp. 31, 254–255, *passim.*

9. The *American Israelite* quoted in *American Jewish Archives,* vol. XVII, no. 2 (Nov. 1965), p. 115; Simon Wolf, *ibid.,* p. 114. See also, Zosa

Szajkowski, "The Attitude of American Jews to East European Jewish Immigration, 1881–1883," *PAJHS*, vol. XL (March 1951), pp. 221–280.

10. Esther Panitz, "In Defense of the Jewish Immigrant (1891–1924)," *American Jewish Historical Quarterly*, vol. LV, no. 1 (Sept., 1965), p. 72. The article contains a useful summary of eventually futile attempts to halt the tide of restrictionism, pp. 57–97. See also Joseph, *op. cit.*, pp. 17–18, 24–25, 209–210, *passim*.

11. Joseph, *op. cit.*, pp. 31, 29, "Deed of Trust . . .," pp. 279–280.

12. "Report of the Trustees of the Baron de Hirsch Fund, 1893," B.D.H.

13. The United Hebrew Charities of New York alone sent back to Europe over 1,000 immigrants in each year from 1887 through 1890: *Annual Reports . . . of the United Hebrew Charities . . . of New York*, quoted by Zosa Szajkowski, "The Attitude of American Jews to East European Jewish Immigration, 1881–1893," *PAJHS*, vol. XL, Part 3 (March, 1951), p. 243. Many were returned by Federal immigration officials enforcing statutes against the admission of paupers or assisted immigrants; see Panitz, *op. cit.*, pp. 58ff.

14. *New York Sun* article, May 3, 1891, in B.D.H.

15. Hebrew Emigrant Aid Society (H.E.A.S.) quoted in Szajkowski, *op. cit.*, pp. 225–226.

16. *New York World*, June 5, 1882, quoted *ibid.*, p. 231.

17. Zosa Szajkowski, "The Alliance Israelite Universelle in the United States, 1860–1949," *PAJHS*, vol. XXXIX, no. 4 (June, 1950), p. 418.

18. Szajkowski, "The Attitude of American Jews . . .," *op. cit.*, pp. 228, 232; see also, "Early Relations: Germans and East Europeans," ch. 5 of Stuart E. Rosenberg, *The Jewish Community in Rochester*, pp. 63–69; Moses Rischin, *The Promised City: New York's Jews*, 1870–1914 (Cambridge, Mass., 1962), pp. 95–111, *passim*.

19. Szajkowski, *op. cit.*, pp. 234–235.

20. *New York Times*, April 27, 1891, Isaacs to Schiff, March 24, 1891; *The Philadelphia Press*, Feb. 18, 1892, B.D.H.

21. Interviews with A. S. Solomons, General Agent, Baron de Hirsch Fund, *New York Times*, April 27, 1891; *New York Herald*, May 27, 1891, B.D.H.

22. *New York Herald*, Dec. 21, 1891, B.D.H.

23. Elias Tcherikower, "Jewish Immigrants to the United States, 1881–1900." *Yivo Annual of Jewish Social Science*, vol. VI, 1951, p. 167. On the failure of the Argentine colonies, see Winsberg's *Coloniá Baron Hirsch*.

24. Quoted in Tcherikower, *op. cit.*, p. 168.

25. Quoted *ibid.*, pp. 169–170.

26. Report of the Trustees of the Baron de Hirsch Fund, 1893, p. 2 (Schiff, Sulzberger, Seligman, Isaacs, Goldman, Hackenburg, James H. Hoffman, Oscar S. Straus, Henry Rice), B.D.H.

27. Sanford Ragins, "The Image of America in Two East European Hebrew Periodicals," *American Jewish Archives,* vol. XVII, no. 2 (Nov. 1965), pp. 143–145, 148.

28. *Ibid.,* pp. 146–147, 151.

29. Szajkowski, *op. cit.,* Appendix B, pp. 265, 270.

30. Ragins, *op. cit.,* p. 145.

31. *Ibid.,* pp. 152–158; the Trenton quote is from p. 161.

32. George M. Price (Leo Shpall trans.), "The Russian Jews in America," *PAJHS,* vol. XLVIII, no. 1 (Sept. 1958), p. 34.

33. For tables based on statistical reports of the United Hebrew Charities, see Price, *op. cit.,* pp. 44–45.

34. George M. Price, *PAJHS,* vol. XLVIII, no. 2 (Dec. 1958), p. 109 (second installment).

35. *Ibid.,* pp. 116–117.

36. *Ibid.,* p. 121.

37. Rosenthal to Hebrew Emigrant Aid Society (H.E.A.S.), May 24, 1882, letter printed in Szajkowski, *op. cit.,* pp. 246–247.

38. Isaacs to Schiff, March 24, 1891, B.D.H.

39. *Ibid.; New York Times,* April 27, 1891; Sabsovich and Rosenthal to Trustees (Agricultural Committee), June 19, 1891, *ibid.* See also, Joseph, *op. cit.,* pp. 48ff.

40. *New York Evening World,* Nov. 29, 1891, B.D.H.

41. Goldman to Trustees, Feb. 29, 1892, *ibid.*

42. *Ibid.*

43. Joseph, *op. cit.,* pp. 50–53.

44. *New York Press,* April 2, 1893, quoted *ibid.,* pp. 53–54.

45. Sabsovich to Dr. Paul Kaplan, May 30, 1892, B.D.H.

46. Henry to "Bayuk and Others" in Alliance, Dec. 31, 1884; "Report of the Residents of Alliance Colony to its Sponsors, 1885 . . . Beloved: . . ." in Appendices E & F, Szajkowski, *op. cit.,* pp. 275–276, 279.

47. Sabsovich to Kaplan, May 30, 1892; *New York World,* Nov. 20, 1892, B.D.H.

48. Isaacs to Schiff, March 24, 1891; petition by "Agudoth Ovde Adomo Ansche Russia," to Dr. M. J. Burstein, May 10, 1890, *ibid.*

49. Public Notice by Woodbine Land and Improvement Company, Sept. 20, 1892, *ibid.*

50. Telegrams: Farmers to Seligman, March 13, 1893; to Reichow, March 13, 1893; to Weber and Solomons, April 4, 1893; Sabsovich to Goldman, March (?) 1893, all in B.D.H.

51. David G. Ludins, *op. cit.*, p. 12.

52. Sabsovich to Goldman, March 15, 1893, *ibid.*

53. Katharine Sabsovich, *op. cit.*, p. 83; text of Sabsovich's reply to the job offer is on pp. 84–85.

54. Sabsovich to Reichow, April 21, 1893, B.D.H.

55. Ludins, *op. cit.*, pp. 10–11.

56. *New York World*, Nov. 20, 1892, B.D.H.

57. *New York World*, Nov. 20, 1892; Goldman to Trustees, Nov. 29, 1892, *ibid.*

58. Katharine Sabsovich, *op. cit.*, pp. 77–78; a somewhat different version of the "ugly incident" appears in Ludins, *op. cit.*, p. 11.

59. K. Sabsovich, *op. cit.*, pp. 75, *passim;* Ludins, *op. cit.*, p. 13.

60. Joseph W. Pincus, "The Jewish Farmers' Best Friend," in Sabsovich, *op. cit.*, p. 195; Goldman, Hackenburg and Weber, "Present State of Affairs at Woodbine," May 6, 1893, B.D.H.

61. Report of the Trustees of the Baron de Hirsch Fund, 1893, B.D.H.

62. "Present State of Affairs at Woodbine," *ibid.*

63. *Ibid.; New York Press*, April 2, 1893, quoted in Joseph, *op. cit.*, p. 54.

64. Ludins, *op. cit.*, pp. 13–14.

65. Letter to Rosenthal (Nachman, *not* Herman), Rosenfeld, Weinstein, Kimel, Sigel, Schore, Hornstein, and Krimsky; signed by Goldman, Seligman, Schiff, Isaacs, May 16, 1893, B.D.H.

66. Sabsovich to Goldman, April 29, 30, 1893, *ibid.*

67. Sabsovich to Goldman, June 14, 1893, *ibid.*

68. Sabsovich to Goldman, June 22, 1893; for the continuing problem of unoccupied farms, see Sabsovich to Weber, Oct. 3, 1893, *ibid.*

69. Isaacs to Schiff, March 24, 1891; *New York Times*, May 8, 1891.

70. "Present State of Affairs at Woodbine," *ibid.*

71. Reichow, Annual Report (1895) of the General Agent, Jan. 20, 1896, *ibid.* See also Reichow to Isaacs, Dec. 15, 1894, *ibid.*

72. Joseph, *op. cit.*, pp. 109–111, *passim;* K. Sabsovich, *op. cit.*, pp. 99–100.

73. Report of the Trustees of the Baron de Hirsch Fund (1893), pp. 6–7, B.D.H.

74. Sabsovich letters in K. Sabsovich, *op. cit.*, pp. 85–87; see also, Joseph, *op. cit.*, pp. 58–61.

75. *Hoard's Dairyman* (1902), quoted in K. Sabsovich, *op. cit.*, pp. 120–121. See all of ch. 15, "A Pioneer of Agricultural Schools," *ibid.*, as well as pp. 58–61, 69–88 in Joseph, *op cit.*, for details of the school's development.

76. Goldhaft, *op. cit.*, pp. 87, 89.

77. *Ibid.*, pp. 224–226.

78. *Jewish Exponent*, Nov. 27, 1900.

79. *Ibid.*, Nov. 30, 1900.

80. Report by Sabsovich, *ibid.*, Feb. 10, 1899. For additional background, *ibid.*, Oct. 11, 18, 1895, Oct. 9, 1896, Dec. 4, 1896; Sabsovich to Solomons, Aug. 31, 1894, B.D.H. "Woodbine Products Win Awards at Cape May County Fair," *American Hebrew*, vol. 61, no. 21 (Sept. 24, 1897), p. 617.

81. Quoted in Davidson, *op. cit.*, p. 258; see also, *Jewish Exponent*, Nov. 27, 1900.

82. *Ibid.*, Oct. 14, 21, 1904.

83. *Ibid.*, Feb. 10, March 24, 1899.

84. *Ibid.*, Oct. 18, 1895; *V.E.J.*, Nov. 28, 1898; *Trenton Gazette*, April 29, 1904.

85. *Jewish Exponent*, Sept. 2, 1898, March 31, May 19, 1899.

86. Schechter address quoted partly *ibid.*, April 1, 1904.

87. *Ibid.*, March 10, 1899; K. Sabsovich, *op. cit.*, pp. 79–81, *passim*.

88. Joseph, *op. cit.*, p. 79; *Jewish Exponent*, April 14, 1911; Woodbine Hebrew School to The Committee of the Baron de Hirsch Fund, Nov. 23, 1908, B.D.H.; Claude Montefiore, "State of Religion in Woodbine," Sept. 6, 1910, *ibid.*

89. Joseph, *op. cit.*, pp. 70, 73, *et passim*.

90. Boris D. Bogen, *Born A Jew*, pp. 69–70, quoted in Joseph, *op. cit.*, pp. 71–72. Later, Bogen edited in New York a Russian-Jewish journal and distinguished himself in Jewish civic leadership, especially with the Joint Distribution Committee.

91. K. Sabsovich, *op. cit.*, p. 120.

92. *Forward*, July 13, 1899 (advertisement), July 10, 13, 1900. The *Abend Blatt, Arbeiter Zeitung*, and *Yiddishe Gazetten* were also critical of Sabsovich.

93. *Jewish Exponent*, Dec. 16, 1904.

94. *Ibid.*, Feb. 15, 1907 (circular letter), May 20, 1910.

95. Quoted *ibid.*, July 3, 1908, July 23, Aug. 6, Oct. 1, 1909.

96. Letters to the Editor, *ibid.*, from Mayerson, Sept. 30, 1910; from Fastman, June 16, 1911.

97. *Ibid.*, May 13, 20, Oct. 21, 1910, Aug. 4, 25, Sept. 22, 1911.

98. Reports of Charles S. Phelps, P. F. Staples, to Goldman, Nov. 7, 1905, B.D.H.

99. "Visitations of Professor J. L. Stone . . . regarding the question: "Are the soil and the environment at Woodbine such that a proper agricultural education can be provided?" Nov. 1905; A. R. Merrill to Harold H. Ballard, Oct. 1905; *Breeder's Gazette*, Nov. 20, 1905, all *ibid.* J.C.A. representative, A. L. Schalit, quoted in Joseph, *op. cit.*, p. 77.

100. Letter from H. L. Sabsovich to the Editor of the *Jewish Exponent*, Aug. 9, 1895.

101. *Jewish Exponent*, Nov. 1, 1895; see also, July 7, Aug. 2, 1895.

102. *Ibid.*

103. *Ibid.*, Jan. 31, Nov. 6, 1896; June 18, 25; July 30, 1897; June 3, 10, 1898.

104. Editorial, *ibid.*, Jan. 13, 1911.

105. *Ibid.*, Nov. 27, 1903; Dec. 2, 1904; Jan. 26, 1906; Feb. 10, March 3, 1911.

106. Joseph, *op. cit.*, p. 85; *Jewish Farmer* (in Yiddish and English), Feb. 1913, p. 42; April 1913, pp. 83ff.; May 1913, p. 107, *et passim.*

107. For the removal proposals, including Peekskill, see Joseph, *op. cit.*, pp. 82–89.

Notes to Chapter V: Rural Factories: New Economic Diversification and the Social Response

1. Early efforts at cigar-making and sewing are described in the *Jewish Record*, Feb. 13, 1883, Jan. 23, 1885; *V.E.J.*, Dec. 8, 1883; July 25, 1884; April 26, 1888; *American Hebrew*, vol. 19, no. 13 (Aug. 8, 1884), p. 201; vol. 20, no. 5 (Sept. 12, 1884), p. 67; *American Israelite*, vol. 31, no. 34 (Feb. 20, 1885), p. 2.

2. *Jewish Exponent*, Aug. 13, 1897; Alliance farmer quoted by George Randorf in the *American Hebrew*, vol. 35, no. 10 (July 13, 1888), p. 152.

3. Klein, *op. cit.*, p. 61.

4. *V.E.J.*, Feb. 4, March 30, Aug. 21, 26, Oct. 25, 1899; Nov. 20, 1901; March 10, May 20, Oct. 5, 1905; Feb. 27, 1906; July 26, 1913; Feb. 18, 1916.

5. *New York Evening World*, Nov. 29, 1891, in B.D.H.; Directors of the Woodbine Land and Improvement Company to the Trustees of the Baron de Hirsch Fund, Feb. 29, 1892, *ibid.* On Woodbine's farm and factory balance see also the account in the *American Hebrew*, vol. 55, no. 20 (Sept. 14, 1894), p. 593.

6. Reports of the Jewish Agricultural and Industrial Aid Society, 1901 and 1902, B.D.H.; *Jewish Exponent,* Aug. 16, 1895; Dec. 4, 1896; July 23, 1897; July 15, 1898; *V.E.J.,* April 14, 1892; Feb. 12, 1895; *American Hebrew,* vol. 56, no. 15 (Feb. 15, 1895), p. 445.

7. H. L. Sabsovich to Nathan Bijur, including copy of Report to the Roosevelt Commission on Country Life, Nov. 19, 1908, B.D.H.

8. H. L. Sabsovich, "Eleventh Annual Report," Jan. 20, 1903, B.D.H.

9. Eugene S. Benjamin to W. B. Yuditzky (President, Woodbine Hat Company), Dec. 14, 1908, *ibid.* For an early statement of this transportation scheme see *V.E.J.,* April 11, 1899.

10. Katharine Sabsovich, *op. cit.,* p. 102; J. J. Schoeneman (Pres., Woodbine Clothing Co.) to L. Siegbert (de Hirsch Fund), Nov. 7, 1908, Siegbert to Schoeneman, Nov. 11, 1908, B.D.H.; Goldstein, *Social Aspects,* p. 21.

11. Sabsovich, *supra,* p. 101, *passim;* Sabsovich to Mayer Sulzberger, March 12, 1908; Eugene S. Benjamin to J. J. Schoeneman, Oct. 28, 1908, B.D.H.

12. Sabsovich to Sulzberger, *ibid., loc. cit.*

13. Quoted in Samuel Joseph, *History of the Baron de Hirsch Fund,* p. 61.

14. *Ibid.,* p. 64 *et passim;* See, for example, letter of Nov. 12, 1901, from Jacob Schiff and Julius Goldman to Messrs. Charles Hallgarten and Julius Plotke, special collection of the American Jewish History Center.

15. *Forward,* Dec. 6, 1900.

16. *Jewish Exponent,* July 15, 1898.

17. Joseph, *op. cit.,* pp. 91–92.

18. *Jewish Exponent,* July 15, 1898.

19. H. L. Sabsovich, Jan. 20, 1904, "Twelfth Annual Report," B.D.H.; Joseph, *op. cit.,* pp. 92–93.

20. *Jewish Exponent,* Jan. 11, 1895.

21. *V.E.J.,* Oct. 13, 1896.

22. Bernard A. Palitz to Sabsovich, March 30, 1908; "Petition from the Residents of Woodbine," B.D.H.

23. Benjamin to J. Joseph Schoeneman, Oct. 28, 1908; Sabsovich to S. G. Rosenbaum, Nov. 18, 1908, *ibid.*

24. *Forward,* Jan. 31, 1900; *V.E.J.,* July 2, 1900.

25. *Forward,* Sept. 14, Dec. 8, 1903.

26. For eviction of D. & B. see Resolution of Oct. 5, 1904, Woodbine Land and Improvement Company; for terms of new agreement, see "Letter of Agreement," Oct. 14, 1904, from the Central Committee of the Baron de Hirsch Fund to the Trustees, B.D.H.

27. Sabsovich to Benjamin, Nov. 5, 1908, *ibid.;* quoted also in Joseph, *op. cit.*, p. 94.

28. Palitz to Sabsovich, Nov. 14, Dec. 4, 1908, B.D.H.

29. Benjamin to Executive Committee, de Hirsch Fund, March 7, 1908; Palitz to Sabsovich, Oct. 26, 1908, *ibid.*

30. Palitz to Sabsovich, Dec. 14, 1908, *ibid.*

31. *Forward*, Aug. 25, Nov. 26, 1902.

32. Louis Siegbert (Fund trustee) to J. J. Schoeneman (partner of Joseph Rabinowitz), Nov. 11, 1908; Sabsovich to Palitz, Feb. 2, 1909; Woodbine Hat Co. to Sabsovich, May 12, 1909, B.D.H.

33. Palitz to Sulzberger, March 12, 1908; Sabsovich to Benjamin, Nov. 3, 1908, *ibid.*

34. Palitz to Sabsovich, Feb. 2, March 2, 8, 4, 25, 1909; Sabsovich to Bayard, Oct. 15, 1909; Bayard to Sabsovich, Oct. 18, 1909; Sabsovich to Benjamin, Oct. 20, 1909, *ibid.*

35. Agreement between Joseph Schoeneman, Jacob Salsburg, and Joseph Rabinowitz, owners of the Woodbine Children's Clothing Company, and local #207, United Garment Workers, Feb. 4, 1911, *ibid.*

36. Louis Cohen (Woodbine Hat Co.) to Sabsovich, June 28, 1909, *ibid.*

37. S. Aleo, President of Kirschbaum & Co. (Philadelphia) to Woodbine Board of Trade, June 24, 1914, *ibid.*

38. Louis Mounier, "Reminiscences," Jan. 22, 1908.

39. *V.E.J.*, Oct. 12, 1906; Aug. 2, Sept. 20, 21, 24, 27, Oct. 7, 21, 1878.

40. *V.E.J.*, June 21, Sept. 6, 1898; July 16, 1902.

41. *Ibid.*, July 12, Oct. 30, 1901; Jan. 24, May 22, Dec. 13, 1913; Oct. 18, 1916; April 26, 1917.

42. John E. Bebout and Roland J. Grele, *Where Cities Meet: The Urbanization of New Jersey*, pp. 5, 35.

43. *V.E.J.*, July 25, 1914.

44. *Ibid.*, Aug. 27, 1914; Dec. 22, 1915.

45. *Ibid.*, Dec. 5, 19, 1906; Jan. 19, 1907.

46. *Ibid.*, Dec. 3, 1907; May 12, 1909; July 2, 1910; for sketches of early Jewish industrialists see also Cumberland County•editions of *Who's Who in New Jersey* (State Library Archives).

47. *V.E.J.*, Oct. 31, Dec. 2, 1903; April 15, July 22, Nov. 10, 1904; March 10, April 15, Oct. 5, 21, 1905.

48. *Ibid.*, March 4, 27, 1907.

49. *Forward*, Jan. 31, 1900; *V.E.J.*, Sept 2, 1910; Oct. 4, 5, 1911; Oct. 28, Nov. 11, 20, 1912.

50. *V.E.J.*, Nov. 30, 1901; Aug. 23, 1907; Jan. 24, 28, Feb. 15, 24, 25, 27, 1913.

51. *Ibid.*, Aug. 30, Sept. 4, Sept. 13, 22, Oct. 6, 10, 1913.

52. *Ibid.*, May 7, July 9, Aug. 23, 26, 29, 1904; Sept. 3, 1907; Feb. 18, 1913.

53. *Ibid.*, Dec. 30, 1907.

54. Goldhaft, *op. cit.*, p. 51.

55. *V.E.J.*, Oct. 21, Nov. 3, 1909; Nov. 9, 1910.

56. "A Call to the Voters of Vineland and Landis Township," *ibid.*, Oct. 11, 1913.

57. Joseph, *op. cit.*, pp. 95–96.

58. *Ibid.*, pp. 99, 101, including post-war contrasts.

59. *V.E.J.*, Nov. 18, 1914; Jan. 2, 26, 1915; July 1, 1916.

60. *Ibid.*, June 8, Sept. 13, 1916; Jan 19, 20, 22, May 24, 1917.

61. *Ibid.*, Dec. 26, 1914; March 31, July 21, Aug. 12, Dec. 23, 1916; Jan. 22, Feb. 1, 1917; Dec. 24, 1919.

62. *Ibid.*, June 27, July 26, 1916.

63. *Ibid.*, March 22, 28, 1917.

64. *Ibid.*, July 15, 1916; Aug. 3, 15, 1917.

65. *Ibid.*, May 24, 25, 1915; June 15, 30, July 26, Aug. 3, 1916.

66. *Ibid.*, Feb. 1, 1917.

67. *Ibid.*, March 18, 1919.

68. *Ibid.*, Nov. 3, 4, 1919.

69. *Ibid.*, Jan. 22, Aug. 17, 21, 22, 1917; Aug. 20, 1918.

70. *Ibid.*, April 20, 29, 30, May 3, 18, 27, 31, 1918.

71. *Ibid.*, April 11, 13, 1918; May 26, 1919.

72. *Ibid.*, July 20, 1918; Joseph, *op. cit.*, pp. 99, 101.

73. Gilbert Seldes, *The Stammering Century*, with a Foreword by Arthur Schlesinger, Jr. (New York and Evanston, 1965), pp. 404–405.

74. *Ibid.*, p. 403.

Notes to Chapter VI: Acceptance and Rejection in the New Society: Aliens, Natives, and German Jews

1. Abraham Cahan, *The Rise of David Levinsky*, originally published in 1917 (New York: Harper Torchbook edition, 1960, with a Foreword by John Higham), p. 528.

2. *Vineland Weekly*, July 14, 1866.

3. *V.E.J.*, Aug. 5, 1882.

4. *Ibid.*, June 11, 1912.

5. *Daily Journal*, March 29, 1879.

6. *Daily Independent*, Oct. 25, 1876.

7. *The Daily Journal*, Oct. 21, 1875.

8. *V.E.J.*, Feb. 11, 1885; interview with William Levin, March 30, 1966.

9. *Vineland Daily Journal*, Jan. 27, 1876; May 8, 1879. For the national picture, see John Higham, *Strangers in the Land* (New Brunswick, 1955), pp. 28–29, *et passim*.

10. *Ibid.*, p. 27.

11. *Vineland Daily Journal*, June 19, 1877, Aug. 2, 1879.

12. *Ibid.*, Nov. 6, 1876, June 14, 1880.

13. Gustavus Myers, *History of Bigotry in the United States* (New York, 1960 ed.), pp. 195–196, 203. Newly edited by Henry M. Christman.

14. *V.E.J.*, May 26, 1914; Jacob Riis quote is from Higham, *op. cit.*, p. 67.

15. *V.E.J.*, May 8, Aug. 9, 11, 1882; May 3, 1883.

16. *Vineland Daily Journal*, July 2, 1877; *ibid.*, March 14, 1902.

17. *V.E.J.*, Jan. 24, 26, 1916.

18. *Ibid.*, June 15, 1916.

19. Wallace N. Jamison, *Religion in New Jersey: A Brief History* (Princeton, 1964), pp. 121–122.

20. *V.E.J.*, June 6, 16, 1882; the *Century* article of June, 1882, by U.S. Consul-General at Beirut, J. Augustus Johnson, was previewed, *V.E.J.*, May 18, 1882.

21. *Ibid.*, July 13, 18, 19, 1882; Sept. 19, 21, 22, 23, 1891 (the 1891 dates deal with the Millville strike).

22. *Ibid.*, Jan. 19, 20, 27, Sept. 5, 1893.

23. *Ibid.*, Aug. 24, 1895; July 20, 28, 29, 1896.

24. *Ibid.*, June 30, 1893 (insurance); July 22, 1898; July 15, 1910; July 27, 1917.

25. *Ibid.*, Jan. 3, 1883; Dec. 17, 1886.

26. *Ibid.*, March 2, July 26, 1892.

27. *Ibid.*, Oct. 25, 1895; Dec. 2, 1896; Feb. 23, 1903; June 26, 1909.

28. *Ibid.*, July 24, 1896; Jan. 1, 8, 1909; Mounier, "A Good Samaritan" (unpublished), July, 1933.

29. *V.E.J.*, June 16, 26, 1883; July 30, 1887.

30. *Ibid.*, March 8, 1883; Oct. 30, 1901; Alliance did not get teachers from Vineland until the decade of 1900–1910.

31. *Ibid.*, Sept. 5, 1881.

32. *Ibid.*, Jan. 31, 1896.

33. *Ibid.*, July 25, 1899; Jan. 24, 27, 1903.

34. *Ibid.*, Dec. 8, 1893; April 11, 1905; June 30, 1909.

35. *Ibid.*, April 4, 1913.

36. *Ibid.*, May 18, 1914.

37. *Ibid.*, April 2, 1914; Sept. 13, 14, 19, 21, 1916.

38. *Ibid.*, June 19, 20, 1918.

39. *Ibid.*, Jan. 27, 1876; May 8, 1879. See also Jamison, *op. cit.*, pp. 134–135.

40. *V.E.J.*, Aug. 9, 1893.

41. *Ibid.*, April 20, 1888; June 26, 27, July 1, 1896.

42. *Ibid.*, Jan. 7, 1899; May 8, 1901; Jan. 13, 1902; Jan. 16, 1905.

43. *Ibid.*, April 24, 1909; Dec. 19, 1911; May 25, Nov. 9, Dec. 29, 1914; Aug. 9, Oct. 18, 1915; May 27, 1916; March 21, June 13, 1917.

44. *Ibid.*, April 26, 1902; Jan. 19, 1920.

45. Quoted from the American Sabbath Union Constitution, *V.E.J.*, April 23, 1889. For Vineland regulations see *ibid.*, June 9, 1866, March 23, 1888.

46. *Ibid.*, Aug. 5, 1893; *Elmer Times*, March 8, 1890.

47. *V.E.J.*, Feb. 23, 1906; July 8, Oct. 29, 1907.

48. *Ibid.*, Jan. 14, 1914.

49. *Ibid.*, March 29, 1909.

50. *Ibid.*, April 29, 1912.

51. *Yoval*, p. 40.

52. *V.E.J.*, May 1, 3, 1912 (the latter issue contains Mounier's complete statement). See also Mounier's *Autobiographical Sketch* (Vineland, 1937), pp. 25, 55–56.

53. *V.E.J.*, May 3, 1912; Feb. 26, 1913. On this matter of Jews observing the Sabbath on Sunday, as some did in the ultra-liberal Reform movement, a comment by Rebecca Gratz on a Savannah Sunday school begun by her niece is enlightening: "Do not call your Sunday *Sabbath* school, my dear Miriam, lest some should mistake your meaning." Quoted in Joseph R. Rosenblum, "Rebecca Gratz and the Jewish Sunday School Movement in Philadelphia," *Publication of the American Jewish Historical Society* (PAJHS), vol. XLVIII, no. 2 (December, 1958), p. 77.

54. For a first-hand account of the tribulations in South Jersey *and* on the Lower East Side see George M. Price, "The Russian Jews in America," trans. Leo Shpall in *PAJHS*, vol. XLVIII, no. 1, pp. 40–41, 52–55, *et passim*.

55. *V.E.J.*, Jan. 30, Feb. 1, 15, 1894.

56. *Ibid.*, Aug. 2, 1893; July 14, 1894; Nov. 9, 1897; April 19, May 28, Nov. 3, 1898.

57. *Ibid.*, Aug. 26, 1895; March 7, 1896; Oct. 9, 1908; Feb. 21, 1910.

58. Martin I. Douglas, "The Vineland Jewish Community," *Vineland Historical Magazine* (Centennial Number), August, 1961. Pages 66–67 offer useful background data. Also, *Social Aspects,* p. 51, on the colonies; *Yoval,* p. 37, *et passim.*

59. *V.E.J.*, Jan. 11, 1905.

60. *Boston Transcript,* quoted *ibid.,* Feb. 29, 1916.

61. Emma Lazarus reply to Madame Ragozin's "Russian Jews and Gentiles," in the May issue of *Century* magazine, quoted in large part by the *V.E.J.*, May 2, 1882 (front-page two-column spread, headed "Russian Christianity versus Modern Judaism").

62. *V.E.J.*, Jan. 4, 1881; follow-up accounts Jan. 6, 21, 1881.

63. *Ibid.*, March 29, 1880; May 16, 19, June 18, Aug. 13, 1881; May 9, 26, Aug. 26, 1882; May 26, 1883.

64. *Ibid.*, Sept. 30, Oct. 2, 3, Nov. 3, 1882.

65. *Ibid.*, Feb. 16, 18, Sept. 27, 1898; Jan. 7, Feb. 2, June 3, Aug. 16, 21, 1899; July 13, 1906.

66. London *Times* quoted in Rufus Learsi, *op. cit.,* p. 171.

67. Solomon, *op. cit.,* p. 41, deals with Henry Adams' position. On the charges against French Rabbi Kahn, see *V.E.J.*, Feb. 2, 1899.

68. *V.E.J.*, Nov. 3, 1890 (see also Dec. 30, 1890); for further details, see Dubnow, *op. cit., passim.* Learsi, *op. cit.,* p. 125.

69. *V.E.J.*, July 31, Oct. 7, 1891.

70. *Reports No. 1177 and No. 1000,* 52nd Congress, 1st Session, quoted in Myers, *op. cit.,* pp. 199–200.

71. *V.E.J.*, May 27, 1903.

72. Theodore Roosevelt quoted in Sachar, *op. cit.,* p. 249.

73. *V.E.J.*, May 4, 1904.

74. *Ibid.*, June 27, Nov. 2, 4, 6, 1905.

75. *V.E.J.*, Nov. 11, 1913; see also Maurice Samuel's scholarly treatment, *Blood Accusation: the Strange Case of Mendel Beilis* (Philadelphia, 1966).

76. Quoted in Learsi, *op. cit.,* p. 224.

77. *V.E.J.*, Nov. 11, 29, 1913; interviews with Harry and Rose Sobelman of Carmel, N.J., June 21, 1967.

78. Georg Brandes, *Impressions of Russia,* pp. 131, 136.

79. *Jewish Record,* Feb. 17, 1882.

80. *Ibid.*, March 3, May 26, 1882.

81. *V.E.J.*, Feb. 21, 1882; Oct. 18, 1890 (Gladstone); May 22, 1903 (Tolstoy).

82. *Ibid.*, May 18, July 13, 1903.

83. *Jewish Exponent,* May 22, 1903.

84. *Forward,* May 5, 12, 1903.

85. *Ibid.*, July 13, 1903.

86. *V.E.J.*, June 27, July 2, 15, 16, 17, 1903.

87. *Ibid.*, Jan. 13, 1920. Salo W. Baron, *The Russian Jew Under Tsars and Soviets,* pp. 211, 219–222, deals with the pogroms during this period of violent transition from Tsarist to Soviet hegemony.

88. *V.E.J.*, June 6, 1911.

89. *Newark News* editorial, quoted *ibid.*, July 25, 1914.

90. Publications of the Immigration Restriction League, quoted in Maldwyn A. Jones, *American Immigration* (New York, 1957) p. 259; Solomon, *op. cit.,* p. 107 (the latter devotes three full chapters of effective analysis to the I.R.L.). See also "Restriction," ch. 8 of Oscar Handlin, ed., *Immigration as a Factor in American History* (Englewood Cliffs, N.J., 1959); Ray Ginger, *Age of Excess* (New York, 1965), pp. 239–244.

91. *V.E.J.*, Dec. 8, 1888.

92. *Ibid.*, Aug. 15, 1877; Aug. 1, 1882.

93. *Ibid.*, Dec. 6, 1890; June 1, 1891.

94. *Ibid.*, Aug. 17, Sept. 10, 1891; see also, Joseph, *op. cit.,* p. 49.

95. *Ibid.*, Sept. 14, 1891; Feb. 18, 1892.

96. Moses Rischin, *The Promised City: New York's Jews, 1870–1914,* p. 54.

97. *V.E.J.*, July 13, 1903.

98. Gompers quoted in Handlin, *op. cit.,* p. 186.

99. Liberal Immigration League, *The Immigrant Jew in America* (New York, 1906), pp. 4–6, 370–371.

100. *Jersey Journal* quoted in *V.E.J.*, Oct. 13, 1914.

101. Rischin, *op. cit.,* p. 263 *et passim;* see also, Ginger, *op. cit.,* pp. 79–80 *et passim;* Jones, *op. cit.,* pp. 256ff. For nativist anti-Semitism see John Higham's "Anti-Semitism in the Gilded Age: A Reinterpretation," *Mississippi Valley Historical Review,* XLIII (March, 1957); his "Social Discrimination Against Jews in America, 1830–1930," *Publication of the American Jewish Historical Society* (PAJHS), vol. XLVII (September, 1957); and Norman Pollack's "The Myth of Populist Anti-Semitism," *American Historical Review,* vol. LXVIII (October, 1962).

102. Heilprin quoted in Joseph, *op. cit.,* p. 7.

103. Quoted in Rischin, *op. cit.*, p. 97.

104. Joseph, *op. cit.*, pp. 17–18, 24–25, and Ch. VIII, "Americanization Activities;" Palitz's Report to the Roosevelt Commission on Country Life (November, 1908), B.D.H.; warnings against a rural "ghetto" in the *American Hebrew*, vol. LXVI (Dec. 15, 1899), p. 198 *et passim*.

Notes to Chapter VII: Struggle for Identity: American and Jewish

1. Moses Klein, *op. cit.*, p. 49; see also, *Jewish Exponent*, Oct. 28, 1887, Nov. 1, 1889, *V.E.J.*, Oct. 28, 1889, *Yoval*, p. 40. *The New York Times*, April 9, 1964, included an article on the quaint history of Salem. See also Wallace N. Jamison, *Religion in New Jersey*.

2. Russian quoted in Klein, *op. cit.*, p. 51; *Elmer Times*, Oct. 22, 1887.

3. Herman Eisenberg, a Norma farm boy later Philadelphia attorney, in *Yoval*, p. 25.

4. *Jewish Record*, July 21, 1882; for Sternberger's reports on religious observance see also *Jewish Messenger*, vol. LI (June 9, 1882), p. 5 and vol. LIII (March 2, 1883), p. 5; *American Hebrew*, vol. II (July 14, 1882), p. 104.

5. *V.E.J.*, May 21, 1883; *Jewish Record*, Feb. 13, 1883; Nov. 27, 1885. The Mendes account is also summarized in the *American Hebrew*, vol. XXIV (Nov. 6, 1885), p. 201. For Randorf's reports to Mendes see *American Hebrew*, vol. XXXIV (April 20, 1888), p. 168; vol. XXXV (May 25, 1888), p. 45.

6. *Jewish Record*, July 11, 1884; *V.E.J.*, March 22, April 17, 1886.

7. *Jewish Exponent*, Dec. 9, 16, 1887.

8. *Ibid.*, Aug. 3, 1888.

9. All of the dedication ceremonies and speeches were reported in detail by the *Jewish Exponent*, Aug. 3, 1888. See also, *Jewish Messenger*, vol. LXIV (Aug. 3, 1888), p. 3; *American Hebrew*, vol. XXXV (Aug. 3, 1888), p. 204.

10. *V.E.J.*, July 13; *Jewish Exponent*, July 19, 1889

11. Klein, *op. cit.*, pp. 83, 49 fn; *Jewish Exponent*, Nov. 1, 1889; see also *Yoval*, pp. 19, 37.

12. *Jewish Exponent*, Oct. 4, 1889; *V.E.J.*, April 22, 1896; Sept. 20, 1901; *Jewish Messenger*, vol. LXIV (Sept. 28, 1888), p. 3.

13. Presentation of Torah, including incident of the eagle, in the *American Hebrew*, vol. XXXVI (Oct. 5, 1888), p. 133; the *Jewish Messenger*, vol. LXIV (Oct. 5, 1888), p. 2; the *Jewish Exponent*, Oct. 12, 1888. All related the story of the eagle quill as a well-nigh miraculous occurrence.

14. For Purim celebrations see *Jewish Messenger,* vol. LXIII (March 9, 1888), on Sabbath observance, *American Hebrew,* vol. XLVII (July 3, 1891), p. 189.

15. Mrs. Charles D. Spivak, "Three Dreams in a Jewish Colony," in *Jewish Exponent,* Aug. 18, 1899. Her husband was a founder of the Jewish Alliance of America in 1891. At this time, Mrs. Spivak was traveling from Denver, Colorado on her way to Europe.

16. Raymond Lipman and Herman Rosenfeld to Trustees, Nov. 23, 1908, Sabsovich to Acting–President Rosenbaum, March 29, 1909, B.D.H.

17. Korolenko, *op. cit., Hadoar* trans., pp. 9–10.

18. "Constitution of the Association of Agudath Achim Anshei Woodbine" (16 pp.).

19. Sabsovich, "Eleventh Annual Report," Jan. 20, 1903, B.D.H.

20. Lewis T. Stevens, *The History of Cape May County* (Cape May City, 1897), p. 403 (a full-page photograph of the synagogue is on p. 402); *Jewish Exponent,* Aug. 16, Oct. 11, Nov. 27, 1896; see also, Joseph, *op. cit.,* p. 57.

21. "Synagogue at Woodbine," *Jewish Exponent,* Nov. 27, Dec. 4, 1896.

22. Moses Freeman, *Fuftsig Yohr Geschichte fun Idishen Leben in Philadelphia, 1879–1929* (Philadelphia, 1932), pp. 30–31.

23. *Yiddishe Gazetten,* April, 1894, quoted in Harold Silver, "Some Attitudes of the East European Jewish Immigrants Toward Organized Charity in the United States in the Years 1890–1900" (typewritten manuscript, Jewish Division, New York Public Library), p. 219.

24. For additional background on relations between German and Russian Jews in America, see, for example, Rischin, *op. cit.,* pp. 95–111, 237–239, 263, *passim.*

25. Historical references relevant to changing trends in American Judaism include such works as the following: Salo W. Baron, *A Social and Religious History of the Jews,* 3 vols. (New York, 1937); Joseph L. Blau, *Modern Varieties of Judaism* (New York, 1966); Moshe Davis, *The Emergence of Conservative Judaism* (Philadelphia, 1965); Louis Finkelstein, ed., *The Jews, Their History, Culture, and Religion,* 2 vols. (Philadelphia, 1960), especially Moshe Davis, "Jewish Religious Life and Institutions in America (A Historical Study)," vol. I, pp. 354–453; Theodore Friedman and Robert Gordis, eds., *Jewish Life in America* (New York, 1955); Oscar I. Janowsky, ed., *The American Jew, A Composite Portrait* (New York, 1942).

26. From correspondents "Maftir" and "Sopher," *The American Israelite,* vol. 29, no. 1 (July, Sept., 1882), pp. 1–2, quoted in Harold Silver, *op. cit.,* p. 46.

27. Magnus Butzel, in *The American Israelite,* vol. 32, no. 48 (May, 1882), p. 378, quoted *ibid.,* pp. 47–48; Benjamin F. Peixotto, "What Shall We

Do With Our Immigrants?" Address before New York YMHA Board, Feb. 2, 1887.

28. *Yiddishe Gazetten*, vol. 19, no. 1 (May, 1894), p. 1, quoted in Silver, *op. cit.*, pp. 25–27; also July, 1898 *Yiddishe Gazetten*, editorial quoted on pp. 28–29.

29. Freeman, *op. cit.*, pp. 36–41, 76–77; see also, A. S. Sachs, *In Kamf far a Beserer Velt: Geklibene Ksovim Vegen Sotsiale Problemen un Revolutsionere Persenlichkeiten* ("Struggle for a Better World: Selections on Social Problems and Revolutionaries") (New York, 1938), pp. 131–134.

30. "Constitution of the Chevra Kadisha of Alliance, N.J."; Constitution and Minutes of Congregation *Emanu-El* (both in Yiddish).

31. Louis Mounier, "Colonial Characters" (unpublished, handwritten memoir), July 29, 1933.

32. *Ibid.*

33. "Carmel's Synagogue," *Jewish Exponent*, Sept. 25, 1908; see also, Aug. 28 and Sept. 11, 1908, *ibid.; Jewish Farmer*, I, no. 7 (Nov. 1908), p. 16. For Goward's role in establishing the Hebrew Literary Society as an institution for the educational and cultural needs of Russian Jews, as well as a forum for discussions, see Freeman, *op. cit.*, p. 58. For the synagogue dedication, see also, *V.E.J.*, Sept. 22, 1908.

34. *Jewish Exponent*, May 1, 1896, April 7, 21, 28, 1899, Dec. 17, 1901. See also Gustav Pollak's *Michael Heilprin and His Sons* (1912), *passim.*

35. *Jewish Exponent*, Sept. 15, 1899, Aug. 19, 1904, March 22, 1907, Dec. 25, 1908; *V.E.J.*, Aug. 5, 1909.

36. Articles by "Ben Amitai" in *Yiddishe Gazetten* (July, 1900), quoted in Silver, *op. cit.*, p. 209. Sabsovich to Rabbi Levinthal, June 2, 1910 B.D.H.

37. *The Jewish Farmer*, Jan. 1911, p. 3; see also, Nov. 1910, p. 176.

38. *Ibid.*, Jan. 1911, p. 5; Feb. 1911, pp. 36, 44.

39. *Ibid.*, April, May, 1911, June, Dec. 1912, Dec. 1913, July, 1914; *Jewish Exponent*, May 10, June 9, 1912.

40. Goldstein, *Centers in My Life*, p. 23.

41. *Social Aspects*, p. 52.

42. Goldstein, *Centers*, pp. 29–30.

43. *Ibid.*, p. 32.

44. Sidney Bailey, "The First Fifty Years," in *Yoval*, p. 16.

45. *Social Aspects*, pp. 44–45.

46. *Jewish Exponent*, Aug. 3, Oct. 26, 1888.

47. Mounier, *Auto-Biographical Sketch*, pp. 8–9. Printed privately, Vineland, 1936.

48. *V.E.J.*, Aug. 6, *Jewish Exponent*, Aug. 19, 1898.

49. Mounier, "Brotmanville in its Hey-Day," June 1933; "Children's Gardens," July 4, 1933 (unpublished manuscripts).

50. Mounier, "A Discovery"; "A Talk with a Native Public School Teacher in Alliance" (unpublished manuscripts).

51. *V.E.J.*, July 18, 1894; Jan. 10, 1907; *Yoval*, pp. 16–17.

52. *Yoval*, pp. 17, 32–33; "Just 80 Years Ago . . .", Atlantic City *Sunday Press*, July 22, 1962; interview with Dr. Tevis Goldhaft, William and Harry Levin, Vineland, March 30–31, 1966.

53. H. L. Sabsovich, "Eleventh Annual Report," Jan. 20, 1903, B.D.H.; *Jewish Exponent*, Dec. 4, 1896; Feb. 10, June 9, 1899; Dec. 14, 1900; April 23, Nov. 13, 1903. *Social Aspects*, pp. 47–48. David Blaustein, "The First Self-Governed Jewish Community Since the Fall of Jerusalem," *Circle: A Modern Department Magazine for all People,* vol. II (1907), pp. 138–140.

54. Sabsovich, B.D.H., *supra; Jewish Exponent*, May 12, 1899, Jan. 11, 1901; April 24, Oct. 23, 1903; June 10, 1904. *The Jewish Farmer* (Nov. 1909), p. 148, reported 450 Woodbine children enrolled in the elementary school program, 50 more than in 1903, and 14 teachers plus a principal; 14 youngsters then attended the Millville High School.

55. Report summarized in Joseph, *op. cit.*, p. 105.

56. Annual Report, Baron de Hirsch Fund, 1902, pp. 4–5, B.D.H.

57. *V.E.J.*, Oct. 11, 1898, Aug. 28, 1905.

58. *Ibid.*, Oct. 12, 19, 20, 1905; see also Martin Douglas, "The Vineland Jewish Community," *op. cit.*, p. 67.

59. *Ibid.*, Oct. 12, 1905; Sept. 24, Oct. 4, 1906; Aug. 21, Sept. 11, 1908; July 28, Aug. 12, 1909.

60. *Ibid.*, Dec. 14, 1904; Oct. 18, 1905; July 31, 1913.

61. *Ibid.*, Sept. 29, 1910; Oct. 3, 1911; March 11, 1912; April 10, April 14, 1913; Sept. 15, 22, 1914.

62. *Ibid.*, Sept. 29, 1913; March 30, 1914.

63. *Ibid.*, Oct. 6, 1909; April 29, 1914; Feb. 24, 1917, July 19, 1919.

64. Joseph Magill, manager, *Jewish Daily News,* to David W. Amram, July 31, 1914; Louis J. Cohen, Superintendent, to David W. Amram, Aug. 5, 1914, B.D.H.

65. Benjamin to Jewish Colonization Association, March 30, 1911, *ibid.*

66. John Daniels, *America Via the Neighborhood,* pp. 50–51, quoted in Joseph, *op. cit.*, p. 105.

67. *V.E.J.*, May 25, 1906.

68. *Ibid.*, Sept. 20, 1913; June 19, 1914; June 13, 1916; June 11, 13, 22, 23, 1917; Sept. 26, 1918.

69. The subject has been treated in a number of historic-sociological works, such as Judith R. Kramer and Seymour Leventman, *Children of the Gilded Ghetto: Conflict Resolutions of Three Generations of American Jews* and Marshall Sklare, ed., *The Jews, Social Patterns of an American Group.*

70. Goldhaft, *op. cit.,* p. 51.

71. *Ibid.,* p. 105.

72. Goldstein, *Centers,* pp. 17–18, *et passim; V.E.J.,* May 23, 1914.

73. *The Diaries of Theodor Herzl* (Marvin Lowenthal, trans. & ed., New York, 1956), pp. 15–19ff., including a detailed account of the encounter with de Hirsch. See also: Alex Bein, *Theodor Herzl* (Maurice Samuel, trans., Philadelphia, 1941), pp. 127–128; Israel Cohen, *Theodor Herzl* (New York, London, 1959), pp. 69–70, *et passim.; The Jewish State* in Arthur Hertzberg, ed., *The Zionist Idea* (New York, 1959), p. 213.

74. Klein, "Zionism and the Coming Conference at Munich," *Jewish Exponent,* June 4, 1897; see also his *Migdal Zophim* (1889), pp. 86–88.

75. *Jewish Exponent,* June 21, 1901; Sept. 9, 1904; *V.E.J.,* March 29, 1902, Sept. 14, Oct. 10, 1903.

76. *Jewish Exponent,* Aug. 9, Oct. 25, 1907; July 24, Oct. 16, 1908; Jan. 8, Feb. 12, 1909.

77. *The Jewish Farmer,* March 1914, p. 55.

78. *Jewish Exponent,* Jan. 21, 1910.

79. *V.E.J.,* April 19, Oct. 4, Nov. 8, 1915.

80. *Ibid.,* Sept. 22, 1915.

81. Louis D. Brandeis, "Zionism and Patriotism," quoted in Alpheus T. Mason, *Brandeis: A Free Man's Life,* pp. 445–446.

82. *V.E.J.,* Nov. 27, 29, 1915; Jan. 20, 22, 1917.

83. *Ibid.,* Dec. 4, 1916.

84. Mounier letter, Dec. 5; Krich's, Dec. 12; Goldstein's, Dec. 23; Mounier's, Dec. 27; Goldhaft's, Dec. 27; all 1916, *ibid.*

85. Goldhaft, *op. cit.,* pp. 17, 281–289.

86. *V.E.J.,* Oct. 25, 1915; Jan. 31, Feb. 17, 1917; for the Ludlow "massacre," see such standard works as Foster Rhea Dulles, *Labor in America,* pp. 195–196.

87. *Ibid.,* March 21, 1916; July 13, 16, 30, 1917.

88. Letter of Simon Wolf and Adolf Kraus to Mayer Sulzberger, quoted in Learsi, *op. cit.,* p. 213.

89. *V.E.J.,* March 13, July 13, 1916; May 28, 29, June 8, 9, Nov. 5, 1917.

90. *Ibid.,* Dec. 11, 13, 31, 1917.

91. *Ibid.,* Dec. 24, 1917.

92. *Ibid.*, Dec. 15, 1917; Jan. 12, 29, July 10, 1918; for the Jewish Legion, see Learsi, *op. cit.*, pp. 255–256, also *ibid.*, March 1, 1918.

93. Henrietta Szold, "Elements of the Jewish Population in the United States" (1903), in *The Russian Jew in the United States,* Charles S. Bernheimer, ed., pp. 14, 16.

94. *V.E.J.*, April 9, 1918; June 20, 1919; April 26, 1920. It was local Zionist leader Dr. N. S. Greenwood who thought of displaying the "Yiddish flag" in Vineland's City Hall.

Notes to Chapter VIII: Within American Society: Toward Democratic Pluralism

1. Bernard A. Palitz, President, Woodbine Board of Education, 1908 Commencement Address, B.D.H.

2. U.S. Immigration Commission, "Hebrews in Agriculture," Part 3, *Recent Immigrants in Agriculture* (Sen. Doc. 633, 61 Cong., 2 Sess., 1911), vol. II, p. 116.

3. *Ibid.*, p. 8.

4. *Ibid.*

5. *Ibid.*, pp. 8–9; for social and economic life of the Jews in the colonies, see pp. 113–116, 134–135, and *passim.*

6. David Blaustein, "The First Self-Governed Jewish Community Since the Fall of Jerusalem," *Circle: A Modern Department Magazine for all People,* vol. II (1907), 138. He was director of New York's Educational Alliance.

7. Editorial, *Cape May County Gazette,* included in "Report to the Roosevelt Commission on Country Life," *loc. cit.*, submitted by Sabsovich to Bijur, Nov. 19, 1908, B.D.H.

8. Sabsovich to Solomons, Jan. 4, 1903, to Benjamin, Jan. 7, 1903; "Resolution for the Incorporation of Woodbine," Jan. 6, 1903, all *ibid.*

9. "Report to the Roosevelt Commission on Country Life," *op. cit.; Social Aspects,* p. 22, *et passim.*

10. Bogen, *Born A Jew,* pp. 67–68, quoted in Joseph, *op. cit.*, p. 104.

11. B. A. Palitz, Commencement Address (1908), B.D.H.

12. "Agreement between the Woodbine Land & Improvement Company and Joseph Rabinowitz," Nov. 15, 1904; Sabsovich to Executive Committee of the Fund, June 16, 1908; Borough Ordinances, 1907–1917, *ibid.;* The Woodbine Planning Board, "A Look at the Past," *Woodbine Comprehensive Plan* (1958), pp. 8–14.

13. "Woodbine Legal Voters' and Taxpayers' Resolution," Jan. 6, 1903; *Jewish Exponent,* Sept. 11, 1903; H. L. Sabsovich in a court appearance

justifying the rejection of applications for liquor licenses, Sept. 1905, B.D.H.

14. Sabsovich, "Eleventh Annual Report," Jan. 20, 1903, *ibid.*

15. Levin to Palitz, Oct. 28; Palitz to Rosenbaum, Oct. 29, 1915, *ibid.*

16. *V.E.J.*, March 28, 1908; Nov. 30, Dec. 28, 1914.

17. *Ibid.*, Feb. 1, 1909; Oct. 11, 1913; Oct. 22, 1914; Feb. 9, April 22, 1915; April 11, 1916; "Hebrews in Agriculture," *op. cit.*, pp. 8–9.

18. *Forward*, Nov. 6, 1901; *V.E.J.*, Oct. 12, 1906; Nov. 3, 1909.

19. *V.E.J.*, March 12, 1907; Aug. 15, 1912.

20. *Ibid.*, Aug. 1, Nov. 9, 1910; Feb. 12, May 28, Sept. 28, Oct. 1, 15, 1912; Oct. 29, 1914.

21. Rudolph J. Vecoli, *The People of New Jersey* (Princeton, 1964), p. 158.

22. *V.E.J.*, Sept. 29, Nov. 3, 6, 1915; Oct. 12, 13, 1916; Jan. 16, Sept. 19, 1917.

23. *Yoval*, pp. 19–20; proceedings of "Alliance Republican Club" (photostats), including document dated Nov. 7, 1892; minutes of Congregation *Emanu-El.*

24. "Hebrews in Agriculture," *op. cit.*, p. 114. For the politics of ethnic-religious groups in New Jersey see ch. 5, "Nativism and Cultural Conflict," Vecoli, *op. cit.*, pp. 131–172.

25. *V.E.J.*, April 8, 1916; June 21, 29, July 16, 19, 20, 21, 23, 25, Aug. 27, Sept. 24, Dec. 17, 1917; Feb. 4, 19, 25, March 25, April 8, 11, 22, May 3, 6, 7, 22, 25, June 17, 24, 26, July 8, Aug. 6, 17, 1918.

26. *Ibid.*, March 8, June 24, 1918.

27. *Ibid.*, Liebman, May 6, 1918; Melletz, Feb. 28, July 22, Aug. 7, 1918; Mennies, July 6, 23, Aug. 2, 1918.

28. *Ibid.*, July 24, Dec. 17, 1917; Jan. 9, 16, Feb. 18, March 27, 1918.

29. *Ibid.*, Aug. 4, Nov. 27, 1917; Feb. 11, May 6, Aug. 10, Sept. 11, 1918; May 3, July 12, 1919.

30. *Ibid.*, Feb. 19, July 31, Oct. 1, 1918; March 3, 26, April 12, June 26, Dec. 18, 1919.

31. *Ibid.*, Aug. 23, 1918.

32. *Ibid.*, March 1, 1918.

33. Learsi, *op. cit.*, pp. 250–251.

34. *Jewish Farmer*, Nov. 1918, p. 243.

35. *V.E.J.*, July 16, 1917.

36. *Jewish Farmer*, May 1918, pp. 149, 156; June 1918, p. 167.

37. *V.E.J.*, April 23, 1918 (Rosenhayn), June 12, 1917.

38. *Ibid.*, Oct. 20, 1917; April 25, 27, Oct. 8, 1918.

39. *V.E.J.*, Sept. 20, 1915; Jan. 17, 1916; July 10, 1917; Sept. 30, Oct. 6, Nov. 10, Dec. 18, 1919.

40. *Ibid.*, June 5, 6, 9, 11, Oct. 29, 1919; April 22, Dec. 15, 1920. For attempts to safeguard the legal position of Polish Jews, as seen by an eyewitness at Versailles, see Cyrus Adler, *I Have Considered the Days*, (Philadelphia, 1941), pp. 306–327.

41. "Hebrews in Agriculture," *op. cit.*, p. 115.

42. Goldhaft, *op. cit.*, pp. 40, 44–45; Lipman, "The South Jersey Colonies," *The Russian Jew in the United States*, Charles S. Bernheimer, ed., pp. 385–386.

43. Louis Mounier, "An Elopement," in "Glimpses of Jewish Life in South Jersey" (June, 1933).

44. Mounier, "Ike Merochnik's Wedding" (Carmel), *ibid.*; *V.E.J.*, Aug. 6, 1896 (Bakerman), Jan. 9, 1904 (Traiman *et al.*). The quotation on Jewish girls is from George W. Simon, Appendix to K. Sabsovich, *op. cit.*, p. 207.

45. Mrs. Gertrude Serata, "Conversations with Papa (Jacob Crystal)," taped interview, May 1966.

46. "Hebrews in Agriculture," *op. cit.*, p. 7.

47. *Ibid.*, pp. 7–9, 113, 116, 136.

48. "Hebrews in Agriculture," *op. cit.*, pp. 94–95. Family and personal details are based on interviews with Jacob Crystal, William Levin, Harry Levin, *et al.*

49. Seldes, *The Stammering Century*, ix, xii, *et passim*. For a vivid description of the Great Depression's first years, see Seldes' *The Years of the Locust: America, 1929–1932* (Boston, 1933).

50. George H. Kotok, *Selected Poems* (Vineland, 1930), including biographical sketch. Poem, "The Wanderer to His Mother," p. 50; preface and biographical sketch by his brother, Justice Frank Kotok.

51. Davidson, *op. cit.*, pp. 177, 179. On Agro-Joint and Rosen's role, see Merle Curti, *American Philanthropy Abroad* (New Brunswick, N. J., 1963), pp. 366–371.

52. *V.E.J.*, May 19, 1914; Feb. 26, June 14, 1916; June 6, 1917.

53. Figures adapted from *Social Aspects*, pp. 18, 22, 29.

54. The Jewish Agricultural Society, *Jews in American Agriculture* (on the occasion of the American Jewish Tercentenary, New York, 1954), pp. 37–38.

55. B. Gorin, "Die Frieherdike Iddishe Farmers Un Die Nie" ("The Old Jewish Farmers and the New"), *Zukunft*, XX (Jan. 1915), pp. 157–163.

The colony in South Dakota was named for Adolphe Crémieux, distinguished Franco-Jewish statesman, founder and president of the *Alliance Israélite Universelle*.

56. *Jewish Farmer*, May, 1915, p. 123, May, 1916, p. 157; quotation from George Herbert by K. Sabsovich, *op. cit.*, p. 153. Fund Executive Committee, April 16, 1915, on death of Sabsovich, B.D.H.

57. Moses Freeman, "More Light on the *Am Olam*," pp. 198–203, in *Fifty Years of Jewish Life in Philadelphia* (Yiddish). He includes quotations from Cahan and Farenberg, p. 198, followed by his own counter-criticism. See also, Farenberg's article in the Yiddish *Day*, Oct. 6, 1928; the reprinted essays of Abraham S. Sachs, *op. cit.*, pp. 159–160, edited and with a Foreword by B. Z. Goldberg, perennial editor of the *Day*.

58. For the social work aspects see Solomon Lowenstein, "A Pioneer Social Worker" (Sabsovich), pp. 163–165, and Palitz, "A Life Nobly Lived," pp. 166–182 (especially pp. 180–182), both appended to K. Sabsovich, *op. cit.*; J. W. Pincus, "Social Work Among Jewish Farmers," *Jewish Exponent*, June 23, 1911.

59. For comparative data on Jewish farmers see George W. Simon, "Leader of Jewish Agriculture," in K. Sabsovich, *op. cit.*, pp. 206–207; The Jewish Agricultural Society, Inc., *Jews in American Agriculture*, pp. 37, 43–44.

60. "Official Annual [Report], Convention of the Federation of Jewish Farmers," Nov. 29–Dec. 2, 1914.

61. Schiff never lost his concern with Jews in agriculture, in spite of his distaste for Jewish "separatism" as represented, to some extent, by the Federation; see Cyrus Adler, *Jacob H. Schiff* (Garden City, New York, 1929), vol. II, p. 296.

62. *Jewish Exponent*, Oct. 16, 1908; *Jewish Farmer,* Jan. 1909, p. 15 (Zangwill); *V.E.J.*, Nov. 14, 1914 (Yiddish plays). For Schiff's interest in Zangwill and his Jewish Territorial Organization, see Adler, *op. cit.*, vol. II, pp. 96–101, especially as related to the use of Galveston and New Orleans as ports of entry for Jewish colonists.

63. *V.E.J.*, March 18, 1903; Nov. 27, 1908; May 8, Oct. 19, 1915; March 14, 1916; April 27, 1918; Jan. 10, 12, 1920.

64. *Jewish Exponent*, Sept. 26, 1888, March 3, 1899; *V.E.J.*, Jan. 9, 1904; Aug. 9, 1911; Nov. 26, 1912; Sept. 6, 1913; Feb. 8, Nov. 8, 1915; June 2, 1917.

65. *Forward*, March 5, 7, 8, 1900; Feb. 4, 1901; *V.E.J.*, Feb. 4, 1907; March 3, 1908; May 1, 1917; Feb. 19, 1919; G. Serata, "Conversations with Papa" (Crystal).

Notes to Chapter IX: Between Two World Wars: Years of "Normalcy" and Crisis

1. *V.E.J.*, Aug. 31, 1924. For the Ku Klux Klan in New Jersey see also, Murray Schonbach, *Radicals and Visionaries: A History of Dissent in New Jersey* (Princeton, 1964), pp. 83–86; Vecoli, *op. cit.*, pp. 210–211, *et passim;* Higham, *op. cit., passim.* See also chs. 20–23 in Myers, *op. cit.*, as well as other treatments, such as William Pierce Randel, *The Ku Klux Klan, A Century of Infamy* (Philadelphia and New York, 1965) and David M. Chalmers, *Hooded Americanism: The First Century of the Ku Klux Klan, 1865–1965* (New York, 1965). Goldhaft on the K.K.K., *op. cit.*, pp. 164–165.

2. *V.E.J.*, Jan. 21, 1921; Jan. 7, Feb. 4, 9, 12, 14, 18, May 26, 1924; also, Goldhaft, *op. cit.*

3. *V.E.J.*, Feb. 9, April 17, 1920.

4. *Ibid.*, Dec. 16, 1920.

5. *Ibid.*, April 29, 1924; *The New York Times*, April 13, 1966, reported on a planned K.K.K. rally in Bridgeton (see also March 27, 1965 for a good journalistic analysis of the K.K.K. and its pervasive influence).

6. Bishop Alma White, *The Ku Klux Klan in Prophecy* (Zarephath, N. J., 1925), pp. 26–27, 45–54, quoted in Vecoli, *op. cit.*, p. 258.

7. *Vineland Evening Times*, Feb. 15, 1933; for the remaining summary of extremist activity in New Jersey, including the Nazis, see Schonbach, *op. cit.*, pp. 83–100, Vecoli, *op. cit.*, pp. 259–264, especially in terms of response by Jewish civic organizations.

8. *V.E.J.*, June 5, 1882; Jan. 10, Oct. 7, 1920.

9. For this survey, the articles and advertising in the *V.E.J.* were essential, especially June 5, 1882, July 24, 1896, March 24, 1900, Dec. 31, 1903 (arbitration), March 29, 1907, Nov. 23, 1908, Feb. 2, 1910, April 11, 1912 (Lipitz), Sept. 3, 1913 (Brown Bros.), March 30, 1914 (Coltun), April 10, July 1, Aug. 13, Sept. 14 (Klure), Sept. 17, all 1915; March 18, April 21 (Lipitz), June 19, Oct. 28, Nov. 2 (autos), all 1916; Jan. 3, 1917, Sept. 10, 1918, July 9, Nov. 3, 1919, Dec. 20, 1920 (Traiman).

10. *Ibid.*, June 25, 1912; Oct. 7, 1915; Sept. 22 (Joseph Bros.), Oct. 27, 1916 (Mrs. Mac George); July 22, 1919 (Mennies); Oct. 20, 1920 (Kotok); Jan. 3, 1921 (R. E. Williams).

11. *Ibid.*, Aug. 25, 1906; Dec. 4, 1908; May 1, 1909.

12. *Ibid.*, Aug. 1, 1896 (Pharmacist Cohen); Sept. 4, 1908 (Rubinoff); April 13 (Kotok); June 9, 1914; July 2, Nov. 13, 1915; Feb. 7, Sept. 13, 1916; Jan. 7, 1919 (M. E. Cohen); Sept. 4, 1920.

13. *Ibid.*, Feb. 21, March 9, April 20, 1920; Jan. 5, 28, 31, 1921.

14. *Vineland Evening Times*, Sept. 11, 1928; July 1, 30, 1932.

15. *Ibid.,* July 9, Oct. 15, 1932; June 6, 26, July 13, 14, Nov. 22, 1933. For Woodbine, see also Joseph, *op. cit.*

16. *Ibid.,* Nov. 9, Dec. 21, 1937; April 5, May 12, 1938. For the state-wide labor picture, see Leo Troy, *Organized Labor in New Jersey* (Princeton, 1965); on the general economic development of the State, with brief historical treatments, see Salomon J. Flink, *et al., The Economy of New Jersey* (New Brunswick, 1958).

In Woodbine's pioneering period, back in the 1890's, Jacob H. Schiff had tried to use his influence in obtaining favorable freight rates to Philadelphia and New York. Toward this end, he asked the aid of Frank Thomson, first vice president of the Pennsylvania Railroad, in hopes of attracting manufacturers to locate in the struggling colony. Schiff continued to follow Woodbine's progress, or lack of it, even during such violent Wall Street upheavals as the one in 1901, when he refused to cancel a previously scheduled visit to South Jersey: Adler, *op. cit.,* vol. II, pp. 89–90.

17. Paul K. Conkin, *Tomorrow a New World* (Ithaca, New York, 1959), pp. 111–112, quoted in *The New York Times,* Feb. 6, 1965, with accompanying article on the West Virginia communities and F.D.R. See also William E. Leuchtenburg, *Franklin D. Roosevelt and The New Deal, 1932–1940* (New York, 1963), pp. 136–137.

18. Goldhaft, *op. cit.,* p. 226.

19. *V.E.J.,* May 8, Nov. 6, 1914; June 10, 1915; May 17, 1917; April 9, Oct. 7, 1918; Jan. 6, 1920; March 10, July 22, 1933; *Vineland Times Journal,* March 29, 1938.

20. *V.E.J.,* Sept. 24, 1906; July 6, 1909; Jan. 3, 1910; Aug. 26, 1914; Sept. 23, 1915; April 25, 1917.

21. *Jewish Exponent,* Aug. 19, 26, 1910; *Jewish Farmer* (Yiddish), June 1913, p. 156; July 1913, p. 165.

22. *Vineland Evening Times,* April 16, 1929; April 5, Oct. 31, 1932; Nov. 25, 1938 (annual bazaar of the N.A.A.).

23. *Ibid.,* Nov. 1, 1932; April 22, July 7, Oct. 12, Dec. 7, 1933; May 18, 1934.

24. *V.E.J.,* Oct. 30, 1924; *Vineland Evening Times,* Nov. 7, 8, 9, 1932; May 17, 1933; May 19, 1934; Aug. 25, 26, Sept. 17, Nov. 7, 9, 1938; Jan. 3, 1939.

25. *Vineland Evening Times,* May 14, 17, 1928; Feb. 14, 15, April 15, 1929; Feb. 15, 20, 1933.

26. *Ibid.,* June 12, 1929; Jan. 30, Oct. 5, 1932; May 8, 1934; Nov. 18, 1938.

27. *Ibid.,* July 19, 1929; Jan. 16, 1930.

28. Herbert Hoover quoted *ibid.,* Jan. 21, 1929.

29. *Ibid.,* July 19, 1929; June 17, 1932; June 23, 1938.

30. Goldhaft, *op. cit.,* p. 38; *Centers,* p. 30; Mrs. G. Serata, "Conversations with Papa" (Crystal).

31. Crystal interviews, *ibid.*; Aaron Pincus collection on Jewish agriculture, YIVO Institute for Jewish Research.

32. Goldhaft, *op. cit.,* p. 244.

33. *Vineland Evening Times,* Sept. 10, Dec. 14, 1928; June 12, 1929; Dec. 9, 1938.

34. *Ibid.,* Dec. 22, 1924 (Rabbi Krueger), April 25, 1925 (Rev. Johnson), Feb. 23, 1928 (De Haas), March 27 (Bender), Oct. 18, 1928, Jan. 4, 1930 (Thomas), June 4, 1934.

35. *Ibid.,* March 6, April 4, 1928; Dec. 27, 1929; March 21, April 14, June 6, 1938.

36. *Ibid.,* Jan. 22, 23, 1925.

37. *Ibid.,* Oct. 4, 7, 1937; March 27, 1939.

38. Douglas, *op. cit.,* p. 67.

39. Reverend Simeon Singer, *Jewish Chronicle* (London), quoted in Klein, *op. cit.,* pp. 67, 69, and Abrahams, Israel, *The Literary Remains of the Reverend Simeon Singer: Lectures and Addresses* (London and New York, 1908), p. 158. For a discerning analysis of the East European exodus, see Lloyd P. Gartner, *The Jewish Immigrant in England, 1870–1914* (London, 1960).

40. B. A. Palitz, "A History of the Borough of Woodbine," 1905, B.D.H.

41. Bureau of Immigration, *Annual Report of the Commissioner-General of Immigration for the Fiscal Year Ended June 30, 1903* (Commissioner-General F. P. Sargent), pp. 59–60.

42. *Hearings on House Resolution No. 166,* 61 Cong., 2 Sess. House Committee on Rules (Washington, 1911), including testimony by William Williams, Commissioner of Immigration at the Port of New York, pp. 52–53, as well as Barondess, Levy, *et al.,* pp. 136ff., *passim.*

43. Mary Antin, *They Who Knock At Our Gates (A Complete Gospel of Immigration),* (Boston and New York, 1914), pp. 10, 34–35, 137, 141.

44. *Ibid.,* pp. 36–37, 139.

45. William Kirsch, *The Jew and The Land,* with preface by Richard T. Ely and Introduction by Sir Horace Plunkett (Madison, Wisconsin, 1920), pp. 3, 42, 45, *passim.* Distributed by the American Association for Agricultural Legislation, University of Wisconsin.

46. Isidor Singer, ed., *A Religion of Truth, Justice, and Peace (A Challenge to Church and Synagogue to Lead in the Realization of the Social and Peace Gospel of the Hebrew Prophets),* (New York, 1924), pp. 28, 101, 281.

47. *Hearings before The Committee on Immigration and Naturalization,* 76 Cong., 3 Sess. (Washington, 1923), pp. 755–757. Heading: "Analysis of the Metal and Dross in America's Modern Melting Pot . . ."

48. Solomon Schechter to Simon Wolf, Aug. 27, 1903, *Thirteenth Annual Report of the Board of Delegates* (Union of American Hebrew Congregations), p. 5050, quoted in Panitz, *op. cit.,* p. 90.

49. Michael B. Scheler, "The 'Back-to-Land' Movement of the Jews," *The Reflex,* vol. VI, no. 1 (Feb. 1930), pp. 32–38.

50. Jacob B. Menkes, "Judah's Sons of the Soil: An Historical Summary dealing with the Jews in Farming . . ." Mimeographed (Cincinnati, 1933), pp. 1, 3, 13, *passim.* In Jewish Division, New York Public Library.

51. The Jewish Agricultural Society, Inc., *Annual Report, 1938,* pp. 12–13, 28.

52. *Ibid.,* pp. 10, 13.

53. *Ibid.,* p. 12.

54. Merle Curti, *American Philanthropy Abroad, op. cit.,* p. 384; among other sources, he cites Herbert Agar's *The Saving Remnant* (New York, 1960), p. 90ff. See also: David Brody on "American Jewry, Refugees, and Immigration Restriction," *PAJHS,* vol. XLV (Sept., 1955 and June, 1956); Kenneth Jacobson, "Franklin D. Roosevelt and the Refugee Problem: 1933–1939," unpublished M.A. thesis, Columbia University (New York, 1966). Ironically, F.D.R. "was the hero of the majority of Slavic-and-Jewish Americans" (Louis Gerson, *The Hyphenate in Recent American Politics and Diplomacy,* p. 255). See Arthur D. Morse, *While Six Million Died: A Chronicle of American Apathy* (New York, 1968), pp. 194–229, *passim.*

55. Freeland League for Jewish Territorial Colonisation, "Memorandum for the Consideration of the Delegates at the International Refugees' Conference at Evian" (Jewish Division, New York Public Library), pp. 1, 3–4.

56. Freeland League, "A Jewish Settlement in Australia" (S. Sedman), "A New Land for Jews," "Jews and the Post-War World (Gabriel Haus), *ibid.*

57. Vladimir Grossman, *The Soil's Calling* (Montreal, 1938), pp. 29, 36, 38, 40–43, 63, 71, 118.

Notes to Chapter X: Dream and Livelihood in South Jersey: New Farm Communities, New Americans

1. Aaron Pincus, Letters to the Editor column, *Day-Morning Journal* (Yiddish), April 14, 1960, part of Pincus collection, YIVO Institute for Jewish Research.

2. Pincus-Rocker letters, June-Aug. 1930, as well as extensive data on Jewish agriculture, YIVO.

3. *The Jewish Farmer* (May, 1958), pp. 100–101.

4. Pincus collection, including Minutes of the Toms River Community of Jewish Farmers, *op. cit. Vineland Times Journal,* June 11, 14, Dec. 2, 1938; Jan. 16, 1939.

5. Jacob S. Joffe, "How Will Jewish Workers be Settled on the Land?" (Yiddish), *The Day,* Feb. 24, 1934. YIVO collection.

6. M. Melamed, "The First School in Clarion" (Utah), *California Jewish Voice* (Yiddish), Sept. 12, 1913, YIVO collection.

7. Albert Einstein's letter and others quoted in press release, Association for Jewish Farm Settlements, March 16, 1934. YIVO collection.

8. Jacob S. Joffe, "On The Agricultural Front" (New York, 1933), a 12 page pamphlet in Yiddish, outlining the Hightstown plan published by The Provisional Commission. YIVO collection.

9. William E. Leuchtenburg, *op. cit.,* p. 136.

10. *The Day,* Feb. 24, 1934; Press releases, Association for Jewish Farm Settlements, YIVO collection. On the New Deal's "subsistence homesteads," see Paul Conkin, *Tomorrow a New World* (Ithaca, 1959), pp. 83, 111–112, *et passim.*

11. Morris Schonbach, *Radicals and Visionaries, op. cit.,* p. 107.

12. Samuel Joseph, *History of the Baron de Hirsch Fund,* pp. 176–178; Goldhaft, *op. cit.,* p. 233; Jewish Agricultural Society (J.A.S.) *Annual Report,* 1930, pp. 10–12.

13. Joseph, *ibid.,* pp. 171–172; Robert Shosteck, "De Hirsch Fund is Still Serving," *The National Jewish Monthly,* vol. LXXX, no. 11 (July–Aug., 1966), 12. From 1934, however, a number of outstanding J.A.S. loans were refunded through the new Farm Credit Administration.

14. Quoted in *Vineland, N. J., Centennial, 1861–1961.*

15. Federal Writers' Project, W.P.A., *Stories of New Jersey* (New York, 1938), pp. 203, 274; John T. Cunningham, *Garden State* (New Brunswick, 1955), p. 45.

16. *V.E.J.,* June 13, Oct. 7, Dec. 18, 1914; July 25, 1916. William C. Coleman, "Fifty Years of Service to South Jersey Poultrymen," *Eastern Feed Merchant* (Dec., 1956).

17. *The Jewish Farmer,* Jan. 1918, p. 6; The Jewish Agricultural Society, *Report for the Period 1900–1924,* pp. 32–33, 60–61; J.A.S. *Annual Report,* 1930, p. 28.

18. *Vineland Evening Times,* March 20, 1925; J.A.S. *Annual Report, 1930,* p. 18.

19. Goldhaft, *The Golden Egg*, pp. 171, 175–176, 190–193, 222ff., 276–282, *passim.*; "Dr. Goldhaft Announces 'Perfect' Vaccines for Tracheitis and Fowl-Pox," *Vineland Times Journal,* June 1, 1938.

20. J.A.S. *Annual Report, 1930,* pp. 5–7.

21. *Vineland Evening Times,* March 3, 1928, Feb. 20, 1932; J.A.S., *The American Jewish Farmer in Changing Times,* pp. 27–28.

22. *Vineland Evening Times,* March 14, 21, July 3, 1929; March 5, 1930; March 1, 24, June 3, July 7, 1932; March 9, 1933.

23. *Ibid.,* Oct. 1, 1932; Aug. 12, 1933.

24. *Ibid.,* July 12, 1933; Sept. 2, 1937.

25. *Ibid.,* May 30, 1934; Aug. 23, Nov. 11, 1938.

26. *Ibid.,* June 22, July 26, Aug. 8, 13, 1928; Aug. 2, 14, 1929; March 18, 1930; Aug. 22, Oct. 31, 1932; Aug. 15, 1933; *Yoval, passim.*

27. Interview with William Levin, Alliance, March 30, 1966.

28. J.A.S., *Annual Report, 1939,* pp. 12–18; Mark Wischnitzer, *op. cit.,* pp. 208–209.

29. Goldhaft, *op. cit.,* pp. 236, 243–244.

30. *Ibid.,* pp. 244–246; Jacob Crystal interview, April 9, 1966. See also: Manfred George, "Geistige Einordnung in die Neue Welt," *Ten Years: American Federation of Jews from Central Europe, 1941–1951,* pp. 78–85; Eric E. Hirshler, ed., *Jews From Germany in the United States* (New York, 1955), pp. 89–100.

31. Jack B. Baer, Financial Secretary, Toms River Community of Jewish Farmers, to President Franklin D. Roosevelt, Dec. 17, 1942, reply from M. H. McIntyre, President's Secretary, Dec. 28, 1942, both in YIVO collection; The Jewish Agricultural Society, *Annual Reports* of 1939, 1940, 1942, 1943, pp. 22–23; 1945, p. 16 *et passim.*

32. J.A.S. *Annual Reports,* 1947, 1948.

33. J.A.S. *Annual Report,* 1952, pp. 6, 20–28.

34. *Ibid.,* pp. 12–13.

35. Miles Lerman, "Jewish Vineland and the Newcomers," *Tenth Anniversary Journal,* J.P.F.A. (1962), p. 43.

36. I. Harry Levin, "Vineland, A Haven for Refugees," in *Tenth Anniversary Journal,* J.P.F.A., p. 6.

37. A. Pelz, Secretary, J.P.F.A., "Greetings . . .," *ibid.,* p. 45. The Goldhaft family was also a source of strength to the new settlers; for Dr. Arthur Goldhaft's cogent description of their trials and successes, see *The Golden Egg,* pp. 262 ff.

38. Sabato Morais quoted in Moshe Davis, *The Emergence of Conservative Judaism: The Historical School in 19th Century America* (Philadelphia, 1965), p. 326.

39. *Tenth Anniversary Journal*, pp. 2, 31.

40. U.S. Department of Agriculture and U.S. Department of Commerce figures, quoted in *The New York Times*, Aug. 14, 1966.

41. J.A.S. *Annual Reports*, 1956, 1957.

42. College of Agriculture and Experiment Station at Rutgers, The State University, *New Jersey Agriculture*, vol. 42, no. 5 (Sept.-Oct., 1960), pp. 4, 13–14; "Helig Finds Farm Life Now Austere," *Vineland Times Journal*, April 10, 1959; its Poultry Section also contained such headlines as "Index Dips on Poultry Market" (down 18% from 1958).

43. Mordecai V. Efron, "Greetings to the Jewish Farmers," *Tenth Anniversary Journal*, p. 47.

44. Yaakov Berman, *Shaliach to Haikar Haoved*, to Dr. Martin J. Douglas, Feb. 9, 1954 (letter and pamphlet); Yaacov Morris, *On The Soil of Israel*, contains ch. 15 on the *Orot* village, pp. 187–198, as well as much valuable information on Americans in Israeli agriculture, including the pioneer efforts of such New Jerseyans as Eliezer Yoffe and Sam Friedlander.

45. Goldhaft, *op. cit.*, pp. 275, 282, *et passim.;* J.A.S., *The American Jewish Farmer in Changing Times*, pp. 92–93.

46. Timothy L. Smith, "New Approaches to the History of Immigration in Twentieth Century America," *American Historical Review*, vol. LXXI, no. 4 (July, 1966), pp. 1265–1275, contains some seminal ideas.

Bibliography
and Sources

I. SOURCE MATERIALS

A. *Manuscript Sources* (Unpublished)

Unless indicated otherwise, documents used are in the collection of the American Jewish History Center, The Jewish Theological Seminary of America.

Agudath Achim Anshei Woodbine. Constitution of. December 7, 1893.

Alliance Land Trust To *Hewra Kadisha,* Certified Copy of Deed. Salem, N.J. Sept. 30, 1910. The American Jewish History Center collection contains a number of private family deeds to land in the Vineland area, as well as other pertinent records, dating back to the 1880's.

Alliance Republican Club. Proceedings.

Baron de Hirsch's Jewish Colonization Scheme, Report. London, 1894.

Baron de Hirsch Fund. Papers (incl. Annual Reports), on microfilm, since 1891.

Chevra Kadisha of Alliance, N.J., Constitution of the.

Chevra Kadisha Society, Alliance Colony. Certificate of Incorporation (Salem, N.J.), Feb. 2, 1891.

Emanu-El Congregation, Alliance, N.J. Constitution and Minutes (in Yiddish).

Federal Writers' Project New Jersey Ethnic Survey. "The Jews in New Jersey," MS., 1940, New Jersey State Archives.

Haberman, Joshua O. "The Jews in New Jersey: A Historical Sketch." MS, New Jersey Collection, Rutgers, the State University, New Brunswick, 1953.

Jewish Alliance of America. Constitution. 1891.

Menkes, Jacob B. "Judah's Sons of the Soil" (Subtitle: "An Historical Summary Dealing with the Jews in Farming, Accompanied by Bibliography and Questions for Discussion"), for the National Federation of Temple Brotherhoods. Cincinnati, 1933. Mimeo. Jewish Division, New York Public Library.

Schiff, Jacob H., Letters (selected from 1891 and 1906).

Serata, Gertrude. "Jewish Agricultural Settlement in the U.S. with Special Reference to the Alliance, New Jersey Colony." (Unpublished paper, The City College of New York, 1961.)

Silver, Harold. "Some Attitudes of the East European Jewish Immigrants Toward Organized Charity in the United States in the Years 1890–1900." Unpublished thesis, New York, 1934. Jewish Division, New York Public Library.

B. *Official Reports* (Printed)

1. Government Agencies
   (Public Documents)

New Jersey Department of Agriculture. *The New Jersey Egg Industry . . . Report of the New Jersey Poultry Industry Steering Committee.* Trenton, N.J., January, 1966.

New Jersey Office of Economic Policy. *Annual Reports.* Trenton, N.J. 1968, 1969.

Stainsby, William. *The Jewish Colonies of South Jersey.* Bureau of Statistics, Trenton, 1901. (New Jersey Division, Newark Public Library.)

United States Congress, House Committee on Rules. *Hearings on House Resolution No. 166, Authorizing The Committee on Immigration and Naturalization to Investigate the Office of Immigration Commissioner at the Port of New York and other Places.* Washington, D.C., 1911.

United States Congress, House. *Hearings before The Committee on Immigration and Naturalization.* 76 Cong., 3 Sess. (Serial 7–C). Washington, D.C., 1923.

401

United States Immigration Commission. "Hebrews in Agriculture," *Recent Immigrants in Agriculture* (part 3, vol. II, 3–148). (Also as 61 Cong., 2 Sess. Senate Doc. 633). Washington, D.C., 1911.

United States Treasury Department, Bureau of Immigration. *Annual Report of the Commissioner–General of Immigration for the Fiscal Year Ended June 30, 1903*. Washington, D.C., 1903.

Vineland, New Jersey. Centennial: 1861–1961. City of Vineland, 1961.

The Woodbine and Cape May County Planning Boards. *Woodbine Comprehensive Plan*. Borough of Woodbine, 1958.

2. Organizations and Institutions

American Federation of Jews from Central Europe. *Ten Years . . . 1941–1951*. New York, 1953.

Congregation Beth Hillel of Carmel, N.J. *Re-Dedication: 75th Anniversary of Carmel*. Carmel, N.J., 1958.

Freeland League for Jewish Territorial Colonisation. "Memorandum Prepared . . . for the Consideration of the Delegation at the International Refugees' Conference at Evian." London, July, 1938.

The Jewish Agricultural Society. *Annual Reports, 1900–1960*.

The Jewish Agricultural Society. *Report of the General Manager and 50th Anniversary Issue of the Jewish Farmer*. New York, 1958.

The Jewish Agricultural Society. *Jews in American Agriculture: The History of Farming by Jews in the United States. Published on the occasion of the American Jewish Tercentenary (and also the 150th anniversary of the founding of Jewish Agricultural colonies in South Russia)*. New York, 1954.

The Jewish Day School of Vineland (Yeshivah Yesod Ha-Torah). *Yearbook, 1946–1967* incl.

Jewish Farmers of America, Federation of. *Conference of Jewish Farmers* (annual, 1909–1914, vols. 1–6).

The Jewish Poultry Farmers' Association of South Jersey, Vineland. *Tenth Anniversary Journal* (English and Yiddish). New York, 1962.

Joseph, Samuel. *History of the Baron de Hirsch Fund: The Americanization of the Jewish Immigrant*. Philadelphia, 1935.

Klein, Moses. *Migdal Zophim* ("The Watch Tower"). *The Jewish Problem and Agriculture as Its Solution* (for the Jewish Emigration Society of Philadelphia). Philadelphia, 1889.

Levine, Herman J., and Miller, Benjamin. *The American Jewish Farmer In Changing Times* (for The Jewish Agricultural Society). New York, 1966.

Liberal Immigration League. *The Immigrant Jew in America* (Edmund J. James, *et al.*). New York, 1906.

C. *Autobiographies, Memoirs, and Speeches*

Abrahams, Israel, ed., *The Literary Remains of the Reverend Simeon Singer: Lectures and Addresses*. London and New York, 1908.

Adler, Cyrus. *I Have Considered the Days*. Philadelphia, 1941.

Bloom, Sol. "Jewish Farm Movement of Today: A Quarter Century of Progress by American-Jewish Farmers." Address to the U.S. House of Representatives, March 2, 1925 (reprint).

Freeman, Moses. *Fuftsig Yohr Geschichte Fun Idishen Leben in Philadelphia, 1879–1929*. ("Fifty Years' History of Jewish Life in Philadelphia"). Philadelphia, 1932.

Goldhaft, Arthur D., edited with an introduction by Meyer Levin. *The Golden Egg*, New York, 1957.

Goldstein, Philip R. *Centers in My Life: A Personal Profile of the Jewish Center Movement*. New York, 1964.

————. *Social Aspects of the Jewish Colonies of South Jersey* (privately printed Ph.D. dissertation). New York, 1921.

Isaacs, Myer S. "Jewish Farmers," from *The Old Guard and other Addresses*. New York, 1906.

Kobrin, Leon. *Meine Fuftsik Yohr in Amerike* ("My Fifty Years in America"). New York, 1966.

Kotok, Frank, ed. *Selected Poems by George Kotok*. Vineland, 1930 (private printing).

Levy, A. R. "Jewish Colonization." Address to the Members of the Lawndale Club of Chicago, 1911.

Ludins, David G. "Memories of Woodbine: 1891–1894," *Jewish Frontier* (June, 1960), pp. 7–15.

Mounier, Louis. *Auto-Biographical Sketch*. Vineland, 1937 (private printing).

————. "Brotmanville in Its Heyday." June 30, 1933. "Children's Gardens." July 4, 1933. "Colonial Characters." July 29, 1933. "A Descriptive Account of the South Jersey Colonies Situated near Vineland." Jan. 22, 1918. "Diphtheria and Scarlatina." May 30, 1933. "A Discovery . . ." June 30, 1933. "A Fight in Carmel." July 1933. "Glimpses of Jewish Life in the Colonies of Southern New Jersey." June, 1933. "A Good Samaritan." May 1933. "Ike Merochnik's Wedding in Carmel." May, 1933. "A Talk with a Native Public School Teacher in Alliance" (n.d.) All from the collections of American Jewish History Center and Mr. Nathaniel Tischler of Jamesburg, N.J.

Peixotto, Benjamin F. "What Shall We Do With Our Immigrants?" Address Delivered At the Thanksgiving Service Centennial of Sir Moses Montefiore's Birth, New York, Feb. 2, 1887. Appendix I, Heilprin, "Jewish Colonies in America." Appendix II, "How to Promote Agriculture Among the Jews." New York, 1887.

Price, George M. (Leo Shpall, trans.) "Memoirs of George Price." *Publication of the American Jewish Historical Society*, vol. XLVII, no. 2 (Dec. 1957), pp. 101–110.

Sabsovich, Katharine. *Adventures in Idealism: A Personal Record of the Life of Professor Sabsovich*. New York, 1922 (private printing).

Sachs, Abraham S. *In Kamf far a Beserer Velt: Geklibene Ksovim Vegen Sotsiale Problemen un Revolutsionere Persenlichkeiten* ("Struggle for a Better World: Selections on Social Problems and Revolutionary Personalities"). Foreword by B. Z. Goldberg, ed. New York, 1938.

"Vineland Journal of Charles K. Landis, Founder of Vineland, New Jersey," *The Vineland Historical Magazine*, vol. XXIII, no. 1 (January, 1938), pp. 166ff.

Yoval: A Symposium Upon the First 50 Years of the Jewish Farming Colonies of Alliance, Norma and Brotmanville, N.J. Sidney Bailey, ed. Philadelphia, 1932.

D. *Interviews*

Rabbi M. V. Efron, Vineland, N.J.

Mr. & Mrs. Eugene Feldman, Woodbine, N.J.

Mr. Fred Fernich, Vineland, N.J.

Dr. & Mrs. Tevis M. Goldhaft, Vineland, N.J.

Mr. Karl Kleeblatt, Bridgeton, N.J.

I. Harry Levin, Esq., Vineland, N.J.

Mr. William Levin, Alliance, N.J.

Mrs. William (Bayuk) Levin

Mrs. Arthur Levy, Woodbine, N.J.

Dr. & Mrs. Milton Nevins, Woodbine, N.J.

Rabbi Baruch Schwartz, Norma, N.J.

Mrs. Gertrude Serata, "Conversations with Papa (Jacob Crystal)," Bridgeton, N.J.

Mr. & Mrs. Harry Sobelman, Carmel, N.J.

II. SECONDARY WORKS

A. Books and Pamphlets

Adler, Cyrus. *Jacob H. Schiff: His Life and Letters* (2 vols.) Garden City, N.Y., 1929.

Antin, Mary. *They Who Knock At Our Gates (A Complete Gospel of Immigration)*. Boston and New York, 1914.

Baron, Salo W. *The Russian Jew Under Tsars and Soviets*. New York and London, 1964.

Bein, Alex. *Theodor Herzl, A Biography.* Maurice Samuel, trans. Philadelphia, 1941.

Bernheimer, Charles S., ed. *The Russian Jew in the United States (Studies of Social Conditions in New York, Philadelphia, and Chicago, With A Description of Rural Settlements).* Philadelphia, 1905.

Brandes, Georg. *Impressions of Russia* (1889). Reprinted, New York, 1966, Herman Ausubel, ed.

Cohen, Israel. *Theodor Herzl: Founder of Political Zionism.* New York, London, 1959.

Cunningham, John T. *New Jersey, America's Main Road.* New York, 1966.

————. *This Is New Jersey, From High Point to Cape May.* New Brunswick, N.J., 1953.

Curti, Merle. *American Philanthropy Abroad.* New Brunswick, N.J., 1963.

Davidson, Gabriel. *Our Jewish Farmers.* New York, 1943.

Davis, Moshe. *The Emergence of Conservative Judaism.* Philadelphia, 1963.

Dubnow, Simon M. *History of the Jews in Russia and Poland From the Earliest Times until the Present Day* (3 vols.), (I. Friedlaender, trans.) Philadelphia, 1920.

Elbogen, Ismar. *A Century of Jewish Life.* (Moses Hadas, trans.) Philadelphia, 1946.

Ellis, Herbert Lee. *New Jersey, The State and Its Government.* New York, 1967.

Finkelstein, Louis. *The Jews, Their History, Culture and Religion.* Philadelphia, 1949.

Fite, Gilbert C. *The Farmers' Frontier, 1865–1900.* New York, 1966.

Gartner, Lloyd P. *The Jewish Immigrant in England, 1870–1914.* London, 1960.

Gerson, Louis L. *The Hyphenate in Recent American Politics and Diplomacy.* Lawrence, Kansas, 1964.

Ginger, Ray. *Age of Excess: The United States From 1877 to 1914.* New York, 1965.

Grayzel, Solomon. *A History of the Jews: From the Babylonian Exile to the End of World War II.* Philadelphia, 1948.

Griswold, A. Whitney. *Farming and Democracy.* New Haven, 1952.

Grossman, Vladimir. *The Soil's Calling.* Montreal, 1938.

Hackett, James P. *The New Jersey Citizen.* New Brunswick, N.J., 1957.

Halcrow, Harold G. *Agricultural Policy of the United States.* Englewood Cliffs, 1953.

Handlin, Oscar. *Adventure in Freedom: Three Hundred Years of Jewish Life in America*. New York, 1954.

Hertzberg, Arthur. *The Zionist Idea, A Historical Analysis and Reader*. Garden City, New York, 1959.

Hicks, John D. *The Populist Revolution: A History of the Farmers' Alliance and the People's Party*. Minneapolis, 1931.

Higbee, Edward. *Farms and Farmers in an Urban Age*. New York, 1963.

Higham, John. *Strangers in the Land: Patterns of American Nativism, 1860–1925*. New Brunswick, N.J., 1955.

Hirschler, Eric E., ed., *Jews From Germany in the United States*. New York, 1955.

Jamison, Wallace N. *Religion in New Jersey: A Brief History* (N.J. Historical Series, vol. 3). Princeton, N.J., 1964.

Jones, Maldwyn Allen. *American Immigration*. New York, 1957.

Kull, Irving S., ed., *New Jersey, A History* (6 vols.). New York, 1930.

Learsi, Rufus. *The Jews in America: A History*. New York, 1954.

Morris, Yaacov. *On the Soil of Israel: Americans and Canadians in Agriculture*. Tel Aviv, 1965.

Morse, Arthur D. *While Six Million Died: A Chronicle of American Apathy*. New York, 1968.

Myers, Gustavus. *History of Bigotry in the United States*. Henry M. Christman, ed. New York, 1960.

Pollak, Gustav. *Michael Heilprin And His Sons: A Biography*. New York, 1912.

Rischin, Moses. *The Promised City: New York's Jews 1870–1914*. Cambridge, Mass., 1962.

Robinson, Leonard G. *The Agricultural Activities of the Jews in America*. New York, 1912.

Rosenberg, Stuart E. *The Jewish Community in Rochester, 1843–1925*. New York, 1954.

Sachar, Howard M. *The Course of Modern Jewish History*. Cleveland and New York, 1958.

Schonbach, Murray. *Radicals and Visionaries: A History of Dissent in New Jersey* (N.J. Historical Series). Princeton, 1964.

Seldes, Gilbert. *The Stammering Century*. Foreword by Arthur Schlesinger, Jr. New York, 1965.

———. *The Years of the Locust: America, 1929–1932*. Boston, 1933.

Shannon, David A. *Twentieth Century America*. Chicago, 1963.

Shannon, Fred A. *The Farmer's Last Frontier*. New York, 1945.

Sherman, C. Bezalel. *The Jew Within American Society. A Study In Ethnic Individuality.* Detroit, 1965.

Singer, Isidor. A. *Religion of Truth, Justice and Peace: A Challenge to Church and Synagogue to Lead in the Realization of the Social and Peace Gospel of the Hebrew Prophets.* Introd. by Edward E. Filene and Epilogue by Israel Zangwill. New York, 1924.

Solomon, Barbara Miller. *Ancestors and Immigrants: A Changing New England Tradition.* New York, 1965.

Stember, Charles H. and others. *Jews in the Mind of America.* New York, 1966.

Stevens, Louis T. *The History of Cape May County.* Cape May City, N.J., 1897.

Tcherikower, Elias, ed. *Geschichte fun der Yidisher Arbeter Bavegung in die Fareinikte Shtatn* ("History of the Jewish Labor Movement in the United States"). 2 vols. New York, 1943. Also in one-vol. trans. and rev. by Aaron Antonovsky, *The Early Jewish Labor Movement in the United States.* New York, 1961.

Vecoli, Rudolph J. *The People of New Jersey* (New Jersey Historical Series). Princeton, N.J., 1964.

Winsberg, Morton D. *Colonia Baron Hirsch: A Jewish Agricultural Colony in Argentina.* Gainesville, Florida, 1964.

Wischnitzer, Mark. *To Dwell in Safety: The Story of Jewish Migration Since 1800.* Philadelphia, 1948.

B. *Articles and Essays*

Black, John D. "Agriculture in the Nation's Economy." *American Economic Review,* vol. XLVI, no. 1 (March, 1956), pp. 1–33.

Blaustein, David. "The First Self-Governed Jewish Community Since the Fall of Jerusalem," *Circle: A Modern Department Magazine for All People,* vol. II (1907), pp. 138–140.

"A Colony in Kansas—1882." *American Jewish Archives,* vol. XVII, no. 2 (Nov. 1965), pp. 114–139.

Darling, Elena J. "The Conception and Founding of Vineland, New Jersey." *The Vineland Historical Magazine* (Centennial Number, 1961), pp. 6–27.

Douglas, Martin I. "The Vineland Jewish Community." *The Vineland Historical Magazine* (Centennial Number, 1961), pp. 64–68.

Gleason, Philip. "The Melting Pot: Symbol of Fusion or Confusion?" *American Quarterly,* vol. XVI, no. 1 (Spring 1964), pp. 20–46.

Gorin, B. "Die Frieherdike Idishe Farmers un die Nie" (The Old Jewish Farmers and the New). *Zukunft,* vol. XX (Jan. 1915), pp. 157–163.

"Idishe Farmerei in America," *The Day-Jewish Journal,* January 18, 1959.

Kirsch, William. *The Jew and the Land.* Preface by Richard T. Ely. Madison, Wisconsin, 1920. Also *Bulletin* of the American Association for Agricultural Legislation (May, 1920).

Korolenko, Vladimir. "Korolenko in Woodbine" (letters of Aug. 30–Sept. 11, 1893), *Hadoar* trans., vol. XXXVII (May 31, 1957), pp. 230–235.

Mason, Bessie B. "Louis Jules Gabriel Mounier," *The Vineland Historical Magazine,* vol. XXIII, no. 1 (January, 1938), pp. 156–160.

Miller, Louis. "Jewish Farm Colonies in South Jersey," *Die Arbeiter Zeitung,* vol. II, no. 32 (Aug. 7, 14, 1891). Yivo Institute for Jewish Research.

Mounier, Louis. "Glimpses of Jewish Life in the Colonies of Southern New Jersey." *The Vineland Historical Magazine* (April, 1965), pp. 477–485.

———. "Trials and Hardships of Immigrants." *The Vineland Historical Magazine,* vol. XVIX, no. 1 (January, 1934), pp. 17–21.

Osofsky, Gilbert. "The Hebrew Emigrant Aid Society of the United States (1881–1883)," *Publication of the American Jewish Historical Society,* vol. XLIX (March, 1960), pp. 173–187.

Price, George M. (Leo Shpall, trans.), *Russkie Yevrei v Amerike* ("The Russian Jews in America"). *Publication of the American Jewish Historical Society,* vol. XLVIII, no. 1 (Sept. 1958), pp. 28–62; no. 2 (Dec. 1958), pp. 78–133.

Scheler, Michael B. "The 'Back–to–Land' Movement of the Jews," *The Reflex,* vol. VI, no. 1 (Feb. 1930), pp. 32–38.

Shpall, Leo. "Jewish Agricultural Colonies in the United States," *Agricultural History,* vol. XXIV (July, 1950), pp. 120–146.

Smith, Timothy L. "New Approaches to the History of Immigration in Twentieth-Century America." *The American Historical Review,* vol. LXXI, no. 4 (July, 1966), pp. 1265–1279.

Szajkowski, Zosa. "The Alliance Israelite Universelle in the United States, 1860–1949." *Publication of the American Jewish Historical Society,* vol. XXXIX, no. 4 (June, 1950), pp. 389–443.

———. "The Attitude of American Jews to East European Jewish Immigration, 1881–1893." *Publication of the American Jewish Historical Society,* vol. XL, part 3 (March, 1951), pp. 221–280.

Tcherikower, Elias. "Jewish Immigrants to the United States, 1881–1900," *Yivo Annual of Jewish Social Science,* vol. VI (1951), pp. 157–176.

"Vie die Ershte Idishe Farmers Hoben Gegrindet a Colonie in Jersey" ("How the First Jewish Farmers Founded a Colony in Jersey"), *The Day-Jewish Journal,* Jan. 25, 1959.

408

Wise, Isaac M. and Davis, Charles K. "An Humble Plea for a Russian Colony," *The American Israelite,* June 30, 1882, reprinted in *American Jewish Archives,* vol. XXVI, no. 2 (Nov. 1965), pp. 116–139.

III. NEWSPAPERS AND PERIODICALS

American Hebrew, vol. XIX (Aug. 8, 1884).

American Israelite, vol. XXXI, no. 34 (Feb. 20, 1885).

Bridgeton Evening News. Bridgeton, N.J. June 8, 1954 (commemorative issue).

Der Nei-Gekumener, Vineland, July, 1963.

Elmer Times. Elmer, N.J., Nov. 1886, Oct. 1887, Oct. 1891.

Freeland: Periodical of the Freeland League for Jewish Territorial Colonization. New York, 1939–1941.

Jewish Daily Forward, 1897–1903.

Jewish Exponent. Philadelphia, 1882–1920.

Jewish Farmer, The (in Yiddish). New York, 1891–1892.

Jewish Farmer, The (Yiddish and English). New York, 1908–1959.

Jewish Messenger. New York, July 21, 1882.

Jewish Record, The. Philadelphia, 1882–1920.

New Jersey Agriculture. New Brunswick, N.J., 1955–1960.

Vineland Evening Journal (successor of the *Vineland Weekly, Daily Independent, The Daily Journal*), 1875–1920.

Vineland Times Journal (successor to the *Vineland Evening Journal*), selective issues since 1920.

The Vineland Historical Magazine. Vineland, N.J. (Centennial Number, 1961, and other issues since 1934.)

Index

Aaron, Maurice, 287
Aaron, Morris, 328
Aaron, Solomon, 297
Accidents, industrial, 153-154
Acculturation, 94, 269-270, 296, 299, 304
Ackley, John A., 159, 261
Adams, Henry, 193
Adler, Cyrus, 82, 103
Agricultural Experiment Station (Fort Collins, Colo.), 45
Agro-Joint, 275, 315
Agronski, Dora, 166
Agronsky, Gershon, 273
Agronsky, Martin, 273
Agudath Achim Anshei Woodbine. *See* United Woodbine Brotherhood
Ahavas Achim (Vineland), 237-238, 239, 267, 302, 331, 333
Alampi, Philip, 334
Aleichem, Sholom, 281
Alexander I (Russia), 45
Alexander III (Russia), 17
Alliance, N.J., 29, 43, 62, 70, 114, 128, 175, 180, 218, 219, 225, 232, 260-261
    agriculture in, 77-78, 97
    anti-Semitism in, 173
    first colony, 4, 27, 28, 51
    industry in, 58, 145-146, 147
    political activity in, 262, 297
    poverty in, 85, 89, 91, 116, 278
    religious observance in, 209-216, 299-301
    Sabbath issue in, 187, 188, 189, 233
    settlement of, 55-60, 129
Alliance Israélite Universelle, 6, 25-27, 28, 46, 58, 104, 107, 109, 111, 112, 199, 211, 212, 343
Alliance Land Trust, 57, 82, 84, 85, 210, 211, 213
Alliance Republican Club, 262, 297
Allivine Canning Co., 66, 80, 130-131
Allivine Farm, 79, 80-81, 237
ALT. *See* Alliance Land Trust
Alterman, Joseph, 297

Am Olam movement, 18-24, 26, 44-45, 47, 67, 278-279, 337, 343
Amalgamated Clothing Workers, 155, 164, 165, 167-168, 291, 315-316; relief service, 294
America Via the Neighborhood (Daniels), 240
American Federation of Labor, 203
American Hebrew, 91, 103, 205, 215
American Hebrew Farmer's Association, proposal for defeated, 39, 94
American Israelite, The, 47, 105, 145, 222
American Jewish Committee, 199, 251, 281; office of war records, 266
American Jewish Congress, 247, 251, 301
American Jewish Joint Agricultural Corporation, 275
American Jewish Joint Distribution Committee, 268-269
American Jewish Relief, 268
American Legion, 288
American Nazi Bund, 287-288, 295
American Protective Association, 200
American Sabbath Union, 186
Americanization, 9, 10, 12, 64-65, 105, 108-110, 124-125, 126, 132, 141-142, 205, 219, 224, 237, 240, 242, 245, 247, 249, 255-256, 269, 273, 282, 334, 344
Amos Society, 306
Anshei Oesterreich, 300
Anti-Catholicism, 173, 174, 175, 200, 285, 287
Anti-immigration movement, 7, 200-205
Anti-Negro bias, 102, 184, 285-286, 287
Anti-Semitism, 5, 16, 18, 19, 21, 22, 41, 133, 171-184, 198-199, 250, 277, 285-288, 303-304, 308, 325; in Europe, reaction to, 192-198, 326
Antin, Mary, 247-248, 249, 305-306
April, Morris, 322
Aqua, Samuel N. (quoted), 137

417